Statue of Liberty–Ellis Island Centennial Series

Board of Editors

Roger Daniels, Chair (University of Cincinnati)
Jay P. Dolan (University of Notre Dame)
Victor Greene (University of Wisconsin–Milwaukee)

A list of books in the series appears at the back of this book.

Contented among Strangers

Contented among Strangers

Rural German-Speaking Women and Their
Families in the Nineteenth-Century Midwest

Linda Schelbitzki Pickle

University of Illinois Press   Urbana and Chicago

Publication of this book was supported by a grant from the
Ellis Island–Statue of Liberty Foundation.

© 1996 by the Board of Trustees of the University of Illinois
Manufactured in the United States of America
1 2 3 4 5 C P 5 4 3 2 1

This book is printed on acid-free paper.

Library of Congress Cataloging-in-Publication Data
Pickle, Linda Schelbitzki, 1942–
    Contented among strangers : rural German-speaking women and their
families in the nineteenth-century Midwest / Linda Schelbitzki
Pickle.
        p.   cm. — (Statute of Liberty–Ellis Island Centennial series)
    Includes bibliographical references (p.   ) and index.
    ISBN 0-252-02182-7 (cloth). —ISBN 0-252-06472-0 (paper)
    1. German American women—Middle West—History—19th century.
2. Farm life—Middle West—History—19th century. 3. Middle West—
Social life and customs. 4. Middle West—Rural conditions.
I. Title. II. Series.
F358.2.G3P53   1996
977'.0043—dc20   95-9849
                                                                      CIP

For

James Anton Schelbitzki
and
Clara Bollettini Schelbitzki,

grandson and daughter of immigrants

Contents

Illustrations follow pages 108 and 138

Acknowledgments

As is true of most authors engaged in projects that entail a decade or more of research and writing, I owe much to others. My participation in a Modern Language Association–National Endowment for the Humanities summer seminar in 1979 sparked my interest in the hidden history of women's lives and greatly advanced my understanding of the particular problems and rewards of working with personal documents. I began the actual research for this book during a Mellon Foundation faculty development seminar at the University of Kansas in the spring of 1982. Two National Endowment for the Humanities Travel to Collections Grants, in 1986 and 1993, enabled me to explore archives in Kansas, Nebraska, Iowa, and Illinois. In 1988, a German Academic Exchange Service (DAAD) Study Visit Grant made possible a month in Germany at the Bochum Immigrant Letter Collection. Westminster College gave me several summer research grants to visit other archives in Missouri and elsewhere and a sabbatical leave, during which I was able to write a sizable portion of the manuscript. Without such backing, I could not have completed this project.

At least as important was the assistance of many individuals. Several scholars saw parts or all of the manuscript at various stages of its development. Glenda Riley, Walter Kamphoefner, Sandra Myers, Wolfgang Helbich, Adolf Schroeder, and Becky Schroeder were generous in their comments and suggestions. Seena Kohl shared her own related work. My patient editors, Karen Hewitt and Jane Mohraz of the University of Illinois Press, made many helpful recommendations that led to improvements in both content and style. This book owes much to the insights of all of these people. Many of its strengths are due to their influence, while I am responsible for any errors or flaws. Lorna Mitchell and Liz Hauer at Reeves Library assisted with data-base searches and interlibrary loans above and beyond the call of duty. The lively personal interest in my work on the part of colleagues at Westminster College helped keep me going as well.

This book represents a personal quest of sorts, so I am particularly grateful to members of my family, who encouraged me in recovering a bit of our collective history. They might have despaired at times of ever seeing the results in print, but if so, they never let on, for which I thank them. My pleasure in completing this project is marred only by the fact that my parents are no longer here to share it with me.

Most of all, I thank my husband and daughter, Charlie and Joyce Pickle, for their unflagging help and support. Among other things, this took the shape of lots of pep talks, reading and commenting on pages and pages of text, assisting in drudge work, tagging along on research trips, and putting up uncomplainingly with many curtailments on family life. *Contented among Strangers* is also the fruit of their loving generosity.

Introduction

Growing up on a Nebraska farm in a neighborhood dominated by the descendants of German-speaking immigrants, I took for granted patterns of individual and family behavior that later no longer seemed self-evident. No doubt living with my Italian-American mother, an "outsider" from Chicago who brought other experiences and perspectives to her new rural life, planted questions in my mind about the world around me, long before I became conscious of wanting to answer them in an organized fashion. My first questions had to do with my father's family, in whose midst we lived, and how they interacted with each other and their neighbors. This book is the final result of an inquiry that began with this unreflected wondering and has led me far from its Nebraska and familial origins to a general investigation of rural German-American immigrant family life and, more specifically, of the role women played in these immigrants' adaptation to the Midwest.

The separation of the sexes and of the spheres to which they were assigned in my community seemed to be exemplified in my grandparents' quiet and essentially harmonious life together. In spite of the outwardly untroubled quality of their relationship, however, I found myself asking certain questions as I matured. Both had been born soon after their parents' immigration and had been shaped by that experience, at least secondarily. Was my quiet, even-tempered, hardworking, frugal, and self-denying grandmother the way she was because of her individual personality, her family background, or her ethnic heritage? Or was it because of her marriage to this particular man, my grandfather? Like some of the other women in the neighborhood, she had left her domestic sphere at times to work alongside her husband and sons. Had she minded distributing the hay the men pitched up to her on the rack or cleaning out the manure piled up to the half-doors of the stalls on the farm bought for my father while he was in the war? Did she really hide her egg and cream money from my grandfather in a crock in the cellar, as I thought as a child? Or was this a communal cache, like the money my grandfather kept in two hiding places and from which my grandmother took cash when her funds ran out?[1] Although she did all the domestic work, her authority in the home was not absolute. Or so it seemed when her daughters-in-law had to intervene and have indoor plumbing installed in her home when she became too frail to pump and haul the water necessary for daily use.

My grandfather's behavior was even more of a puzzle in certain ways. A man who had dedicated his energy to accumulating land, he distributed it all equally among his four children and retired to a life of enforced idleness in late middle age. Even less interested in other worldly possessions than my grandmother was, he displayed no outward appreciation of her contributions to their accomplishments or her care of him and their home. Instead, he grumbled about "women always wanting something." At the suggestion of his children, however, he bought his wife a watch when she recovered from a mid-life illness. The sketchy entries in his account books between 1900 and 1941 indicate that he considered all the major farm income and liabilities "his" and that he provided contributions to the domestic sphere with the purchase of large items (a refrigerator in 1929 and a washing machine in 1930, for example). He recorded payments only to himself from the farm income, but he also paid the doctor bills for the births of his children and unusual family expenses, such as my aunt's graduation dress and pictures in 1929 and my father's first car in 1936. The only daily household goods he seems to have bought in those years were four bags of flour, indicating that my grandmother produced everything else that the family needed. This is probably also not completely accurate, however, for my aunt remembers that my grandmother once took a few dollars from my grandfather's billfold, because "it was hard for her to ever ask him for money."[2]

Important as my grandmother's contributions were to the family success in accumulating land while leading relatively comfortable lives, all major economic decisions had been my grandfather's. If he consulted her on what land to buy and when, it was not apparent. Nonetheless, he was judged in the family as generous for having taken in his wife's orphaned niece and helping pay for her education and for allowing his widowed mother-in-law to live in his home for long periods. What balancing act between authority in the male and the female spheres and between emotional and economic family demands did my grandparents live out? Were they unusual in the impulses behind their relationship, or did they follow patterns familiar from their cultural heritage and prevalent among the Old World stock around them?

If my grandparents' work and economic lives seemed not to touch very directly, was their emotional life equally separate? I never witnessed displays of affection between them, nor did their children, but anger and arguments had not been part of the atmosphere of my father's childhood either. The contrast between my father's parents and my mother's could not have been greater in this regard. Yet even these undemonstrative people did have emotions. Taciturn and seemingly impassive though he was, my grandfather drove several miles to our farm with tears streaming down his face after being present at his brother's death from cancer. My grandmother's terse response to my mother's concern was simply yes, he would be alright. Reserve was a general family characteristic, one shared by most of our rural neighbors. Was it also an ethnic quality?

Other questions arose as I grew older. What had life been like for the immigrant frontier ancestors of the stolid people around me? Physically hard, no doubt, but few stories had been passed down about this in my family and next to nothing about the emotive dimension of those experiences. How had my great-grandmother felt, living in a dug-out in a creek bed for several years and helping her husband break prairie? She lost four of her first seven babies soon after the birth of each, and her oldest surviving child, a daughter, was born a stunted cripple. Did she make the connection, as I wanted to, that these melancholy events were because of the hardships and privations of her life? If she did, was she resentful or resigned? Had these people, especially these women, felt at a disadvantage with their English-speaking neighbors? Had friendly relations existed? Or had they kept within their own immigrant groups, as the dense clustering of their descendants suggested?

Like too many others of my generation, I did not set about answering my questions until my grandparents and others who might have helped me do so were gone from this world. When I turned to printed texts to fill in the broad picture of German-speaking immigrants, I found much that was helpful in understanding the background and dynamics of the movement of these people to the United States during the nineteenth century. Some of the things I had noted in my childhood were confirmed as typical in the wider context of Midwest rural history: the agricultural success and staying power of the immigrants and their descendants, their tendency to settle in clusters and eventually to buy out their Anglo-American neighbors, the importance of the rural immigrant church in their social lives.

At least one scholar, Dietmar Kügler, also ascribed to this group of immigrant pioneers a central significance in the development of the midwestern and American character:

Here in the Midwest "the American" came into existence. . . . Hardened, battered, and challenged by the land in which everything that was weak was destroyed, a new race developed: self-confident, strong, armed with an iron ability to survive. They were suspicious, self-willed, trusting only themselves and marked by aggressive individualism and a pronounced consciousness of freedom.

The opening of the great plains, decried as a desert for agriculture, was to a large measure the accomplishment of the German immigrants. They knew how to look after themselves. They survived the dry summers and the merciless winters. They didn't give up when their grain shriveled on the stalk in the first year, when a hail storm devastated their fields and killed their livestock in the pastures in the second year and when the locusts ate their crops in the third year. With tireless energy they continued their efforts to transform the prairies into a land of culture.[3]

I was not sure that these assertions corresponded to the reality that I had experienced in my Nebraska community. Certainly my family and their neighbors were a hardworking, enduring people, but could I really attribute to them and their ancestors this larger-than-life role as civilizers? Even more than this, I was bothered by the essentially male model of the aggressively individualistic, self-reliant, freedom-loving pioneer that lies at the heart of this picture. What about the domestic and communal relationships of interdependency that I knew also existed? What about the women among the immigrants? Had they shared in the individualism and love of freedom that Kügler assigns to all of them? I felt that women's actions and contributions had been different, but in what ways?

My readings about the American frontier made it clear that the image of the rural pioneer has attained archetypal proportions in the national consciousness. We are all, if we accept what Kügler asserts, midwesterners marked by our frontier past: self-confident, tenacious, toughened by hardship, individualistic, and freedom-loving. Underlying this archetype is Frederick Jackson Turner's thesis of the frontier as a crucible that reduced people to primitive conditions, stripping off "the garments of civilization" and fostering these typically "American" qualities.[4] Later writers refuted Turner's view of the frontier, but it nevertheless captured the imagination of many. It has been further embellished in reference to ethnic immigrants who, in literary works like Willa Cather's *My Ántonia* and Ole Rölvaag's *Giants in the Earth,* were given near-mythic stature as archetypal representatives of the pioneer experience.

We know that Germans played an important role in American agricultural history, and we may indeed believe that the contributions of German-speakers were substantial, particularly in the Midwest, where a third to half of the present population claims German ancestry.[5] But can we justifiably credit them with much of the settling and "civilizing" of this area, as Kügler does? What was the nature of their contributions? Were they, as Kügler implies, more "American" than the Anglo-Americans? Did they mark American society forever with their own hard work and persistence? Were they not changed by their frontier experiences? Did they accomplish what they did in a cultural vacuum or in interaction with settlers of other backgrounds? As I attempted to find answers to these questions, I began to look at the stories of individual immigrants. This led to other, related questions, as the following "typical" family history illustrates.

In 1860 two young Germans, Louisa Roenigk and Adolph Roenigk, born in Ufhofen, Thuringia, sailed to America. Louisa was seventeen and her brother thirteen, and they were embarking on a long-term family venture. Their journey was probably one of the many small expeditions headed by former villagers who returned to the Old Country to visit or to lead family members back and who, perhaps only incidentally, also recruited others to join them in America. Louise's and Adolph's parents gave them money and extra clothes before they left with twelve others. They spent the next two years on a farm in Wisconsin, Louisa as a domestic and Adolph as a hired hand. Their next move was to Madison, where Louisa again entered domestic service and Adolph was apprenticed to a saddler. In 1864 they went to St. Louis with a family that had persuaded Louisa to work in its home. Adolph found a job in the saddler trade. After the Civil War, Louisa married a Danish immigrant, Mates Rasmussen, and they moved to Leavenworth, Kansas, where Mates took up his trade as a bookbinder until they could acquire a farm. In 1868 Adolph joined them. Three years later Adolph took a homestead in Clay County, Kansas, near Louisa and Mates, who had already established themselves on a homestead there. Soon after this, Louisa's and Adolph's parents, three brothers, and two sisters joined them in Clay County and took homesteads. Eleven years after Louisa and Adolph left Thuringia, the Roenigk family had attained its dream of economic independence and a better future for all.[6]

The general contours of this family history resemble those of many families who immigrated to the New World in the last three or four centuries. Successful immigration to the United States has largely been accomplished by families through cooperative efforts sustained over time. We do not know a great deal about the concrete processes and structures accompanying these efforts or about the subjective dimensions of immigration and adaptation to the new environment. The Roenigk family history left me with important questions about these processes, structures, and subjective reactions. What bonds linked these young people, whom we would think of today as children, to their parents and siblings thousands of miles away, bonds that endured a new environment, financial and personal independence, new emotional and familial ties, and the passing of many years? How typical was their attitude and the behavior that accompanied it? What were its origins? How much was due to the idiosyncrasies of these particular individuals or this particular family? To cultural characteristics peculiar to Germans? Adolph Roenigk wrote only this in his biographical sketch: "While we were practically alone here among strangers, we were contented, although separated from our parents, brothers and sisters, by thousands of miles, the Atlantic ocean between us. We looked forward with hopes of a prosperous future and to meet our parents and the rest of the family at some future time. Their influence remained with us and we intended to make good."[7] Louisa and Adolph were contented among strangers. They do not seem to have seen themselves as civilizers, and individual self-realization and freedom were not their primary goals. Instead, strategies of cooperation, hard work, and perseverance enabled them to reunite their family so they could to continue patterns of mutual aid and interdependence.

When reading about the Roenigks, I was struck by the important role Louisa played in this story. She was entrusted with her younger brother's care and future, and she eventually drew her husband into the effort to achieve the reunification of her family in the New World. I felt strongly that her influence was not unique, although women have been generally ignored in studies of German-American immigrants. Women's contributions and the complexity of family relationships have been taken for granted and gone unremarked and unrecorded, just as they were in my family. My research has shown me that their traditional role as conservators of traditions and rural family values made women central players in this immigrant group's adaptation to America. Their contributions deserve to be acknowledged.[8]

Even the important and fascinating scholarship of recent years examining women on the American frontier proved to be incomplete and biased about German-Americans. When historians of women on the American frontier have referred to European immigrants who did not speak English, they have generally asserted that women in such groups faced a second, cultural barrier and thus had a more difficult time.[9] I eventually came to the conclusion that the reality was more complex than this. Their home- and family-centered lives tended to shelter them from the more traumatic experiences of cultural alienation. In addition, European culture prepared many immigrant women to make vital contributions to frontier adaptation with less alienation than many Anglo-

American women felt. Indeed, I assert in this study that more often than not, German-speaking frontierswomen were, as Adolph Roenigk said of himself and his sister Louisa, contented among strangers.

* * *

My study examines German-speaking women's actions and reactions before, during, and after immigration to America. Their contributions to the family and the building of rural society and their legacy in the family, the ethnic community, and the community at large are also of particular interest. Women's roles and experiences are a little-explored field that has much to offer in revealing the economic, social, and interpersonal dynamics of rural family life and frontier society.[10] At the same time, my study acknowledges the interdependence of women's history with that of men, families, communities, and states. It seeks to work, as one scholar of German-American women's history has put it, within "a theoretical framework which . . . does not assume a dichotomy between public (male) and private (female) spheres."[11]

Many studies have examined the history of German-speaking immigrants in the United States, but few have concentrated on rural frontier immigrants.[12] As I use it here, the word *rural* refers to residence on a farm. The farm might not have been the immigrants' first dwelling place in the United States, or their last, for the German-speakers, although generally more "persistent" in settling than other groups, did move about, for one reason or another. For a few German-speakers, the farm income might have been supplemented by work in town, but it is their residence on the farm and what led up to it that primarily interest me.

The term *frontier* requires clarification as well. I use it in the conventional way to refer to the first years of settlement in a newly opened region and the conditions usually associated with that period. Typical of the early frontier years were harsh physical conditions and the gradual establishment of communal and legal institutions. It is important to remember, however, that the frontier was not always readily identifiable. It certainly was never a clearly defined line. People settled first along rivers and later along railroads. They tended to settle in clusters and to choose the choicest land first, leaving large and small inner tracts for later settlers. In 1890, when the U.S. Census Bureau declared that it could no longer clearly distinguish between populated and unpopulated areas, the common wisdom was that the frontier was closed, but frontier conditions continued in certain areas and for some individuals well into the twentieth century.

Frontier conditions were particularly long-lasting in large parts of the Great Plains, in rural areas in general, and especially for ethnic immigrants in those areas. Because of physical isolation and conservative social patterns, rural residents experienced the end of frontier conditions later than people in towns and cities did. Ethnic immigrants tended to come to new areas later than Anglo-Americans and therefore went through this process later. Even if they were not the first to farm the land they settled on, ethnic immigrants were often slower to improve their living conditions because they came with fewer assets than their neighbors had. They sometimes had to learn new techniques of agricultural and domestic production. They had to adjust to the structures of a new society or build communal structures of their own. For all of these reasons, some ethnic immigrants experienced frontier conditions longer and later than did many Anglo-Americans, even in the same neighborhood. The material in my study may therefore not, on the surface, seem to fit the temporal or spatial limitations of the raw frontier in its stereotypical manifestations of unbroken prairie, marauding Indians, and general lawlessness.

Examining the history of German-speakers throughout the rural United States, even during the nineteenth century, would be a vast undertaking. I have therefore limited my study to German-speakers who came to farms in Illinois, Missouri, Iowa, Kansas, and Nebraska. For reasons I discuss more fully later, the area examined here mirrors the complexity of German-speaking immigration to the United States and merits the designation of "the representative Midwest."

* * *

German-speaking migration to the United States in the nineteenth century presents a complex picture. This complexity is evident in the migrants' nation of origin. In the first decades of the 1800s, a dozen large states and many smaller principalities occupied the territory that in 1871 united to form the German imperial nation. The emigration of German-speakers from Switzerland, Luxembourg, Alsace, and the Austrian Empire, and from the Volga and Bessarabian areas in Russia colonized in the previous century, further complicates the picture. Outer manifestations of differences among the German-speakers, such as dialect and dress, paralleled deeply embedded variations in social and legal traditions and customs. This pattern of regionalism, bolstered by strong religious allegiances, fostered the parochialism and traditionalism that marked German-speakers at home and abroad.[13]

Although Anglo-Americans lumped all of these groups and individuals together as "Germans," the personal and public documents of nineteenth-century German-Americans strongly support the persistence of a sense of difference and sometimes even animosity among them. This is equally true of the area under consideration. For example, the Hannoverian immigrant Georg Isernhagen recounted the first conversation he had with his future in-laws, neighboring homesteaders in western Kansas. They were German colonists from Bessarabia, who spoke a dialect that Isernhagen had difficulty understanding. They, in turn, characterized Low German–speakers in the vicinity as "coarse, dirty people," who in Russia would have earned the appellation *Katchuppa.* Antagonisms between religious denominations could lead to such tricks as draining the water in the baptistery of another sect's rural church. A Luxembourgian-American from Iowa remembered when his countrymen there engaged in fights with Prussian immigrants because of Old World enmities.[14] The hardships and isolation of the frontier did not nullify the prejudices that various German-speakers felt toward one another, even though they often drew together to work and socialize.

Not only were rural German-speakers dissimilar in speech patterns and their loyalties to their historical and national origins, but they also came at different times, because of various historical and personal forces in their homelands and lives, and in response to varying historical and personal forces in America.[15] Many studies have documented increases in emigration from German states in response to crop failures, the pressure of industrialization on cottage industries, the imposition of the military draft, and political upheavals. In the first half of the nineteenth century, immigrants came primarily from southwest Germany, the first wave from the Pfalz, Württemberg, and Baden after the 1817 famine. The depression in the home weaving industry in northern Westphalia, along with poor harvests, led to a surge in emigration from that area in the 1840s, while poor harvests combined with the worst decline for decades in wine production to drive the emigration numbers in southwest Germany to record highs in the 1850s.[16] St. Charles and Warren counties in Missouri, for example, reaped some of the benefits of this influx of German peasants and handworkers, who often settled near one another and proved to be diligent and persistent farmers in less than ideal circumstances.[17]

Immigrant settlement patterns were, in part, a response to the availability of cheap land as the American frontier expanded westward. German-speakers moved into Missouri and Illinois in the 1830s and 1840s, into Iowa in the 1840s and 1850s, and into Kansas and Nebraska in the 1850s and after the Civil War, when each of these territories was opened to immigration.[18] (See figures 1–4.)

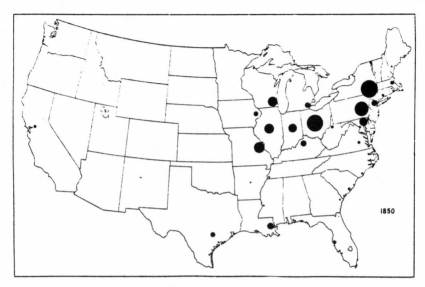

Figure 1. Dispersal of 584,000 German-born immigrants, constituting 2.5 percent of the U.S. population, in 1850. The smallest dot represents one hundred German-born, with increasing size of dots and circles indicating correspondingly larger numbers of the immigrants. (Max Hannemann, *Das Deutschtum in den Vereinigten Staaten,* Petermanns Mitteilungen, Ergänzungsheft No. 224 [Gotha: Perthes, 1936], 11, 62).

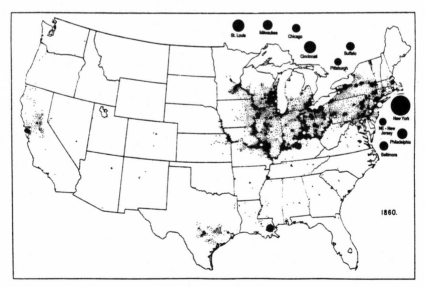

Figure 2. Dispersal of 1,276,000 German-born immigrants, constituting 4.1 percent of the U.S. population, in 1860. (Hannemann, 62.)

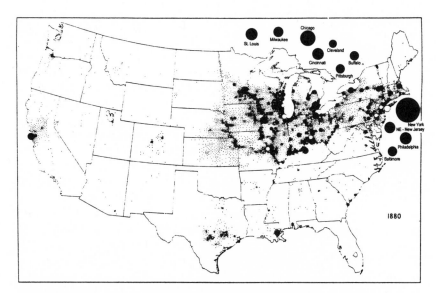

Figure 3. Dispersal of 1,967,000 German-born immigrants, constituting 3.9 percent of the U.S. population, in 1880. (Hannemann, 62.)

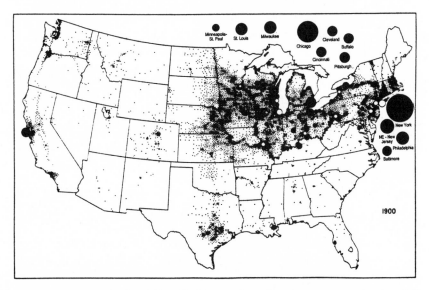

Figure 4. Dispersal of 2,663,000 German-born immigrants, constituting 3.5 percent of the U.S. population and 10.5 percent of the "foreign white stock," in 1900. In 1890, the number of German-born immigrants had reached its peak at 2,785,000, or 4.4 percent of the general population. (Hannemann, 62.)

Family and neighborhood ties in the Old World, however, were often the crucial factor in individual and group decisions on whether to migrate and where to settle, as the well-documented phenomenon of chain immigration shows.[19] Clusters of immigrants connected by blood, marriage, or Old World acquaintanceship were probably more typical than a random scattering of German-speakers from different places of origin, even in areas that had a low percentage of such immigrants.[20] Personal ties, as well as economic opportunity, brought German-speakers to different areas of the Midwest at different times. Once they arrived, the physical and climatic nature of the areas in which they settled necessitated different adaptations, so some of the immigrants were forced to change their patterns of living more than others. American political and social events caused the tide of immigration to ebb and flow as well. This was particularly evident during 1855 and 1856, in response to the xenophobia of the Know-Nothing nativism movement, and in the period of the Civil War. (See figure 5.)

The diversity among the German-speakers was because of their Old World origins, their various settlement patterns, and their different motives for emigration. The vast majority came to America with the goal of economic improvement for themselves and their families. Many hoped to gain this through landownership. A government official in Trier reported in 1847 that the unprecedented level of emigration from that part of the Rhineland the previous year had had to do with the peasants' poor economic prospects in their homeland. He went on to explain: "By contrast, America opens up to them the seductive prospect of being able to acquire with a small capital a considerable property and to leave to their children and their children's children a farm capable of providing them with an abundant livelihood."[21] Landownership was such an ingrained mark of prosperity that even those who had been unable to make their living through agriculture in Europe were lured to America by available land. Louisa Roenigk's husband, Mates Rasmussen, might have been one of these. My great-grandfathers, the one a baker and the other a weaver, certainly were. Sometimes whole communities were made up of immigrants from the artisan and cottager classes. One group of peasants and cottage weavers, the latter deprived of their livelihood by mechanization of the textile industry, left Dietzenbach near Darmstadt and founded a new Darmstadt on Mud Creek Prairie in Illinois. Between 1833 and 1868, thirty-four families, twenty-six of them headed by weavers, immigrated to that location. We are told that most of the immigrants had to learn how to farm, but they must have been successful in this. This rural American community remained remarkably German far into the twentieth century.[22]

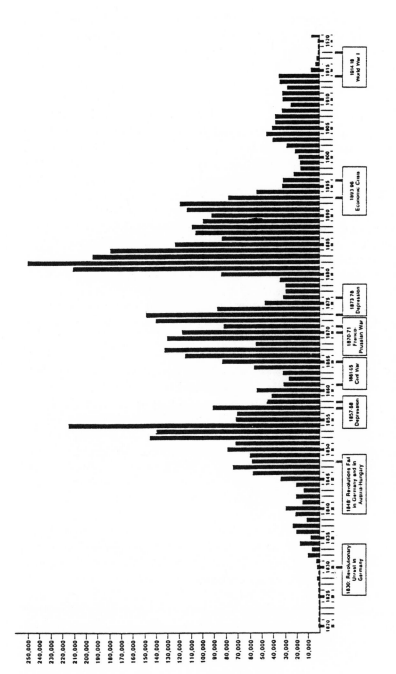

Figure 5. Immigration from Germany, 1820-1920. (Adapted with permission from the original by Jürgen Eichhoff, German House Research.)

The hunger for land of the German-speaking peasant and cottager immigrants and their view of the land as a trust to be handed on to future generations rather than a speculative, short-term investment were noted and extolled by nineteenth-century German-Americans and confirmed by later scholarly studies.[23] Their persistence on the land and the intensity and productivity of their farming practices were part of a family strategy that often made these immigrants particularly successful, much as my paternal ancestors were. Another important factor in immigrant geographic persistence was the opportunity rural American society afforded the immigrants to maintain traditional social relationships while bettering their economic status. Studies of "transplanted" rural immigrant communities demonstrate the relationship between membership in such communities, especially as indicated by membership in an immigrant church, and economic success and persistence.[24] Later sections of this study explore the demographic aspects of German-speakers' immigration in nineteenth-century America (see appendix B) and the family and community values and strategies that influenced the economics of their frontier experience.

Economic motivations for emigration were secondary to religious, philosophical, and political goals for significant subgroups of German-speakers. Members of emigration societies, led by intellectuals and professionals alienated by the repressive political events of 1830–31 (hence the name attached to them, the Dreißiger), came to the United States in the early years of that decade to form communities that would realize the dreams of German liberal democracy dashed at home. The Dreißiger settled throughout the Midwest, often in rural areas, where they hoped to attain financial and cultural independence and create an ideal German community. The leaders, called Latin farmers by their neighbors because they knew Latin so much better than they knew farming, often gave up farming in fairly short order and moved to the cities. The largest and arguably the most disastrous attempt to found a German colony in America was undertaken from 1844 until 1847 by the Society for the Protection of German Immigrants in Texas, the so-called Mainzer Adelsverein.[25] After this notorious venture, those in German lands viewed emigration societies quite skeptically in general.

A decade or more later, after the failed revolutions of 1848, other disillusioned middle-class intellectuals fled German lands for political reasons. Unlike the Dreißiger, however, the so-called Forty-Eighters seldom aspired to form separate German societies in the New World. They tended to come as individuals or in family groups and usually went directly to the more congenial urban areas of America, where they, like the Dreißiger before them, often became significant forces in journalism, politics, and education.

The desire for greater religious freedom was also a factor in the emigration of German-speakers. Religious minorities, although they made up a small percentage of all the nineteenth-century immigrants, were overrepresented relative to their strength in the Old World. Their efforts at group settlement were generally more successful than the politically motivated efforts. This may mean that such immigrants experienced their faith as a unifying force, whereas the political and philosophical ideas of other groups tended to be sources of divisiveness. Charismatic leadership in such religious settlements was perhaps also able to marshal the survival skills of the community more effectively than the loosely organized, cooperative membership of the groups headed by the Dreißiger. Groups founded on religious principles often lived as separately as possible from the wider community. They were also among the last to adapt to American ways and therefore were often the most distinctive among the German-speaking immigrants. Even today, the groups that have clung most fiercely to the German language and Old World ways, the Old Order Amish and the Hutterites, are those that have always separated themselves most strictly from the mainstream society around them.

Let us turn now more specifically to the area that this study encompasses. The territory of present-day Illinois, Missouri, Iowa, Kansas, and Nebraska is representative in many ways of the American nineteenth-century rural frontier. Its geography includes the mixed prairie and woodland of Illinois; the Mississippi and Missouri river basins; the rolling, wooded hills of the Ozarks; the rich, flat farmlands of Iowa; and the Great Plains. The climate ranges from the relative mildness and generous precipitation of the Mississippi Valley to the aridity and temperature extremes of western Kansas and the Nebraska Sandhills. In short, all of the environmental variations of the Midwest are present, with the exception of that typical of the Great Lakes shorelines and the northern forests.[26]

This five-state region received large numbers of German-speaking immigrants, for it was opened to settlement by whites during the course of the nineteenth century, when the great influx of foreign-born immigrants occurred. By the end of that flood of immigration, the Germans were the most numerous foreign-born group in all the states in question.[27] Citizens of every German state and nation, along with significant numbers of Swiss, Austrians, and Germans from Russia, came to this part of America. In 1870, the German-born population in Missouri was 113,618, out of a total population of 1,721,295. If one adds the 11,000 immigrants born in Switzerland and Austria, German-speakers made up approximately 7 percent of the population. In Kansas, out of 1,413,999 residents in 1880, 38,566 were German-speakers. According to the 1900 Nebraska census, persons of German stock (first and second generation) constituted 18 percent of the total population.[28] In certain townships, of course, the numbers could be as high as 80 or 90 percent, as was the case in my neighborhood.

The patterns of settlement that evolved among the German-speakers in this region are typical of those throughout the Midwest.[29] Areas of dense settlement, often by people from the same Old World place of origin, were scattered among areas with almost no foreigners. In Illinois, St. Clair County along the Mississippi, as well as the areas around Darmstadt, Warsaw, Teutopolis, and New Trier, were all German communities, and Highland was German-Swiss. Missouri Germans were concentrated in a "crescent moon" of counties along the Missouri and Mississippi rivers called the Missouri Rhineland, but they were also scattered throughout the state. In counties with many German-speaking settlers, clustering occurred at the township level and was even more apparent in church parishes. The same thing may be observed in the other states examined in this study.[30]

The first Germans from Russia who came to Kansas in the 1870s attempted to buy large tracts of adjoining land to re-create the colonies they had left behind, and Ellis, Harvey, McPherson, and Marion counties are still dominated by the descendants of these immigrants. They were, however, not successful in rebuilding the centralized village structures of their Old World past. Nor was this group of German-speakers heterogeneous. They continued to live in separate communities of Catholics, Lutherans, and Mennonites and were differentiated by their place of origin in Russia (e.g., the "Volga Germans," the "Black Sea Germans").[31]

Such diversity of the German-speaking population is also part of the representative quality of this part of the Midwest. Identifiable settlements of German-speakers from virtually all of the German-speaking states and regions were located here in the nineteenth century.[32] Individuals of various national and regional backgrounds were often scattered among these. Conflicts among the various groups were also not unusual. Sometimes these had to do with language, as when a resident of Clarinda, Iowa, recalled the resentment that Low Germans felt at having to learn High German in their Missouri Synod Lutheran parochial school and remembered that the children who spoke High German at home "made fun of those who couldn't."[33] On other occasions, religious, cultural, or class differences led to conflict. The educated, middle-class Dreißiger often had little understanding for the impoverished peasants who had immigrated during the same period. When Friedrich Gustorf rode through the area between Washington and Union, Missouri, in the summer of 1835, he noted in his diary the filth that prevailed in the homes of the twenty-some families from Osnabrück that had settled there. In spite of the heat, he even refused to accept water from women who appeared too dirty to him.[34] In the St. Louis newspaper *Anzeiger des Westen,* the radical freethinker Heinrich Koch did not hesitate to criticize the newly arrived group of Old Lutherans from Saxony, who were preparing to go to their colony in Perry County, Missouri. On March 2, 1839, he went so far as to harangue them for the wretchedness of their living conditions and to accuse them of undercutting the wages other German day laborers were receiving.

Less public but no less real were the conflicts in rural neighborhoods. In Butler County, Iowa, a gravel road split the German community into two very distinct units, with the High Germans and the Evangelical church on one side and the Low Germans and the Reformed Church of Christ on the other. The perceived differences were long-lived in this community. In 1980, a resident of the High German community remembered that "the Low German people were card players and liked to go to dances" and that the two groups helped each other out but attended different schools and "continued to act as if they were on different social levels."[35]

Close-knit settlements like those of the Germans from Russia, who immigrated in groups and had an already developed sense of shared identity, were able to maintain structures and institutions that helped shield them from the necessity of adapting completely and quickly to Anglo-American culture and society. For all German-speakers in rural areas, the most important institution was the immigrant church. The church gave the immigrants a place of spiritual solace and a center for the development of community and the preservation of language and culture.[36] It was a place where other differences among the German-speakers could be subordinated to a broader sense of shared values, although this did not always happen without conflicts and resentments, as the language conflict in Clarinda, Iowa, shows.

Many areas inhabited by German-speakers who were divided by differences of class (including wealth, education, and social status), regional background, and religious affiliation failed to develop strong communal structures or the sense of a common ethnic identity. For example, the German element in Cooper County, Missouri, was made up of immigrants from places as diverse as Denmark, Holland, Switzerland, Nassau, Alsace, Holstein, Hanover, Bavaria, Baden, Hesse, and Saxony. They were clustered in certain townships and in the county seat, Boonville. Several of the earliest German immigrants, especially those who were relatively wealthy and had few German-speaking neighbors, seem to have associated almost solely with Americans after the first generation. They intermarried with Americans in the second and third generations and, in a few instances, Americanized their names. A diffusion of the ethnic population among several immigrant churches also mitigated against the development of large, unified German communities. Cooper County illustrates this as well. No fewer than seven German-language churches had been organized in Cooper County by 1860, including a Methodist, four Evangelical, one Lutheran, and one Catholic. A second German Catholic church was established in the 1890s as a mission from a Swiss Benedictine abbey near St. Joseph.[37]

German-speakers immigrated to the Midwest for all the reasons cited earlier. In rural areas, as elsewhere in America, the primary motivation was economic. Ihnke Kleihauer (born in 1834) was the heir of his parents' East Frisian farm, but he emigrated at the age of twenty to avoid military induction and, one suspects, to pass a few years fruitfully until his father was ready to turn the farm over to him. He found he liked America and spent the next few years working as a farmhand in Illinois near his oldest sister and her family, where he eventually rented and then bought some land. His letters in this period contain one reason after another why he could not comply with his family's requests that he return. The following excerpt is representative of his letters:

> In the letter that I last wrote to you I promised to return to you. But because I had bought some land here, which you probably already know, but until now had no opportunity to sell it without incurring a loss, I had to wait two more months in order to get the money after I had sold it. That is why I cannot come at the time I promised. But I would also like to ask you something else, because I heard that war is beginning again in Germany. If that is the case, then perhaps it wouldn't be so good if I came. Secondly, when I think about how things are there, that one works the whole year and then has to pay half of the profits to the authorities, and third, a person who has been in America for a while doesn't like the work over there any more. In general farming is much more difficult there than here. One can also eat and drink a lot better here than there, which is the most important thing for a person.[38]

Kleihauer's family eventually stopped trying to persuade him to return, gave him the permission to stay that he requested, and made one of his older sisters the heir to the family holdings. Kleihauer moved to eastern Nebraska in 1865 and died on his farm near Johnson in 1919.

Similar personal statements and stories abound in the Midwest. Kamphoefner has stated that the reasons for immigration found in the memoirs or biographies of most of the impoverished immigrants who came to St. Charles and Warren counties, Missouri, are unclear. They made vague assertions about the possibilities in America and often connected these with the concept of freedom, but it is hard to say whether freedom (*Freiheit*) in its more abstract, political sense or the freedom to attain economic well-being (*Wohlstand*) was foremost or how the two concepts were interrelated.[39] The letters of Friedrich G. Hillenkamp, an educated Dreißiger in St. Charles County, illustrate this. Nine years after his arrival, he wrote an old friend that

> young, hardy people who are used to work belong in America's West. Nature has provided much here, if it is only handled properly, the government is very favorably inclined toward farmers. However, things are bad in some ways for some people in respect to religion, for example, the old women in Velmede [Westphalia] would certainly cross and bless themselves if they heard that I never go to church, eat meat three times a day during Lent, that my children are not even baptized, etc., and that I nevertheless intend to get into the same heaven as all those who punctually observe all of this useless clerical make-work. For my part, I live like the old patriarchs and pray in the great book of nature, live honestly and righteously as always, and concern myself little with the fairy tale of original sin. But enough of this, I am in a free land and you, my friend, in an un-free; here people can express their opinions freely and openly, but you must be silent. . . .

Hillenkamp's other letters contain a similar mixture of reasons for immigration, ranging from personal and political freedom to economic advancement and independence, along with the attractions of the hunt in the American wilderness.[40]

The Midwest is also rich in examples of German-speakers who came to America for reasons other than the economic ones cited by many immigrants. Latin farmers of the 1830s settled in rural areas of Missouri, Illinois, and Iowa. A significant number, perhaps Friedrich Hillenkamp among them, were drawn to Missouri through the bucolic representations in Gottfried Duden's 1829 *Report on a Journey to the Western States of North America*.[41] Among these was a group of about five hundred organized by the Giessen Emigrant Society (Gießener Auswanderer Gesellschaft), led by Paul Follenius and Friedrich Muench. The founders of this group, disillusioned after the failure of the 1830 revolution and hoping to create a model republic in the American West, deliberately chose a cross section of German social classes. The fate of the Giessen Emigrant Society was typical of other groups led in the 1830s and 1840s by German intellectuals who had political and philosophical motivations for emigration. Made up of two contingents that sailed to America in 1834, they were so demoralized by illness and strife during the voyage that they split the common funds soon after arrival in St. Louis and gave up the idea of a closed settlement. Although some of the Giessen Society settled in Warren County near Duden's former home, eventually most of these also became discouraged and disillusioned with pioneer life in the Missouri wilds and moved to the city.[42] Other, smaller groups of Dreißiger had more luck in establishing themselves in Missouri. The Berlin Society of intellectuals, founded by the genial Mecklenberger Wilhelm von Bock in 1832 at Dutzow near Duden's cabin, is one, and the Solingen Society, headed by the Steines family, another. These, too, were short-lived anomalies that had virtually no impact on German emigration or on the developing rural German-American society.[43]

This part of the Midwest also received its share of utopian and religious immigrant groups. Several of these were longer-lasting and had a more significant impact on German-American life and broader American society than those founded by the Dreißiger. The Amana Society, or Community of True Inspiration, in Iowa is among the best known. Bethel in Missouri was the home of one of the longest-lasting German-American communes. The Saxon Old Lutherans, protesting the forced union of the Lutheran and Reformed churches in German lands, arrived in Missouri in late 1838 and established a colony in Perry County and a congregation in St. Louis, seeds of the Missouri Synod church. From the early 1870s, Germans from Russia went to Kansas and Nebraska to avoid having their young men subject to the military draft. Even today the descendants of many of these groups have a strong sense of identity closely linked to their immigrant roots. All of these groups, along with the much larger and more anonymous mass of German-speaking immigrants, receive attention in the following pages.

* * *

This study of rural midwestern German-speakers focuses primarily on the women among them. Because nineteenth-century farm women were first and foremost members of families, it necessarily explores the structural, interpersonal, gender, and economic dynamics of family life. Since agricultural communal life, in both the ethnic community and the wider society, was important to women as well, it is also important to this study.

To gauge the power of ethnicity in these immigrants' lives, I looked for signs of cultural adaptation among rural German-speakers in general and women in particular. Here it is important to compare the behavior of such immigrants with what we might expect of people who brought with them the cultural structures, attitudes, and values we know typified rural European culture and society, as well as with the behavior that characterized the dominant American culture. Chapter 1 explores this Old World "cultural baggage." Individual and group adaptation to the new society is measured by the identifiable influence of American patterns on female, family, and community life among German-speaking farm people in the Midwest.

The core material of the study begins in the second chapter with the examination of concrete aspects of immigrant life: women's roles and contributions in settlement, evidence of the impact of the new physical and cultural environment on women's lives, and general signs of women's cultural adaptation and retention. This material helps assess the "civilizing" contributions rural German-speaking women and their families made to Midwest society. The third chapter gathers information on the subjective impact of immigration by examining in some detail individuals who, because of their backgrounds, stage in life, or personal experiences, can be considered representative of many German-speaking women. This crucial material helps answer the question of whether rural German-speaking women were indeed "contented among strangers." The fourth chapter looks at groups that differed from the broader mass of German-Americans by virtue of their settlement patterns, frontier activities, or communal lives. The chapter focuses on how residence in such communities affected women's frontier experience. The final chapter evaluates the significance of German-speaking immigrants in the cultural and social history of the Midwest, as this has been revealed through women's lives and experiences.

My study of the lives and experiences of rural German-speaking women and their families has led me into other areas of general historical concern. In the final chapter I also look at the history of German-speakers, as the largest non-English-speaking Euro-ethnic immigrant group in nineteenth-century America, for the information it provides about the immigration process in general and about the role of ethnicity in American cultural history in particular. The United States is still facing the complications of a multi-ethnic society. Our incomplete understanding of ethnicity and its impact on the American experience has left many questions only partially answered. How do immigrants react to their new environment? How do Americans react to immigrants? How does the new environment shape them, and how do they alter it over time? After asking these questions about nineteenth-century German-speaking farm families in the Midwest, I am able to assess the validity of Dietar Kügler's assertions, cited earlier in this introduction, that German farmers made extraordinary contributions in the settling of the Midwest and that they transformed Americans with the cultural behavior they brought with them. The central concern throughout my study is, however, elucidating women's roles in all of this and evaluating the degree of their "contentment" in the lives immigration had thrust upon them.

The appendixes provide the reader interested in the broader aspects of my subject matter a framework for understanding my methodology and "hard" evidence about the immigration of German-speakers. Appendix A discusses the resources available to the investigator of the history of German-speaking female immigrants and the limitations inherent in these resources. Appendix B analyzes statistical evidence of the migration, focusing on women and the presence of these female immigrants in the five midwestern states. This background information contributes to a fuller understanding of these rural women in their historical and social context.

1

"The Best Household Utensil": *Women and Families before Emigration*

Where there is no wife, the best household utensil is missing.

A few of the women among the German-speaking immigrants in the Midwest lived on their own, but the majority were in family units. Before we can appreciate what family life in America meant for nineteenth-century German-speaking immigrant women or judge whether residence in America changed it for them, we must know something about the social and historical environment they left. Although this varied somewhat, certain factors were common to virtually all women. Most important, they shared similar cultural and historical backgrounds that determined the ways in which they and their families viewed female roles and behavior.

Women had few legal rights in nineteenth-century Europe, but as the century wore on, women in German lands became relatively worse off in this regard. The establishment of the German nation in 1871 did not bring with it, for example, a married women's property act. A woman could acquire property but not administer it, even if she was single or widowed. As only one of many related folk sayings put it, "Husband and wife have no separate property" ("Mann und Weib haben kein verschieden Gut").[1] The property she brought into marriage became her husband's. Married women were in the legal guardianship of their husbands, and unmarried women in that of their nearest male relative. It was 1949 before married women in East and West Germany gained legal equality in the care and governance of their children. The education of women lagged behind that available to English and French women, partly because industrialization came later to the German-speaking lands and partly because of the strong conservative influences of the Christian churches in those lands. Women were not allowed to attend German universities as regular students until the twentieth century, and almost all professions were closed to them. Folk wisdom held education to be as inappropriate for a woman as forwardness was: "A woman with Latin and a hired girl who contradicts you, neither are worth anything" ("Eine Frau mit Latein und eine Magd, die widerspricht, taugen beide nicht" [Wander 1:1115]). Women also had fewer opportunities at the lower levels of education and tended to be more poorly educated than men. A common saying communicated differing attitudes toward male and female children and their potential: "Boys turn into people. Girls turn into brides" ("Aus Knaben werden Leute. Aus Mädchen werden Bräute").[2] More ominous, other proverbs expressed women's vulnerable social and legal status: "Women and eggs, the more you beat them, the better they get" ("Frauen und Eier, je mehr geschlagen, je besser werden sie" [Wander, 1:1123]). Until 1900, German common law allowed husbands to use physical means to discipline their wives. Similar laws and customs prevailed throughout Europe in the nineteenth century.[3]

If the laws of a land are some indication of the intended power structures of a society, then it is certain that women were meant to be the subordinates of men in nineteenth-century German-speaking lands. On the individual level and within the family sphere, however, things could be different. Women of the middle and upper classes were usually not as bad off as their legal status would suggest. Women of the aristocracy had, of course, long enjoyed the personal and public privileges that wealth and status bring. The Enlightenment, although not as influential in German-speaking lands as elsewhere in eighteenth-century Europe, had propounded women's and men's intellectual equality. In that same century, Pietism encouraged an emotional approach to spiritual self-realization. This religious movement permeated most of German Protestantism and raised the status of women. In Pietism, women were viewed as creatures ruled by their emotions, which proved to be beneficial for women for it enhanced their possibilities for expressing themselves publicly and exercising authority in spiritual and moral questions. Women of the growing middle classes were the ones to profit most from this. As the century went on, they became more influential in cultural life, had more opportunities for education, and founded a movement calling for women's political and social rights.[4]

The changing attitudes among some sectors of the educated classes in the eighteenth century did not significantly alter the lives of women of the lower classes, though. Agrarian reform and the change to a centralized, capitalist economy that accompanied nineteenth-century industrialization had a much more direct impact on the family lives of large segments of the population than did political and social theory. It is important to keep in mind, however, that industrialization and the shift to a market economy affected some parts of society much more than others and that different national and geographic sectors of the German-speaking lands felt the consequences at different times. For these reasons, the following summary should be regarded as a general model, one not valid in every respect for each individual.[5]

In preindustrial European society, the family was essentially a production unit in which each member had a role. The cooperative nature of family labor ensured that women's labor would be recognized and valued. Proverbs like the following collaborate this: "The wife is the key to the house" ("Die Frau ist der Schlüßel des Hauses" [Wander, 1:1107]); "Where there is no wife, the best household utensil is missing" ("Wo keine Frau ist, da fehlt's am besten Hausrat" [Beyer and Beyer, 169]). More directly related to women's role as household producers are such sayings as these: "Where a wife is in charge of the household, the bacon grows from the rafters" ("Wo die Frau wirthschaftet, wächst der Speck am Balkan" [Wander, 1:1139]); "A thrifty wife fills the house up to the roof" ("Eine sorgliche Frau füllt das Haus bis unters Dach" [Wander, 1:1119]). In fact, one scholar points to women's status as "the first workers in the household" as the economic reason behind their legal subordination; they were simply too valuable to be allowed autonomy.[6]

A recent study by David W. Sabean shows that lower-class and peasant women strongly resisted nineteenth-century official rhetoric and policies that sought to reify a hierarchical, male-dominated control over them and the property they brought into marriage. Sabean's study throws into doubt assertions of German-speaking women's uniform submission to the men in their lives and subordination to the patriarchal constructs and dialogue of the state. The realities of women's lives and their awareness, solidified by their everyday experience, of their importance and contributions to the family economic enterprise strengthened them in this resistance.[7]

Whether they lived in rural or urban areas, women did productive labor of a seasonal and interruptible nature in or near the home. They were in charge of the raising, procurement, preparation, and storage of food. They usually spun the thread and wove the cloth from which they manufactured the family's clothes. They had the main care of the children and oversaw their contributions to the family labor. If they were rural women, they were in charge of the livestock and the products (eggs, milk, and butter) of the livestock and, with their children, did most of the garden work. Women who lived in cities probably also had a garden and small animals to tend, and they helped the men of the family in their business or handicraft. Farm women were called on to work in the fields at peak labor periods. In poorer families, married women's control over decisions and work having to do with the family's nutrition probably gave them considerable power, for food was the main family expense.[8] All women made important and visible contributions to the family's livelihood in the preindustrial family. Agricultural traditions and economy demanded the maintenance of this way of life and of the productive role for rural women long after industrialization radically changed most other women's existence in the German-speaking lands.

Industrialization removed the center of production from the family. The separation of labor spheres and the move toward a capital-oriented economy brought changes to women's status and contributions within the family, particularly, at first, in urban areas. Families of the growing middle class, which most immediately profited by the rise of industrialism and capitalism, were the first to show the effects. The realm of labor, in the capitalist sense of employment for wages and profit, moved outside the home to the workplace of the male head of the household. Women were left in charge of the household, which had lost its economic status within both the family and society at large. Labor was divided into paid and unpaid labor, which also came to mean recognized and unrecognized labor. With the household's loss in economic status came a loss in status and power for those associated with it: primarily women but servants and minor children as well. By the second half of the nineteenth century, household domestic production in middle-class families had changed into consumerism.[9]

The removal of the center of productive labor from the home left the married middle-class woman with one primary purpose: the care of the home as a refuge from what increasingly came to be seen as the harsh, cold world of commerce. Although she continued to contribute in concrete ways to the economic viability of the family through her work in the home and the labor she supervised there, as she had in preindustrial times, sentiment grew in middle-class circles that what she did should not appear as work, in order to differentiate the home and "shield" the family as much as possible from the hectic and morally threatening male work sphere. Eventually, household work was thought of as "beneath" the bourgeois housewife, and the number of servant girls in the home became a measure of middle-class status. Particularly after the failure of the 1848 revolutions, a tendency toward the "aristocratizing" of the German-speaking middle classes became stronger. The second generation often withdrew from active involvement in the family business and devoted a great deal of time and energy to the outer presentation of wealth and status.[10] Although proportionately few upper-middle-class German-speaking families were among those who immigrated to America, we cannot discount an awareness of such models of behavior among other middle-class and lower-middle-class immigrants in their reactions and adjustments to American conditions, especially since the dominant culture in the New World shared these ideals of female behavior.

The traditional view of women as subjective and emotional also contributed to the role the middle-class wife and mother assumed as the center of the intimate, emotional life of the family. The division of spheres of work and influence supported separatist ideas about gender. The conviction developed in middle- and upper-class circles that there were "typical" masculine and feminine qualities, perhaps partly as a justification for that division. Men came to be identified with certain qualities and behavior: rationalism and objectivity, lack of emotion, and vulnerability to corruption through the outside world. Women were thought to be subjective, passive, and innately moral. As one scholar has put it, "Women's identity and men's seemed to diverge so radically in the nineteenth century that all human communication across the gender-boundary was impaired."[11]

The growing divergence of the intellectual and emotional realms of the sexes did not take place to the same extent among the majority of the poorer, less educated German-speakers, however. Again, this stemmed from economic conditions. The division of labor between the public and the private spheres because of industrialization did not proceed as quickly or as completely in rural areas or among the lower classes. In the families of some successful craftsmen and small businessmen, women continued to play almost the same central productive, preindustrial role in the twentieth century that they had in the nineteenth.[12] In many parts of the German-speaking lands and in some social groups, however, this way of family life was threatened by many factors. Rising population and decreasing mortality in Europe in the eighteenth and nineteenth centuries led to a higher marriage rate and a lower average age at marriage,[13] but the founding of more families lagged behind the ability of the protoindustrial economy to absorb the growing labor supply. In addition, the spread of mass-produced products, such as textiles and shoes, and the centralization of services and production put craftspeople and small businesspeople out of work.

Craftspeople who combined their trade with small landholdings, cottagers, and day-laborer families in rural areas were especially vulnerable. They had managed to attain some security and relative prosperity in the latter eighteenth century by adding a cottage industry, such as weaving, to the family craft and agricultural production. Often the unmarried daughters were the ones who contributed these wage earnings to the family income. An interesting consequence of cottage industry was that it tended to increase women's status in the family and to break down gender-determined work roles, since the entire family cooperated to gain and maintain economic independence.[14] It was at this time that such sayings as the following arose: "The best place for women is at the distaff" ("Der Frauen bester Ort ist am Spinnrocken" [Wander, 1:1105]). As industrialization eliminated cottage industries, however, some families could no longer survive as independent economic units. They had little choice except to join the growing ranks of the urban proletariate or, if they wanted to continue their accustomed way of life, to start anew elsewhere.[15]

The continuation of preindustrial patterns of labor and family structure throughout the nineteenth century was probably more prevalent among women engaged in agriculture than among those married to skilled laborers, small businessmen, and workers of the new urban proletariate.[16] Young, unmarried rural women did work outside the home in the preindustrial era as farm workers and maids, and they also earned supplemental income in cottage industries, such as spinning and weaving. Wages earned in this way, essentially in the home environment, were considered part of the family income, though. This pattern persisted among European peasant families even after industrialization was well established. The daughters in such families were sent to work in sectors of the economy in which they had worked at home: as housemaids or hired girls and in the garment-making and textile industries. Peasant families could thus maintain traditional values of interdependence and cooperative labor. This was probably also true of most lower-class families in predominantly rural areas. The persistence of these family strategies, values, and structures helps explain why nineteenth-century industrialization did not "emancipate" women of the lower classes or cause them to clamor for political enfranchisement. A woman's only acceptable course for ensuring some measure of personal and financial independence was marriage and the founding of her own household.[17]

Since rural family and social patterns persisted in many German-speaking areas throughout the nineteenth century, it is important to examine these patterns to better understand emigrants from such sectors of society. German-speaking parts of Europe remained predominantly rural in nature throughout the nineteenth century. For example, in 1871, when the German nation was founded, 64 percent of its residents still lived in communities of less than two thousand, and half of the population earned their living in agriculture.[18] The large number of emigrants from agricultural areas also makes it important to examine these attitudes and patterns. Between 1840 and 1855, 46 percent to 51 percent of the emigrants from Baden were farmers, for example, and the percentage of Prussian agricultural workers in the emigration between 1862 and 1880 was comparable.[19] Many of these came to the midwestern United States.

In the Old World, many young rural men and women, if they were not the sole heir of a farm, were not needed in the family farm labor force, or were not engaged in a cottage industry as a contribution to the family income, worked as hired hands on other farms during adolescence and young adulthood. Rural families viewed this employment for women as training for marriage, not as a break with the family. At least in the first half of the century in the German-speaking lands, a woman was also considered part of the extended family of the farm on which she worked, so in a sense she remained in the familiar relationships of her home. A reflection of the familylike status of hired help and an indication of the power relationships within the extended farm household is the fact that German law governing the conditions and duties of farm servants allowed the physical punishment of hired hands by their masters and mistresses until 1900, just as it allowed wife-beating. The more positive familial aspects of farm-servant status in the preindustrial era included the tradition that servants ate at the same table and slept under the same roof as their masters and mistresses. This remained so until agrarian reform, the pressures of the market economy, and the infiltration of urban middle-class cultural values and patterns created a two-class rural society and thus altered social relationships in peasant communities.[20]

As a hired hand, a woman might be asked to do anything that a hired man would do, but she was also expected to cook, clean, darn, sew, and (until 1900) spin. In peak labor periods, fourteen- to sixteen-hour workdays were not uncommon for all peasant women.[21] A hired girl's entire existence was oriented toward her future marriage. The savings she accumulated, the dowry of linen and thread she made or was given, the agricultural and household skills she developed, the reputation she earned as a worker and person in the rural community determined her future and that of any children she might have. If she was successful in making an appropriate and secure marriage, she gained a lasting place in the rural community.[22]

Her place as wife, to be sure, was marked by very hard work. It was no accident that Swabian farm girls said, "Happy, when we're single—sad, when we marry" ("Lustig, wenn mer ledig sind—traurig, wenn mer hauset").[23] Even more bluntly, it was also said, "A woman who marries must have a pig's snout [to consume the family's leavings] and a donkey's back" ("Eine Frau, die heirathet, muß ein Schweinsmaul und einen Eselrücken haben" [Wander, 1:1113]).

In addition to the hard work and self-denial that society expected of her, the woman who married also lost whatever autonomy she might have had as a single wage earner or property owner. She would live the rest of her life limited by the authority of her husband, an authority that derived to a large extent from his public role in the village pub, the communal meetings, the church council, and, most important, the commercial livestock and grain markets. The disparity between men's and women's power in marriage was less in areas of subsistence farming but changed in favor of the man whenever the farm economy was altered by an increase in mechanization or a switch to production for centralized markets. In general, a woman's power was restricted to the household. Although the wife on a larger farm might have considerable authority within those confines, in the view of society and all its institutions, it was her husband who granted it to her.[24] Men did not always grant even this authority graciously: "He who wants peace in his house must do what his wife wants" ("Wer in seinem Haus Friede haben will, der muß tun, was die Frau will" [Beyer and Beyer, 169]).

The alternatives to marriage for rural women were the religious life (in Catholic areas) or the life of celibate family member or life-long servant. The religious life effectively removed women from society, and the status of the unmarried woman in the household was low. The exploitation of female farm labor, noted in many German-speaking areas well into the twentieth century, indicates the low status of women in rural areas. This could take particularly pernicious forms, at least from a modern point of view. In some parts of Swabia (as elsewhere in Europe), the intellectual development of one daughter in the family might be intentionally inhibited so she could be kept at home to serve as cheap labor and to care for aged parents. Such a girl was referred to as *dubbelig,* or simple (rather than *blöd,* the common term for mental retardation), and it was said in the village that she was "kept as a simpleton" (*als Dubbel gehalten*). Such exploitation of rural women by family members was not typical, perhaps, but it is indicative of the instrumentality that underlay attitudes toward women and the treatment of women.[25]

A host of nineteenth-century proverbs attests to women's low status and the misogynist attitudes prevalent in the culture of German-speakers. Women were criticized for their vanity: "Every woman loves the woman in the mirror" ("Jede Frau liebt die Frau im Spiegel" [Wander, 1:1127]). Although their future depended on the marriage they could make, their beauty made them suspect: "He who has a beautiful wife is never without worries" ("Wer ein schönes Weib hat, ist nie ohne Sorgen" [Beyer and Beyer, 662]). Restricted in opportunities for education and training, women were portrayed as irrational and frivolous creatures: "Women, wind, and luck change in a moment" ("Frauen, Wind und Glück wechseln im Augenblick" [Wander, 1:1124]); "Women have long hair, short thoughts, whoever doesn't believe that will experience it" ("Frauen haben lange Haar, kurtze Sinn, wers nicht glaubt, der wird es inn" [Wander, 1:1125]). Their preferred activity was talking: "Even if a woman is stupid, she is never silent" ("Ist eine Frau auch dumm, doch ist sie niemals stumm" [Wander, 1:1127]); "Who can know how often women gossip and dogs piss" ("Wie oft die Frauen schwatzen und die Hunde pissen, wer kann das wissen" [Wander, 1:1138]). Women were untrustworthy and prone to mendacity: "Women do tell the truth—but never all of it" ("Die Frauen sagen wohl die Wahrheit—aber nie ganz" [Wander, 1:1108]). If given half a chance, women would rule over their husbands: "He who takes a wife takes a master" ("Wer eine Frau nimmt, der nimmt einen Herrn" [Beyer and Beyer, 169]). Although it was said that "he who has a wife and land and a house can endure life" ("Wer eine Frau hat und Acker und Haus, der hält das Leben aus" [Wander, 1:1135]), another proverb stated that woman's presence in the house could not make up for the lack of material possessions: "He who has nothing better has to make do with his wife" ("Wer nichts Besseres hat, muß mit seiner Frau vorliebnehmen" [Beyer and Beyer, 169]). Long-held attitudes among German-speakers, bolstered by Pauline traditions in the church, held ultimately that "all women are Eve's daughters" ("Alle Frauen sind Evas Töchter" [Beyer and Beyer, 169]).

Economic factors, influenced by the centrality of the family holding in peasant life, also help explain unmarried women's low status. European and German-speaking peasant family life centered around the strategies necessary for the continuation of the land-based household.[26] The size of the family farm established the place of the family in the community as well as the availability of meaningful roles for individuals in the productive life of the farm and the community. A small farm could support only a limited number of people, and the average size of peasant families in early nineteenth-century western Europe was around five persons. On smallholdings, children consequently were often sent away to work in other families as early as the age of nine or ten.[27] Since women's labor was paid more poorly than men's, their contributions to their family were less.[28] They also were often unable to accumulate enough resources themselves to secure an independent existence, particularly as the years of their greatest physical strength passed. If they were the daughters of smallholders, their eventual inheritance portion would probably not be large enough to help them. Unmarried children, even if they worked away from home, were a potential burden to the family as an economic unit. If they became ill, they often had to be cared for at home. In many German-speaking areas, the illegitimate children of the daughters of the house were often regarded as an additional burden, whereas the legitimate children of married peasants were a potential source of labor.[29] For all concerned, it was therefore generally better if rural women established their own households.

Young rural men and women did not always find it easy to marry, however. During the course of the nineteenth century, local authorities placed restrictions on the marriage of poor people in many German-speaking areas. These laws and statutes were an attempt to limit the establishment of more such families, which grew in number as the century went on. The restrictions, however, did little except increase the number of illegitimate births and arouse the underclasses' hostility toward the government.[30]

Inheritance laws and customs also sometimes frustrated people's hopes of marriage. Two dominant patterns of inheritance obtained in nineteenth-century German lands: partible and impartible. In areas with partible inheritance (which included most of the western and southwestern German lands), the family property was split equally among the sons and daughters upon the death or retirement of the parents. Often one of the children would buy or rent the land of the other siblings to keep most or all of the family land intact and to have an economically viable farm. The family residence usually passed to a single heir, in return for extra compensation to the parents or other heirs. This pattern led to increasingly small peasant holdings during the course of the nineteenth century.

The territories with impartible inheritance (most of Prussia, Westphalia, Bavaria, and Austria) were those in which families tended to live on large farms in separate houses, instead of traveling to their land from villages. The attachment to the family holding was particularly strong in these areas, for the residence was passed on, along with the land, to only one child. A sign that the holding was more important than the family is that the name of the house was the one used to refer to the family residing in it. It was the holding that had continuity rather than the family per se.[31] Since the child inheriting the holding (always a man, except in the absence of a male heir) could not attain independence until his parents were ready to turn the farm over to him, he often married and shared the family residence with his parents for a number of years. Two- and three-generational "stem" families resulted. Upon the parents' death or retirement, the heir had to recompense his siblings in money or property for their share in the family holding. Often the wife's dowry was the source for such payments. Both partible and impartible inheritance, by focusing everyone's efforts on passing on the family holdings as intact as possible, had the effect of enhancing intergenerational ties in the family and links to the village and community.[32]

These inheritance patterns also had negative aspects. They were built on the subordination of individual wishes to the broader good of the family. Strong as the pressures of family tradition, communal expectations, and legal structures were in enforcing family-centered attitudes and behavior, however, resistance is evident. Economically based antagonism between siblings and between parents and children was common. It was sometimes a contributing factor in the decision to emigrate. Thirty years after leaving Germany, Louis Osterholt wrote his parents, "I wouldn't want to be dead there with you in Germany, where the oldest son gets everything and the other children, one can say, nothing. If that is just, than anything is. I am always glad that I left Germany in my youth and that what I have and have saved is all mine. Don't have to thank you or anyone else for it."[33] Children had to wait for their parents to die or step down from active life before they could come into their own economic majority. Once parents had retired, children were often reluctant to support them, as the many laws governing such support indicate. Young people, even heirs, delayed marriage until their mid- to late-twenties, or sometimes well into their thirties because they had to accumulate enough capital or property to establish an independent household. Even aside from restrictions on marriages among the economically disadvantaged, the practicalities of life were enough to ensure that people generally married only when they could afford to do so.

In areas of impartible legacy, the noninheriting siblings were even more likely than the primary heir to postpone or forego marriage. Peasant women were at a general disadvantage regarding marriage. Since they were unlikely to be the main heir, they had to accumulate as much capital as possible to marry on a level equal to that of their family. Because this was difficult to do, they often had to "marry down" if they wanted to marry at all. Most people did want to marry, not only for self-gratification and survival but also because this step integrated them into the close kinship structures of rural communities.[34]

Several scholars of the German peasantry have pointed to the centrality of economic concerns in marriage and family life among rural residents as the basis for an apparent lack of emotional attachment in their personal relationships.[35] The conflict and competition among siblings and generations discussed earlier no doubt strained those relations at times. This is apparent in many of the letters emigrants wrote home. Certainly the economic basis for marriage contracts between landowning families sometimes resulted in incompatible couples, but the relative homogeneity and closeness of the rural community, which was a network of intermarriages going back for generations, might have made such mismatches less common than among the propertied middle and upper classes.[36] Probably the centrality of preserving and, if possible, increasing the family holding, along with the cooperative nature of working life between farm men and women, made the emotional content of marriage secondary to its pragmatic aspects. A Swabian proverb expressed what was important in a peasant marriage: "So let those who bind themselves to each other for eternity think about how the meadow will be added to the field" ("Drum prüfe, wer sich ewig bindet, wie sich die Wies zum Acker findet").[37] The eternal bonds of peasant marriage had very concrete earthly dimensions.

It is easy to conclude from our contemporary perspective that marriages founded on such considerations lacked all subjective depth and meaning, but the daily shared life of labor could build bonds of mutual respect that were perhaps more enduring than those of sexual attraction. Indeed, another proverb claimed, "Equality is the bond of love" ("Gleichheit ist der Liebe Band" [Beyer and Beyer, 222]). Many other proverbs also praised mutuality in marital relations, especially that based on the sharing of resources and of good household management: "The husband makes the wife and the wife the husband" ("Der Mann macht die Frau und die Frau den Mann" [Wander, 3:377]); "In the household the wife should be the left and the husband the right eye" ("Die Frau soll im Haus das linke, der Mann das rechte Auge sein" [Wander, 1:1107]); "Husband and wife are one body" ("Mann und Weib sind ein Leib" [Wander, 3:420]). Such folk sayings assert the possibility and even the desirability of a oneness within marriage, which, although it might be based in pragmatic considerations, had emotional dimensions as well.

Protoindustry in rural areas also increased the possibilities of marrying for love instead of property. An indication of this is the markedly lower marriage ages of both women and men in areas of strong cottage industries. Young people could follow their hearts rather than the dictates of purse and family and establish independent households. It is, of course, impossible to know if such marriages were any happier in the long run than those arranged primarily for economic considerations. What seems likely, however, is that such couples were quicker to assume bourgeois attitudes toward marriage and personal relationships.[38]

It is in any case difficult to explore or document the subjective dimension of ordinary people's lives in earlier times, since they left few personal records. Again, proverbial sayings give us some clues. Economic equality between potential marriage partners was desirable, as several proverbs proclaimed: "Equal partners dance best together" ("Gleiche Paare geben den besten Tanz"); "Equal horses pull best" ("Gleiche Pferde ziehen am besten"); "The best peace exists among equals" ("Unter Gleichen ist der beste Friede" [Beyer and Beyer, 221]). Whatever their initial economic status, husbands and wives were urged to deal with each other equally once united in marriage: "Once the blanket is over their heads, the married couple is equally rich" ("Ist die Decke über dem Kopf, so sind die Eheleute gleich reich"); "In marriage there can be no peace if it is ruled by 'mine' and 'thine'" ("In der Ehe kann kein Frieden sein regiert darin das Mein und Dein" [Beyer and Beyer, 168]).

The wife had the power to make or break the household, depending on whether she was thrifty or a spendthrift: "A woman can carry away more in her apron than a man drives in with the hayrack" ("Eine Frau kann mehr mit der Schürze forttragen, als der Mann mit dem Heuwagen einfährt" [Wander, 1:1114]). The same was true of the husband: "Women make talers out of pennies; men make pennies out of talers" ("Frauen machen aus Pfennigen Taler; Männer aus Talern Pfennige" [Beyer and Beyer, 168]). The contributions of each marriage partner to the union were sometimes summed up thusly, emphasizing the importance of women's material wealth: "If the wife has nothing and the husband does nothing, the marriage is seldom good" ("Wenn die Frau nichts hat und der Mann nichts tut, ist die Ehe selten gut" [Beyer and Beyer, 168]).

Women's social and legal status as men's property also comes through in sayings that equated them with other objects: "One shouldn't loan out women, horses, and clocks" ("Frauen, Pferde und Uhren soll man nicht verleihen"); "One must check out horses and women equally carefully" ("Pferde und Frauen muß man gleich beschauen" [Beyer and Beyer, 168]). A bald statement of women's economic status and value is contained in the following widespread saying: "The death of a wife causes no harm, but the death of horses makes a beggar out of a farmer" ("Weibersterben bringt kein Verderben, aber Pferde im Grab bringen den Bauer an den Bettelstab" [Wander, 5:74]).[39] A new wife could replace the old one and possibly add another dowry to the family holdings, but the replacement of livestock meant an outlay of capital, a loss to the family finances. Similarly, it was said, "If your wives die on you and your horses foal, your wealth increases" ("Wem die Frauen sterben und die Pferde fohlen, dem wächst das Vermögen" [Wander, 1:1121]).

These and similar sayings certainly point to German-speakers' basic attitudes toward women and their economic function and roles. Nevertheless, we should also remind ourselves that proverbs express only part of the way people think and feel about common situations and aspects of human life. The husband who had just lost a wife with whom he had had children and built a life for several years was no doubt unlikely to think first of how fortunate he was that his prize draft mare did not die instead. The intertwining of practical interests, common experiences, and the shared bonds of work, family, and community formed ties that probably were at least as strong and deep as most today. In spite of women's inferior legal and social status, woman's central significance for family life was certainly felt: "The wife is the husband's life" ("Die Frau ist des Mannes Leben" [Wander, 1:1107]).

Nineteenth-century contemporaries from the middle class sometimes commented on the paucity of emotional life they witnessed among German-speaking rural populations.[40] Again, the economic basis of family life was probably a factor in the deemphasis of its emotional dimension. We should remember, however, that these witnesses were also viewing peasant life from their own perspective, one imbued with the emotional value family life had acquired in bourgeois society during the eighteenth and nineteenth centuries, partly as a result of the separation of the workplace from the home.[41] Rural families in the nineteenth century, unless they owned large amounts of land and employed many servants, had to work prodigiously and probably had little extra energy for displays of affection in the conventional sense. That they did not show it in front of middle-class outsiders might also be a reflection of shyness or traditional reticence rather than a lack of emotion.

Scholars have also raised questions concerning the status of children in rural and working-class families and parents' emotional attachment to young children. In the typical rural family, children had a role in production by the age of five or six. Until then, it has been asserted, they were given little special attention or care because horrendous mortality rates discouraged the investment of emotion in them.[42] This is arguable, though. The economic conditions that forced women to do hard physical labor just before and after giving birth and prevented them from adequately caring for their infants certainly drove infant mortality rates higher. Desperate economic conditions could well have made people consider a new child another burden. This does not mean that poor women and men did not love their children or that they would not have better cared for them if they had been able. It may be that poor people protected themselves from the pain of losing so many children by adopting habits of mind and patterns of behavior that permitted greater acceptance of and resignation to the harsh reality of their losses.[43]

Certainly letters home indicate that many immigrants loved and cherished their children. Wilhelm Niggemeier, having accumulated enough money working as a shoemaker in St. Louis to send for his wife and five children, wrote a letter detailing the food and cooking equipment she should take aboard ship and admonishing her three times to keep watch on the children, lest they fall overboard during the voyage. Amalia Rückels wrote to her mother-in-law in 1861, "Hardly an hour goes by that I do not think of you and remember many a thing, that you always took care of me and my little Augusta, and yet I had to lose the dear child so early, which still makes me cry sometimes." The toddler had died soon after the Rückels arrived in St. Louis in 1857. Amalia's husband Gottfried wrote in late 1871 of a farm accident the previous spring in which their next child, a son fourteen years old at the time, had been killed: "Oh, dear sister, you cannot believe how my heart has been wounded by this blow. Every day the tears roll from my eyes when I think of my dear son." Two years later, after the birth of their tenth child, Gottfried wrote that he would not mind having another dozen: "Children are my joy."[44] Were people like Wilhelm Niggemeier and Gottfried and Amalia Rückels atypical for German-speaking rural residents?

The testimony that Johannes Gillhoff drew from immigrant letters sent to his pastor father, Gottlieb, by former parishioners in the Mecklenburg-Vorpommern village of Glaisin may be useful in this context. Gillhoff, himself a teacher, created from the letters a composite figure, Jürnjakob Swehn. In the enormously popular book-length collection that resulted, Gillhoff had "Swehn" tell how he immigrated to Iowa in 1868 with others from his Mecklenburg village, married a village girl who had also immigrated, and with her eventually established his family on their own farm. Although we cannot know how accurately and completely the bourgeois schoolteacher cited the immigrants' letters as he edited them (we cannot even be sure of the sex of the writers), the authenticity of the immigrant experience speaks so strongly through Gillhoff's figure that I believe it justifiable to use his book to supplement the primary sources we can verify. To remind the reader of the composite nature of this testimony, however, I place Swehn's name in quotation marks whenever I cite from the work.

The letters of "Swehn" contain evidence of the emotional bonds between poor Germans and their children. About thirty years after immigrating, "Swehn" sent his mother, the widow of a rural day laborer, a ticket to join them, and she spent the last six years of her life in Iowa. The letter that "Swehn" wrote his Mecklenburg schoolteacher (Gillhoff) upon his mother's death speaks movingly of the love he and his mother felt for each other, even though they did not show it outwardly. At her deathbed, the following exchange took place:

> Then she said very softly, as if she were ashamed: "Jürnjakob," she said, "you can give me a kiss. No one has kissed me for such a long time. I've only gotten a kiss three times in my life. Once, when I married Jürnjochen. The next time when you were born. The third time, when Jürnjochen died. Now I want to get ready to follow him. So you can give me one for the journey." And I said: "Mother, that's how things are with me, too, and I see that I am your son. So we both have something to catch up on."
>
> So I bent over her gently and gave her a good kiss, and she caressed my cheek as if I were still her little boy. Then she lay back and was content.

"Swehn" closes his account of his mother's death by saying how often he thought of her and the harshness of her life and how the trusting piety of her death consoles him. He concludes, "I was still a very little boy. On one Pentecost morning I had slept late, which really is not good, because then one is a *Pingstekarr* [the last one to drive the livestock out to pasture]. Then suddenly I woke up, because I felt something soft on my face. My mother was standing at my bed. She was bending over me and tickling my face with a little sprig of lilac. She was doing that very softly. And as she did it, she was looking at me kindly. See, that is my first memory of my mother." Such testimony indicates that deep wells of emotional attachment could exist among family members, even without demonstrativeness. What "Swehn" said about himself and those from his part of Germany might have been typical of many rural German-speakers: "That's just how it is: the North German keeps inner things to himself."[45] Certainly these and related readings about the nineteenth-century German peasantry have helped me better understand the emotional restraint in my father's family and in the rural neighborhood in which I grew up.

*   *   *

A strong case can be built for the endurance of many patterns of rural family and community life among German-speakers throughout the nineteenth century, even though industrialization and the move toward a market economy produced pressures for change. Families still attempted to operate cooperatively as production units and to maintain family and community continuity through marriage and inheritance structures. This became increasingly difficult as the century went on, however. Peasant emancipation legislation and related agrarian reforms that were gradually instituted in the first half of the century also contributed to this. The old rural landscape of compact villages surrounded by open fields, characterized by common pastures and three-crop rotation (summer grain, winter grain, and fallow land), had endured for two centuries or more, but pressure toward crop specialization, brought about by the increased population and development of urban centers, was growing, even in the backward German lands.

The Napoleonic reforms of 1807–8 began a process that continued throughout the first half of the century in western Europe. The common village landholdings were eliminated, and laws that had bound peasants to the soil in varying degrees were abolished. The new freedom resulted in greater productivity for landowners, but it also meant the loss of security for those who had had the guaranteed protection of a manorial lord and the end of a marginal livelihood for those little farmers who had supplemented their smallholdings with the village common fields for their few heads of livestock. Landless agricultural workers—farm servants, contractual farm workers, and day laborers—also suffered from the economic and social disruptions that ensued. As German lands moved toward a money-based, large-scale capitalistic organization of agriculture, a rural proletariat was created, a class of people who had no control over the means of agricultural production. They were vulnerable to exploitation by the landowners in control of those means and were increasingly vulnerable to general economic conditions as well as the vagaries of poor crops and weather-related calamities.[46]

Women proved to be especially at risk in rural areas as these economies became increasingly specialized and mechanized. Their traditional labor was often the first to be affected, and they found themselves less and less in control of when and how much they could or had to work. High maternity and infant mortality rates among peasants in German lands resulted, particularly in areas that developed specialized crops requiring seasonal labor.[47] Poor nutrition, increasingly typical of the peasant diet as the century wore on, was a factor in increased mortality among women and children. The potato became the staple of the poor family's diet. The toy makers of Sonneberg in Thuringia had the saying, "Potatoes in the morning, at noon in broth, in the evening in their jackets, potatoes in eternity" ("Kartoffeln in der Früh, zum Mittag in der Brüh, des abends mitsamt dem Kleid, Kartoffeln in Ewigkeit").[48] It is no wonder that the failure of the potato crop in the 1850s led to massive emigration from southwest Germany, for example. Meat was rarely served in poor households, perhaps only on holidays. The meat a family had at its disposal often came from the one pig it could afford to raise each year. The family took butter and eggs to market instead of consuming them.[49] In some areas, people who owned no land were not even allowed to raise their own poultry. Of course, hunting and trapping had long been strictly regulated and restricted to property owners. Not surprisingly, many immigrants' letters to relatives in Germany comment on the amount of protein in their diet in America.

In the nineteenth century, it became impossible for many economically marginal rural residents in German-speaking lands to continue family and community life as they had known it. Cottage industry, which for a time had given the smallholders and landless members of rural society the chance to compete financially with landowning peasants, proved to be even more vulnerable to economic disaster than had earlier marginal agricultural life. The possession of land had been for centuries the single, unchallenged measure of one's place in rural society. As members of the rural community, the underclasses had shared the traditional, conservative values of peasant society, even though they were relegated to the lower rungs of that society by the landowning peasantry.[50] It should not surprise us, then, that if they immigrated to America, these families displayed behavior very similar to that which was characteristic of the society they had left behind and that they viewed landownership as a family goal worth the greatest sacrifices.

Some have argued that most families, especially those from nineteenth-century rural areas, emigrated to preserve their threatened way of life. Mack Walker has said that emigrants like these "went to America less to build something new than to regain and conserve something old, which they remembered or thought they did: to till new fields and find new customers, true enough, but ultimately to keep the ways of life they were used to . . . they were conservatives, who acted radically in order to preserve, and who journeyed to another world to keep their homes."[51] In the following pages, I seek evidence of such conservatism, as well as cultural change, in the lives of women and their families who came to the Midwest in the nineteenth century. Let us begin by turning to the general aspects of women's activities and roles both before and after emigration.

2

Arriving, Settling In, and Surviving: Emigration and the Concrete Aspects of Adaptation

Farewell, O you dear fatherland,
To fare thee well we raise our hand;
Our gaze does grow sad, of course,
But fortune's eyes do smile on us;
At home just fear and poverty,
Typhus, starvation, and misery;
Thus a new home do we seek,
America, we turn to thee. . . .
—Christian Hansern, "Song of the Emigrants
    upon Their Departure for America"

Most of the German-speakers who came to rural areas of the Midwest seeking new homes free from the travails of their old life came as members of families. They knew that in all probability they were leaving their homeland forever. By traveling with family members, they had a bulwark against total estrangement in the new land, but they also knew that their lives would never be the same as they had been. For adult women, whose lives had revolved around the home and the kinship structures of the rural community, this must have been a daunting prospect. Would they be able to preserve their old ways, while of necessity adapting to their new environment? What strategies, conditioned by their ethnic and cultural background, could they employ to accomplish this? This chapter explores women's contributions in the process of emigration and the adaptation to the new environment. Family structure—that is, the context of power relations in the family—is one of the primary focuses.

In most cases we do not know what role German-speaking women played in the decision to emigrate. Their personal documents usually do not comment on this or why they emigrated since the writer and her audience already knew.[1] Because economic considerations usually set the emigration in motion and because most of those who eventually became Midwest farmers did so as part of families, it is likely that women, whose lives and work were centered in their families, were willing participants. Louisa Roenigk was certainly acting in her family's long-term interest when she left Thuringia with her thirteen-year-old brother, worked on a farm and then as a domestic in Madison and St. Louis before marrying, and later helped her parents and siblings come to Kansas. Other German-born women were eager to emigrate for similar reasons. Ferdinand and Augusta (Holtz) Beulke left Pommerania ten years after their marriage in 1877 because of family concerns: "due to the serious illnesses and disappointments in losing their four children they decided to leave their homeland." Katharine Ensinger Reinim, an impoverished widow, went to the Belleville, Illinois, area with her six children in response to a letter from her childless cousin, who had recently lost his wife. He made it clear he was at least as interested in gaining her three strong teenage boys for his farm as he was in marrying her. (Katharine Reinim's youngest son eventually inherited his uncle/stepfather's farm.) Mathias Blommer was grateful that his mother had been willing to migrate with him and his family to Osage County, Missouri, in 1840: "If my old mother had not decided to travel with us, we might have had to stay for a long time in poverty-stricken Germany and would have raised our children for other people and for the old sinner and misguided religious persecutor [Kaiser] Wilhelm." Blommer's mother died soon after their arrival, but, as he said, by supporting their decision to migrate, she had helped give her descendants the opportunity to make "much better progress than in poor Germany."[2]

The revolutionary idea that it was legitimate for the underclasses to seek to improve their place in society had become generally accepted by the early 1800s, leading to an easing of many regional restrictions on peasants' lives and movements.[3] The more adventurous among these groups were consequently freer as well as more willing to emigrate. This class-based change in attitude and self-image was one that women no doubt shared. More concrete political considerations lay behind the emigration of other German-speakers, particularly those of the middle class. Women, because they had so little share in public life, were unlikely to initiate emigration for political reasons. Their influence in such cases was actually based on family considerations. For example, a few, like the widow Anna Pohlman, left Europe to help their sons evade military obligations. Others exercised some influence in the timing of politically motivated emigration, as did Elizabeth Koepfi, who persuaded her Swiss physician husband to wait fourteen years, until the eldest sons were through with their education and the other children were old enough to be helpful, before settling in Illinois. Writing from

St. Louis, Hermann Steines, a Dreißiger scout, warned his mother and sisters of the importance of their willing participation: "If you feel strong enough in body to endure the hardships of the journey, and buoyant enough in spirit to participate in the attempt of realizing the fond dream of your men folks, then we shall all be happy and greatly benefited. The older members of our family will not be materially benefited by coming here, but your interest in your children must be the deciding factor if you take this step. You women must have a clear understanding with your men." The next year the Steines family emigrated. The actions of other women also indicate support of their husbands' desire to leave an uncongenial political environment. Ulrike Haeger Gellhorn ran an apothecary and sandwich shop in Pommerania for a year, caring for five young children at the same time, until her husband could send the money for the family to join him.[4]

Yet because married women seldom acted as free agents in emigration, some were less supportive than others. Their unwillingness to leave familiar surroundings was common enough to generate broadsides like the following exchange between a husband and wife:

> Husband:
> O wife, how many pretty wares
> Come from there, America!
> Why should we any longer tarry,
> So good could we two have it there.
> Here's nothing but trouble, day after day
> And not enough bread to make it pay.
> How wonderful our life would be there,
> If we were in America . . .
>
> Wife:
> O husband, how can you think that?
> I want you to forget it now,
> Or if you don't I'll feel so bad,
> 'Cause I'm not goin', no way, no how.
> Now if I were to leave my friends
> And never see them again,
> I'd die a troubled death, I would
> So what good's America, tell me, what good? . . .[5]

The song ends with the husband's winning the argument. Of course, more women than we can know succeeded in keeping their families in Europe. Though we have no record of such cases, we do know that after emigration some women persuaded their husbands to return to Europe.[6] They were usually bourgeois women, whose families had the financial means to return and who probably had relatively less to gain by emigration. Their husbands might also have been less authoritarian in their families than rural men were. Other women could only acquiesce to their husbands' decision and voice their protest within the family circle. Most women, whether they were enthusiastic about emigration or not, seem to have put the best face possible on it.

The memoir of Helena Friesen Eitzen, written near Inman, Kansas, in 1919, when she was fifty-three, offers an interesting example of the motivations behind immigration and the way in which a woman could forestall it, at least for a time. Helena Eitzen came from a poor family in southern Russia. At fifteen she had begun to contribute to her family's support through her sewing. At twenty she was contracted to work for an aunt for a two-year period, during which time she was ill-treated, which might have contributed to the emotional problems she exhibited later. She then married a carpenter, who seems to have had a small farm as well. Soon thereafter she suffered a nervous breakdown and had to be nursed two months by her mother. After the birth of Helena Eitzen's first daughter in 1889, crops failed and work opportunities for her husband slowed down. He began pressing her to agree to go to America, something he had suggested as a possibility even before they married. Helena wrote later, "At the time I gave my consent, but now when the question really arose I didn't agree so readily, for it meant I would have to leave all those I loved, never to see them again." In about 1891, after the birth of a second daughter, things became even harder for the Eitzens. Helena was ill for a long time after the birth and could not take in sewing, and her husband injured his hand and could not work for twenty-six weeks. His requests that she agree to emigrate became ever more frequent and importunate. Viewing her resistance as contrary to the God-willed order, Helena began to pray: "I began to examine myself, also prayed a great deal because of this, but I could not say: 'Lord, may not my will but yours be fulfilled,' for the reason that I didn't want this."[7]

The next section of Helena Eitzen's memoir describes what led to her final acquiescence:

> I kept going into the barn to pray, that was my little room where I was alone with my God and where I poured out all my sorrow. I prayed that the dear God might show me in piety what I should do and what would be the best for me. Then I swore that I would also consent to do whatever I dreamed. But I dreamed nothing having to do with leaving until I had repeated the vow three times, and also had promised each time to do it [i.e., whatever she dreamed].
>
> Then I dreamed one night we were getting ready for the trip to America. My beloved mother was helping me, and we were singing together

as we worked. Then I woke up, but, but my request had been fulfilled, I had dreamed, but now I also had to keep my promise, and right away the Tempter was at my side. He gave me the idea that no one knew what I had prayed or promised, that I shouldn't tell anyone anything about it, and I could stay there [in Russia]. I was tempted in this way for two weeks, didn't tell anyone what I had prayed and also not what I had dreamed. My husband kept asking me if I was sick, for I was very depressed. He was worried that I would again have a nervous breakdown. But I didn't stop praying and the dear Lord helped me vanquish, and may praise and thanks be to God, I have experienced this so often, if I am true, He is glad to help. Thus it was at that time, too. One morning, when we got up, I confided in my husband that I had prayed thusly, and also that I had promised to obey and that I now had conquered [myself] and was ready to comply with his desire [to emigrate].[8]

Few extant documents contain such explicit testimony about the inner processes of a woman's reconciliation to emigration. Helena Eitzen's memoir reveals the role a woman's piety and her acceptance of the divinely ordained subordination to her husband could play in this. Her statements confirm other aspects of a woman's role in the decision to emigrate. In this case, her husband had to seek her agreement before the plans to leave could go forward. It is also clear that deciding to leave was not easy, no matter how difficult the financial conditions from which people fled. Helena Eitzen's family supported her decision, and her mother even praised her for having been willing "to do what the Lord had showed [her]." When it was time to go to the train station to depart, though, Helena fainted and did not come to until they were already under way: "It was for me like the funeral day of my entire family."[9]

Helena Eitzen's memoir offers insights into what might have been typical of many poor women's motivations and experiences prior to emigration. In contrast, it is probably safe to guess that few women came to America for the same reason that Sophie Luise Weitbrecht did: to escape an unwanted marriage. More common is the second part of her story. On shipboard she met an Evangelical Lutheran minister on his way to take over a German parish in Red Bud, Illinois, and married him two days after their arrival in New Orleans.[10] Many women married just before departing for America, and others came to America to begin married life. Some of them were completing arrangements that had been made in Europe and were bringing a dowry payment that would help establish the newlyweds on a farm, much as would have happened in Europe. This was the case with Luise Rodekopp, whose fiancé Heinrich Steinwald (who had emigrated in 1881) threatened to marry a rich German-American farmer's daughter in Illinois if Luise's mother did not send a large enough dowry. Luise came to America and worked for relatives while Heinrich bargained with her mother. Eventually the money came, the two married, bought a farm, and had what was said to be a happy life together.[11] Other women had had no contact with their husbands-to-be beyond the exchange of a few letters. The pragmatic nature of arrangements like this, which was quite in keeping with what we know about marital relationships in rural German lands, is apparent in what Rosina Scwendleman Reusser said in later years about her wedding day, celebrated right after she arrived by train in Iowa: "Marriage in the forenoon, hoeing potatoes in the afternoon."[12]

Other economic aspects of the emigration of both married and single women reflect family and social structures of the day. A few women brought the money into their marriages that enabled the emigration. Some had the advantage of sharing the sale of their original family's holdings, and these women were better able to secure a good start for themselves and their families as American farmers. Others entered into work agreements that allowed them to pay off their fares and thus had lives in America much like those they would have had as hired help in Europe. Some single women had enough money to pay their own fare and the skills to find work in America.[13] Most, however, probably came with less capital than single males did, a reflection of the low status of female labor in the nineteenth century. Walter Kamphoefner found that four-fifths of the single women from Osnabrück who immigrated to St. Charles and Warren counties in Missouri between 1832 and 1858 had been agricultural workers or domestics, while a few others listed the profession of seamstress or midwife. The thirty-two women who came from the rural lower class took only 49.9 percent of the average amount of assets for all the immigrants to those counties during that period, while the twenty-five who were the daughters of propertied peasants took 88.2 percent of the average. One hundred and twenty-five other single women, who did not indicate their father's occupation, brought 62.6 percent of the average amount of assets.[14]

Nineteenth-century publications were full of advice on who should emigrate, where the emigrants should settle, what awaited them there, and what they should take along. Almost all the material directed at women assumed that they would be traveling as family members. The material intended for single women emphasized the perils of traveling alone. One leaflet warned that among the conditions awaiting women who emigrated were "the dangers of white slavery": "Houses of prostitution in foreign lands are filled with German women. Women and girls are seduced by agents under the guise of offering them good positions. Do not accept any job offer in a foreign land without consulting with emigrant advisory offices."[15] It is hard to know if this warning was justified. Virtually no information about German-speaking "fallen women" has been uncovered. The fact that Anglo-American women's associations were also concerned about the sexual vulnerability of immigrant women indicates that such warnings contained at least a kernel of truth.[16]

Publications for emigrants encouraged women in charge of setting up households to bring material that would make them self-reliant, and every woman brought as much of her household goods as possible. Bedding and linen were particularly important and were often part of a woman's dowry. A chest could supply sheets, towels, and clothing for the crucial early years, as it did for one Kansas sod house family. Featherbeds were prized so highly that one women made sure they were safe in the creek bed when a Kansas prairie fire threatened. Families usually left their furniture behind (which women sometimes sorely regretted), but silver and clocks made the transatlantic journey, as did family bibles and other keepsakes. The more valuable of such items were sometimes sold for cash in hard times, foiling women's attempts to maintain household continuity.[17] Generally, emigrants tried to anticipate their future needs and took only what they believed would be useful and not readily or more cheaply available in America. The common wisdom, especially among newly arrived immigrants, was that American goods were inferior. Letters in the first years of settlement contain requests for clothing, material, and household items that were not to be had in the United States. Emigrants traveling to farms sometimes took plant and orchard cuttings, and many women took flower, herb, and vegetable seeds to have a bit of home in their new surroundings and for their practical uses.

Women packed most of the baggage that accompanied the German-speaking emigrants. Women's help would be necessary once they arrived. No matter to what degree women had initiated and supported the decision to emigrate, their role would be central to the success of the family venture. They were therefore encouraged to foster the self-sacrificing qualities that would ensure success. An emigrant adviser declared:

> QUALITIES
> which the emigrating woman must possess:
> A strong resilient body
> Robust health

A resilient soul
Strong nerves
A great lack of consideration for herself
Friendly obligingness to others.[18]

This exhortation is, in several ways, a description of what was already expected of rural women in German lands, but in America, at least on the agricultural frontier, hard physical work would be required of all women, no matter what their background.

The power relations in the farm family of the antebellum Midwest entailed male domination and female exploitation. John Mack Faragher has used the term *patriarchy* to describe this family structure. He summarizes its features in this way: (1) the family and household operated as the basic unit of labor; (2) both sexes were involved in the family division of labor, with women playing central roles in both productive and reproductive work; (3) women bore more children than in simpler foraging societies or in more complex industrialized ones; and (4) the husband's rule in the household was legitimized by the sexually segregated public domain.[19] In other words, the rural family structure of the American premarket economy was much like that prevalent in rural areas of nineteenth-century German lands. American rural society would have seemed familiar to most German-speakers, although as the century wore on, the immigrants continued to live according to family structures that became outdated in many parts of the United States.

In objective terms, frontierswomen, no matter what their place of birth and mother tongue, faced similar conditions and did much the same kind of work. Glenda Riley has established the existence of a "female frontier" based on gender as the common experience of both prairie and plains women in the nineteenth century. Riley contends that shared experiences, life-styles, responsibilities, and sensibilities that transcended geography marked the patterns of women settlers' lives.[20] To no small extent, they also transcended ethnic and cultural differences. Many writers have noted that the unpaid labor of women and children was the resource that enabled farm families to survive hard years.[21] Others, in considering the broader picture of American agriculture, have asserted that this labor pool and the diversification of the areas of women's production made it possible for the farm family to withstand the elements of risk and heavy capital investment that characterize farm life. The cost to women was often immense, as it was to their husbands and children, but the agrarian ideology that praised the simple, independent, and physically and morally healthy life-style gained through harmonious family work undergirded this economic system and provided a social and cultural framework of support. The rural sociologists Cornelia Flora and Jan Flora have said, "The relations of production (that the same unit, the household, provided management, capital and labor to the enterprise, with little labor bought or sold) helps explain the fact that all in the enterprise were expected to contribute to the whole to make it work. Women's culture contributed to that sense of family, life style, and community—and has helped to mobilize the needed labor at key moments in the production cycle."[22] German-speaking women were culturally conditioned to be ready to participate in the family effort that made frontier success possible.[23]

The same emigrant literature that urged women's self-sacrifice also warned them of the physical travails of emigration. They would be expected to work without surcease in primitive living conditions, helping in the most difficult of frontier tasks: clearing forests, removing tree stumps and preparing virgin land, building houses, planting and weeding crops, tending animals and gardens. For these jobs, they should take sturdy shoes and work clothes, including trousers and bellybands (to help prevent rupture). They also had to be ready to provide family health care and to educate their children in the isolation of the wilderness.[24] German-speaking women in the Midwest did all of these things and sometimes more. For example, in the 1830s Margaret Blauff Hillenkamp helped her husband clear twenty *Morgen* (about forty acres) of forested land in St. Charles County, Missouri, for crops and a seven-acre peach and apple orchard, in between bearing several children. Elisabeth Beckbird Biehler-Meyer quarried all the stone and helped lay up the walls for the first house built on her family's Kansas farm.[25]

Labor such as this was difficult and out of the ordinary. Much more common and widespread was field work. In this regard, German-speakers continued work patterns established in Europe, even though some emigrant literature warned that this was not common among Americans and would bring disapproval.[26] Katharina Wolf Langendorf Tiek wrote her parents in February of 1869 from Moro in Madison County, Illinois, about an accident caused by a "wild" horse with which she had plowed a potato field the previous spring:

> As we came up a hill and I wanted to turn the horse, it knocked me over and struck me in the back with its hooves and the plow caught in my skirt and took me along. There I lay like dead in the field. My husband took me home. You can imagine what pain I suffered. Four days later I had a little girl on the first Pentecost morning. But what I had to en-

dure until she was born! I didn't think that I could survive it. Then I
got up on the third day and had been so badly hurt that I had to stay
in bed for three more weeks. No one thought that I would get better.[27]

The daughter born after that accident in the spring of 1868 did not
survive to be counted in the 1870 census.[28] A decade later, Katharina
Tiek wrote that she was expecting her seventh child in a few weeks and
that of the six children born to her, four had survived. Her hard life
had taken its toll on her body, she said, and she had two ruptures. She
assured her mother, however, that they "never suffered want in America
and eat meat and sausage three times a day," and then she added, "But
there's never a lack of work, either."[29] The details of Katharina Tiek's
life are unclear. We know that she married again after her first husband's
death and eventually had ten children, of whom only three survived
childhood and adolescence. Scanty and inarticulate though they are,
her letters confirm the harsh demands farm life made on women and
the extent to which German-speaking women were willing to sacrifice
themselves to meet those demands. The costs to them and their families in terms of women's health and child mortality are obvious.[30]

Childbirth was a hazardous thing in the nineteenth century, and
nowhere more so than on the frontier. Friederika Oesterreich Staatz
had the distinction of giving birth to the first white child in Dickinson County, Kansas. Having arrived in May 1857, she and her new
husband spent the summer living in their wagon until they could prepare a home. In June a daughter was born, but the baby died in October.[31] Friederika Staatz had the help of other immigrant women, but
others were not so fortunate. They gave birth alone or with the help
of a husband or even a child.[32] When women died as a result of childbirth, illness, or years of exertion, other immigrant women often took
their place caring for the family.

In difficult economic circumstances, women and men were frequently forced to neglect the children that survived and to drive them just
as hard as they drove themselves. One young mother often left her
infant and toddler locked up in the house, "guarded" by a big black
dog, while she went to sew and wash for neighbors. Another helped
her husband shock wheat with their one- or two-year-old son tied to
the back of one of the horses.[33] Children were put out to work as early as eight, and their wages went to their parents to purchase supplies,
pay taxes, or buy land. Some of these children had bitter memories of
childhoods dedicated to work and the care of younger siblings. Others were matter-of-fact about these things, while still others emphasized the happy and funny things that happened. In northwest Nebras-

ka in the 1880s, the Steinhaus boys teased their youngest brother in dangerous ways: hanging him out of the upstairs window by his suspenders, rolling him down the hill in the baby carriage, and getting him to chew tobacco at the age of five. Their mother "never knew any of this—she was so busy."[34]

None of these difficult and potentially tragic circumstances of family life was different from the experiences many rural immigrants had had in their homelands. There, too, women worked hard throughout their pregnancies and even gave birth alone on occasion. Women aged prematurely and died young. Many infants perished because they had poor prenatal and postnatal care and nutrition and because their mothers had to work and could not care for them properly. Infants and toddlers in poor rural families in German lands were sometimes left on their own while their parents worked. In all farm families, young children were often in the care of older children for most of the time, and children were put to work early and sent away to earn wages.[35]

In other words, the strategies that had been necessary for survival in Europe were still necessary for survival in America. The difference was that now a family could see that by pooling its labor and wages, family members could do more than just survive. They had a chance of advancement. A German who worked for a time on the farm of a Forty-Eighter in Illinois noted that the immigrants who had done best were those who had had family members work for others as soon as possible. After about ten years, the accumulated wages and interest enabled the family to buy a large farm, build a house, work the land with the now-grown children, and send the nonessential family members out for more wages to repeat the process. In a letter discussing the prospects for immigrants in America, Friedrich G. Hillenkamp acknowledged that he had had difficulty establishing his Missouri farm, even though he had started with a good sum of money and had had a hardworking wife who had helped him with all his work. Nevertheless, Hillenkamp believed that an impoverished relative with several children could do well in America: "His sturdy children, who are surely used to working, would be his capital." This is what Johann Diedrich Wilkens meant when he spoke of his young children (ages one month to seven years) as the future hired help (*Knechte* and *Magd*) for his farm.[36]

At the age of eighty, my grandmother wrote down a few lines about her family history that illustrate the cooperative strategy that made it possible for immigrants to get ahead. Her parents, Anton and Karolina (Miller) Krause, had been weavers and agricultural workers in Austria. They came to Nebraska in 1882, at the height of the German-speaking immigration, with six children, age twelve and under. The youngest, an infant, died soon after their arrival, and two more babies, including my grandmother, were born in Nebraska. Of their first years, my grandmother wrote:

> My parents were not among the very first settlers in this community, so therefore there was no homestead land for them left to settle upon but they thought nothing of living in a rented house and working to earn money to buy a farm and also feed and clothe themselves and family. Mrs. Krause's work consisted partly of walking about twelve miles every day to work in the harvest field in midsummer and to shuck corn in the late fall. Mr. Krause obtained work in the town of Exeter. He applied for work on the railroad line they were laying, they found him not able to do this heavy work so he planted and cultivated gardens for the families who were working on the railroad. This job meant for him about a 20 mile walk at weekends. There was not much pleasure in those long walks in the early days as on a starless night one could very easily be walking around in circles and get nowhere. I remember Mother putting several slices of bread in her pocket and going to meet him when he had not arrived home by dark.
>
> The older children contributed toward living expenses by working for neighbors and friends at herding cattle or minding younger children, earning their clothes, room and board. Herding cattle was assigned to youngsters as there were few fences. I remember the task in the summer when the tall grass hid numerous snakes and in the winter when the ground was cold to walk on, ofttimes covered with ice and snow.

My grandmother wrote nothing about who was doing the family's own farm work during the years (at least ten and probably more) that her parents and siblings worked away from home. The oldest child, the only son, no doubt did a great deal of it, along with his mother and older sisters, since Anton Krause's health never allowed him to do much hard labor. In her brief memoir, my grandmother wrote at greatest length about the strong musical tradition in her family and about her father's accomplishments as a musician. She mentioned Karolina Krause's "clear soprano voice" and the happy memories she had of her parents and the family singing together at their chores. In contrast, the hard work they all did to accomplish the family goal of landownership she depicted only in the matter-of-fact way seen above. She took this so much for granted, I think, that she did not linger on those more negative memories.[37]

In America, women were important as wage earners both before and after marriage. Their savings enabled them to marry and begin farming, much as had been the case in Europe. For instance, "Wieschen

Schröder Swehn," the wife of "Jürnjakob Swehn," saved the money she earned as an Iowa farm worker for two and a half years. Her $200, added to her husband's $350, allowed them to start farming. Others continued the work they had trained for, if this could be done along with their domestic work. Nurses and midwives like Mary Cresence Berhalter Maichel found plenty of opportunity to practice their professions. From her homestead southwest of Lawrence, Kansas, she continued to practice the nursing she had learned in a Württemberg hospital. Margaret Hiebert Schroeder, a German Mennonite from Russia who immigrated to Kansas, is an unusual example of a rural professional immigrant woman. She studied medicine in America in fulfillment of a vow she made to God. After beginning her practice in 1900 at the age of forty-two, she presided at fifteen hundred births. Gesche Mahnken Block, one of the founders of the German Lutheran community of Block, Kansas, served as the district's midwife and general health care deliverer until her death in 1911. She was highly respected by area doctors as well as her patients. In the forty-two years of her work as midwife in the Block area, only four stillborn births were recorded. Within three years after her death, seven women were delivered of stillborn babies. A recent study by Charlotte Borst identifies European birthing traditions and the readiness with which midwifery lent itself to integration in a woman's domestic life as reasons for its prominence as a profession for immigrant wives and mothers.[38]

So many women took in washing, sewing, and boarders at one time or another that they cannot be enumerated here. A striking example worth mentioning is Maria Bayer Pelzer, who took her baby along when she worked as a domestic and field hand and then kept house for a year for a widower with seven children, as well as for a single man and her own husband and child. In some areas, women developed cottage industries to earn extra income. As had been true in Europe and for women of American parentage, as long as they had a husband, their paid activities were considered supplemental, however. On rare occasions, if their husband was unable to support them, they might seek work publicly, as did a Mrs. Glaubitz of Hillsboro, Kansas, in 1888. She wanted sewing work to tide the family over until her husband could find work.[39] Like Mrs. Glaubitz, women generally did only work that could be considered an extension of their domestic functions and that was in keeping with the female roles acceptable in their time and culture.[40]

The same was true of the domestic work their daughters did to supplement the family income. Such work was in demand, in the country as well as in the towns and cities. Hired girls in America usually did only housework, even on farms. Countless immigrants wrote home, urging sisters and other single women to come to America, where they could earn decent wages without having to do the heavy labor and live under the close personal control that was typical in German-speaking lands. Katarina Wolf Tiek's sister Maria Wolf Förschler wrote her twenty-four-year old sister, Mina, who had stayed with their parents in Germany: "Dear Mina, you write that you have to work hard. I believe you, because I was also stiff from work when I left my homeland. Here I don't need to guide the oxen and stumble around all day in the field like I had to do at home. Here it is better for you, Mina."[41] Much as they might have done in Europe, girls like Maria Wolf were learning and practicing the skills they would need someday in their own households. At the same time, they often gained language and domestic skills that would ease their and their family's adaptation to the new culture. If they gave their wages to their parents, young rural women were also ensuring their future inheritance. The comparatively high pay and reasonable working conditions, the relative lack of restrictions on behavior, and the freedom of movement from one job to another made work as servants appealing to German-speakers at a time when Anglo-Americans considered it degrading.[42]

One rare instance of illicit activity by a rural German-speaking family should be noted as an acknowledgement of the potential for variety among the immigrants. This family, the so-called bloody Benders of Kansas, included a son and a beautiful young daughter, Kate. In 1871, the family set up a grocery store and offered meals and lodging. A year later, Kate advertised her healing and spiritualistic gifts in a flyer. After the family precipitously departed by train in April 1873, nine bodies were discovered on the family premises. In a way, Kate, too, thought to be the bait attracting hapless men who were then killed and robbed and whom the early twentieth-century account paints in lurid colors as a bloodthirsty seductress, was working in traditional, if unacceptable, female ways for her family. The Benders were not, of course, typical rural residents, yet we cannot be sure that their deadly family business was not a way-station to a more respectable farm, though it is unlikely. They were never brought to justice.[43]

More typical rural German-speaking women contributed to the family economy in less colorful ways. Much of what they did was unpaid and involved production for the family's own consumption. Some spun wool for stockings and operated looms to weave linen and carpets. All of them sewed the family clothes and made quilts, blankets, and curtains. Until the latter decades of the century, women did this all by hand. Later, a sewing machine was likely to be the single mechanized piece of equipment a farm woman had. The cost of a sewing machine fell to about $30 by 1870, which made it affordable for family use (although some farm women had to pay more than twice that, perhaps because of transportation costs). When we remember that the price for a cow at that time was $18–20, however, it is not difficult to imagine that many farm families would have thought long and hard about making such a large investment.[44] Women who got this coveted item often let their neighbors use it. This could be an opportunity to visit or, at times, an imposition. Such sharing also reveals the community network of family and friends. Most German-speaking women probably loaned their sewing machines to or did sewing for other German-speakers only, as did Ulrike Gellhorn in Iowa, for instance.[45]

Some husbands gave their wives a sewing machine after a good harvest or upon the sale of livestock. Other women earned the cash for it themselves with their butter and egg money. Unless the family farm emphasized dairy or poultry production, this income was usually a woman's to manage, although it was almost always used for the benefit of the family. Butter and egg money bought the staples (flour, sugar, salt, coffee, calico, and the like) that the family could not produce, it paid the taxes in a lean year, and it made small improvements to the home possible. One woman decided to buy a dress with the money that she had saved, penny by penny, to buy tar paper for a roof for the family soddy. Another paid the bill on her husband's wedding suit.[46] This female income served as a cushion against the unpredictability of the grain market. In 1888, one woman wrote from Kansas that high egg and poultry prices would help offset the low prices the family could get for their grain harvest.[47] On a diversified farm, a woman's income could make up a substantial proportion of the family resources. This was true well into the twentieth century, as my own grandmother proved.[48]

The 1880 agriculture census offers provocative evidence that women's egg and butter income was more than mere "chicken feed." In Warren and St. Charles counties in Missouri, where many German-speakers farmed, small amounts of milk were sold to factories (144 and 30 gallons, respectively). Farm women produced large amounts of butter, however: 263,278 pounds in Warren County and 207,941 in St. Charles County. On farms in St. Charles County, women had also made 10,100 pounds of cheese. During the same year, barnyard poultry in Warren County had produced 369,167 dozen eggs, and those in St. Charles County, 430,882 dozen. The proximity to markets, geography, and other factors no doubt influenced the extent to which women and their families engaged in such production. The German-speakers in Marion County, Kansas, for instance, probably participated in that area's relatively intensive dairy production, as indicated by the 58,238 gallons of milk sold to factories in 1880 (produced by 3,086 milk cows, 2,470 fewer than in St. Charles County). At the same time, the women in Marion County must have been heavily engaged in the production of butter and cheese: 439,616 and 14,321 pounds, respectively. The same can be said of the German-speaking residents of Clinton County, Iowa, where 18,079 milk cows produced 373,026 gallons of milk sold to factories, barnyard poultry laid 491,609 dozen eggs, and farm women made 1,394,707 pounds of butter.[49]

Women's cash earnings were probably generally more important than the women, their husbands, or their children realized, although once in a while one comes across the acknowledgement that a woman's butter or egg production "kept the family from starving."[50] On occasion, the importance of women's traditional sources of income is indicated by the fact that the husband took credit for them. Friedrich G. Hillenkamp, for instance, wrote that *he* had planted an apple and peach orchard that produced enough fruit to warrant a trip to St. Louis, and when *he* took the fruit to market, *he* could take along several hundred dozen eggs, for which *he* could buy the necessary household things.[51] The language of this text reveals the power relations in some immigrant families. Everyone took for granted that women would contribute to the establishment and maintenance of the family enterprise and that this did not necessarily grant them power or even ownership of the returns on their production. The everyday, domestic nature of women's contributions also helped mask their significance. Nevertheless, some women no doubt gained some claim to autonomy through the money they earned. This might have been partly why some men thought of such earnings disparagingly as "pin money" and resented the time their wives gave to their churning and chickens instead of to field work or other livestock.[52] The traditional separation of a woman's income from a man's in rural society also helps explain why my grandmother kept her income in "female space," a crock in the cellar. Her wish to maintain control over it was probably also the reason that she kept it "hidden" from my grandfather, even though he must have known where it was and would not have been likely to take any of it from her anyway.

All farm women, with the help of children, tended large gardens, for food production was one of their most important activities. They planted, weeded, watered, and hoed the plants and then harvested the fruit and vegetables when they were ripe. Some produce was stored away as it was, but large quantities had to be preserved in some fashion. In the late nineteenth century, as the process became less expensive, women began to can much of their produce. On butchering days, women supervised the making of the sausages and headcheese that German-speaking families enjoyed.[53]

The children might take extra foodstuffs to sell in town. Women, however, often bartered among themselves and with merchants for what they wanted. One woman caught her biggest turkey and sent it to town with her son in exchange for the other groceries needed for a Thanksgiving dinner. Another traded the thirty pounds of butter and the fourteen seven-pound cheeses she had made for a wagonload of apples, a kraut cutter, a sausage cutter, and a raincoat. Louise Nickel, a milliner in Hillsboro, Kansas, declared her willingness to take eggs in payment for her work.[54] With hard work, good management, and luck, a woman could supplement her family's income and diet in important ways without leaving home.[55]

In spite of the immense amount of work they did, women in rural areas were in some ways better off than their city sisters. To judge by Dorothee Schneider's study of working-class families in New York in the early 1880s, most married German-American women in the urban areas did not earn wages, unlike the women in many other working-class families. Their families were consequently worse off than Anglo-American families. Some of the New York families who responded to a newspaper inquiry about their weekly budget were eating only somewhat better than they had in Germany, with potatoes still forming the staple of their diet.[56] In contrast, rural women could earn extra money without "going out" to work. The low percentage of foreign-born women between the ages of sixteen and thirty-four working for wages in agricultural pursuits compared with native-born women (see table B12 in appendix B) indicates that young women in this age group, when they were likely to have small children, did not willingly work outside the home. Rural German-speaking women's cash earnings through butter, eggs, and produce sales, however, gave them some autonomy and authority and helped the family progress. Rural families also benefited immediately, since they ate better for less because of this unpaid labor.

Women sometimes also played a role in the success of the family venture by acquiring or maintaining property on their own. One woman was awarded one share of the capital stock of a Nebraska town company, equal to ten average lots in the town, "in recognition of her true pioneering spirit in being the first woman to locate in Columbus."[57] More common were German-speaking women's accomplishments as independent farmers. As we would expect from the demographic analysis in appendix B (see especially tables B12 and B13), it almost always was a widow who sought to secure or maintain a future for her family in this way. It is likely that most of the successful female farmers had spent time on an American farm before feeling confident enough to tackle one on their own. To succeed, their children, whether boys or girls, had to be old enough to help. Two such Kansas widows, women "of physical vigor and forceful will," managed to run large farms with the help of young children or daughters. After her husband had an incapacitating stroke, an Iowa woman "acted as hired man and girl both" and did all the farming with a son for the next sixteen years. A few young widows with little children managed to stick it out long enough, with help from neighbors or relatives, to meet the obligations of residence and property improvements necessary "to prove up" on a homestead.[58]

After passage of the Homestead Act in 1862, single women and female heads of households could gain 160 acres of land by residing on and improving it over a five-year period. Given the attraction land had for German-speaking immigrants, we might expect that the women among them would have taken advantage of this opportunity in numbers at least proportional to their presence in rural areas and certainly proportional to those of Anglo-American female homesteaders. H. Elaine Lindgren has estimated that in the last four decades of the nineteenth century, women gained title to approximately 5 to 10 percent of the land acquired through homesteading, preemption, or timber culture in the Great Plains. The percentage increased as the century came to a close and grew to as much as 15 and even 30 percent in some areas of the Dakotas after 1900. In an analysis of several townships in North Dakota, however, Lindgren found that German-born women were unlikely to take advantage of the Homestead Act in the first two decades after it went into effect. Women in groups that immigrated somewhat later, like the Germans from Russia, were more likely to do so, unless they were Catholic. The differences among the various ethnic groups and subgroups in Lindgren's sample became relatively insignificant as time went on. Lindgren concludes that ethnicity played a complex role in these patterns and in the lives of individual women. Certainly German-speaking women shared their men's hunger for land. While some of them might have homesteaded as agents for men—their fathers or future husbands, for instance—others did it for themselves and for the family members dependent on them. More work needs to be done in this area of ethnic American women's history, as in so many others, before the cultural influences are clear.[59]

Inheritance is another fuzzy area. One woman believed her father was "unusually progressive" for having divided his property equally "among the boys *and girls,* not just among the boys as so many Germans did."[60] There is collaborative evidence that males were favored over females in inheritance in the families of German-speakers. Daughters received less land than sons, or they received cash, livestock, and household goods instead of land. For example, when the children of Claus Sieck, a Schleswig farmer, received their inheritance in Iowa in the 1870s, the sons were able to pay off twice as much on their American farms as the daughters did.[61] There is evidence to the contrary as well, though. A study of one area of Illinois has shown that German-Americans from the Frisian moorlands, where partible inheritance was traditional, continued the practice of dividing the land equally among all the siblings. To accomplish this, while at the same time perpetuating the tradition of farming within the family, the number of children was kept small after the first generation, and parents retired early. Other studies of the same area by the same author show that ethnically derived family and farming choices and goals, repeated over several generations, explain the contemporary replication of early farming patterns (i.e., relatively small, diversified farms) among German-Americans there.[62]

The Old World custom of parents' retiring early and passing on their land to heirs persisted elsewhere in America, even into the second generation, as my grandparents proved. Kamphoefner's study in Missouri showed that "only about half of all German men over 60 were still heads of households, compared to three-fourths of such Americans."[63] The Germans from Russia primarily practiced male ultimogeniture, although one source indicates that in the Black Sea colonies, men and women could inherit equally. Whether they actually did so has not been verified.[64] European traditions probably influenced inheritance among German-speakers in America, although the extent to which that was the case is unclear and no doubt varied greatly. The homogeneity of the immigrant community would have been an important factor in the perpetuation of such customs.[65]

American tradition and force of law also played a role. The American pattern of equal inheritance was, by and large, congenial to German-speakers. Whether they came from traditions of partible or impartible inheritance, the idea of attempting to treat all children equally was widespread, although in practice inequities had been the rule. Now they had the opportunity of fulfilling that ideal without having to pass on a family holding diminished by having been split into many smaller pieces. The hard work and family cooperative effort could result in the accumulation of enough land for all the children.[66]

To provide additional insight into inheritance patterns among German-speaking immigrants, I conducted a study of the wills of immigrants who came to Cooper County, Missouri, in the nineteenth century. I identified the individuals and families by searching through an early twentieth-century county commemorative history. Then I located their wills or other related documents, to the extent that such existed, in the county probate court archives.[67] I included individuals and families who had engaged in activities other than farming in the study, since the largest town, Boonville, remained an essentially rural community throughout the nineteenth century. In any case, farming, either as the main occupation or as a second family enterprise, was the dominant way of life for at least 90 percent of those included in the study. My search yielded 101 documents, dating between 1854 and 1957, of which 18 related to the estates of individuals (12 men and 6 women) who had died intestate. Of the remaining 83, 69 involved the wills of men and 14 those of women.

The higher number of men in the sample indicates the economic dominance of males, but this is somewhat deceptive. Fewer women than men wrote their own will, partly because married women in Missouri could not legally write a will until 1864. Women also had no property rights in the state until 1875. Before this, a woman could own land, but all rent and earnings from it were her husband's to control, as were her wages and any personal property she might have brought into the marriage. Not until 1889 could a married woman own and control her own real estate and be held liable for her own debts. It was therefore customary for the husband's will to be written in such a way as to dispose of the couple's property after the wife's death, should he predecease her. Thirty of the men whose wives were still living at the time the wills were written left their spouses a life interest in the estate, and many expressed confidence in their wives' ability and willingness to manage the estate to the advantage of the children. Others who divided the family property included provisions for the wife: a child's share (five), considerable sums in the form of notes or money to be put out at interest (six), or a part of the property greater than that of a child's share (two). Where the couple's personal property was mentioned, the wife inherited all or part of it in all except one case. These provisions demonstrate an intention to provide for widows. That twenty-nine of the fifty-two men still married to the mothers of their children named their wives as executors of their estates also indicates these men's confidence in their wives' administrative abilities.

Some of the wills specify how the settling of the estate was to proceed in order to clear debts owed it by children or to repay services children had performed. Many of the immigrants, however, split their property in ways that seem, at least on the surface, inequitable. One heir or more seems to be at an advantage in thirty-one of the wills men wrote and in eight of those written by women. Without doing an exhaustive study of land transfers and legal documents, however, I cannot be sure that what looks like inequities in a will are not attempts to make good on earlier advantages that other children had had in the form of loans for land purchase or sales of land (at low prices) to them. Given that caveat, however, certain patterns in these documents are reminiscent of European inheritance customs.

One man's will seems to be modeled on Old World *Altenteil* agreements, whereby the support of the retired farm couple was outlined. Georg Neff, who came to Cooper County in 1848 and died in November 1854, deeded his wife the "new house," half of the household furniture, and half of the livestock, while Jacob, the eldest of two sons, inherited the home farm and farm equipment. Jacob was also to give his mother one-third of the crops "free of expenses" and furnish and deliver her firewood and water free for the rest of her life. The similarity between this provision for Georg's widow and the typical third of the crops given the Midwest landlord indicates that German immigrants were probably often able to meet the cultural expectations and legal demands of their new society in regard to inheritance while disposing of their property according to the customs of their former homeland. Another Old World aspect of this will is the attempt to keep the family holdings intact while giving other children money or property of equal value. The will required Jacob to pay his brother half of the value of the farm and livestock when his brother came of age.[68]

The primacy of males in European peasant inheritance also shows up in the Cooper County wills. Fifteen men and four women wrote wills favoring one or more of their sons. The advantages male heirs enjoyed took a variety of forms. In a version of primogeniture, three parents encouraged the maintenance of the home place within the male line of the family by giving it outright to the oldest (or sole) son or by giving him the first option of buying it from his siblings. Therese Schmidt stated, "It is my wish and desire that my aforesaid farm, which for many years has been my homestead, shall continue to be owned by some member of my family, and therefore direct and will that in the event my said son . . . does not wish to purchase said farm as aforesaid, then a preference right to purchase said land is given to my second son." Although she also had two daughters, she did not expressly encourage them to buy the farm.[69]

Several fathers deeded land to sons but money to daughters. Sometimes the money gifts were close in value to the land given the sons, as when Wilhelm Kahle left each of his four older sons 100 to 140 acres, with the proviso that each had to pay one of his sisters $3,000. In a version of ultimogeniture, the home place was to be the youngest son's upon the death of Wilhelm's wife, Johanna, but he was to pay the youngest, as yet single, girl of the family $3,000. An additional 40 acres were given the five sons to share as they wished, while the couple's personal property was to remain Johanna's until her death, when the five daughters were to divide it. When Johanna died, however, twelve years after her husband, two of their five daughters had predeceased her. These women and their heirs therefore did not enjoy the advantage of that portion of the estate. In a similar instance, a father excluded two sons who had already received their share of the estate and divided what was left among his wife, three other sons, a daughter, and the children of a deceased daughter. The final settlement to each heir was just under $900. The excluded sons might have received more or less than this, but in any case they had had the use of their inheritance longer than their siblings had.[70]

Other documents also point to possible discrimination in favor of male heirs. Theobald Theiss deeded $5 to his married daughter, his house and personal property in the village Prairie Farm to his unmarried daughter, and 80 acres each to his two sons. Two other fathers gave their only sons large sums of money, while their four daughters shared the remaining cash or property. Another willed his youngest daughter $300 and his youngest son $600 "for their education."[71] Unequal treatment of female heirs existed in other cases but was not apparent in probate documents. One will, which on the surface appears to treat the man's three sons and two daughters equally, contains nothing about the three farms that the county history says he had sold to his sons.[72] Some women also seem to have favored their sons. One had inherited $7,000 from her husband. She left $1,000 to each of her four sons and the widow of the fifth, $500 to her daughter, and everything else to her third son and his family. Another gave her oldest son $2,000 and divided the rest of her estate equally among her children.[73]

Such documents indicate that legacy traditions tended to disadvantage women in German-speaking families in America. Their economic vulnerability is revealed in other ways as well. Four wills attempt to protect a daughter's inheritance from her husband's debts or control. Blasius Efinger specified that the cash and real estate given his oldest child, daughter Louise Friedrich, "shall be held and owned by her as her separate estate, to her sole, separate and exclusive use and benefit, free from all control of her husband and from any interest of her husband." Whether such stipulations were totally successful is another question. Blasius Efinger died in 1904. In the Cooper County commemorative history book published a few years later, his home place was said to belong to Charles Friedrich, Louise's husband.[74] This may, of course, be merely a convention of speech rather than an indication of authority and power. Charles and Louise Friedrich did not write wills, evidently having divested themselves of their property before their deaths, so we cannot know if Louise exercised some control over the family real estate she inherited. That four fathers in my survey attempted to protect family property from sons-in-law reveals women's economic subordination to their husbands and the desire to keep family holdings intact. In only one will were restrictions placed on the property bequeathed a son. In that case, too, the father apparently intended to protect the continuity of the family land. He entrusted the son's inherited property to the latter's older brother to keep the younger man, who was financially delinquent, from squandering his legacy.[75]

In other instances, daughters seem to have been favored. In seven of the nine such cases, however, their larger inheritances were probably due to their having cared for their aged parent(s). A telling example is that of Andrew Steigleder. He willed his wife $2,000 that he had gotten from her, perhaps as a dowry, as well as a life interest in his property. His three sons and four married daughters were then to share the estate after a seventy-acre farm had been set aside for his single daughter, Louvenia, "on account of her staying at home so long and keeping house for me, and having no home."[76] Another man, however, gave one of his two daughters $1 as her share in his estate: "I do this because of [*sic*] my daughter, Margaret, has not shown to me and to her mother during her lifetime, the love and affection that I feel a daughter should show to her parents."[77]

The wills of the women in the study tended to be somewhat more personal and idiosyncratic documents than those of the men. Whereas thirty-eight of the sixty-nine wills by men specified the equal distribution of the property or equal awards of money to all the children (although many of these were token gifts of $1 to $5 to minor children), only one of the women did so, and her estate was so diminished when she died that four of her children had to split the settlement costs.[78] Most of the women were left with only small estates of cash or personal property at the time of their death, which perhaps explains why they felt they could designate the recipients of personal items without being grossly unfair to their children. An interesting example is that of Sophia King. The terms of her husband's will had determined the disposition of most of her estate. John King had left eighty acres to each of his heirs: his son, his four daughters, and his wife, with the latter piece of property to revert to Lizzie Toellner, the only child of a deceased daughter, upon Sophia's death. Further, Sophia was to have a lifetime use of two forty-acre pieces of land, which their only son could then buy from the other heirs upon his mother's death. The legacy of one daughter, Ella Toellner, was to be kept free of her husband's debts and passed on to only her "bodily heirs."[79] Four years later Sophia wrote a will in which she specified:

> I direct that my large brass kettle and the large family bible, and all meat that may be on hand at the time of my death, shall be kept on the place I now occupy, for use of the family after my death. I further direct that all the carpets and rugs which may be on the floor of the dwelling house I now occupy, shall remain thereon after my death. I give and bequeath the two large pictures of myself and my late husband John King, dec'd, unto Ella Toellner, if she be living at the time of my death, if not, then said pictures to remain in the dwelling house I now occupy. I further direct that the pictures of my father and mother now on the wall of my said dwelling house shall remain thereon after my death. I give, and bequeath unto my said grand-daughter, Lizzie Toellner, six dozen chickens, one cow, and one hog, and sufficient feed to keep the same until she can get some feed of her own for that purpose. I further direct that all my fruit which may be in the cellar at the time of my death, shall remain therein for family use.[80]

This is certainly a much more personal listing of bequests than that in John King's will. Sophia King's desire to set her granddaughter up as a farm wife is apparent. Her directions about the family bible and the pictures of her parents show she also was concerned about family continuity on a subjective level. Her bequest of the pictures of herself and her husband to her daughter Ella Toellner might also have been a gesture of reconciliation, to soothe any ruffled feelings John King's will might have caused.[81]

The problems associated with inheritance in Europe could not be avoided in America. Strife among children was no doubt common, even with their parents' attempt at equality. For example, John Schnuck left everything to his wife, with $2,100 to be given each child when they came of age or "started in life for themselves." Some of these payments were made, but when John's wife's estate was settled, the widow of a deceased son had to sue the other heirs, his siblings, to get her husband's share.[82]

Other problems associated with property distribution also appear in this sample of wills. Even in America, where land-hungry immigrants had the opportunity to accumulate real estate, families did not always avoid the injustices and financial dangers of partible inheritance patterns. Louis Roth deeded all of his property to his wife, Mary. After her death, his oldest son was to inherit a 200-acre farm and the oldest daughter 80 acres. His two youngest sons, Frank and Fred, were to inherit the 160-acre home place, but this farm was encumbered with a $700 lien as the inheritance of Louis's second daughter and with a lien of $2,000 for his second son. The four youngest children were to divide the personal property in the estate. Mary died soon after Louis, and the couple's personal property was appraised—at $29.85. This German-born couple had lived economically to accumulate 440 acres of Missouri farmland. They had also committed their sons Frank and Fred to similar lives of frugality to pay off the debts incurred in dividing the value of the estate without dividing the real estate holdings.[83]

On the basis of this sampling, we cannot be sure to what extent German-speakers were influenced by the legacy traditions of their homeland. Probably the prevailing inheritance customs in the area in which they settled as well as the land transfer patterns they were used to in Europe affected their behavior in America.[84] It may be significant that in two cases, a mother administered her dead husband's estate for minor children and then seems to have passed it on to them intact, without taking the child's share to which she was entitled by Missouri law. In both cases, the mother had remarried. The self-sacrificing behavior encouraged in German-speaking women by their culture may be showing up here.[85] What does seem clear from the wills included in this study is that women as a group tended to be at a disadvantage when it came to inheritance. German-speaking immigrants passed on land to sons more often than to daughters and in greater quantities to male heirs. A significant number of the documents also show women's inferior legal and traditional status regarding property rights.

* * *

Studies of the agricultural Midwest have posed a variety of questions about the influence of ethnicity on concrete aspects of settlement among rural German-speakers. Were the immigrants influenced by the type of soil and the geographic lay of the land available to them? Did they come to frontier areas later than Anglo-Americans and choose improved rather than unimproved land where possible? Were they more mobile and more likely to be renters than Anglo-Americans were? Did they retain European farming practices and crop production? Were they more discouraged by the inhospitable qualities of the Great Plains environment than other groups were?[86] Generally, these studies have found few significant differences between German-speakers and other frontier settlers, except in isolated instances of communities founded by homogenous groups of religiously motivated immigrants. The following sections examine the ways in which rural German-speaking women were affected by concrete aspects of their new environment and identify areas of the frontier experience in which they and their compatriots differed from the population at large.

Like everyone else in the Midwest, German-speakers often settled on isolated farms. This was probably more difficult for women than men, since women did not come into contact with the outside world as often.[87] The German-speaking immigrants, however, made the same accommodations to this aspect of their new environment as other settlers, often locating their farmstead across the road from or at a corner of the farm close to the residence of their neighbors. In some areas, immigrants formed string villages, like those they were familiar with at home, but for the most part they responded to the constraints of land division as everyone else in the Midwest did.[88]

Similarly, German-speakers adjusted to geographic and climatic differences. Many letters comment on the discomfort those born in the cool, temperate European climate suffered during their first Midwest summer. One woman put it this way: "I was completely done in much of the time. Everyone who comes from Germany has a hard time the first summer because of the great heat."[89] The immigrants also suffered from other aspects of the Midwest climate. The spectacular lightning and thunderstorms of the prairies and plains were new and often frightening. The Swiss-born Louise Ritter wrote that "the sky looked like fire, and the thunder rumbled constantly so that we trembled all the time." An Ursuline nun on the edge of St. Louis wrote of one thunderstorm that lasted three days.[90]

Other German-speakers found the new landscape uncongenial. Swiss Benedictine sisters asked their mother convent to send a picture of the "dear mountains" of their homeland, and the same nuns complained of the constant winds on the wide-open northwest Missouri prairie.[91] Some women wept in despair upon confronting the "Great American Desert." Karoline Glass Zerfass, a Bukovinia German immigrant to Ellis County in June 1893, lay down weeping on the dry Kansas ground and rolled about in despair, crying, "Why did we leave our good home? What are we going to do here? We're going to starve!" Later, during the trip from their first home—a dugout—to their next—a dilapidated sod house—Karoline was frightened by her first sight of fireflies and cried out, "See, that's the devil! There it is! What are we doing in this country?" The Zerfasses, like most other immigrants, did not have the funds to return to the green, forested, rolling plains of their homeland.[92]

In spite of such anecdotes, German-speakers were no less willing than other ethnic groups to face these new elements. The extreme climate and geography of the Great Plains did not unduly discourage most of them. Indeed, many Germans from Russia were quite familiar with such conditions because of their long sojourn on the steppes, so they were particularly successful. They are credited with having developed in Russia and then introduced in America the hardy red winter wheat that helped make Kansas and the other Great Plains states the breadbasket of the nation. E. P. Hutchinson found that in 1920 the first- and second-generation Germans from Russia were especially heavily represented in the Dakotas (two to four times the national average for that group). Only the Scandinavian stock constituted an equally strong segment of the population in these states. The concentration of the first- and second-generation German stock was also well above the national average in the Great Plains states in 1920, except in Kansas, where it nonetheless approached the national average.[93]

On the frontier, woman's domain—the home—was likely to be a primitive log cabin or even a sod house or dugout. The cost or simple unavailability of finished building materials made other types of construction difficult if not impossible in many areas. Such living conditions were particularly discouraging for women who had been used to decent residences in Europe.[94] Others from more modest economic backgrounds were probably less taken aback by these primitive shelters. Many women of the poorer classes had lived miserably in Europe, so they probably found conditions comparable in America. Educated Germans and Anglo-Americans were often disgusted by the poor and dirty living conditions of such immigrants.[95] Most women, however, found they were generally too busy in the early years to be very concerned with careful housekeeping anyway. Nevertheless, many found it difficult to adjust to dugouts and sod houses. Louisa Bartsch, for example, first saw the family dugout during a heavy rain, when part of the roof had washed in and a foot of water stood in the recessed floor. Only after her husband had bailed out the water and settled the children did she agree "to enter, and take up the duties of a homesteader's wife."[96] Like other frontierswomen, the German-speakers complained of the creatures with whom they had to share these dwellings and the tendency of the roof to drip mud during rains. A sod house could also be a dangerous place, for sometimes large animals fell through the top or the structure would collapse in a storm. Elizabeth Ewy Hirschler's aunt was killed when the main beam supporting the sod house roof fell on her during a heavy rain, and Elizabeth herself, several months pregnant, hurt her leg badly. It is no wonder she was deeply depressed for some time after this.[97]

German-speaking women generally accepted sod houses and dugouts as necessary and temporary housing on the timberless Great Plains, though. Sometimes they even appreciated their practical qualities: dirt floors that did not warp as cottonwood planks did and cool solidity in the hot summer winds.[98] Sod houses also were warmer in winter than the tar-paper shacks or plank houses that women had thought would be an improvement. There are many stories of snow sifting through the chinks in such walls and of entire families going to bed for days at a time to stay warm. Caroline Emanuel and her mother took turns lying in bed with Caroline's first baby to keep her warm enough to survive the winter of 1870 in a drafty Nebraska wooden house. The family eventually put bricks and plaster on the inside walls of the house, and Caroline bore thirteen more children there before they moved, twenty-some years later, into a ten-room house.[99]

Accessibility to water was one of the frontierswoman's main concerns. Like Anglo-American women, German-speakers thought themselves lucky if they had reliable running water or a well close at hand. Still, carrying water for household use as well as for gardens and livestock was one of the heaviest chores women and children did. Testimony at a North Carolina Farmers Alliance meeting in 1886 indicated that a woman walked more than 150 miles a year fetching and carrying water for household use if her well or spring was sixty yards from the house.[100] Wells could also give out in dry weather. Emilie Joss-Bigler remembered a summer when all seven wells on her widowed mother's Illinois farm went dry. One night a voice awakened her: "There in the moonlight stood her mother, dressed in her Swiss national costume which she wore only for important occasions, telling God what it was like to have seven dry wells and no water. She was praying for rain."[101] Women like Elizabeth Bigler would have had at the least an ironic smile for Gottfried Duden's idyllic description of how everything, even wash day, was more pleasant in the Missouri woods: "For most of the harder work of housekeeping there are ways of making the labor easier. If, for instance, laundry is to be done, a fire is lighted next to a near-by brook and a kettle is hung over it. The bleaching ground cannot be far away either, and it is a matter of course that during the summer a shady place is chosen."[102] As one might guess, Duden was not speaking from personal experience here. He had a manservant to take care of such tasks for him.

In general, the adjustment to the prairies of Illinois, Missouri, and

Iowa was not as difficult for settlers as adjusting to the Great Plains. There, in the "Great American Desert," scarceness of water, the vagaries of the weather, invasions of grasshoppers, the danger of prairie fire, and the treeless landscape posed particular challenges that not all cared to meet. Mary Wall Regier's family was finishing its frame house when a Kansas wind and hail storm struck, flattening the house and the wheat crop and injuring Mary and her brother. She remembered well that her family and others they knew would have gladly returned to Russia, had they had the means.[103] All areas of the Midwest frontier could try the mettle of farmers. Some immigrants had the support of strong religious faith to help them face setbacks. A diary kept by David and Katherine (Strohm) Ruth, members of a group of Mennonite families that settled in Iowa, contains the following passage from 1855:

> About two weeks before harvest time a small insect they called bugs (probably chinch bugs) came in millions and covered the ground, even in the houses they covered the walls and we were inclined to feel sorrowful as they reminded us of the Egyptian plague. They attacked the fine looking stand of wheat and in a few days sapped this so that it lost its strength, bleached to a deadly color and it soon was evident that only a few grains remained in the heads. This was not general through this section, our farm seemed to be one of those the most afflicted, oats too also yielded but very little, but we had a good crop of corn.
> About harvest time a continuous wet weather set in so that it was difficult and tiresome to harvest and take care of the grain. But thanks and praise be to the Lord, he has kept us and taken care of us and his will be done with us in the future.[104]

Other women and men had a sense of adventure or humor to help them face the difficulties of the frontier. One German-born woman prided herself on the prairie fires she had helped fight. Christian Krehbiel made his wife and family laugh about their economic woes with exaggerated assertions about their hopeful future. "Jürnjakob" and "Wieschen Swehn" joked about "not believing in" wooden corner posts anymore after one in their log cabin broke during an Iowa blizzard. After that they built a stone house.[105]

No matter what their ethnic heritage, those pioneers who settled in the Great Plains region and survived its harshness came to be marked by the culture its ecology shaped. The climate and landscape directly determined many aspects of Great Plains culture. Indirectly, the market pressures of the cash economy that evolved there early because of the restricted crop-growing possibilities also played a role. Vulnerability to these influences caused the inhabitants of this region to develop a fatalistic attitude toward their own efforts, evident in the Ruths' diary entry quoted above. At the same time, they came to redefine *success* in terms of perseverance and self-reliance. John Ise's *Sod and Stubble* and Mari Sandoz's *Old Jules* are great chronicles of the simple endurance immigrants (and others) found necessary to "succeed" on the Great Plains frontier.[106]

In many respects, people on the frontier responded to their environment in similar ways. What differences did exist between Anglo-American and German-speaking farmers often were due to the persistence of Old World agricultural habits and family production methods. An important study of agricultural practice in Nebraska in 1880 indicates that immigrant farmers did not hesitate to change their traditional crop production in response to new environmental demands. Differences in the extent to which Nebraska Germans and Germans from Russia raised small grains (wheat, in particular) might have been culturally determined, though.[107]

To some degree, other differences in agricultural practice between German-speaking immigrants and Anglo-Americans were due to certain patterns in women's roles. Many scholars have noted that the farms of German-speakers were generally more diversified than those of Anglo-Americans and that the tendency to cling to subsistence or yeoman farming typified these immigrants. In my view, this is connected to the centrality of women in farm production among German-speakers. A Nebraska study shows that German-American farmers had more poultry and cattle and were more likely to raise swine and sheep than were Anglo-Americans. This probably had to do with the traditional importance of female agricultural and domestic production as well as cultural and culinary preferences. Women, we should remember, were usually responsible for farm animals in German-speaking lands. A relatively large but diversified investment in livestock reflects certain expectations about women's participation in that sector of agricultural production.[108]

German-speaking women's support of the continuation of certain aspects of subsistence domestic production influenced farming practices in various ways. They wanted sheep's wool for the stockings many of them knit, for example. In some areas, they had their husbands plant flax for the production of homespun clothing. Since many German-speakers considered alcoholic beverages an inherent part of their diet, they grew the grapes necessary for their own wine.[109] No garden would have been complete without potatoes. German-speakers did not add some new foodstuffs, like sweet potatoes and native game, to their diet.[110]

The literature for immigrants, written almost solely by men and intended primarily for men and male enterprises, seldom gave women specific advice on how to accomplish the many demanding and often new tasks facing them.[111] Self-reliant, subsistence farming in the early years of settlement, without the support of the Old World village, meant a reversion to old methods of food and clothing production for many women. Some of them, wives of skilled laborers or of middle-class professionals, for example, were not familiar with these methods. All European immigrant women had to learn how to deal with new situations and new materials, either from American women or from countrywomen who had immigrated earlier.[112] This was sometimes difficult. The wives of the Latin farmers had to learn how to milk cows and cook over an open fire, sometimes with discouraging results. Most German-speakers found corn, that staple Midwest grain, unpalatable, but women had to learn how to use it, even in noodles and pancakes. Baking bread was also new to some women, and the "right" flour and even familiar leavening were not always available.[113] The process for making soap had to be learned, and once mastered, it became part of the activities frugal German-speaking housewives engaged in during the annual hog butchering.[114]

In their primary sphere of influence—the home—German-speaking women accommodated themselves to the pressures of their new environment through hard work and the willingness to accept what could not be altered. This strategy, which worked well for the family's general adaptation to American conditions, also helped women lead meaningful and productive lives in spite of the many changes in their domestic arrangements.

Outside of the home, however, immigrant women had less control of their new environment. This could have frightening and even dangerous aspects, though few German-speaking women in the Midwest suffered the fate of Stine Lauritzen and a young Mrs. Weichel. Stine Lauritzen was killed and scalped in a raid by Cheyenne Indians in the Kansas Salina River valley in 1869. In the same uprising, Mrs. Weichel's husband was also killed, and she was captured, just a week after their arrival in Kansas. When the cavalry caught up with the Cheyennes a few weeks later, Mrs. Weichel was seriously wounded in the battle to free her. Although many German-speaking women (like their Anglo-American sisters) were terrified of Indians, most contacts they had with Native Americans were harmless.[115]

Conflict of a different kind had its origins in American society and politics. The Know-Nothing movement was not felt as strongly in the Midwest as elsewhere. This area was not yet heavily settled by German-speakers in the 1850s, and the movement had its most violent expressions in urban areas. Other political and social forces, however, did play an important role in the lives of German-speakers. Abolition was one of these. German-speaking immigrants were usually not slaveholders.[116] Slavery violated their basic belief in personal liberty, an ideal many associated with their immigration to America. The extension of slavery into the western territories through the 1854 Kansas-Nebraska Bill also threatened the opportunities for immigrants in that area. Most were therefore firm supporters of the Union cause, which made them particular targets of attack by rebel troops and guerrillas. Elise Dubach Isely remembered tension between Anglo-Americans and immigrants in Kansas in the 1850s because immigrants could take out naturalization papers after a six month residence, which made them voters in Kansas or Nebraska under the 1854 bill. In their Doniphan County homestead area, a friendly neighbor warned the German-Swiss Dubachs and other "Free-Soilers" to put a white cloth on their chimney to fool border ruffians into thinking they were Anglo-Americans and proslavery. Conflicts of this sort did widow some German-speaking women, and others lost their husbands, sons, and brothers in the German Union regiments that were formed in the Civil War. In one Missouri incident in 1862, a woman's English language skills helped her gain her Lutheran minister husband's release after he and several German men had been captured in a Rebel bushwhacker raid. The other Germans were shot.[117]

Two other political and social issues in the American arena were more immediately pertinent to women: woman suffrage and temperance. It has been well documented that German-speakers did not support either movement. In general, it seems that women agreed with men on these issues. In keeping with their lack of involvement in public life, they rarely addressed such topics in their personal writings, although they could read a great deal about them in German-American publications. A riddle in the 1 August 1867 edition of the Missouri Synod Lutheran biweekly, *Die Abendschule*, indicates traditional attitudes toward the franchise for women:

> If only the first and the second [syllables] are the honor of a man and
>   of the house,
> As the Scripture and reason so clearly prescribe to them:
> They surely don't intend to beg for the third and fourth,
> Which are of value to the citizen, but don't suit the apron.

The answer, given in the 15 August edition, was *Frauenstimmrecht*, "women's franchise." German-language publications carried numer-

ous articles and features that communicated in greater detail the ethnic community's opposition to suffrage for women. On 26 January
1876, for example, the *Wöchentliche Kansas Freie Presse* in Leavenworth
reported on the push for the vote in Iowa, connected this movement
to temperance, and declared that the legislature was henpecked by the
"tyrants" at home. In July of 1881, the *Kansas Staats-Anzeiger* (Atchison) ran sarcastic stories about *die halbverrückte, Blumenkleid-tragende
Frauenrechtlerin* (the "half-crazy woman's rights advocate who wears
flowered dresses") who wanted to run for the New York state senate.
The *Nebraska Staats-Anzeiger* opposed suffrage on the grounds that
women were liable to yield to control by clergymen and thus become
political tools of the churches.[118] Bourgeois German-American views
about the domestic and maternal nature of women and religious teachings about their roles no doubt negatively influenced German-speaking women's participation in the suffrage movement.[119] Anecdotal
evidence underscores published proof of German-speaking men's opposition to suffrage. On one occasion, for instance, a man heckled
woman's rights speakers on a Nebraska street and drowned them out
by ringing a large bell and shouting, "Oh! the vimmins, the vimmins!
You can hear them every day. Vat you vant to hear them now for?"[120]

Women's inaction suggests they shared men's attitudes toward
woman suffrage and temperance. For example, there were very few
German-American woman suffrage groups, and little if any contact
between these (urban) groups and the American women's movement.
There are no Germanic names on the membership lists of a variety of
organizations in Kansas and Nebraska that advocated woman suffrage
in the late nineteenth century. Recent studies conclude that the German-American press (with the exception of a few urban socialist publications) supported traditional gender roles for both men and wom-
en and offered almost no information about the American women's
movement. It probably did not help that movement gain adherents
among the immigrants when in the late nineteenth century some leaders of the suffrage movement argued that the franchise was needed to
combat the foreign vote.[121]

Although German-speaking women were certainly aware of the
abuses of alcohol and the extent to which some women and their families suffered from men's excessive indulgence, there is little evidence
that they supported temperance. The weight of custom and tradition
was much too strong for this movement to take hold among German-
speakers, unless they were unaffiliated with the ethnic community or
were among the few ethnic immigrants who eschewed alcoholic beverages for religious reasons. Beer and wine were an inherent part of

the ethnic diet and social scene, and beer halls and beer gardens were gathering places for whole families on Sundays.[122] Such behavior institutionalized the enjoyment of alcohol as part of family life and made it, in the view of the ethnic community, relatively harmless. This was, of course, a source of tension and conflict with American society, but rural women were generally isolated from such contacts and influences. They might confiscate the jug when their men were drinking to excess, but they also thought of beer and wine as dietary staples. One Iowa woman, upon hearing that her son, home on a visit from college, had not had the money to try the local beer there, brought up a bucket from the cellar as an immediate solution to his deficient diet.[123]

A common opinion among German-speaking immigrants was that women had many rights in America, perhaps even more than was good for them. One recently arrived immigrant wrote from Illinois, "This is the best land for women. It is not the custom for them to work and they have many rights here. Therefore all the Germans like it here. My wife thinks a lot about home, but she is quite healthy, for she weighs one hundred and eighty pounds."[124] The sequence of his ideas may indicate that he feared America was spoiling his wife, causing her to become fat and lazy. Many German-born immigrants commented on the laziness of American women and on the extent to which they ruled their husbands. This was not an aspect of American society German-born men wanted their women to emulate.[125] Mathias Blommer, however, seemed to think it was good that women in America could take the fathers of their illegitimate children to court and sue for monetary recompense: "It doesn't work here in America like in Germany, that the poor creatures have to bear their trouble and shame all their life long with no compensation."[126]

Women in rural areas apparently did not oppose the traditional pattern of female subordination after their arrival in America. There were exceptions, of course. In Missouri, a Mrs. Kloenne made her husband sell a good, but isolated, farm and move the family to a poorer one "on the left bank of the Osage in order to be able to visit more easily in Jefferson City and to receive company from there." It is likely, however, that this reflects not the Americanization of Mrs. Kloenne but her force of will and her bourgeois background.[127] The traditional European power relations in marriage and the family persisted in rural America. The following are typical expressions of the roles each assumed:

Father was the breadwinner and the Supreme Court; Mother was the tutor and manager of the house.

The great leavening factor between the children and their father was Anna, their mother. She was the first person they went to with any plans or everyday problems. Oftentimes Anna and the children would combine forces to get around the habits or inclinations of [their father].[128]

Sometimes male domination of women led to physical abuse. One immigrant tied his wife to a stake in the sun as punishment because, after having prepared food two days in a row for threshers who never appeared, she refused to do so again on the third day. A moral tale in the 19 January 1899 *O'Fallon Hausfreund,* a Missouri Catholic weekly, indicates that some German-speakers beat their wives in America, as they had had the right to do in Europe. In rural areas, communal pressure might have been strong enough to make this less common than in cities, but there is certainly evidence that it did occur.[129] It is unclear whether women felt emboldened by the protection of American law to complain to the authorities about such abuse. It is more likely that they used the familiar arbitrators of family and church in such cases, much as they had in Europe.

The work German-speaking women did at home and in the fields gained them some measure of authority and respect, but it did not result in true gender equality, even in work relationships.[130] It did not mean reciprocity. That is, women did men's work, but men rarely did women's. Young boys or even those past the age of puberty helped their mothers with housework, but only if no female child was present or capable of doing it.[131] It was considered very unusual and inappropriate for a married man to do housework, which was reflected in the December 1888 appeal in the *Marion County Anzeiger* (Kansas) to its readers to help Franz Voigt, whose wife's illness had forced him to be both *Hausfrau* and *Hausherr.*

The American environment called forth certain new forms of behavior in women, but this did not mean their basic attitudes changed. For example, women learned to ride horseback (and even, sometimes, to enjoy doing so), and they traveled alone to visit neighbors. Such unaccustomed behavior was necessitated by new circumstances, however, not an expression of newfound freedom. Riding *astride* was frowned upon by middle-class immigrants, who sometimes criticized farm women for such "immoral" behavior.[132] German-speaking women might work out in the fields, but they were reluctant to wear men's clothing to do so.[133] Women who were left alone on farms and homesteads for long periods while their husbands worked elsewhere for cash wages had to think and act independently as farm managers. Occasionally a woman took advantage of her husband's absence to carry out a project he would not have approved, especially when she could complete it before his return. But this, too, was probably the result of an individual woman's personality or the exigencies of the situation rather than the influence of the much-vaunted freedom of America.[134]

The following verse, written by a second-generation German-American in her daughter's autograph book, shows that the tradition of self-effacement among German-speaking women did not fade.

> Mother said
> When I asked her
> Don't always speak, when you know something
> Don't trust the friend who only calls himself such.
> Keep yourself quiet and pious and pure
> As your mother's beloved little daughter.[135]

These lines call upon the authority of a female heritage that demanded modesty, piety, propriety, and purity in women. Such precepts might have served to perpetuate patriarchal relationships, but women accepted them as valid and sought to instill them in their daughters.

Other evidence indicates rural German-speaking communities retained familiar patterns of gender relations in their new surroundings. The disapproval of public displays of affection between men and women is an example. Near the end of the century, members of a Kansas German-language immigrant church were disgusted by the first "modern" wedding celebrated there, which included a kiss at the altar. The congregation hid its laughter, but members later muttered that if the young couple had to act in such an animal-like manner, they could at least "lick each other" in private. Among the Germans from Russia, it was the custom for the wife to walk a few steps behind her husband, as a sign of deference as well as subordination. The women in this group considered the more affectionate public behavior of Americans shocking. Even the sight of married couples strolling together or holding hands in public made them cringe. As Carol Coburn has said of the families she studied at Block, Kansas, "A strong sense of family pride and privacy required that problems be kept from nonfamily members, and public displays of affection or anger were highly unusual."[136] The behavior in my Nebraska community also corresponds to this cultural demeanor of reticence and self-control, still evident in the third generation.

Lauren Kattner's study of young women in New Braunfels, Texas, indicates that general patterns of female development persisted several generations after immigration. A girl in that German-American community spent the five- to ten-year *Wartezeit* (waiting period) between her confirmation and her marriage (or career or unwed motherhood) much as she would have in Europe, by learning household and hand-craft skills. The adolescent Bukovinia Germans of western Kansas ended their schooling with confirmation and helped out at home or went out to work for other farmers, as did the children of Block, Kansas. Studies of other closely knit German-American communities in the Midwest would probably reveal similar social and cultural patterns.[137]

Many immigrants were slow to change traditional ways of contracting marriages. Young people who were supporting themselves made their own arrangements, as had been the case among the rural laborers in Europe. Such couples were still concerned about the economic aspects of their union, however, and often postponed their marriage until they had earned enough cash to start farming. In other instances, a man would approach the father of his prospective bride to ask for her hand and to determine what help would be given her to marry. Or he would ask his father to speak with the young woman's father, and her acceptance would be communicated to him indirectly.[138] The role of mothers in such matters was probably important behind the scenes, just as the bride's acquiescence was often accomplished in the privacy of the home. The public role of males indicates the importance of economic considerations in these arrangements. As had been the case in Europe, men took the leading role in transactions that involved the present or future transfer of property. The ability of a woman to bring property to a marriage remained important. Among Germans from Russia, a girl who had nothing but her clothes to contribute was called *die mit den* [sic] *kahlen Arsch* (the girl with the bare ass).[139] Although the descendants of the immigrants gradually adopted the more individualistic patterns of marital choice of Anglo-American society, in some areas of the Midwest the land-based traditions were still evident in the latter half of the twentieth century.[140]

Residence in rural America did not cause German-speaking immigrants to alter their traditional gender relations. After all, most of them had not come to America to effect change of that sort in their lives.[141] Yet it should not be forgotten that within her sphere, a woman traditionally had power and influence. The Boonville, Missouri, German-language weekly *Central Missourier* cited the following joke in 1874: "Who advances the fastest? Answer: Women. Scarcely is the courtship over and they have already become corporals, and soon after that they are also in command."[142] Sometimes this domestic leverage indirectly extended to public matters via a woman's husband. "Jürnjakob Swehn" told the story of how a man agreed to help build the first community church after members of the congregation made it clear to his wife that building the church meant they would no longer track snow and mud into her house when it was her turn to host the services. Such stories indicate the influence women could wield in the wider community, even though their power was masked by the public actions only men could take.[143]

In their desire for continuity and conservation of their accustomed way of life, German-speakers sought the support of an ethnic community. Letters and memoirs indicate that such factors as the cost of the land and its proximity to relatives, Old World neighbors, and other German-speakers figured more prominently in the immigrants' choice of land than did soil type and its physical configuration. German-speakers were willing to rent or buy smaller and poorer parcels of land than did Anglo-Americans and live frugally on them until they could buy or rent more, especially if they were in an ethnic neighborhood. Emil Pieschl remembered this about his parents, Austrian immigrants in Kansas: "As long as there were some German families in our locality, Dad and Mom thought they should live there, buy the land and improve it for their home." Mathias Blommer's two daughters and their families decided to settle in Nebraska rather than Kansas, because Kansas had only Irish, no German-speaking, priests.[144] The ethnic community and its institutions helped determine an immigrant family's satisfaction and therefore their persistence on a particular farmstead. Studies in Iowa and Kansas confirm this connection. In areas of relatively high concentrations of German-speakers, immigrant farmers were very persistent, but they were quite mobile where they were a small portion of the rural population.[145]

In rural areas, German-speakers moved quickly to establish community institutions that would sustain ethnic life and at the same time provide frameworks for adaptation. Schools and churches were the most important. These institutions, particularly the ethnic church, played a vital role in providing a center for the immigrants' cultural and communal life. The ethnic identity and cultural cohesiveness that resulted encouraged the immigrants to send down roots to ensure their future and their children's. After the frontier era, ethnic clubs and societies also formed in some of the villages that served as market centers for German-speakers.[146] Although women participated in this institutional life, their roles in founding and supporting schools, churches, and clubs are not well documented.

It is rare that women's contributions to immigrant churches were acknowledged. Certainly they often played a role, as the story "Jürnjakob Swehn" told about the housewife who wanted to end church services in her home illustrates. Many German-speaking women took their spirituality seriously. Indeed, the church was one of the few areas in which nineteenth-century women could acceptably exercise some autonomy, as the well-known maxim about their proper domains indicates: *Kinder, Küche, Kirche* (children, kitchen, church). Yet here, too, there were limitations. Women were not allowed to take a public role in church work and life in the major German denominations until well into the twentieth century. Some German-American ministers' wives might have married their husbands to serve their church in a more direct fashion than otherwise would have been possible. One woman articulated this in 1842, as she sailed to America to marry, sight unseen, a German missionary. Julie Turnau had wanted to do missionary work in Africa, but the German Evangelical missionary societies would not accept single female workers. In her shipboard diary, she expressed the hope that she would make her husband's domestic life easier and thus provide him more time for his pastoral duties: "I am happy that I shall be able to be active in God's work through such ordinary housework, if not directly, at any rate indirectly."[147]

Because women's contributions were for the most part indirect, nineteenth-century church documents and histories rarely documented them.[148] The visits of circuit preachers and missionaries over a period of several years often preceded the establishment of a church. That women put up the traveling ministers, opened their (often primitive) homes for the services, and supplied meals for dozens of people afterwards is usually merely mentioned in passing, though.[149] The actual founding of a church was publicly attributed to the men and exceptional women (almost always widows) who had land or money to contribute.[150] The separation of women's private, domestic sphere from the public arena is again evident in this. It is likely, however, that many women played an important role in the contributions of land and money that made the immigrant church possible. The participatory nature of women in these processes comes out in their writings, for instance, when a woman comments on the land she and her husband contributed for a school or church. Barbara Strohm Kraemer's diary is an example: "On the 17th of August 1855 our new School House was dedicated. It was built upon our land in the Franklin Prairie. We donated an acre and 11 rods for the purpose of building a Mennonite Church and School. This was given as a memorial to us after we are gone." A year later the Kraemers moved from Iowa to Illinois and hosted church services every other Sunday for the next two years in a large room on the first floor of their house: "It was just the right thing for it." Friedrich and Dorothea Wegener made sure they would not do without church services in their new Thayer County, Nebraska, home in 1884. They built a twelve-room house, one room of which was for the pastor and another for church services. Women like these agreed with their husband's public stance and supported it with the domestic economy under their control, but it was improper for women to do more than this openly.[151]

These cultural attitudes kept women from taking a public role in policy-making in the rural churches. Local control was one of the things that differentiated the American immigrant church from the Old World church and that made it more appealing to men than had been the case in Europe. "Jürnjakob Swehn" wrote to his old schoolteacher that the country church's walls were closer together than the parish church back home; "on the other hand it is also fuller on Sundays than yours. We are also more interested here in church matters. We don't just have to pay here. We also have the obligation of speaking up and making decisions."[152] German-speaking women, however, did not openly take part in this aspect of American church life. Like their Anglo-American sisters, they made many other behind-the-scene contributions to the founding and support of the rural church. They did this in ways that paralleled their accepted roles as nurturers and farm wives. They kept the church property clean, cooked food for church affairs, and conducted a variety of fund-raisers for the benefit of the church. Sometimes their efforts resulted in special additions to the church: for example, the new organ that the Nebraska City First Evangelical Lutheran Church board asked the Ladies' Church Society to finance in 1879 or the crystal chandelier that Mrs. Henry Kalkmann convinced the captain of a river boat to donate to the first Catholic church in Nebraska City.[153] Certainly the immigrant churches, like the Anglo-American ones, could not have functioned or, sometimes, survived without the ongoing work women performed: the annual cleanings, the weekly altar decorating, and the numerous bake sales and soup suppers.[154]

These duties and activities were arduous, but they were also opportunities for rural immigrant women to see each other, exchange news, and maintain their female networks. Most German-speaking women had few chances to leave their farms and see others outside of their family circle, except for the Sunday church services.[155] Even church-related women's groups were uncommon at first. German-language churches in America were rather slow to authorize the founding of women's missionary groups.[156] It took time for men to relinquish control in some of these areas. Men dominated the American ethnic church, the center for community recreational life, much as they had the village pub in Europe. In some parishes in Iowa, for instance, men took part in fellowship and choral groups, but women were not allowed to participate in similar activities until the late 1920s and 1930s.[157] Nonetheless, aggressive female leadership could make a difference. When St. John's German Evangelical Church of rural Cooper County, Missouri, got its second full-time minister in 1899, it also got his dynamic wife and two grown daughters. Within two years, these three women had established a *Frauenverein* (women's club), a *Jugendverein* (youth club), and the church's first choir. They also made the parsonage into a social center for young people of the entire neighborhood.[158]

The heart of the rural community was the ethnic church. It supported the value system that emphasized the preservation of family farming as a way of life for future generations. It mirrored the roles expected of and practiced by those who attended it. As was the case in their homes and families, women were vital to its functioning, but their status and power within the church were not equal to men's. The rural school was the other important social and community institution in farm areas. Here, however, ethnic pioneers often had to accommodate their desire to maintain their native language and culture to the demands of public authorities.

Documenting women's contributions to frontier schools and the education of children is very difficult. What evidence we have is primarily anecdotal. As was the case with the founding of immigrant churches, women probably supported their husbands' donating land for a school and money to pay a teacher. Again, men are given the credit for these efforts. Indeed, a typical German-American attitude toward women taking too public an interest in their children's education is indicated by the praise given "a reasonable woman" in Iowa who declined nomination to the school board because she had family obligations and no desire to "shine in public."[159]

It was no doubt the case that in German-speaking communities, the traditional prerogatives of the father in the education of the children were transferred to America. The weak tradition of formal education among the European rural population was also transferred, with children in country areas often attending school only when they were not needed to work at home. Similarly, girls were generally not encouraged to get an education. Mothers were often no more supportive than fathers in this. Since a girl would, it was thought, marry and stay at home, an education would be wasted on her. Anna Goetsch, who had supported her eldest son's desire to go to college, did not intervene when her only daughter wanted to attend high school and the girl's father and brothers disapproved. Gottfried Walz wrote a niece from Bouton, Iowa, advising her not to undergo teacher training, for as a member of the school board he had too often seen such education go to waste among young women.[160]

German-speaking immigrants generally did not approve of female schoolteachers. They were used to the cultural and educational traditions of the Old World. The respect accorded education and the high status granted educators in German culture was not thought to be compatible with the relatively low status to which women were generally relegated. Particularly in rural areas in Europe, pastors and priests had often doubled as schoolteachers. Even where this was not the case, Old World teachers had been men, for women were not admitted to institutions of higher learning until mid-century and those trained as teachers had almost always stayed in urban areas. In America, German-speaking women were slow to enter one of the few professions open to their sex in the late nineteenth century. In 1900, first- and second-generation German-American women accounted for only 86 of the 314,269 female teachers and professors in the United States, far below the number one might expect from their share in the population.[161] Schools specializing in training German-language teachers were established by church denominations, conservative institutions that for the most part continued assumptions about the inappropriateness of women's pursuing careers outside the domestic sphere. The Missouri Synod church, which developed one of the largest systems of parochial schools and founded highly structured and demanding teachers' training schools, opposed for doctrinal reasons the training or hiring of women as teachers until after World War I. Only a teacher shortage or financial exigency induced some parochial schools to break the ban on hiring women, even as teaching assistants for the elementary grades and at a third the salary of a male teacher.[162]

Partly because of conservative German-American churches' opposition to women becoming teachers and partly because of old patterns of rural gender roles, many German-speakers thought girls did not need to learn anything more than was necessary to function adequately as a homemaker. For a few, however, teaching was a respectable alternative to working as a domestic to earn extra money for the family. Two of Heinrich and Ulrike Gellhorn's daughters, Martha and Louise, attended schools at Union and Steamboat Rock, Iowa, after their father's death in 1880 to help their crippled mother and other siblings pay off a $1,000 debt on their farm. That these young women became teachers, a relatively rare phenomenon for German-speakers at the time, was probably the result of several factors. The girls had been toddlers when they immigrated in 1868 and had thus grown up in America and in a family that had many contacts with Americans. Their parents, of the urban lower middle class, were themselves moderately well-educated. Perhaps most important, the Gellhorns lived in a neighborhood with relatively few German-speakers and attended an English-language rural school, where they had had female teachers.[163]

The Gellhorn family shows there were exceptions to German-speakers' negative attitudes toward the education of women. Another example is Ella Sillars's mother. She had gone to work at fourteen in a boardinghouse. Her own hard youth made her want her children to have an education, contrary to what "most of the other old Germans" in the neighborhood wanted.[164] Many rural immigrant women, however, probably did not share the belief in the value of general education that came to be part of the American dream as time went on. Instead, they, like their husbands, were much more supportive of the parochial schools that were often founded in association with the rural church. Indeed, these schools competed successfully with public schools for students, money, and supplies in many parts of the Midwest.[165] The Catholics and the Missouri Synod Lutherans were particularly successful in establishing such schools. Missouri Synod Lutherans explicitly connected the use of German in the church, home, and school with *reine Lehre* (pure doctrine). Even other German-speaking immigrants saw such schools as the best way to combat the too-rapid assimilation of their children into American society. A comment by "Jürnjakob Swehn" is representative: "We founded the parish school so that our children will learn German and stay German, and so that they will become good Christians."[166] Many immigrants believed that these intertwined goals—language mastery, cultural retention, and religious education—could be met better in the parochial school than in the public school.

In the relative isolation of the countryside, German-speaking immigrants were free to develop an ethnic identity and cultural life without the constant, intense pressure toward assimilation typical of urban areas. Wherever they settled densely enough to form an ethnic church, their religious identification was central to their social lives. This affiliation was strong enough to link like-minded German-speakers from various countries. Secular clubs usually formed later. Although important in helping forge a "Pan-German-American" group ethnicity, such clubs, through their essentially American structures, gradually played a role in the acculturation of the immigrants. This acculturation proceeded slowly and indirectly at first, but as time went on, even the rural ethnic community responded to the demand that the immigrants adapt to the dominant culture. For example, the constitution of the Keystone, Iowa, *Turnverein,* founded on 21 December 1892, stated that it was an "association of men of free moral character, seeking physical and intellectual development, desirous of attaining and disseminating a social brotherly communion and upright American citizenship." Members had to be eighteen years of age or older and citizens or planning to become citizens.[167]

The most important German-American clubs in rural areas were the *Turner* (physical fitness and political awareness) societies and the choral groups. These did not exist everywhere in the Midwest, but most counties with large concentrations of German-speakers had at least one such organization. For example, to make up for the lack of music on the American frontier, Dietzenbach immigrants founded a "Musikchor" that performed in their rural Illinois area.[168] Women's direct participation in such clubs varied somewhat. They generally did not join or form choral groups until after World War I, since this was traditionally a male activity. Similarly, they usually served in an auxiliary function in the *Turner* societies, in keeping with the male-only origins of the movement. The records of the Brunswick, Missouri, *Turnverein,* for example, show that it was composed of men only; however, it sponsored family picnics and balls and on one occasion spent money for forty-three-and-a-half yards of chintz print and two spools of thread. In the same period, they paid a carpenter to build a stage in their hall. Their wives and daughters evidently sewed for the production. They might have also had roles in staged dramas and taken part in musical performances.[169]

In some of the Midwest towns and counties with heavy concentrations of German-speakers, women and children also had gymnastics classes at the *Turnverein* and formed affiliated clubs. Although it is unlikely that most rural women would have had the opportunity to travel to town to regular club meetings or gymnastic classes, they probably did come with their husbands and children to some of the dances, Christmas parties, and picnics the *Turner* societies sponsored. For example, the German-language *Leavenworth Post* contained many references to the activities of what must have been a large and very active *Turnverein* in Leavenworth, Kansas. Between 2 and 15 December 1887, it announced or reported on several events sponsored by the women's gymnastic club (*Turnschwestern-Verein*) or glee club (*Liederkranz*): a Christmas celebration for children of the German-English school, evening entertainment featuring a vocal and instrumental concert followed by a dance, and a "necktie party," at which supper was served and a hundred couples danced until four in the morning. These events were in addition to meetings of such men's groups as the glee club (*Männergesangverein*) and the Swabian Club (*Schwabenverein*). Washington, Missouri, had such an active club life that it, like St. Louis, was a seat of the City Federation of German Clubs. The Washington Turner Society (founded in 1859) produced German-language plays for more than half a century.[170] It is difficult to know to what extent women and families of peasant background participated in such activities, even as part of the audience, but similar club-sponsored events gave midwestern farm women the opportunity to come in contact with the larger society in a relatively comfortable and unintimidating environment. At the same time, the organizational structures and principles and the public and often "non-Germanic" nature of the events such clubs sponsored (neck-tie parties, for example) also contributed to the assimilative function such groups and activities had.

Much more work is yet to be done on the history of rural immigrant women's secular associations. From sketchy evidence, it seems that German-speaking farm women were unlikely to join clubs founded by native-born women. They might have profited by some of the activities those clubs sponsored, though. One example is the waiting rooms and child care facilities set up in small towns for the benefit of farm women who came to shop on Saturdays. German-American women also seem to have been slow to establish parallel groups, perhaps because they found all the social and cultural stimulation they had interest in and time for within the immigrant church. They had important and time-consuming work to do as conservators of tradition in the home and the ethnic community.[171]

Women had an especially important role in diminishing the shock of cultural adaptation. In all immigrant groups, they were traditionally the conservators of culture and language. In the home, the immigrants could preserve their old ways without coming into overt, direct conflict with the new culture around them. On the farm, the food ways, life-style, holiday customs, and language could be maintained while the immigrants accommodated their agricultural enterprise to the American economy.[172]

Many scholars and commentators have noted the linguistic conservatism of German-speaking women.[173] The children and grandchildren of German-speaking immigrants also often remarked on the inability of their female ancestors to speak English, and the manuscript census shows this as well.[174] Women themselves sometimes complained about the difficulties and bother of learning English, particularly when they had little pressing need to do so. This no doubt increased their isolation. Even residence among German-speakers was not always a guarantee against such feelings of linguistic solitude. For example, Pauline

Gauß Wendt wrote to her sister-in-law eight years after arriving in Iowa from Berlin: "I am so alone here. Everyone is American. The Germans are Low Germans and gossipy so that I have no one to whom I can pour out my heart." Louise Ritter wrote of the same alienation from other immigrants who spoke different dialects: "we don't have that cozy living here and the language is different . . . they speak High German instead of Swiss-German." After twenty-eight years in Nebraska, she also wrote that she could not speak English because she lacked the opportunity to do so but that she could "get about fairly well in the shops and so." She regretted that her sons never learned to write High German and that her grandchildren knew only English because their mothers were not Swiss-German-speakers.[175] Rural German-speaking women in ethnic enclaves attempted to maintain their children's native language skills and were largely successful in this; however, this often led to women's partial or complete isolation from the Anglo-American society of which their descendants increasingly became a part.

In their housekeeping practices, German-speaking women could usually maintain traditional ways without risk of conflict with the dominant culture. Their cleanliness was legendary, and generally they deserved that reputation. Emilie Bigler remembered how her mother insisted on having her cooking kettles scrubbed until white paper rubbed on the bottoms remained white.[176] They brought featherbeds and bolsters with them and kept geese to renew their bedding. In some areas, they baked bread in the large brick outdoor ovens they knew from their homelands. Other women made European cheeses, like the "Quarkkäse" of the Luxembourgers, and stuffed sausages and put up sauerkraut.[177] Sometimes non-German-speakers objected to their ethnic culinary practices (e.g., Anglo-American schoolteachers refused to lodge with them and share their diet of pork and sauerkraut, and neighbors criticized Germans from Russia for having their children mix sauerkraut by stomping it with their feet in the crocks). In other cases, they learned from foreign-born women (e.g., a Swiss woman taught her neighbors to make cheese).[178]

The immigrants did not, of course, retain all their European household traditions. For instance, the peasant practice of family members' eating out of a large common bowl was abandoned, along with the protein-impoverished diet of the Old World. Instead of rye, German-speakers now baked white bread, in Europe the food of the wealthy. They ate together at the same table, instead of separating the children and hired help from the adult farm family members, as had been the custom in some households of larger landowners in Europe. Now there was often a tablecloth on the table, although it was no longer used to cover a loaf of bread.[179] In spite of such adaptations to American ways, food, if not always the manner in which it was served, remained an area for German-speaking women's ethnic expression.

The clothing women were used to wearing in Europe had to change in their new surroundings. Climatic changes dictated this, as did women's sense of appropriateness and fashion. Burdened by her woolen clothing, a German immigrant fashioned a cotton skirt out of a blanket during the Atlantic journey. One woman remembered her shame at American women's stares when she got off the train in Kansas in her Russian felt boots and peasant-style costume and was grateful for the "ordinary" clothing given her by kind American women. Other peasant women in rural areas, however, probably felt no need (or could not afford) to Americanize their dress. American observers sometimes noted the oddness of immigrant women's clothing, particularly their drab colors and headscarves. Regional costumes (*Trachten*), which were sometimes even institutionalized by law in the Old World, could retain special significance for immigrant women. Elizabeth Bigler kept her Bernese costume for important occasions, donning it, for example, when she gave a meditation at her husband's burial and when she prayed to God during a drought.[180] In America, the distinctions of social class and region that had been observed in European dress were not maintained. Some of the middle-class immigrants found it offensive that hired domestics could and did dress as stylishly as women from their own circles. But in America, only money and taste dictated what one wore. A general conformity to what was considered urban style shaped female fashion, and this was viewed as another (albeit superficial) indication of equality in American society.[181]

Women also made important contributions to the retention of ethnic holiday practices. In some Swiss families, the New Year began with a visit from a Ruprecht-like figure and continued the next day with gifts for the children and a big family meal of roast goose or pig. Easter was celebrated with the coloring of eggs, games, and another special meal.[182] A "Saxon-traditionalist" neighborhood of Lutherans at Cooper Hill in Osage County, Missouri, continued the pre-Christmas visits of "Belsnickels" (a threatening figure calculated to frighten children into good behavior), erected Christmas trees, and celebrated December 26 as well as Christmas Day as a holiday in the early twentieth century. The holiday and folk customs of Luxembourgian-Americans centered on their Catholic identity. Women expressed this in their homes, keeping rosaries, pictures of saints, the crucifix, and a holy water container in their parlors. They and their husbands gave their children the same saints' names they had in Europe, although distances from the church necessitated their waiting until the Sunday after the birth to baptize the baby. Luxembourgian-American wakes and baptisms were conducted more quietly than in the old country, but weddings were celebrated in the traditional exuberant fashion. Some old Luxembourgian customs had disappeared by the end of the century, however. The visits of St. Nicolas, for instance, gave way to the erection of Christmas trees, a custom imported by other German-speaking groups. Some Luxembourgian-Americans commemorated *Kirmes,* the anniversary celebration of the dedication of the immigrants' European church, with family and neighbors in America, but this often ended with the passing of the first generation. Not always though. For example, the descendants of immigrants from Dietzenbach near Darmstadt continued to celebrate "die Dietzenbacher Kerb" (the anniversary of the founding date of the Dietzenbach parish church) during the last weekend of October for three or four generations after the main wave of settlement around Darmstadt, Illinois, which took place between 1837 and 1850. Annual mission festivals held in Lutheran parishes and similar church celebrations in other denominations were customs congenial to German-speakers used to church-based community holidays in Europe.[183]

Similar customs were common in many parts of the Midwest. Some differences due to varying European backgrounds persisted among the various immigrant groups. Generally, customs connected to religious holidays and events in the life cycle were the most common and the longest lasting. The 28 June 1876 *Wöchentliche Kansas Freie Press* in Leavenworth reported on a Pentecost celebration organized by the German settlement on Deer Creek in Douglas County. "In accordance with Swiss custom," a *Brautbitter* (wedding invitor) announced the wedding of the American-born daughter of Elizabeth Bigler. This was thirty-one years after the Bigler family had immigrated to Illinois.[184] *Brautbitter* and shivarees were also traditional practices in German-American areas in Missouri, Kansas, and Nebraska for many years after immigration. My own parents were shivareed when they moved into their farm house after World War II. German ethnic practices and rural conviviality combined on these occasions as strategies for community building. Women's concern with family and church made them important supporters and conveyors of such traditions.[185]

*   *   *

The midwestern states of Illinois, Iowa, Missouri, Kansas, and Nebraska were proving grounds for the ability of German-speaking immigrants to succeed economically in family-farming ventures. This area offered an appropriate environment and many of the conditions necessary for such success: arable land in large quantities at affordable prices; a growing economy that rewarded hard work and frugality with the opportunity to accumulate property and wealth; a native (white) culture that shared many of the family values and structures of the immigrants, ignored their relatively unobtrusive cultural differences, and, until 1914, tolerated their efforts to build an ethnic community as a bulwark against too-rapid assimilation. For their part, the German-speakers benefited from their habits of industriousness, thriftiness, and self-imposed moderation in personal wants that their often marginal existences in the Old World had imposed on them. The high value they placed on establishing, holding, and, if possible, enlarging the family holding also motivated them to persist in difficult frontier conditions and to take advantage of others' lack of such persistence.

Much of the credit for German-speakers' ability to maintain their presence in rural areas of the Midwest must go to women. Their culture had conditioned them to be hardworking and self-sacrificing, and they had ample opportunity to continue this pattern on the American frontier. They were willing to bear large numbers of children and to supervise their contributions to the family endeavor, even if that came at the cost of their own health and the well-being and education of their children. The household skills and the knowledge of animal husbandry many of them had developed in Europe were also put to good use. These contributions to subsistence farming often enabled their families to weather economic difficulties that might have broken others. Women's domestic economy also made immigrant farm families less susceptible to the pressures of acculturation that a more thorough integration into the growing American agricultural market economy would have caused.

These immigrant women were anxious to continue the home- and family-centered lives they had led. Isolation in the countryside enabled them to do so. Women also were important in the establishment of the immigrant community institutions that supported this isolation and simultaneously created a relatively familiar cultural sphere. Within the rural ethnic community, women's traditional place in the family, with its limited but comfortably familiar autonomy, could be continued. Rural German-speaking women were therefore unlikely to find the comparative independence of American women attractive or to bring gender conflict into the home. Moreover, they could be counted on to support the language, customs, and cultural traditions of the Old World through their domestic activities and in their daily interactions with family members. This domestic ethnic culture was a "safe space" within which the immigrants and their children could more gradually learn about and accommodate themselves to American society.

The cultural conditioning of German-speaking women generally proved beneficial for their families on the frontier. Their inclination toward self-sacrifice and hard work, toward the subjection of their own wishes to those of others and of individual desires to long-term goals, made many of them efficient and effective frontierswomen. Traditional family power structures among German-speakers, with female subordination at its center, suited the work patterns and long-term family goals of the subsistence frontier farmer. Through my research, I have come to regard my own family's success in accumulating land and passing it on to succeeding generations as fitting in the larger framework of the European peasant tradition. My grandfather's relatively early retirement from farming also fits this pattern. I now see my grandmother's character and behavior in a different light as well, and I view the contributions of the women in my family, more felt than documented, as typical rather than extraordinary.

For all the reasons discussed in this chapter, most rural German-speaking women were generally "contented among strangers," but human beings live on an emotional level as well as in the concrete world. Some immigrant women experienced their frontier lives as continuations of their old existences. For others, the familiar family structures and the creation of an ethnic community did not always make up for the inner displacement they felt. In the next chapter, I explore the personal, subjective dimensions of women's frontier experience.

3

Adventure, Alienation, and Adaptation: The Subjective Experiences of Immigrant Life

Our women here have a significant and difficult task, but they sense its importance, are never plagued with boredom, and are content with what they accomplish every day for the good of their loved ones.
—Friedrich Muench, *Der Staat Missouri*

With these words Friedrich Muench asserted the existence of a simple, straightforward subjective reality that the words and actions of German-speaking immigrant women often belied. For example, a Howard County, Nebraska, history tells about a Mrs. Koch who was left alone while her husband went to work on the railroad. According to this story, Mrs. Koch killed herself and her three children because she was "lonely in a strange land and unable to communicate with her neighbors in a strange tongue."[1] Somewhere between the despair and alienation of Mrs. Koch and the serene contentment Muench extolled lies the broader reality of immigrant women's inner experience of their lives in America. Like my own great-grandmothers, most of them persevered. Did they do so in spite of despondency, or were they generally content or even happy in their new lives?

"A man can only be content if his wife is as well," wrote Muench when he addressed the situation of German women in his 1859 book describing immigrant life in Missouri. While acknowledging that some better-educated women were "disconsolate" (*trostlos*) because of their material losses and the work they had to do under frontier conditions, Muench nevertheless maintained that "the great majority of the German women adapt themselves to the new conditions with that good and honest will which is characteristic of the better ones among them, . . . and are their husband's most essential support." He cautioned the immigrants against the "pernicious habit" of keeping servants, which cost too much and just caused trouble. In any case, he went on, the vain, frivolous life of a wealthy woman was unworthy of her duty to be of value to humankind. Instead, he asserted, the immigrant women worked hard milking, preserving, making soap, gardening, taking care of children and poultry, and weaving cloth: "And in spite of all this they do not stop living as educated persons" in the midst of their happy, helpful families, where all daughters married and sons did not have to become soldiers.[2]

Muench's ideas reflect his own bourgeois background and the intended audience for his book. It is interesting that while Muench thought keeping servants was a waste of money, he did not find it contradictory to have kept a black female slave as a domestic servant. It is also significant that he wrote these words twenty-five years after he himself had immigrated. Muench might well have written quite differently in those early years, when he was worn out from unaccustomed physical labor and watched his wife attempt to cope with bearing and raising several children while keeping a frontier household. Like many immigrants, he tended to gloss over the hard times from the retrospective of many years of residence in America. The incomplete and sometimes (unconsciously) deceptive nature of the first- and second-person information about immigrants' feelings accessible to us complicates our interpretation of that information.

Other factors also interfere with determining the full story of German-speaking women's subjective experiences as nineteenth-century immigrants. First and foremost, the sparseness of the evidence makes it impossible to gather a large pool of samples. The forms in which such evidence has come down to us sometimes also complicate our proper understanding of it. For example, the testimony of two German Evangelical ministers' wives, Adelheid von Borries-Garlich and Sophie Luise Weitbrecht, is quite different, even though they had similar family backgrounds and bourgeois upbringings. Both of them came as young married women to the Missouri and Illinois frontiers at approximately the same time (the 1830s and 1840s). They and their husbands served impoverished, sparsely populated parishes. Both lived and had their first children under circumstances that were much more primitive than any they had experienced in Germany. Yet the tone of their personal writing differs greatly. One has the impression that Adelheid Garlich was better able to cope with these circumstances than was Sophie Luise Weitbrecht, but this may be erroneous. Part of the reason for this impression is that Adelheid Garlich shared her diary, our source of information, with her husband and sent it to her family in Germany a few years after immigrating, so she probably did not document negative events or feelings that might have upset her husband or her relatives. Sophie Luise Weitbrecht, on the other hand, wrote her memoir many years later, after the death of her husband, for her children's information, so it is perhaps not surprising that her memoir is much more informative about the difficulties ministers and their families endured in remote areas than is Adelheid Garlich's diary. Sophie Luise Weitbrecht could be more forthright in her statements.[3]

Our perspectives and prejudices as modern readers and contemporary Americans also are forces to be reckoned with as we attempt to understand the lives of people who lived a century or more ago. It is important to remain cognizant of the fact that we look at the past "by the light of our own values," as John Demos has said. In particular, he reminds us, we must keep in mind the context of the earlier time as clearly and as completely as possible. Difficult to accomplish, but at least as important, is the need to differentiate among various emotions and to "separate ideas about emotion from the actual emotional experience."[4] Although these demands on us as readers and interpreters of historical documents and case studies are great, in this chapter I attempt to establish some general patterns of women's subjective experiences as immigrants in the nineteenth-century rural Midwest, while acknowledging the individuality and general diversity of such experiences.

* * *

> The women who come from the fatherland,
> Not as young as once they were,
> There's nothing that meets their eye that's right,
> They curse the land by day and night.[5]

As this Hessian broadside implies, one of the most important factors in a woman's adaptation to America and the frontier was her age at immigration. Generally speaking, the younger a woman was, the easier her adaptation. The flexibility of youth and, in the case of immigrant children, the contact with American culture and society through the public schools were factors. The degree of a woman's eventual integration into American society and her desire for integration were also, at least in part, determined by her age at immigration, as the following examples illustrate.

Louisa Gellhorn was a year old in 1868 when she, her mother, and her five older siblings came to Iowa to join her father. Written in the early 1930s, Louisa's memories of growing up were generally positive. She was young enough to be uninvolved in most of the hard work her parents and the oldest children did during the first years. In her memoir, she expanded most on the results of their labor: her mother's baking and sewing, bins full of potatoes and vegetables, the smoked meats in their cellar, and "those happy winter evenings" when the family popped corn and ate Michigan apples. For her, the Iowa prairie was a place of beauty and bounty. Gathering wild fruits was an opportunity to explore for wildflowers and the occasion for a pleasant family outing rather than work. She did not record any difficulties in adjusting. For example, she remembered with interest rather than concern the friendly Indians who visited her family, including one who followed them, singing in a monotonous and "rather weird" fashion, as they picked corn. She mentions cultural conflict in passing, when she reports that Anglo-Americans called the German immigrants in the neighborhood "dirty Dutch." This prejudice did not strike close to home, however, for Louisa had once overheard a woman say that "Mrs. Gellhorn was such a clean housekeeper you could eat off of her floor."[6]

Living in a mixed ethnic neighborhood, the Gellhorns had Anglo-American neighbors and seem to have been fairly closely integrated into the dominant society. Mrs. Gellhorn did sewing for and traded other favors with neighboring German women, the family exchanged harvesting work with all their neighbors, and the Gellhorn children played with all of the area children. The Gellhorns also attended an English-language church, where neighbors appreciated their singing German Christmas carols at the annual program. As the girls of the family finished the country grade school, they went to work for Americans in nearby towns. Louisa recorded some of the difficulties her mother had after her father's death in 1880 and the hard work she had to do to help, but her narrative is generally positive in both tone and content. It ends when she left home to attend normal school. Eventually Louisa Gellhorn married an Anglo-American.

Elise Dubach was integrated into American society more thoroughly and more quickly than Louisa Gellhorn, even though she was twelve when she immigrated in 1854. This was because her mother died two weeks after Elise, her parents, and two younger brothers arrived in St. Joseph, Missouri, from Switzerland, and, as she said later, "in the same grave with my mother I buried my childhood."[7] To prepare Elise for managing the household of the homestead her father soon bought across the Missouri River in Kansas, her aunt gave her a cursory introduction to "American housekeeping." Elise also attended a convent school for a short time. There she and her brother endured the taunts of other children for being "Dutch," and her brother was beaten up and muddied at the public pump. With minimal English and household skills, Elise, now thirteen years old, moved with her family to their frontier homestead. Neighbor women, members of an extended Kentucky family, took her under their wing and taught her everything she needed to know about frontier housekeeping. Like these women, she attended and hosted sewing and quilting bees and walked across the frozen Missouri to St. Joseph to trade eggs and butter for dry goods and groceries. Although her brothers were able to attend school and perfect their English skills, Elise had too much to do at home and had to learn English more informally. The family became integrated into the broader frontier community, but it maintained its ethnic identity by attending a German Methodist country church.

In 1859, when her father married a widow with five children, Elise went back to her uncle and aunt in St. Joseph and had "additional opportunity to complete [her] Americanization in a bustling city."[8] She attended the English-language Presbyterian church and met her future husband, a man who was also anxious to become assimilated into American society as much as possible. Christian H. Isely had also been born in Switzerland. In the late 1850s, he left the insular German-American community in Ohio in which he had grown up because he believed "he could not become a real American if he remained" there.[9] He broke off his first attempt to homestead in Nebraska because the Ohioans he came with wanted to keep the settlement Swiss-German. Elise and Christian married shortly before the Civil War, he joined the Union army, and in 1865, after his return, they settled in St. Joseph, where Christian made a living as a carpenter. Seven years later, they bought land that had been set aside by the railroad for schools in Brown County, Kansas, and began life as well-integrated members of a predominately native-born rural neighborhood.

Only a few qualities marked Elise Isely's life as different from that of an Anglo-American woman. She taught other women how to make cheese like her family had made in their Old World dairy enterprise. She marked her butter rolls with a mold of a scroll of oak leaves, sent to her by Swiss relatives. Neighbors sent her wayfarers who did not speak English, since she knew both German and French.[10] In all other respects, however, the Iselys lived very "American" frontier lives. They took part in American singing and debating societies, joined the rural Congregational church that was formed as a sectarian compromise among the settlers, and were even active in the local prohibition movement. They were contributing members of the "Fairview Community Chest," Elise's term for the neighborly helpfulness, pioneer hospitality, and communal support in their township.[11] None of their children spoke German well, and most of them married Anglo-Americans.

Both Louisa Gellhorn's and Elise Isely's narratives are generally affirmative reminiscences. Even Elise Isely, forced as she was to assume an adult role in an alien environment at such a young age, placed her memories in a positive framework wherever possible. This was probably due in part to the memoir genre and the perspective of old age. It is natural to want to remember the happy times and successes that validate past experience, especially in a narration intended for family members. Although the positive tone may originate in part from a (conscious or unconscious) reinterpretation of reality, the reader must conclude that both did indeed have positive frontier experiences. Obviously, their individual personalities played an incalculable role in this, but the resilience and adaptability of youth were also important factors. They adapted naturally, as part of growing up, to the American environment. Their young age at immigration also meant that they had little nostalgic attachment to their old homeland. This freed them to form attachments to their new home without suffering inner conflict for wanting to belong to American society.

The letters Barbara Rueß wrote her parents from Spring Bay, Illinois, give us a clearer idea of the thoughts and feelings of a young, single immigrant woman during her first months in America. These letters do not tell everything, however, for it turns out that Barbara had some reason to conceal her thoughts and feelings from her parents. Accompanied by her mother's brother, she came to work at another uncle's Illinois home in 1868 and was probably in her late teens at the time. Before immigrating, she seems to have worked as an agricultural worker in the Augsburg area. Her first letters from Illinois express her astonishment at the quality and quantity of the food served daily and her gratitude for the generosity of her uncle and his wife. Each letter refers to how wonderful she found America and to the relatively light work load she had, with no field work and several afternoons a week free for her own sewing. She urged her family to join her.

In the spring of 1869, however, Barbara Rueß left her uncle's home, first saying she would go to Peoria to find work but then marrying a German-American saddler, whose mother had befriended her. Subsequent letters reveal the conflict between her and her uncles that preceded and followed her actions. A year later, Barbara and her husband, Jacob Meister, were in Kansas City, where he was working to accumulate money to buy land farther west. The letters break off in early 1871, when Barbara was expecting their first child.[12]

Barbara Rueß Meister never expressed regrets at leaving Germany. Above all, she seems to have valued the relative freedom she now enjoyed. She characterized the transatlantic trip as "the happiest life"[13] and chafed under the supervision of her uncle and aunt. She believed that things were better for women, especially poor women, in America. Writing of how she came to marry Jacob Meister, she said:

a rich farmer's widow who had wanted me to work for her for a long time took me in . . . and after a while she urged me to marry her son. At first I refused . . . I couldn't get it in my head, for I said every time that I didn't have anything and everytime [she] answered that I didn't need anything, which indeed wouldn't work at home. But here the girl doesn't need anything; if the boy has a little something, then they can get ahead. . . . We have had until now quite a good life. I have it really good now. Here one is a different woman than in Germany. One seldom hears the term *Weib* here.[14]

Immigration offered young, single women like Barbara Rueß an opportunity for self-determination that was difficult to attain as a member of the German underclasses. Because she did not have the restraining influence of her parents, she could give her streak of independence free rein, at least within the bounds of respectable behavior for a pious Catholic girl. She married in the church and wrote her parents that she was now able to attend mass every day, in contrast to the two times she had attended during the ten months with her uncle.

We do not get the whole story from Barbara Rueß's letters, of course. After she eloped, both uncles in America wrote her parents letters in which they called her ungrateful, careless, and ill-tempered.[15] Perhaps she was a headstrong, problematic daughter the family had hoped would do better in a new environment. The correspondence breaks off before we can be sure that she remained as content with her new life as her letters lead us to believe she was a year after she married. We do know that Barbara advised her parents to stay in their familiar homeland, because she believed they would be unable to make the necessary adjustments. Of herself, however, she said, "But I am wilder and here one has to be or else one can't make it."[16] Although Barbara Rueß might have done little that we would consider "wild" today, for a girl of her background she had acted in a very independent way.

Barbara Rueß's letters show that separation from family and homeland could be exciting and enlivening. Young, single, or newlywed women were the most likely to experience separation in this way. Some could even find adventure in the prospect of homesteading on the Great Plains. Elizabeth Oelder Krebs, who had emigrated from Switzerland at the age of seven and had grown up in Ohio, came with her new husband and nine other recently arrived German-speaking immigrants to farm near Hiawatha, Kansas, in 1870. She told a friend in 1927, "We were both homeless, full of energy, and love of adventure and when we heard of the wonders of Kansas we thought that was just the place to make us a home. I was delighted with the idea of seeing

Indians and the name Hiawatha put on the finishing touch of my dream for our home." In 1875, however, after a grasshopper plague and an infestation of poultry cholera, the Krebses "gathered up the few things [they] had and traded for two lots and a house in Hiawatha."[17] The sense of adventure paled under the onslaught of frontier reality.

In the letters of Pauline Osterholt Greving, we can find hints of how a woman's attitude might change as she evolved from a young newly-wed to a frontier homemaker and mother. Pauline's first extant letter from Hanover in western Kansas contains news about the good crops, the wealth she and her bridegroom hoped to accumulate soon, and the fun she had been having:

> I am very happy here, am visited very often by our neighbor women, and am often invited over, they sometimes complain that we come so seldom. The Sunday before last we were at Frank Gerleve's, he is so happy with his dear Fine. We had a great celebration on their wedding day, there were about 50–60 people there, four musicians, we really danced, didn't get home until the next morning. Three weeks ago we had beer in the schoolhouse, which is near our farm. The neighbor men put their money together for beer and cigars, the women brought all kinds of cakes, and we ate and drank to our hearts' content. The benches were taken out and then we danced, my Henry was the musician. We had a great time. I can tell you that people have a lot of fun here. We don't live as isolated here as you perhaps think. In Hanover, too, there are often balls and plays.[18]

Four years later, after the birth of three children and the death of the first, the tone of Pauline's letter to her recently widowed mother is different: "Since I now have some free time, I want to write you a few lines. Everyone is still healthy and happy here. Lilie can now help me work some and little Paul can already walk by holding on to the chairs. As I heard from Johanna Greving, you, my dear mother, were almost completely lame but kept your spirits all the while, one must be able to put up with everything, burdens and misery are the lot of human-kind, after all." Pauline's own stressful life experiences help explain the change in tone. After her first child's birth, she had been seriously ill with a pelvic infection, from which she never recovered her former strength. Although Pauline wrote that she and her husband still hoped to save enough to visit Germany "if [they] got good years," the harsh-ness of the Great Plains shattered their hopes and dreams.[19]

Pauline and Henry Greving did not give up their ambition for ru-ral prosperity completely, however. In 1892, after the births of the next two children, they sold their Kansas farm and homesteaded in Idaho, where they had four more children. They also opened a grocery store, which quickly became their primary source of income, and finally achieved material comfort and security. Interacting daily with Anglo-American society through their business, the Grevings and their children quickly lost their ethnic identity, stopped speaking German, and became virtually indistinguishable from those around them.[20] As time passed and her growing family and new business placed increasing demands on her, Pauline Greving's desire to return home for a visit might have diminished. She seems to have written her relatives only rarely, stopped writing entirely when her mother died, and never made the trip back to Germany.

It was no accident that the immigrants as a group were disproportionately young or that immigrant letters frequently advised friends and relatives to emigrate while they were still young. The health and vigor of youth were important assets, but so were adaptability and flexibility of mind and habit. As "Jürnjakob Swehn" said, speaking of his mother, "Old trees don't transplant well."[21] Even a middle-aged woman could have great difficulties adjusting to life in America. The letters of Pauline Gauß Wendt illustrate this. In 1889, when she was in her mid-forties, she and her two daughters, Käthe, age twenty, and Emma, ten years old, came to Calhoun County, Iowa, from Berlin. She soon married a widower with six children, a marriage arranged by her first husband's uncle, who lived in the same part of Iowa.

Although Pauline Gauß Wendt usually tried to put the best face possible on her situation in the letters she wrote her former in-laws, her deep-seated unhappiness could not be hidden. She certainly had special difficulties. Coming from a large European city to an American farm would have been hard in itself. Although Pauline wrote on several occasions that she liked the farm better than the city, her enthusiastic description of a trip to Milwaukee with her husband in February of 1897 indicates how much she missed city life.[22] Her daughter Käthe Gauß Baumann was more openly negative in her letters. Eight years after accompanying her mother to Iowa, she wrote, "Mother would have been able to do better in Germany than here, for there is only one Berlin and that is my abandoned father-city. Even if [we were] so very poor, [we were] in our homeland."[23]

Pauline Gauß Wendt also had special family problems. Her younger daughter, Emma, died in 1896 after a three-year illness. In 1899, when she feared that Käthe had developed mouth cancer, she wrote that she now had no one for whom she was working. Her six stepchildren were a burden to her rather than an enrichment in her life. She wrote, "I lack nothing, thank God, and also have a good husband, but eight children, there is always something going on that is troublesome."[24] Again, her daughter Käthe was blunter. She blamed her mother's ill health on having to deal with the stepchildren, who Käthe said were "stupid and smart-alecky. She has to swallow too much and always has annoyances. That makes her even sicker than she is."[25]

It is in her frequent complaints of loneliness that we sense Pauline Gauß Wendt's unhappiness most strongly. She came to an established farm community and thus did not have to face the harsh early years, but this might have contributed to her outsider status, for she did not share the experience of communal bonding that accompanied that period. Regional differences among the immigrants also increased her sense of isolation in the mixed ethnic neighborhood. Perhaps partly because of her urban background, she does not seem to have found congenial company in the German-speaking women around her. In her first letter from Iowa, she complained that her uncle-in-law's second wife was a big-mouthed, slandering woman from Stetten, who tried to make trouble between her and her future husband.[26] On one of the many occasions when she expressed a longing for the companionship of an understanding female friend, she wrote her sister-in-law Albertine Gauß, "I am so totally alone here. Everyone is English here. The Germans are Low German and gossipy so that I have no one to whom I can pour out my heart. Believe me, my thoughts are with you very often and I would often like to exchange my innermost feelings with you."[27] Two years later, writing of her loneliness, she again urged Albertine and her husband to emigrate and gave women's better position in America as another reason for them to do so: "I only wish, Albertine, that you were here. That would be better for both of us. We could both exchange our experiences.—For here women have no [troubles?]. Here the man must take care of her and that is easy for the woman."[28] Even after her sister-in-law died in the spring of 1903, she continued to urge her niece to come to America. These are her last extant letters. Pauline Gauß Wendt had used her correspondence with her first husband's family to air her unhappiness, an unhappiness that was rooted in her age at immigration and her stage in the female life cycle, as well as in the particulars of her individual situation.

A married woman who came to the rural Midwest with young children faced the prospect of caring for them at the same time she was establishing a household under often difficult circumstances and making her own personal adjustments to a new environment. She could have a particularly difficult time if she did not have the assistance of close family members. Anna Barbara Immendorf Ruppenthal was in this situation. In 1877, at the age of thirty-seven, she came with her husband and children to homestead in western Kansas. She was, to judge by her son's testimony, a "reluctant pioneer" who regretted the move for years. She did not miss her native Hesse, however, but longed for Philadelphia, where she had spent twenty-four years and where the rest of her family remained. Although she never openly opposed her husband, she confided to others that "had it not been for five small children, [she] might have steadfastly refused to go West, but . . . did not know what to do with them if the father persisted in going to Kansas." Perhaps in part because of her European upbringing, she felt she owed her husband the obedience that her son described: "None of his family ever questioned his views or his judgement openly, but bowed as to the inevitable."[29]

Anna Barbara Ruppenthal had reason to be reluctant to go to the frontier, for her older sister's hardships as a pioneer woman in Minnesota had culminated in her being gored to death by a bull. Anna Barbara's dread of the difficulties of frontier life proved well-founded. The Ruppenthals had to carry water by a yoke for half a mile for the first five months in Kansas, and eighteen- or twenty-hour workdays were usual for Anna Barbara for the next fifteen years. According to her son, she thought she had no time even to go to church for the first ten years. She had three more children in Kansas, two of them with the help of neighbors and one with the assistance of her thirteen-year-old son. (Her husband and two other sons were on the family ranch eight miles away.) In her son's view, all this brought her to an early grave at the age of fifty-eight.

Adding to Anna Barbara Ruppenthal's travails were her worries about the poor quality of her children's education. As a young girl, she had worked as a servant for Americans (after discovering that they paid better than Germans) and then ran a grocery store with her brothers before her marriage. A city woman, she knew the value of education for getting ahead in America and feared that her children "might grow up into rude, uncouth, ignorant, backwoodsmen," so she attempted to supplement their education at home with readings from the Bible and magazines. At the same time, she supervised the work the children did and their moral development, inculcating them with the virtues of "truth, chastity, justice, honesty and industry."[30] To judge by her son's words, she was eventually rewarded for her efforts by her children's success.

Louise Siegenthaler Ritter had a physically less demanding life than Anna Barbara Ruppenthal, but the negative aspects of her immigrant experience contain a stronger ethnic component. She came to northeast Nebraska in 1893, about twenty years after the area had been first settled. She was thirty years old and the mother of three boys, and she would never see any of the members of her immediate family again. In each of the many letters she sent her parents and sisters until her death in 1925, she wrote how much she missed and wished to be with them. She realized that she and her husband could never have attained the material security of their American life in the old country. She also knew family members were unlikely to leave their secure and relatively prosperous lives in Switzerland to come to the United States, but she wished repeatedly that she might see and talk to them. The presence of most of her husband's family could not substitute for her own.[31]

Louise Ritter's first letters reflect the difficulty older immigrants had adjusting to the new physical environment. She wrote of "snakes which horrify us," the fright of having Indians camp on their land, "terrible" and "gruesome" electric storms, and the constant winds and nearly unbearable heat. Later that first year she reported the impact of the drought on their corn crop, the "gruesome" howling of wolves at night, and a "grimly beautiful" ice storm. She began the Christmas 1893 letter by saying, "I can never be really happy although we are getting along all right; it is the homesickness that will plague me here in America." She was capable of seeing what was good in her new home: the wild grapes, plums, and cherries that formed a canopy along the creek, the labor-saving mechanization of farm work and of women's work, and even the beauty of a field of corn with the plants standing "in rows close together like soldiers." She continued to feel lonely, however, especially at holidays and during stressful times, such as after the summer of drought in their second year in Nebraska: "Everything seems to go wrong, and often I have wished we were still in our old homeland, although I have it better here. If it only were not so terribly far so that we could get together at least once a year." After the difficult birth of her fifth son, her slow recovery, and the serious illness of the second-oldest boy, she again wrote, "I am often very lonesome. We are doing well here, but those who are happy in Switzerland should remain there." The distance from her family was especially hard for her to deal with when members of her family died: first her sister, then her father, and eventually her mother. "If only we were not so far away, then I could be of some help, too," she wrote in June 1901, thinking of her sister's motherless children. After receiving news of her father's death, she wrote her mother in March 1905, "Never again can I look into the eyes of my dear father; maybe not into yours either. I shed hot tears for both of you." She was right; her mother died in 1920 without having seen Louise again.[32]

Motherhood also caused Louise Ritter difficulty in her life in America. She resented the inadequacy of education during the short school year at the country school, for she had had a good education in Switzerland. For the children's sake, she missed some of the Swiss cultural practices. Worst of all, her third son, Rudolf, an infant when the family immigrated, died at the age of ten from an accident while handling work horses. Louise was inconsolable:

> I believe I shall never overcome it. Already five months have passed—I don't know how it can be possible, how I still can be alive; and yet I have to thank the Lord that He lets the time go by and with that my last hour is coming closer when I will be able to find again my darling. . . . Even now I can hardly put a short letter together; it is turning and twisting in my head—oh, I have often been afraid of losing my senses. Oh, God not that also—do take me away from this unhappy world before that.

In every holiday letter after this, she noted how old this son would have been. As she wrote at the first Christmas after the accident, "The year has passed, but my grief will only cease with my death."[33]

Louise Ritter might have lost one of her children (although perhaps not while working with horses) had the family stayed in Switzerland, but she would not have lost her close cultural connection with them, as happened in America. The family's Swiss-German dialect was not the norm among her German-speaking neighbors. In an early letter she complained that her parents "would not be happy here," partly because "the language is different." Swiss relatives and neighbors had intermarried with High German–speakers, and she did not feel comfortable with this. She and her husband made an effort to underpin their sons' oral knowledge of Swiss-German with language instruction at their German-language church, but this was only partly successful. The distance to the town church where classes were held made it difficult for the older boys to attend, and a crabby pastor aroused the third son's resistance to learning German. Louise had to admit that her boys really could not write High German.[34]

Louise Ritter might have felt even more strongly the partial estrangement from her grandchildren that language differences caused. She never learned English well, and none of her grandchildren knew or ever would know German. She was sad about this but understood that because her sons' wives did not speak the Swiss dialect, they could not use it in their homes. She also alluded to the animosity against German-speakers during World War I: "The nasty aftereffect of hatred one will feel for a long time." As a farm woman, however, she was able to avoid much of that animosity. A woman like Louise Ritter, who "had too little opportunity to learn English," could make her home a cultural haven from an alien world as long as her family and friends shared that culture. She and many other female immigrants probably suffered most when they did not.[35]

The younger a woman was at immigration, the easier (and potentially the more thorough) her adaptation to America was likely to be, as the experiences of Louisa Gellhorn and Elise Dubach Isely illustrate. Barbara Rueß's story shows that young, unattached women might be influenced by the relative independence American culture allowed them. Changes in female behavior could then lead to conflict with or even alienation from other family members. If a woman was single or newly married and childless, she could take a lighthearted, even adventurous approach to her new surroundings. The difficulties of rural frontier life were sobering, however, as Elizabeth Krebs and Pauline Greving found out. The presence of children in women's lives added a layer of complications and worries as well. Anna Barbara Ruppenthal, Louise Ritter, and Pauline Gauß Wendt all experienced this. The older the woman was, the harder her own adaptation to her new environment. She could attempt to protect herself from the stress of cultural alienation by associating with other immigrants and conserving cultural practices within the family and ethnic community, but the difficulty of maintaining bonds with those left in Europe and the unhappiness that resulted are apparent in the letters of women like Pauline Gauß Wendt and Louise Ritter.

*   *   *

Pauline Gauß Wendt's and Louise Ritter's letters also show how important the presence of sympathetic family and friends was for a woman's contentment. We might predict that the women most likely to be unhappy were recent immigrants with young children who came to the frontier with no close family members and resided in an area with few other German-speakers. The crying spells "Wieschen Swehn" experienced in the first years of settlement in the Iowa wilds were symptomatic of women's unhappiness in such situations of isolation. "Jürnjakob Swehn" often found his wife weeping after they bought their own farm in an as yet unsettled part of Iowa, where land was still cheap ("in the middle of the bush and miles away from the next neighbor"). She said their log cabin was inferior to a pig sty in Germany and often cried until the children came along: "Then she had no more time to be sad." The bride of a German Methodist minister "buoyed her [own] spirits" by using field glasses to watch for her husband's return when he made the rounds from one Nebraska sod house church to another in 1887 and 1888. Another woman burst into tears when her former employers' son happened to meet her in 1846 at her isolated cabin two hours from Hermann, Missouri: "She said she was getting along fine, except she couldn't bear this desolation. For eight days she had seen no one but her husband and child."[36]

Contrary evidence also exists, however. Frederica Hecker Fischer was a bride of twenty-eight when she came from Württemberg to her fiancé's log cabin in Kansas in 1869. She thought he must be joking at first when they drove up to it. She stayed on, however, encouraged by "an occasional visit with her English neighbor with whom she could not converse except by signs, caring for her neighbor when another life came into the house or being cared for in like manner."[37] Frederica Fischer might not have been happy in those early days, but she was not plunged into despair. She communicated, if only by signs, with her closest female neighbor and shared with her events of the (cross-cultural) female life cycle.[38]

Other women were not able to adjust as readily. Helena Friesen Eitzen, whose memoir was cited in chapter 2, had spent a hard, impoverished youth in southern Russia. Soon after her marriage at the age of twenty-two, she suffered a nervous breakdown. Her emotional balance remained precarious for sometime and might have been a factor in the health problems she had upon her arrival in Kansas. Although times were bad in Russia, she resisted her husband's urgings to emigrate as long as she could. When she left her mother, three sisters, and two brothers, she knew she would never see them again. The Eitzens' trip was arduous, for they traveled alone with two small children, and after their arrival would have returned if they had had the means. The remainder of Helena Eitzen's memoir chronicles the births of four more children, illnesses and financial hard times in the family, and the solace and support she got from her religious faith. She persevered in spite of her isolation from family and friends, but her memoir indicates that this was no easy task. The trauma of her early immigrant life is what she chose to record in middle age, not the "triumph" of persistence.

Since immigrants tended to settle near friends and relatives, many rural German-speaking women were able to perpetuate the close kinship and communal relationships of Europe. Barbara Strohm Ruth Kraemer's diary for the years 1852–58 records the widespread net of relatives with whom she and her family immigrated and near whom they settled. Those who left Worms together in 1852 included the families of her three sisters and her sister-in-law (by her first marriage), who were married to men by the names of Weber, Ruth, and Leisy. The complex intermarriage patterns among these relatively well-off

Mennonites are seen in Barbara's record of a visit the families made to other relatives in western Illinois in 1853. The same family names reappear, along with those of people Barbara identified as cousins. In the next year, another brother and brother-in-law arrived with their families, but the Iowa Mennonite community began to crumble as family after family moved to Illinois. By 1856, many who had first come to Iowa resettled in Illinois, in spite of the fact that land was 50 percent more expensive there. New relatives emigrating from Germany and Bavaria now came to western Illinois. By 1856, Barbara reported a total of twenty-one Mennonite families in that area, and when two of her children were married in a double wedding in 1858, she proudly wrote that "there were 93 people present, all Mennonites except 16."[39]

Other German-speakers also continued to have close family relationships in their new lives, if not always to the extent that Barbara Kraemer had. The support system of mothers and daughters, sisters and sisters-in-law helped women share the hard work and alleviated the loneliness of life on their scattered American farms.[40] Two such families were those of Regina Kessel and Amalia (Malchen) Rückels, who had farms on Mississippi River bottomland in Randolph County, Illinois, south of Barbara Kraemer's neighborhood. Malchen was married to Regina's brother Gottfried and was also a cousin of the Rückels on their mother's side. Fritz Kessel's mother, who accompanied her son and other children to Illinois, was a sister of Regina Kessel's mother. The two families, interrelated and from the same area in Germany, bought land near each other in 1857. They had a difficult beginning, for the river flooded in 1858, wiping out their crops and drowning most of their livestock. They also had to contend with adjusting to a new country: "No language, no familiarity with the customs, no friends," as Gottfried Rückels put it years later.[41] The rich bottomland and their hard work and frugality eventually paid off, though. By 1881, each family owned at least three farms, some of which they farmed themselves with the help of hired men, and the rest they rented.[42]

The women, however, did not have hired help, even though the family's progress depended on their contributions, as was the case with other German-speakers. In 1875, Gottfried Rückels wrote that Malchen had done all her work alone since they had arrived in America. He acknowledged the difficulty of this but seemed to expect it of her: "this was certainly also a difficult job, on such a big farm and it's getting bigger from year to year, but nevertheless you just get down to it: Tackle a chore energetically and it's half done."[43] How did Malchen Rückels manage her work load, at the same time she was pregnant with and caring for the nine children she had had by 1875? (Six were still alive at that time.) Especially in the early years, before their children were old enough to help them, Malchen and her sister-in-law Regina Kessel pooled their resources, cooked together for threshers, and saw each other almost every day.[44] Regina's mother-in-law and a brother-in-law lived with her and Fritz for the first few years, and her references to this old woman (who was also her maternal aunt) show how important the companionship of another woman was. On one occasion, she wrote to her parents, "And so we always were talking about you some, you can well imagine that. Mother and I sometimes shorten the time by talking about Germany, for brother-in-law Johann and my Fritz are usually in the field or cutting wood. And so we live quite happy and content." Two years later, Regina wrote that she and her mother-in-law were planning to color Easter eggs in memory of their family in Germany and were commiserating with each other about how they regretted not having fully appreciated being able to visit Regina's parents in days past.[45]

Regina Kessel and Malchen Rückels shared more than work in their new lives. They seem to have been good friends as well, sharing their hopes and fears with each other. For example, on 6 September 1862, Malchen wrote that they were worried that their husbands would be drafted to fight in the Civil War, leaving her and Regina alone in this "strange world." The two women reported on each other's work, well-being, pregnancies, and births. Their husbands and children were friends, and their families spent holidays together, even staying overnight at each other's homes.[46] On 4 February 1861, Malchen wrote that at the age of thirty Regina still was not expecting a child but that at least she was thus spared "the burden of children." Malchen herself, a year younger, had had three, only one of whom survived. She would lose two more before dying sometime after the birth of her tenth child. Unfortunately, none of the Kessel-Rückels letters between 1877 and 1881, when Malchen died, still exist, so we do not know with what words Regina might have expressed her sorrow or how she would have evaluated their relationship. Surely, though, she would have grieved for the loss of the woman with whom she had had so many common experiences.

The Hirschler and Ewy families were similarly connected by the close relationships among the women. Elizabeth Ewy came to Halstead, Kansas, in 1882, a few months before her parents and six brothers. They were members of a Mennonite community in the Austrian Carpathians, whom other Mennonites aided in immigrating to Kansas. About a year later, she married Chris Hirschler, a German immigrant. Soon after the birth of their first child, the Hirschlers joined Elizabeth's newlywed brother, Pete, and his wife, Mary, on a trip to Hodgeman County, where they homesteaded two miles from each other. The two young women supported each other in their isolation. When their husbands went back to eastern Kansas to earn money on several occasions, they even lived together, once with two other women and their young children in an "'Amazonian' settlement."[47] Mrs. Ewy, Elizabeth's and Pete's mother, came to be with the young women when they were expecting babies, even though "the prairie never did appeal to [her], and if she could have had her way about the matter, her children would have never come out here."[48]

After five years and several life-threatening accidents, Elizabeth Hirschler followed her mother's counsel and convinced her husband to return to eastern Kansas. Pete and Mary Ewy also decided to leave, and both families rented land near Moundridge from 1889 until 1893. With some misgivings, Mary then conceded to Pete's wish to go to Oklahoma to homestead in the Cherokee Strip. Two years later, she wrote how much she and the children missed Elizabeth and her children, so in 1895 the Hirschlers also moved to Oklahoma, accompanied by Elizabeth's now-widowed mother. We do not have personal testimony of the relations between Elizabeth and Mary or among Mrs. Ewy, her daughter Elizabeth, and her daughter-in-law Mary, but the movements of these families along the frontier and the strategies the women employed to support each other indicate the importance of those relationships.

German-speaking women who were not part of close family groups had to build female communities among their neighbors to enjoy some of the same advantages. John Ise's book *Sod and Stubble,* narrated largely from his mother's point of view, contains much information about both the concrete and the subjective aspects of women's lives in an ethnically diverse rural community. The Ises were early settlers in Osborne County, Kansas. Their farm was located between an ethnically mixed community and an area thickly settled by German-speakers ("Germans from Iowa, Germans from Pennsylvania, 'low Dutch,' 'high Dutch,')."[49] Their only relatives nearby were Rosie Ise's brother and wife, who returned to eastern Kansas three years after the two families arrived in 1873. Rosie built close relationships with other German-speaking women, primarily through their sharing of similar life experiences. Her best friend was Louisa Bartsch, two miles away, who came to be with Rosie when her first babies were born and whose children worked for the Ises after the birth of a baby or when Henry Ise was ill. Louisa was with Rosie when her first baby died and, older than Rosie, served as a motherly adviser to her in a variety of ways over the years.

The Krause family (ca. 1890). Karolina and Anton Krause migrated from the Austrian Empire to Fillmore County, Nebraska, in 1882. *Back row:* Rosina (1874–1952), Gustav (1870–1951), Maria (1875–1937), and Anna (1873–1958). *Front row:* Anton Krause (1843–1918); on Anton's lap, Albine (1887–1970); Sophie (1878–1915); Francheska (1883–1959); and Karolina Miller Krause (1844–1932), wearing her wedding dress. (Courtesy of Lillian Schelbitzki Meistrell.)

The Schelbitzki family (ca. 1910). Maria and Wenzel Schelbitzki, born in the Austrian Empire, met and married in Fillmore County, Nebraska, in 1875. Eight of their thirteen children survived into adulthood. *Back row:* Henry (1891–1969), Frank (1882–1959), Anton (1879–1960), Mary (1881–1966), Antonia (1884–1933), and Anna (1886–1988). *Front row:* Gustav (1895–1979), Wenzel Schelbitzki (1843–1928), Maria Kruta Schelbitzki (1851–1916), and Sarah (1877–1952). (Courtesy of the author.)

Louise Ritter and family, Tilden, Nebraska (1902). Their spacious, well-kept home and team of four horses attest to the prosperity they attained in America. In the foreground with Louise (1863–1929) are her sons (*left to right*): Ernest, on Louise's lap (b. 1901); Fred (1887–1975); Willie (1894–1969); Hans (1888–1956); and Rudolf (1892–1903), who died in a farm accident a year after this photo was taken. In the background, Louise's husband, Fritz (1859–1949), holds the horses. (Courtesy of Darlene M. Ritter.)

Henriette Geisberg Bruns (ca. 1863). The daughter of well-to-do bourgeois parents, Jette had difficulties adjusting to rural life in Missouri.
(Courtesy of Carla Schulz-Geisberg and Adolf E. Schroeder.)

Susanna and Christian Krehbiel and children (ca. 1885). The Reverend Krehbiel's duties for the Mennonite church often took him away from home, leaving Susanna to care for the family and farm. *Back row, left to right:* Katharina (1867–1949), Susanna (1871–1924), Henry (1862–1940), John (1860–1939), Jacob (1864–1916), Christian (1869–1948), and Daniel (1868–1921). *Front row, left to right:* Bernhard (1873–1946); behind, Edward (1878–1950); mother Susanna (1840–1920), holding Lucas (b. 1884); Paul (1882–1956); Martha (1876–1947); and father Christian (1832–1909). (Courtesy of the Mennonite Library and Archives, North Newton, Kansas.)

Family of Albert Schaffer, East Custer County, Nebraska (1888). Wearing their best clothes, these multigenerational homesteaders display some of their prize possessions, including house plants that made it through the harsh winter in this well-constructed sod house. (Courtesy of the S. D. Butcher Collection, Nebraska State Historical Society, Lincoln.)

Mrs. (first name unknown) Bader, in front of a dilapidated sod house near Milburn, Nebraska (1904). (Courtesy of the S. D. Butcher Collection, Nebraska State Historical Society, Lincoln.)

Women in the Ises' neighborhood showed their friendship for each other by helping when one of them became sick or a new baby arrived, by laying out and keeping watch over deceased members of each other's families, and by sharing cooking chores at school and church activities. Physical proximity determined some of these exchanges, especially in the early years, so Rosie traded such services with Anglo-American women as well as with German-speakers. She helped line the coffin of the little daughter of American neighbors and organized a sewing bee for the newborn twins of her American neighbor across the road. Kate Winters, who came with her family to Kansas in 1886, became a special friend as well, helping when there was illness and when Henry Ise died.[50] When Rosie got a new sewing machine in 1878, neighbor women came from all around to use it or to have Rosie sew with it for them. She often found this inconvenient but also thought of the machine as "in a real sense a community institution."[51]

It was with her German neighbors, however, that Rosie had her closest relationships. Martha Hunker once carried fresh lettuce five miles around the flooded river when Rosie's stomach was upset during her ninth pregnancy. Rosie took Swiss-born Lisa Meirhoffer, isolated in a remote area with her abusive husband, to eastern Kansas to visit Lisa's brother, whom she had not seen in more than twenty years.[52] Such actions reveal a network of support and caring that went deeper than the sharing of chores.

Conflicts also existed in this neighborhood, however. They sometimes took shape at least partly along ethnic lines, as the growing animosity between the Ises and their Anglo-American neighbors the Altheys shows. More often, however, strife had to do with school and church politics or economic issues: straying livestock, loaned money and tools, road relocations, and the like. In such cases, common language and culture were no guarantee against estrangement between individuals and families. Indeed, the reader of *Sod and Stubble* begins to feel that the communal ties in "mixed" neighborhoods like this one, where people shared few close bonds of family or religion, were often precarious. In the early years, harsh frontier conditions caused people to draw together, to support those among them who had been especially hard hit by misfortune, and to show understanding for the faults and weaknesses of others. Later, when conditions were better and families tended to center their interests and energies on themselves, communal dynamics changed. Some conflicts ended in estrangements between families that lasted decades. Even within the rural ethnic church that the Ises attended, seemingly minor or even petty disagreements (who should lead the hymns, whether to allow organ accompaniment for hymns) could grow into full-scale fights, drawing friends and neighbors into enemy camps.[53] Yet when disaster struck, frontier neighborliness often manifested itself again, and people tended to act generously toward each other, as is the way in small communities where people have known each other for many years.

The conflict in neighborhoods like this has a familial aspect, for bonds that do not originally exist can develop over decades of living close together and sharing good and bad times. As Rosie Ise said, when her children urged her to move with them to Lawrence, "We would never find another neighborhood where there are so many good friends—the kind of friends that you have tried out for forty years and know are your friends."[54]

Rosie Ise's experience shows that women who came to frontier areas without family or Old World ties could and did establish bonds with other women and families for mutual support. She missed her mother and siblings, especially in the early years as a young, inexperienced, and overworked mother. Her life likely would have been easier with close family members to share her work, her joys, and her trials, but she was a pragmatic, energetic woman who accepted what she believed she could not change, so she lost few tears over what she did not have and did her best with what she did have. She was fortunate in having a good and kind man for her husband and in suffering relatively few health or developmental problems with her eleven surviving children. Although having had so many children was embarrassing to Rosie Ise at times, her large family became almost a community unto itself. To some extent, especially as children grew older, a woman's immediate family could substitute for other relatives who were not present and could give her a sense of connectedness in the rural community.

The early years in the new environment were stressful for all immigrants, especially for women who lived isolated lives with little or no contact with family members or even other German-speakers. The stronger and more immediately present a woman's familial and communal ties were, the easier it was for her to submerge herself in such intimate surroundings and protect herself from some of the strain of adaptation to a new language, new customs, and new institutions, as Barbara Kraemer's diary implies. Women like Louise Ritter, who lived in a community with a high percentage of German-speakers, could spend their lives in America without learning English and without surrendering Old World cultural affiliation. Others, like Elise Isely and Rosie Ise, adapted more completely and with little apparent stress because they were young when they came to the frontier areas and because, having settled on their own in areas with relatively few German-speakers, they could not avoid interacting with Anglo-Americans and even, perhaps, developing close, positive relationships with some.[55]

Many women were able to give each other both material and emotional support in their new lives. This probably happened most often among women related by blood or marriage. Such personal and familial closeness was particularly important to women. Since their primary life activities revolved around the home and family, they were unlikely to have their activities affirmed through contact with the broader community. Even the numerical strength of the ethnic community was not as important as the presence of sympathetic women, especially those bound to each other by family ties. For example, although German-speakers were a distinct minority in Hodgeman County in the early 1880s,[56] Elizabeth Hirschler and Mary Ewy did not seem to be especially affected by this during their homesteading days there. They depended much more on each other than on people outside the family. Pauline Gauß Wendt in Calhoun County, Iowa, and Regine Kessel and Malchen Rückels in Randolph County, Illinois, lived in areas with about the same percentage of German-speakers (12–14 percent),[57] but they seem to have had quite different inner experiences. The proximity of close female friends and relatives is what Pauline Wendt missed most, while Regine Kessel and Malchen Rückels could support each other under conditions that were more difficult than those Pauline Wendt encountered.

* * *

Undoubtedly, social and economic background also influenced how women experienced their new lives. A comparison of two immigrants, Jette Bruns and Susanna Krehbiel, who in many ways had much in common, illustrates this. In 1843, Henriette (Jette) Geisburg Bruns wrote her family in Germany that her brother Bernhard should think long and hard before returning to Missouri to attempt farming once again: "even if he gets so far that he can expect some profit from his cattle and his produce, then he has far more needs than people who have been long accustomed to living in modest circumstances. It takes an extraordinary amount of contentedness to remain calm and happy."[58] Jette knew what she was saying. A member of a prosperous, upper-middle-class family from the Westphalian city of Oelde, she came to the Missouri wilderness at the age of twenty-three with her husband, young son, two brothers, and a maid. Her father had been mayor and then a tax collector in Oelde. After her mother's death, she had been sent at the age of thirteen to the beautiful old city of Münster, where she lived with her father's brothers and was educated for two years.

In both Münster and Oelde, she participated in the social scene appropriate for the daughters of well-to-do families in merchant and administrative circles. In her autobiography, she wrote of travels along the Rhine, dances and balls, musical clubs and events, and frequent visits among families of their acquaintance.[59] Soon after her father's death in 1831, when she was eighteen, she married Dr. Bernhard Bruns, a man her uncles did not entirely favor.

Soon Bruns gave the Geisberg family more reason to dislike him. Dissatisfied with the struggle of establishing his medical practice in Oelde and caught up in the emigration fever fueled by the reports of Gottfried Duden and others, he decided that his children would have a better chance of getting ahead in America. His family were farmers, and he thought of the cheap land in America as the key to wealth. He persisted in his plans to emigrate until Jette, against her deepest feelings, agreed to go, as she wrote in a letter of 6 November 1838, to "a land that only Bruns knew and to which my relationship with him rather than my own inclination drew me."[60] Intensifying her reluctance was the feeling that she, as the oldest child, was abandoning her duty to her six orphaned siblings. This sense of guilt was to torment her for many years, even though she tried to alleviate it by taking two of her four brothers with her, to give them the opportunities that she and Bruns hoped for, for their own children. Her brothers' lack of success was therefore especially galling to her, since she felt responsible for their disappointments. The Brunses, too, had many financial difficulties and reverses and only intermittently attained the wealth and comfort they had envisioned.

Jette Bruns's life in America was in several ways similar to that of many other immigrant women. She had trouble learning English and found American people and their ways alien and unsympathetic. She had to work hard and learn new ways of doing things. Her husband was gone a great deal with his medical practice, and she had to take charge of the farm and handle his various business ventures: a mill, a store, and a ferry. She raised one brother's three children along with her own and agonized over the other brother's growing madness. Many of those close to her died: five of the ten children she bore; one of the brothers who came to America with her; another brother in Germany; a sister-in-law, who had tuberculosis; a son and a nephew she had raised, who both died in the Civil War; and her husband, when she was fifty-one. Bruns left Jette so deeply in debt when he died in 1864 that she had to declare bankruptcy and take in boarders, sell garden produce, and give piano lessons to support herself and her young children.

All of these difficulties were compounded by Jette's cultural alienation. She found it hard to summon up the "extraordinary amount of contentedness" that she knew was necessary, as she wrote, "to remain calm and happy." This was partly because of the kind of person she was but also because her social background and education were very different from that of the typical immigrant farmer's wife. Her expectations simply could not be met in the Missouri backwoods. Frustrations with learning English were particularly irritating to a woman who had developed the skills of gracious conversation in educated society. In August 1837, a year after her arrival in the settlement that her husband and brother helped found and was named Westphalia because of all the immigrants from that state, she wrote, "I have progressed with my English speaking so far that I can understand occasionally a few common little sentences and can reproduce them. I must really learn more, for it annoys me tremendously when I stand there like a blockhead and cannot answer."[61] Almost ten years later, on 18 October 1846, she triumphantly reported that she amazed all the gentlemen present when she conversed with a visiting bishop in English. This progress in English language abilities had its negative side, however. Like Louise Ritter, she had to face the fact that her children and grandchildren were more American than German in their own language usage and cultural inclinations. In later years, she apologized for her children not writing to their German relatives, for although they spoke German fluently, they did not write it well.[62]

Like many other immigrant women on the early frontier, Jette experienced intense feelings of loneliness. These feelings arose even though she was surrounded by a predominantly German-speaking community and even though she had her two brothers in her own household for long periods of time, as well as her husband and children. Some of her in-laws also lived fairly close by, she and her husband visited other Dreißiger families in the area, and Westphalia soon had its own German-language Catholic church. Nonetheless, for many years Jette complained about the lack of culture she had been used to in Germany. She particularly missed the association with educated, cultivated people.[63] Along with this, she felt the lack of sympathetic women companions. Thinking of old friends of her youth, she was moved to write in 1840, "Here, how lonely I am; there is not another congenial female being with whom I could exchange now and then my feelings when I need some relief and would forget the daily worries and cares and set these aside for a short time.—Yet what difference does it make, for I tell Bruns everything and he listens patiently even though he cannot get so deeply involved."[64] This is eloquent testimony to the need for female friendship that many immigrant women felt, even when they had their husband's sympathetic understanding.

Jette was often nagged by concerns about maintaining her social position and achieving the material progress that had precipitated their emigration. Some of these concerns were based on the demands the American environment made on all but the most privileged women. The absence of reliable help meant that she, like other wives of the educated Dreißiger farmers, had to do much hard physical work. In her first letter, she portrayed this positively: "You cannot believe how satisfying it is to work. I probably have had few days in which I was ever as busy as I am here, that is, having to do hard work, but I'm quite happy in doing it, and like all the others I have a tremendous appetite and sleep soundly." Later, she gave voice to the burdensome aspects of this labor, which often had to do with the many extra men she cared for: her brothers, hired hands, and workers on various construction projects. On one occasion, she complained about cooking for weeks for the men building the Brunses' mill and wished that her brother would marry to make her own burden less. When her German relatives expressed their surprise that the Brunses had black slaves in their household (taken in partial payment of a debt owed Bruns), she wrote how difficult it was to find and keep a hired domestic and exclaimed, "Oh, you people who are not at all capable of helping yourselves, you can easily talk! How often have I said that I would rather preside over the household alone if only I could live alone with my husband and children!"[65]

Although Jette realized that hard work was not out of the ordinary for women in America, she could not help chafing at it on occasion. Certainly in comparison with the lives her relatives led in Germany, hers was much more arduous and less in keeping with her social origins. Her two brothers in Germany received good educations and attained respected administrative positions. One of her sisters married a man who became mayor of Münster, and the other sister's husband was a court counselor in that city. The Brunses themselves were not without good social connections in America, though. They associated with some of the most famous Dreißiger immigrants in Missouri. Thomas Hart Benton respected Bernard Bruns so highly that he sent two of his sons to live with the Brunses for several months to learn German and study medicine. After the Brunses moved to Jefferson City in 1853, Dr. Bruns became active in politics and was mayor when he died eleven years later. Jette then took in many of the most prominent German-American legislators as boarders, which gave her house the nickname of "the radical corner."[66] Yet such connections, however satisfying they were, were largely those of the German-American subculture and thus were not equal to those her family in Germany enjoyed.

Jette never expressed envy of her German family's successes, but she might have felt, with some reason, that she and her family had "come down in the world." In 1841, her brother Franz married the young woman Jette had employed as a domestic a year and a half earlier. Although she tried to put the best face on this, her conflicting feelings are reflected in the letter she wrote home about her new sister-in-law: "She has a good heart and more feeling than one could expect. I also hope that she will do well in the house; at least I will have to believe so after having had a year and a half of experience. I live on very friendly terms with her; however, I want to confess to you that the changed relationship is still somewhat strange to me, and she has probably gotten a very critical relative."[67] Jette could not hope to have gained in her brother's wife the congenial friend for whom she longed. Later, she worried about her children's education and prospects. She and her husband had little confidence in the American public schools and educated their children privately. Her oldest son did not continue his studies at St. Louis University, developed drinking problems, and was unable to make a success of the various career and business opportunities his father arranged for him. Although she was ashamed to stay in Jefferson City after having to declare bankruptcy, friends convinced her that her daughters' prospects for marriage were best in this community, where the family was known and respected. None of her children made a notable mark in the world.

The disastrous condition of her husband's finances, which Jette did not fully comprehend until his death, was a galling revelation to someone of her background, concerned as she was with respectability and social standing. It tormented her to think of the damage this did to her husband's reputation, as well as to her own and her family's. It was particularly demoralizing when she discovered that he had never repaid loans her family in Germany had made to them many years earlier. Her letters between 1864 and 1868 are filled with expressions of shame and dismay and with various plans and strategies for dealing with this situation. It so intensified the sorrow she experienced upon his death that she felt she had no reason for living, except to do what she could for her young children's futures.

Jette Bruns was, however, a resilient woman who "always found strength and courage at the right time and was never completely discouraged," as she wrote in 1883. Yet a sense of cultural and social displacement is one of the prominent undertones of many of her letters. When portraying to her brother how happy he would be when he ended his studies and moved to Münster, she quickly slipped into a comparison with how unhappy she often was:

> You will be close to our old, good uncle, our caring aunt, our sisters, you will have the close relationships with friends, a free nature where every flower, every straw, every bush represents an acquaintance of your youth that will bud anew again and again. Familiar situations, even though changed, cannot upset or reverse everything. You cannot imagine how hard it is to become accustomed to things here. The customs, the morals, the language, people without feeling, everything is foreign and cold. At home I could take pleasure in the outdoors, and I became happy as a child after a walk. Here it makes me melancholy to see the wild, desolate abundance of plants and trees. The disadvantages make walking disagreeable, the ticks, all kinds of hindrances such as burrs, the lack of well-built roads.

The absence of family, friends, familiar ways of life, and even "civilized" nature caused her sorrow. The sense of loss underlying this passage explains why she never really got over her homesickness for her homeland and her family. Thirty-two years after immigrating, she wrote that she still felt the desire to take her children back to Germany to her brother and sisters: "I will have to keep them together here and must not continue to think that I should be back united with you. I have constantly longed for you during all these long years."[68]

Jette Bruns used her letters as an outlet for expressing some of her innermost feelings. Indeed, lacking a sympathetic female friend, she might have written often when she felt like confiding negative feelings that she could not easily unburden elsewhere. Even if her letters were not completely typical of her everyday sentiments, they no doubt expressed genuine emotions and the inner experiences of her life in America. They testify to the particular difficulties that educated bourgeois women faced when immigrating to remote frontier areas.

Women who were accustomed to living in more modest circumstances did not have to confront these difficulties. That does not mean, however, that they had fewer or less significant problems than bourgeois women did. The autobiography of Susanna Ruth Krehbiel illustrates this.[69] Susanna was one of Barbara Kraemer's Mennonite relatives who left Bavaria for Iowa in 1852. She came with her father, the Reverend David Ruth, and her mother, Katharine Strohm Ruth, who was Barbara Kraemer's sister. In 1858, when she was eighteen, Susanna married Christian Krehbiel, a man who became prominent in American Mennonite circles and later worked in Kansas with the Mennonite German immigrants from Russia.

In some superficial ways, Susanna Krehbiel's life resembles Jette

Bruns's. After her marriage, Susanna shared her home for most of her life with people outside her immediate family circle. Writing her autobiography after her husband's death, she expressed regret that the only time she and he had been alone was when he was recovering from a stroke, soon after their golden wedding anniversary. Susanna was more fortunate than Jette, however, in that most of the time female relatives were among those joining her household. Early in 1860, she and her younger, newlywed sister, Barbara Lehmann, moved with their husbands and Susanna's small son to Illinois, where they shared homemaking in two shanties on a farm that their parents bought for them and their husbands. In August of that year, Barbara's second son was born. She wrote later that her sister took charge of that infant: "We two busy with the children could help each other get over our homesickness." Another sister, Katherine, came to stay with Susanna from December through March, and then her brother Henry came to work with Christian for the spring and summer of 1862. By this time, Susanna and Barbara were able to set up separate households. Susanna and Christian also took in his widowed cousin and three children in 1862 for more than a year. A lifelong friendship developed that bound Susanna to this woman, "a dear friend and efficient helper." Susanna's parents and two sisters came to spend the summer of 1863 in her home, and two years later they moved close to her in Illinois. A few years after this, her sister Barbara was widowed, and she and her three young children lived in Susanna's home for eight years. Still later, her sister Katherine also spent several years with the Krehbiels after Katherine's husband died. Susanna, unlike Jette Bruns, did not suffer from a dearth of female relatives to provide companionship and share her work and concerns.[70]

Susanna's autobiography leaves no doubt about the work she and her female relatives shared. It was the traditional hard labor expected of rural women in German society. During the early years in Illinois, Christian Krehbiel and David Lehmann often had bouts with malaria, which left Susanna and Barbara to do all the farm work. Susanna also remembered the strenuous work that women had to do at harvest time. Preparing meals for a dozen or more men, including those who came to work with the threshing machine, and carrying midmorning and midafternoon lunches out to the fields with only Barbara's help, left little time for anything but food preparation: "so you see why I couldn't sleep in until day-break, and that I had to work late into the evening. There was no time for curling hair, nor for making ruffles or starching linen. We had to get to work early and stay at it late, for wages were very high and we tried to save in that area." For her, later improvements in harvest machinery meant reductions in her work as well, for fewer men had to be fed. Susanna also remembered that in the first summer or two in Illinois, she and Barbara bound and shocked the cut wheat her father's McCormick reaper left in their fields, while their men used the machine on other farms to earn extra cash. The women's work had to be done very early or late in the day, because otherwise the twine broke. The reaper left the stalks of grain so dry and brittle that "it hurt one's hands even more than the old method of binding."[71] Such comments and memories indicate that German-speaking farm women, used to work as they were, nevertheless were aware of how hard their labor was and how much was being asked of them. They were, however, unlikely to feel that they worked harder than other women of their backgrounds would or did. In contrast, Jette Bruns, although she did not do field work and had a hired girl or a slave to help her in the house most of her life, did feel that she worked much more than a woman of her upbringing and social position might have expected.

Probably because of Susanna Krehbiel's youth at immigration and her integration into a large and close-knit family and religious community, she did not write anything in her autobiography that hints at cultural alienation. Since she seems to have had no significant contact with Anglo-American society, she did not suffer the cultural displacement evident in Jette Bruns's letters. Many of Susanna's difficulties as a frontier wife were more individual. They bear a resemblance to some Jette Bruns felt in that her husband was the source. Christian Krehbiel was a hardworking, God-fearing man, who set up a small family altar in the bedroom on their wedding night and asked God's blessing on their life together. He often worked away from home as a butcher and carpenter in the first years of their marriage, then became a Mennonite minister, and from 1866 on undertook lengthy trips as a representative to the Mennonite Conference. These additional responsibilities put a strain on both marriage partners. Christian literally worked night and day at times, during the fall plowing and planting in the day and shucking corn at night. Susanna wrote later, "It should also be said here to our humiliation that under such tense conditions the human being behaves sometimes like a human being, that this caused us many a difficult hour, and that this reminded us that we are only weak mortals, and as such we needed our Father's guidance." Susanna may well have resented the extra work her husband's church caused her. In her autobiography, however, she wrote only of disliking the independence (and, by implication, the responsibility) that Christian's absences forced on her. She saw later that she had had to learn a great deal in the "school of life" to "fulfill the place that fell to" her as Christian Krehbiel's wife. Above all, she had to become self-sufficient, and for that she needed training, training that she had not had in her culture.[72]

Christian's extra duties meant that Susanna became increasingly responsible for running the farm as well as the household. She found it especially hard to accept her husband's long trips away from home. When remembering the first one, in the summer of 1866, she wrote, "Probably no one ever knew how difficult it was for me to conform to this, alone with the children, having to run the place with strange hired hands, and to complain—No, the only thing to do was to go on in God's name. This experience was repeated very often from now on, but it never was easy for me. . . ." She even indicated that Christian's frequent absences were indirectly the cause of illnesses to which she fell prey almost every time he was gone. Years later, when her widowed sister Katherine was living with her, Katherine said to Susanna, "If I had had as little from my husband as you have from yours, I would not have been satisfied."[73] Susanna Krehbiel's inclusion of this statement, in an autobiography intended for her children, may indicate that her uncomplaining demeanor masked deep discontent with some aspects of her marital relationship.

As a committed member of her religious community and as a woman from a culture that expected subordination from a wife, she had to respect her husband's decisions. Her autobiography does, however, indicate that her marriage had some degree of mutuality. She wrote that the blessing upon their life together for which her husband prayed on their wedding night prevailed: "Even if there were also many mistakes and weaknesses, through which we often made life difficult for ourselves, yet we always found the right path that brings peace. And this only really served to make us realize that we were human beings, and as such had our faults, and that the one had to put up with the other patiently." Since Christian Krehbiel did not include personal matters when he wrote his own autobiography, we cannot know to what extent he felt he made compromises for the sake of his wife and family. On the surface, however, it would seem that his wife had more to accommodate herself to than he.[74]

This was so particularly when Christian Krehbiel decided to move the family from Illinois to Kansas, where he had been instrumental in helping the first groups of Mennonite Germans from Russia establish a colony. Susanna was reluctant: "I found it difficult to reconcile myself to the migration to Kansas, to live on wild, raw prairie, so near to the Indians." Nevertheless, she eventually agreed, and the family moved its livestock and goods in stages, with the teenage boys in charge of the move and the breaking of land on the new farm near Halstead. This, too, bothered Susanna, but she wrote, "Father placed much trust in his little boys, which was probably good for them; the responsibility made them grow up, but for me it was not an easy thing."[75]

Susanna Krehbiel had to accept and adapt to her husband's calling in the Mennonite community and the many demands it placed on his time and energies. Similarly, Jette Bruns supported her husband's various efforts to capitalize on frontier opportunities and to establish himself and his family as prosperous, respected members of early Missouri society. Jette did this by participating actively in the family businesses and, it seems, by refraining from criticism of him and his lack of good sense and prudence in financial dealings. The one occasion on which she did vent her irritation had to do with Bernhard Bruns's lackadaisical dealings with her brother's estate: "If only I could be Bruns for a while!"[76] Both women's lives were complicated and made more difficult by their husband's activities. But it seems that Jette Bruns did not reap the long-term rewards, either material or social, that Susanna Krehbiel did, indirectly, through her husband. Instead, Bernhard Bruns's incompetency cost Jette not only her financial security but also, what may have been even harder for her to accept, her pride.

Because Susanna Krehbiel wrote so long after most of the events of her life had transpired, we cannot know how negatively she felt about some of them at the time. Her autobiography does not shirk mention of the hard times she experienced, particularly those during the first years of her marriage. She also hints at irritations and difficulties in her relationship with her husband. But she couches such references in homilies to her audience, that is, to her children. For example, the poverty of the first years explained her thriftiness and taught her gratefulness for what she had. Similarly, she portrays the conflicts in her marriage as lessons in the importance of conciliation in human relations.[77] No doubt the separation in time from the events of her life and the purposes for which she wrote her autobiography affect its tone and content.

It is likely that, were we able to read a diary or letters by Susanna Krehbiel, we could better judge the extent to which she mustered the "extraordinary amount of contentedness to remain calm and happy" on the American frontier of which Jette Bruns wrote. We do, however, know that Susanna and those around her met the main criterion that Jette mentioned as necessary for contentedness, for they were "long accustomed to living in modest circumstances." It is therefore perhaps legitimate to assume that Susanna Krehbiel was able to feel content more often and more readily than Jette Bruns. Other factors played a role as well. Susanna came to America as a twelve-year-old and had six years to adjust to her new surroundings before taking on the duties of wife and mother. She also had the support of close female relatives throughout her life. Perhaps most important, Susanna was closely integrated into an immigrant community united by common religious and Old World origins. She, unlike Jette Bruns, must have always felt that she was living among her social and cultural peers. Jette Bruns spent her life in rural Missouri isolated, at least in her own mind, from a supportive community that shared her social and educational background.

Friedrich Muench believed that the wives of the Dreißiger could fulfill their "human duty" (*menschliche Aufgabe*) of being of value to humankind better by living hard lives on the Missouri frontier than by living the "vain, frivolous life" of a wealthy woman in Germany. Jette Bruns might have agreed with this assertion, but her subjective experience of life in early rural Missouri certainly conflicts with Muench's assertion that "the best" among these women were never bored and were content with what they could do for their families.[78] Perhaps Muench would not have counted Jette among "the best" (although he was one of the German-American legislators who later boarded in her Jefferson City home). Or, more likely, he might have mistaken Jette's quiet, self-effacing demeanor for complete contentment.

* * *

It is misleading to portray any single German-speaking woman's experience as typical. As was the case with Anglo-American women, individual differences and outside factors made variation from "the norm" far more likely than conformity to any pattern that I might establish or identify in this study. This was especially true because of differences in personality. Women's writings show us how great these differences were. Susanna Krehbiel and Jette Bruns, for example, reacted differently to what appeared to be similar situations. They both lived in close proximity to relatives and immigrants from the same part of Germany, they shared religious beliefs with their neighbors, they both worked hard, they were married to busy and ambitious men who often left them to cope with everyday life on their own and who took them to a raw frontier area against their inclinations. Susanna Krehbiel kept her unhappiness largely to herself and reinterpreted it as positively as she could, in accord with the expectations of her rural and religious upbringing. Jette Bruns felt isolated from her social peers in spite of the large number of German-speakers around her and at times expressed her discontent openly to her husband and her family, a "right" that her education and background accorded her. Her expectations made it more difficult for her to process her experiences in an equanimous manner. Susanna's and Jette's personalities, to the degree they had been shaped by their upbringing and social environment, thus played a role in their adaptation to their new surroundings.

Some women, like Helena Eitzen, faced an even more difficult adjustment because of deep-seated personality problems. Helena's mental fragility colored her experience, making her reluctant to emigrate, timid in her interchanges with Americans, and perhaps susceptible to the illnesses she suffered from during the early years in Kansas. A tendency to depression may be at the base of the melancholy undercurrent perceptible in her autobiography. Nor can the more positive tone of Elise Isely's memoir be attributed solely to her young age at immigration or her eventual integration into American society. Some of Elise's early experiences could have made her portray her life more negatively than she did: her mother's early death, her sudden isolation as a child homemaker in the Missouri River backwoods, and her eventual separation from her father and brothers. We are left with the feeling that Elise Isely simply had more resiliency of personality and character and a more positive outlook to help her in her adjustments than did Helena Eitzen.

The role that a woman's husband played was particularly important in helping determine how happy she might be. Käthe Gauß was only twenty when she came with her widowed mother and sister to Iowa. We might expect her to have adjusted relatively easily to America, as Barbara Rueß did. Although Käthe soon learned English and worked in the Anglo-American community, she missed Berlin and evidently could not find her place in the family into which her mother married. Most important, perhaps, she made an unfortunate marriage soon after immigrating in 1889. Her husband left her in the summer of 1897, returned in September of that year, but then sold their house and rented a furnished room at his brother's in Chicago, leaving Käthe to fend for herself as best she could. It is no wonder that soon after this she wrote, "I wish I had never in the world seen America. It is called a free land, but it is not free." Several years later she expressed the same feelings: "It is said that America is Malerica, and that's how it is."[79] In 1903, although still married, she was working as a restaurant cook. The hope of an easier and more prosperous life did not materialize for this young woman. She blamed America, even though she might have been in the same situation had she and her mother stayed in Berlin.

Few examples of German-speaking women's comments on their husband's neglect exist. Käthe Gauß did not allude directly to her marital problems in her letters. Nor did Trienke Kleihauer Rahmann. Her husband, Heinrich, left her and their two young sons alone in Illinois for three years while he sought his fortune in the California gold fields. She wrote her parents annually, commenting factually on Heinrich's absence and the lack of news from him. Perhaps she wanted to reassure them that she was doing all right, living on savings and raising garden crops to support herself while he was gone, even facing the death of one of their sons alone. Upon his return, they seem to have continued their life together as if nothing had happened.[80] Trienke's letters during this period and related comments by her brother Ihnke, who arrived in America just after Heinrich had left, seem remarkably restrained, considering the uncertainty in which she must have lived. Given the dearth of subjective evidence in documents like Trienke's letters, Susanna Krehbiel's and Jette Bruns's hints of discontent with their husbands are especially valuable in gaining a fuller picture of married immigrant women's lives and experiences.

Men's letters and memoirs are sometimes tantalizingly noncommunicative about their marital relationships. Adolf Frick seems to have been sent to America with family funds to set up a store and make his fortune. He did not announce his marriage to Alwina Vitt until 1858, after his mother had already found out about it indirectly and after their first child was born. Was he ashamed of having married her? He said that she was the daughter of a large farmer from Prussia, and the 1860 census shows that John E. Vitt was worth more than Frick himself. Did Adolf Frick assume his family would think he had "come down in the world" by marrying the daughter of a farmer, no matter how well-off his in-laws were by American and even German standards?[81]

Georg Isernhagen never even names his wife in his lengthy memoir. This might be simply the consequence of his having written them for his children, but we also know from oral interviews that many years after immigrating and marrying, he wrote his former sweetheart to join him in America. The editor of Isernhagen's memoir speculates that the fact that Elizabeth Zweigardt Isernhagen was born two months before her parents married lowered her in her husband's eyes.[82] The self-satisfied garrulousness of Isernhagen's memoir, however, also leads me to speculate that he was simply arrogant enough to believe he had the right to maintain a long-term, long-distance relationship with his Old World sweetheart and to invite her to join him and his wife of many years in a companionable ménage à trois. (His old sweetheart did not take him up on the invitation, however.)

Some men did communicate more positive sentiments about their wives in their writings. "Jürnjakob Swehn" often mentioned his wife with affection and admiration in his letters. She was a woman of common sense and few words, who nevertheless was able to articulate for him some of his deepest feelings to which he could not put a name. He also recognized women's wisdom and authority in some areas of life: "But in certain things the woman is the man, and his house is sometimes governed by the opposite world order."[83] "Jürnjakob" might have kept most "inward things" to himself, as he wrote, but "Wieschen Swehn" probably felt sure of his love and support. This must have made her feel better about sharing her life with him far from their homeland.

Men's actions also lead one to speculate on women's subjective experiences. For example, three sewing machine stories hint at the various levels of support women had from their husbands. Christian Krehbiel and Christian Isely bought their wives sewing machines when they were still quite expensive. Susanna Krehbiel got hers in 1872 for $80, a purchase she remembered as being necessary since she made all of her husband's and sons' clothing, as well as her own. Her husband must have been sympathetic to her needs, perhaps in part because he seems to have been one of those Mennonites in the forefront of farm mechanization. Elise Isely's machine cost $60 in 1873, a sum a shocked neighbor woman said the Iselys "couldn't afford." Elise's response indicates an awareness of the generally low status assigned women's labor and consequently the low priority some rural Americans accorded purchases to diminish it: "While sixty dollars was a large sum to pay for a machine which accomplished nothing but the lightening of woman's toil, yet my husband was able to pay for it from the profits he made that year from an unusually bounteous corn crop." Elise Isely might not have gotten her machine as early as she did without that good corn crop, but it seems her husband did not begrudge it her when they could reasonably afford it.[84]

A contrasting story is that of Mrs. C. F. D. Wyneken, wife of an early and prominent Missouri Synod minister. Her relatives in Germany sent money on several occasions for a sewing machine, but her husband "always found what he considered a more important use of this money." Finally a family friend happened to be present when another money draft arrived, and she insisted that Mrs. Wyneken get the sewing machine.[85] This was in the 1870s, just before the birth of the Wynekens' thirteenth child. The modern woman's mind balks at the thought of caring for the clothing needs of such a large family without a machine, but evidently Reverent Wyneken had not seen it that way. Few clear records of the negotiations and power dynamics in German-speakers' marriages exist, but incidents like these show that women's traditional subordination to their husbands was practiced to varying degrees in America, as in Europe. It is probably safe to surmise that women also experienced varying degrees of satisfaction in their marital relationships as a result.

Subjective experience is often dependent on chance events. That was no less the case for German-speaking immigrant women in the nineteenth century. Their letters and memoirs often speak of the devastating effect sickness and death had on them in both subjective and objective terms. Even the loss of livestock could be felt deeply, for this might determine the family's economic survival. From 1876 until 1878, Katharina Martin lived alone in a sod house with her six small children near Osceola, Nebraska, while her husband plied his shoemaking trade in town from Monday morning through Saturday evening. While he was gone sometime in the first summer, one of their horses drowned, and soon after this a cow died. Katharina burst into tears. This unusual behavior upset her children, and they remembered it as symptomatic of how difficult those early years were.[86]

More often, however, we are at a loss to know how women reacted to similar misfortunes. Heinrich and Clara Boeckers came to a farm near Moscow, Iowa, in 1858. Heinrich's letters to his sister and brother-in-law end on 22 December 1861. Discouraged by a poor fruit harvest the previous year, the Confederate blockade of the Mississippi, and a frightening episode in which a rabid dog bit many pigs in his herd that necessitated their destruction, he had sold his farm to a neighbor at a loss. Clara, pregnant at the time, narrowly missed being bit as well and gave birth a few weeks later to a stillborn son. We do not know if Clara Boeckers shared her husband's discouragement or if her perhaps negative reactions to these events augmented his. We only know that the Boeckerses returned to the Rhineland.[87]

The letters of Jette Bruns following the deaths of three of her four children testify eloquently to the blow such events dealt women. The actions of other women speak to this as well. Adolf Frick wrote in 1865 of the death of their third daughter from a fever the previous year: "We still cannot forget this loss. My dear wife took a lot of effort last summer with the grave, planting flowers, and the verbenas are still blooming on it. It is located on a rise on our place, shaded by three large oak trees and beautifully situated. We visit it very often." Further evidence of the pain women felt upon the deaths of their children is found in the letters Käthchen (Katharine) Hamm sent her sister Dina (Christine) Venus. The sisters do not seem to have seen each other after they spent time together in St. Louis soon after immigrating in 1849. At the time of the 1850 census, Käthchen Hamm had two sons, Wilhelm and Augustus, the latter born in Missouri. Augustus evidently died sometime in the next year or two, for she does not mention him again in the extant correspondence. In 1853, Käthchen wrote that she had lost a newborn baby in the summer because of "bad medicine." Three years later, she sent an anguished letter, reporting the drowning of her only remaining child, eight-year-old Wilhelm. After the death of her fourth (and last) child in about 1860, she gave her sister a detailed description of how she had washed and dressed the little girl's corpse "just as if she were alive" and laid the child out with flowers. The poignant passages leave no doubt about the pain Käthchen felt on all these occasions and the sympathy she knew she would get from her sister.[88]

Losing a child was a hard blow, but losing her husband meant a woman had lost her life companion and probably her economic mainstay as well. Louise Ritter reported on her sister-in-law's reaction to the sudden death of the latter's husband: "I will never forget how Elise screamed when I went over to her in the afternoon: 'They took my husband, my dear husband!' It was terrible, and in the beginning we feared she would lose her mind. Now she is somewhat calmer, but she almost grieves herself to death. Yes, such a grief almost breaks the human heart; the world turns dark when the grave closes over a beloved one."[89] Elise Ritter Friedli and her husband had been in Nebraska only seven months when he died of a stroke. She debated about returning to Switzerland but stayed in Nebraska near her siblings. She was fortunate in that she could make a new life for herself on the land her husband had bought.

Other women were sometimes stricken themselves. This was especially hard when the children were young and there were no close family members nearby. Amy Holmes Bilsland (born Mary Buchow) was a year old when her mother was struck by lightening. Mrs. Buchow's mental powers were impaired, and Mr. Buchow left his six children in an orphanage so he could take her back to Germany for treatment. The Buchows had one more baby in Germany, but Mrs. Buchow never recovered. She "didn't know anything, just blank." By the time Mr. Buchow came back for the children, they had all been adopted by various families. Mr. Buchow's efforts show that some German-born husbands did all they could on their wives' behalf, even if this threatened the integrity of the family.[90]

The death or absence of the mother was indeed a threat to family integrity. Most families survived it, however, with the help of others and by adopting a philosophical attitude. Albertine Messinck Quandt came to Charter Oak, Iowa, with her husband, Hermann, and three small sons in 1886. She died in 1895 of a hemorrhage when she got up to do the washing three days after giving birth to her ninth child. Neighbors took this baby in for the first six months of his life, and the other children got along as best they could with their father and part-time housekeepers. Two of Albertine's children remembered how many personal hardships the death of their mother caused. They were left alone a great deal while their father and the oldest sons worked in the field, they had to do without the important food production in garden and orchard their mother had done, and they had no cake or pie until the oldest daughter took cooking lessons a few years later. They also remembered other families in which the mother had died: "They got along, too."[91]

The Quandt children adapted to this situation it seems. It may be that Herman Quandt found it more difficult. We know that he did not remarry until 1908. Another German-born man, Ferdinand Erhardt, spoke directly of the pain he felt after a similar loss: "While I was in the United States Service during the Civil War I lost my wife and two children from typhoid fever. It was a hard blow for me and shattered my hope for the future. I had a boy of four years left who was taken care of by friendly neighbors. I then lived a single life for seven years. By that time I had gotten over my bereavement. I had a good claim and was considered well fixed for those days. I then met my present wife and in 1870 I decided to marry again."[92] Such words prove that at least some men, like some women, thought of their marriages as much more than mere economic relationships.

*   *   *

Age at immigration, the presence of family (especially of female relatives), the strength of the ethnic community and its institutions, economic conditions, the affection and support of her husband, and her health and that of her family were important factors in how a woman felt about her life in America, as we have seen in the writings and lives discussed. Other more elusive factors, particularly personality and psychological makeup, also were important in determining how an individual woman (or man) responded to events and conditions. The diversity and unpredictable quality of women's subjective reactions to life in America were due to the endless combinations of these elements. For example, Jules Sandoz's widowed mother-in-law seems to have had no trouble adjusting to life in America, in spite of her age at immigration. In rural Nebraska, in the Sandozes' Swiss and German neighborhood, she led the life that she would have led in Switzerland: "The quiet, man-subordinated little woman effaced herself as well as possible, and she was not unhappy in this strange America with this strangest of all men, this son-in-law. She knitted and mended and kept an eye on the children. . . ."[93] Mary Sandoz's mother was able to adjust so successfully to America because the traditional European pattern of female subordination and domesticity gave her a meaningful role in her daughter's household. Her quiet, nonabrasive temperament also allowed her to live peacefully with her difficult son-in-law. Her attitude and behavior illustrate both the unpredictable and the typical in individual women's immigration experience.

Immigrants certainly were aware that women's unhappiness and dissatisfaction could cause the failure of their new beginning in America. Women's wholehearted cooperation was particularly important on farms, where their labor was so essential. Henry Ruegg saw evidence of this when scouting the Fancy Creek area, west of Manhattan, Kansas, for land in 1867. Ulrich Metzger, a fellow Swiss, had done nothing to prepare for his wife's arrival on his claim, and she responded by falling ill and complaining to everyone that she did not like it in America. Ruegg and the other Swiss farmers criticized Metzger for his treatment of his wife and thought he should have left her in Switzerland. In spite of beginning her new life in a mood of alienation rather than adventure (thanks to her negligent husband), she seems to have accepted what she could not change and to have adapted to her unenviable situation.[94]

Such adaptation was probably never complete, however. Even women in established and "successful" immigrant families who had been in America for many years could succumb to attacks of homesickness. Thomas Hart Benton's daughter Jessie Benton Frémont wrote of encountering such a woman during an overnight stay in Washington, Missouri, in the fall of 1853. The unnamed woman had a large, clean, attractive home and headed a grown family that entertained the guests that evening with "piece after piece of such music as only the Germans can play rightly,—occasionally all joining in a lovely song." The mother of the family, however, burst into tears as she was helping Jesse Frémont with her fine clothes and gloves, exclaiming that they reminded her of those worn by aristocratic ladies at home in Cassel. She then explained that she had come to Washington from Cassel twenty-four years earlier and had never left the little town, although her husband sometimes went to St. Louis. It turned out to be the German-born couple's wedding anniversary, which may have been another reason for her emotional outburst. She soon composed herself, however, and Jessie Frémont enjoyed her short stay in this immigrant home, which she found to be, in its cleanliness, decor, and general atmosphere, "Germany itself."[95]

Like this Missouri family, many German-speaking immigrants were able to compensate for the loss of their homeland by re-creating that environment, as much as possible, in the New World. They did this by settling near family members and Old World neighbors when they could, by reconstructing community institutions that approximated or substituted for those they had known in their homelands, and by maintaining in their homes the old customs and folkways. A rural environment allowed them to do this with less conflict with the dominant culture than was possible in urban areas. Others, like Elise Isely, found it easier to "throw their memories overboard and hang their German coat up on a nail," as "Jürnjakob Swehn" put it. "Swehn," however, was like many immigrants, male and female, who never felt totally at home in America. He could not simply "hang up his German coat" and put on an American one: "That's not how it is with me. Nor with many others. We all carry some soil from our home village around on our boots. Until we finally take them off. The one sand, the other clay. That doesn't make walking any easier; but I wouldn't want to do without the home soil on my boots."[96] Some of the women whose testimony we have examined felt this way as well. Jette Bruns had the dust of the Münster streets on her shoes and Luise Ritter that of the Bernese highlands on hers all the years they spent in America.

Immigrants who lived the relatively isolated life of farmers were probably especially likely to maintain their emotional links to their past. Some might have developed a certain schizophrenic split in their attachments, as "Jürnjakob Swehn" did. In his old age, after living almost fifty years in Iowa, he was moved to mull this over when his wife said the reason they so often spoke about their old village was that they were homesick: "How can that be homesickness, when Wieschen is with you, and the children were born and grew up here? Here you have your own house, you have sown and harvested here on your own land. . . . How can you get homesick? You have made progress here and not over there; almost only people from your homeland live around you, and God's sun shines here just as it does over there. What could you be homesick for? Surely not for the old hut with its poverty or for the young faces, of whom you no longer know one?" A year and a half later, still turning this over in his mind and increasingly alienated by the anti-German sentiments preceding World War I, he wrote, "I have noticed that inside I have little to do with the land America. I have here on earth two homes. One is our old village, the other is my farm. But the land America is not my home. Inside I stayed German all these years."[97] That is not to say that "Wieschen" and "Jürnjakob Swehn," or immigrants like them, were unhappy in America. In spite of their essential contentment, however, many of them might not have felt fully "at home."

The women whose lives I have examined in this chapter offer varied and even contradictory evidence of the diverse and unpredictable nature of immigrant women's subjective and objective experiences. Some clung tenaciously to their ethnic identity and managed to attain contentment within the family and ethnic community. Others, eagerly or reluctantly, adapted to their foreign surroundings and thereby were relatively satisfied with their new lives. Still others probably isolated certain parts of their selves from the intrusions of American life and culture. In this, German-speaking women would have had a certain advantage over men in the nineteenth century, since they were expected to keep to their home, a place they had some power and influence to shape as they wished.

Certain broad patterns are discernible in the overall picture: married women with young children and old women were generally unhappier in their first years in America than young, unmarried women, for instance; the presence of close female family members could alleviate some of a woman's emotional pain at being separated from familiar surroundings. The infinite variety of existences, however, makes it impossible to be sure how individual women responded to what seem to be similar circumstances. Moreover, we cannot come to definite conclusions about the inner life of each German-speaking immigrant woman because we almost always lack the necessary personal testimony about it. Nonetheless, the words and actions of the women presented in this chapter show the range of emotions that no doubt accompanied other women's lives in America.

4

Strangers in a Strange Land: Women and Their Families in Special Groups

The majority of immigrant German-speakers in the rural Midwest, having come to America as part of family units, found their primary identity as members of those families. My great-grandfather bought his three sons land located within a mile of each other, so they could share work. Their wives worked together as well, and their children found most of their closest friends in each other's families. The sons, my father's generation, who inherited the land continued the pattern of mutual assistance established by their parents. Many of the immigrants I have mentioned thus far—the Roenigks, Kessels, Rückelses, Krehbiels—led similar family-centered lives.

Most immigrants probably viewed themselves secondarily as members of rural neighborhoods, which were often centered on ethnic churches and other immigrant associations and linked by personal and economic ties. Because of such affiliations, they might have also thought of themselves as Catholics, Lutherans, or freethinkers. Where chain immigration had been a strong element in the area's settlement, German-speakers also identified themselves as Westphalians or Austrians, as distinctive from their Holstein or Swiss neighbors, for example.

Other forces influenced many German-speakers to think of themselves in ways that were antithetical to a narrowly ethnic self-identification, though. Viewing them from the outside, Anglo-Americans ignored the immigrants' diverse national, regional, and linguistic origins and, on the basis of the common roots of their native dialects, characterized them simply as "Germans." American public institutions expected the immigrants to behave in ways congruent with indigenous cultural, political, and economic structures. The pressure on the German-speakers to conform to their new environment and the immigrants' own desires to "get ahead" and "belong" in America contributed to the often-noted rapidity with which many German-speakers deemphasized their ethnic differences and became virtually indistinguishable from the dominant society within one or two generations of immigration. This process, slowed though it often was in some areas of rural isolation and ethnic concentration, held true for the majority of the immigrants and their descendants. It was also true for rural women, even though they were generally sheltered from the most immediate pressures to adapt since their activities were restricted to the home, family, and rural neighborhood. Neither of my immigrant great-grandmothers learned to speak English, but their children were all bi- and even tri-lingual (Czech being the second language in the Schelbitzki line). This second generation, however, spoke English almost exclusively in the home. I grew up without knowing that my grandparents spoke German at all. In our mixed neighborhood, the original settlers had had trouble understanding each other's Austrian, Low German, and Hessian dialects and had had few objections to using English as a lingua franca.

Certain immigrant groups, however, bolstered by the support of commonly held beliefs and life-styles and aided by the relative isolation of rural life, resisted the pressures and the temptations of cultural assimilation much more effectively than did other German-speakers. Sometimes they even identified themselves primarily with a doctrinal group, rather than with a consanguineal family. This chapter examines several such special groups of immigrants in the Midwest: the Germans from Russia who attempted to re-create their Old World settlements in Kansas and Nebraska; the Saxon Old Lutherans who came to Perry County, Missouri, in the 1830s; the utopian communistic colonies at Amana and Communia in Iowa and at Bethel in Missouri; and foundations established by German-speaking nuns in rural areas of Illinois and Missouri.

All of these groups shared certain qualities. They did not seek integration into the dominant American culture and sometimes even avoided contact with other German-speakers. They therefore tended to retain cultural differences longer than other immigrants. Their sense of separateness often stemmed from shared religious or philosophical beliefs that had already drawn them together as a group. Adaptation to American culture and society was generally slower for those in concentrated settlements large enough to achieve economic stability and retain group identity. The situation was different for many women in Catholic religious orders, whose groups were small and whose work in American communities thrust them, often with little preparation, into the larger society.

With the exception of the Roman Catholic nuns, very little personal testimony exists to tell us about the lives of the women in these groups. Their motivation for immigration had been conservative, and part of what they sought to conserve was the relationship between the genders that gave women a respected and important role but one confined almost totally to the private sphere. These women generally were not moved to record their personal experiences for others or even for themselves. Indeed, some groups regarded such activity as prideful and inappropriate. Women's activities, in both the home and the ethnic community, were also so taken for granted that they usually received little official attention and went unrecorded. Nonetheless, the extant documentation does permit us to explore the following questions: (1) how did women's lives in these groups differ from those of other more "mainstream" German-speaking women, and (2) did women's membership in such more or less isolationist groups cause them to experience greater or lesser disruption and stress as a result of immigration to America? In other words, was their experience as strangers in a strange land made more bearable by virtue of their membership in these immigrant subgroups?

* * *

The Germans from Russia carried to America a cultural habit of mind of being different and holding one's group separate from the dominant culture. They had developed these patterns of thought and behavior during decades of life as colonists in Russia. First invited by Catherine the Great in the 1760s to colonize the frontier along the Volga, land-hungry German-speaking peasants took advantage of the free land and privileged status accorded them, especially those from areas ravaged by the Seven Years War and later by the Napoleonic wars. The Russians opened up other areas to colonization in southern Russia, along the Black Sea and in the Crimean steppe, later in the eighteenth century. In addition to land grants of up to 175 acres per family, enticements included exemption from military service, local self-government, and the right to conduct German-language public schools.

During the eighteenth and nineteenth centuries, the German colonies grew and prospered, fulfilling the hopes of the Russian government for development of the areas they inhabited. They formed distinctive communities, generally centered on the village church and dominated by its influences. Along the Volga, Catholics and Lutherans grew to number about 250,000 by the 1860s. Mennonites, the third-largest group, were concentrated in southern Russia and numbered about 40,000 at that time. Many of the Mennonites were Dutch by heritage. Their ancestors had colonized areas of East Prussia in the seventeenth century because of religious persecution in their homeland and had adopted the German language as their own. Other Mennonites who came to southern Russia and the Ukraine were Swiss, also seeking to escape an uncongenial environment.[1]

A variety of circumstances contributed to the decision on the part of a sizable minority of these German-speaking colonists to leave their adopted homeland during the 1870s and attempt to establish new communities in America. The very success of the colonists had resulted in burgeoning populations and a subsequent scarcity of land and livelihood for many. By the 1860s, a significant proportion of the German-speaking populations (approximately one-third among the Mennonites) had become a landless proletariat. At the same time, changing conditions in Russia threatened the privileged economic, political, and cultural status of the colonists. Taxes went up 25 percent between 1840 and 1868, grain prices fell because of competition from the United States, and certain economic advantages the colonists enjoyed, such as exclusive licenses for brewing beer, were withdrawn. The Russian authorities made moves to apply midcentury land reforms and a general liberal-rational course of modernization, intended to improve the situation of the Russian peasantry, to the colonists as well. This especially disturbed the richest Mennonites, who had accumulated thousands of acres and were now being forced to contribute land and supplies to their landless brothers and sisters. The Russian government also threatened the cultural integrity of the colonies by pressing for the use of Russian in the schools and local government. The military reform law of 1874, designed to make everyone equally subject to the draft, might have served as the final catalyst for some. It was especially repugnant to the Mennonites, although alternate service in forestry work was eventually made available to them.[2]

This set of "push" circumstances in Russia coincided with favorable "pull" conditions in America. In the 1870s, the United States was just coming out of a recession, and development was booming in the new western states. Acts of Congress had set aside millions of acres in alternate sections for twenty miles on each side of the railroad lines built through Kansas and Nebraska in the 1860s and 1870s. The railroads were now looking for experienced farmers to develop this land. They were ready to compete with each other to offer large tracts at low prices to desirable settlers, and in the Germans from Russia they saw just such settlers. The first German immigrants from Russia, for their part, were anxious to settle together in colonies and perpetuate their communal life. The availability of huge areas of inexpensive land, much of it geographically similar to what they were used to in Russia, meant they could do so while securing their economic future.[3]

For some of the first immigrants from Russia, the religious reasons for emigration were as important as the economic reasons. In the second half of the nineteenth century, religious controversy stemming from the infiltration of west European pietism and sectarianism had torn apart several Russian colonies. German Baptist and Methodist movements gained converts among the Lutherans and even the Catholics. Doctrinal controversy intensified the Mennonite tradition of founding daughter colonies. Many families in the Alexanderwohl Mennonite colony, split by such controversy in the 1860s, left for Kansas in the 1870s. The splinter group that called itself the Krimmer (Crimean) Mennonite Brethren immigrated en masse to Kansas. The freedom to practice the religion of their choice was immensely attractive to these immigrants. It was no doubt also an incentive for some Mennonites that in 1874 the Kansas legislature and in 1877 the Nebraska legislature passed acts exempting from the state militia those who belonged to a religious group whose creed forbade the bearing of arms.[4]

Germans from Russia were not, however, able to reestablish the village life they had pursued for a century or more along the Volga, in southern Russia, and elsewhere in eastern Europe. The Krimmer Mennonite Brethren settlement at Gnadenau in Marion County, Kansas, came closest to achieving this goal. The village was plated in the middle of one of the twelve sections of land the congregation bought, with half-mile strips of land stretching behind the forty house lots. The four adjoining sections of land were similarly divided, with each family farming a mile-long strip of land in every section and plans for the other seven sections to be used first for grazing and later for farming. As in the Old World, a village council of three men governed Gnadenau, determining the crops sown, planning public improvements, and appointing the village herdsmen. The village took on a Russian appearance, with straw-thatched "adobe" buildings, homes that combined the house with the barn and granary, a communal well, well-tended flower beds and orchards, and neighboring fields of sunflowers and watermelons.[5] Within two or three years, however, the village residence system broke down, the settlers redivided the land to consolidate each family's holdings, and eventually the town of Gnadenau ceased to exist.[6]

In a less dramatic fashion, the Volga Germans of Ellis County, Kansas, were more successful in adapting some Old World aspects of village life to New World circumstances. Until after World War I, the descendants of these immigrants retained the custom of maintaining two houses, one on the farm as the main residence, and another in town, used for family gatherings on Sundays and presided over by the mother or an older daughter during the school months. After the automobile made transportation to the farm easier, some continued into the late twentieth century the European pattern of living in town and traveling to the land to work it. For several decades after immigration, the settlers maintained communal holding of land for grazing and gardening purposes in the sections of land on which they established the towns of Munjor, Catharine, Pfeifer, and Schoenchen.[7]

In spite of failures to reestablish village life in the old sense, communal life continued among the various groups of Germans from Russia. This was based on not only long-standing family and village ties but also religious bonds forged in the Old World.[8] Almost all accounts of Germans from Russia emphasize the continued centrality of the church in their immigrant communities. For example, the Bukovina Germans who had come to the Ellis area in Kansas in the 1880s, although scattered throughout three counties at distances of fifty miles or more from each other, were bound by family ties, their Swabian dialect, and their Lutheran faith. For several generations, the only group with which they intermarried was the Lutheran Volga German group in the Ellis area. As had been the case in Europe, they had little or no social contact with members of other ethnic or religious groups until the last half of the twentieth century.[9] Ellis County German-speakers from the Volga area also practiced strict endogamy for the first decades of their residence in America, even continuing Old World prejudices against marrying persons from other Volga German villages.[10]

The clannishness of the ethnic German immigrants from Russia was one of the strongest carryovers from the Old World, which led them to associate almost exclusively with those who could claim common origins of faith and place (often in the narrowest sense). It strengthened communal bonds while it slowed assimilation into American culture.[11] Their special status in Russia had led to an alienation from that political and social culture, which carried over into their lives in America. With the exception of school board elections, rural Germans from Russia, whether Mennonite, Lutheran, or Catholic, did not participate in American political life. They had correspondingly little influence in it.[12]

Certain things peculiar to these immigrants vanished within a few years of immigration, however. The men replaced their Russian-style embroidered shirts and full pants gathered into knee-high boots as these garments wore out. Some of the women discarded their felt boots, kerchiefs, and aprons even before they wore out, especially if they lived in town.[13] Women in rural areas, who rarely went to town and socialized primarily with their neighbors and in ethnic churches, were slow to adopt American fashions. First-generation immigrants often kept their native dress until their death, although some might carry a hat in a bag to wear instead of a kerchief when attending church outside of the community.[14]

Other ethnic peculiarities of the immigrant settlers also were phased out over the years. They stopped building housebarns and constructed their buildings out of native materials rather than the sunbaked puddled or "adobe" brick common in the southern Russian steppes.[15] The straw- and manure-burning brick ovens they built in their first structures made way for American-style stoves, although well into the twentieth century many Ellis County Volga Germans preferred their homemade manure-based fuel (*Mistholz*), sunflower stalks, and corn cobs to coal, which they called "burned money."[16] Eventually, the immigrants moved their beds, piled high with featherbeds and pillows, out of their kitchens and sitting rooms and adopted American home furnishings. A few activities in which women had been heavily involved in Russia were soon abandoned in Kansas as impractical, in particular the production of tobacco and silk. Left were the rows of mulberry trees typical of the farms of Germans from Russia.[17]

This group maintained other characteristic aspects of female behavior and family life in the New World. Women continued to dedicate their energies to the family farming enterprise, to marry young, and to bear many children. One sample of 205 first-generation Volga German families revealed an average of 9.3 children per family, while the number of children in the families of those born in the United States from 1895–1910 averaged 8.1.[18] Observers and descendants often emphasized women's willingness to bear large families and the contentment they exhibited in spite of their large number of children and their confinement to the domestic sphere.[19] Women seem to have done the hard work expected of them without complaining and to have inculcated the same expectations in their daughters.[20] Contemporary scholars have concluded that the success of these families in the marginal farming areas of Kansas was often due to the willingness of wives to contribute their earnings to the accumulation of land and to daughters' willingness to work for wages that were also dedicated to that endeavor.[21] The descendants of such women rarely documented what these demands on a woman's time and energy could cost her and her family in health problems and emotional impoverishment.[22]

The traditional expectations for women persisted long after immigration. In the Ellis, Kansas, area in the 1940s, rural women still seemed to be living the hard lives of their ancestors. In the Russian colonies, women had been reminded of their burdens by their girlfriends on their wedding day, as their bridal wreath was lifted from their heads:

> O comrade, what are you thinking of?
> Now you will turn away from us.
> You have taken a husband
> And entered the estate of marriage,
> The estate of marriage, of suffering,
> Where one knows no joy.[23]

In America, married women still had "little leisure time and few recreational pleasures," and virtually all women married within their community. They also did not continue to work outside the home after marriage.[24]

Women's subordination to men was deeply ingrained among the Germans from Russia. It was supported by church doctrine and teachings and expressed in community attitudes, customs, and practices, many of which continued to manifest themselves in America. Wedding customs among the Volga Germans in Kansas manifested this, for example, in the custom of the bride preceding the groom to the ceremony but walking behind him to the wedding celebration and for all the rest of her married life. The ethnic community aimed its disapproval of divorce and illegitimacy at women in particular. As part of the Catholic church's encouragement of large families, Ellis County priests taught women that it was their Christian duty to submit to their husbands' sexual demands. Some Mennonite elders also felt that the growth of the church was more important than the personal wishes of the woman or the family. In one instance, an elder visited a small family to inquire why they had so few children. When told it was because further pregnancies would endanger the wife's life, he responded that it would be to the greater glory of the church for her to risk this.[25]

Economic practices, influenced by the prevailing ones in Russia, generally disadvantaged women. In Russia, inheritance customs usually prohibited women from inheriting land unless there were no male heirs. The same inheritance patterns continued in America for the first generations after immigration. The situation was even more difficult for women among the Volga Germans, who had adopted the Russian mir system of land distribution in their colonies. Under that system, land was allocated according to how many men lived in a household. A family of girls therefore meant poverty. In America, families coming from this Old World tradition generally gave daughters a cash dowry and sons land.[26]

Interior of a Mennonite kitchen belonging to German immigrants from Russia in McPherson County, Kansas (1878). Note the woman's kerchief, embroidered apron, and short skirt, legacies of these German-speakers' sojourn in Russia. (From the *American Agriculturist* 37 [1878]: 472.)

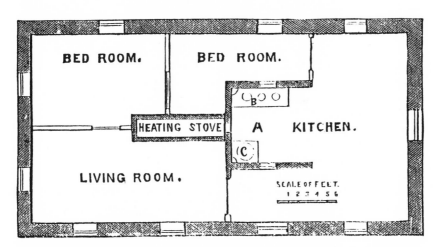

The floor plan of a Kansas Mennonite home shows how a heating stove warmed the rooms connected to it, an Old World technology found for several decades after immigration. In the winter, women also used these stoves for baking. (From the *American Agriculturist* 37 [1878]: 472.)

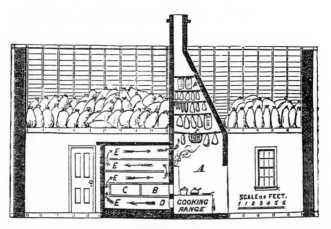

While dinner cooked on the range top of the Kansas Mennonites' stove, the escaping smoke cured meat and sausages suspended in the chimney, as this cross section shows. (From the *American Agriculturist* 37 [1878]: 472.)

Kitchen crew sorting green beans at the Moerschel community kitchen, in Homestead, one of the Amana colonies (date unknown). Amana women routinely cooperated in domestic duties. (Photographer John Eichacker; courtesy of the Amana Heritage Society, Amana, Iowa.)

Wedding photograph of Joseph Jr. and Clementina (Dreher) Hertel, German immigrants from Russia, in Ellis County, Kansas (date unknown). Note the traditional bridal headdress and the groom's ribbon corsage. (Courtesy of the Kansas State Historical Society, Topeka.)

A woman braiding a corn husk rug in the Amana colonies (date unknown). (Courtesy of the State Historical Society of Iowa, Iowa City.)

An Amana resident, wearing the traditional colony churchgoing garb, is continuing her contributions to family and community life by knitting (date unknown). (Photographer William F. Noe; courtesy of the Amana Heritage Society, Amana, Iowa.)

Residence of the George Kopp family, Communia, Iowa (1889). This was the original colony residence, bought by the Kopp family when Communia was dissolved in 1864. It contained the communal dining hall and kitchen, five separate family apartments, and sleeping space for single members in the attic and two cellars. (Courtesy of the State Historical Society of Iowa, Iowa City.)

Christine Klein Venus with daughter Louise (ca. 1867). Soon after immigrating in 1849, Christine Klein married Joseph Venus, one of the founders of Communia Colony in Clayton County, Iowa. Louise, one of seven children, was born in 1857. (Courtesy of the State Historical Society of Iowa, Iowa City.)

Mother Clementine Zerr (ca. 1870). With a small group of immigrant nuns from Baden, Mother Clementine founded a pioneering mission in rural Illinois. (Courtesy of the Archives, Provincial House, Adorers of the Blood of Christ, Ruma, Illinois.)

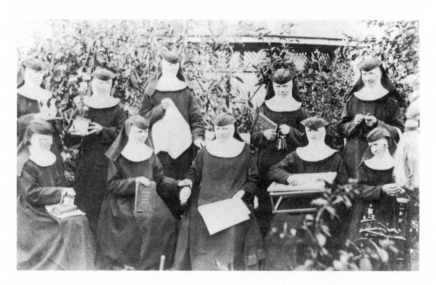

Members of the order of Benedictine Sisters of Perpetual Adoration in Switzerland who established a mission in Nodaway County, Missouri (ca. 1870). Mother Anselma Felber (*front row, second from right*) was the first American superior. Mother Gertrude Leupi (*front row, center*), who had founded the Swiss order, also established missions in South Dakota. (Courtesy of the Archives, Congregation of Benedictine Sisters of Perpetual Adoration, St. Louis, Missouri.)

The mir system also meant that a woman went to live with her in-laws after the wedding and had to conform to the new household's customs while doing the hardest work as its newest member. Her mother-in-law was in charge of the household and often proved to be a hard mistress, perhaps to make up for the difficult years she had had to endure as a young woman. Some immigrants continued these patrilocal and matriarchal customs in America for a time. The Ellis County Volga Germans continued it until World War I.[27] Such practices, however, seem to have broken down fairly quickly elsewhere. One testimony indicates that families stopped living together because there were too many arguments between the mother-in-law and her son's wife, but this was probably only the most obvious reason and nothing new in family relations.[28] Certainly the tension of living in such extended families could be considerable. Some Ellis County women said "that when they were sixteen or seventeen and married and had to live with their in-laws, they cried themselves to sleep many a night and often wished they were dead."[29] It is more likely that the main reason for the abandonment of the multigenerational living arrangements was economic. It was often financially feasible for the young couple in America to have their own home and unnecessary for them to live with their parents to increase the family's allocation of land.

The transition to the new style of family life was no doubt difficult for some, especially for those of the older generation. Women who had attained and expected to maintain a position of domestic power in their later years had to relinquish those expectations. The account of the Bruntz family documents the effect this could have in family life. The grandmother had been reluctant to leave the Volga, knowing she would have to give up her privileged position as widow of the village supervisor (*Vorsteher*). Once in Nebraska, the family continued to hand over all their earnings to her and deferred to her judgment for several years. Eventually the daughter-in-law Eva, at the urging of her sons and after checking with other immigrant women, decided to keep her own earnings and then talked her husband into turning his paycheck over to her rather than to his mother. Eva "felt like a free woman now," but *Großmutter* was distressed, viewing this as further evidence of the lack of respect accorded elderly people in America.[30]

Other older women, however, recognized that America offered them and their daughters possibilities for breaking out of depending on men for their financial welfare. Christina Heine and her daughters homesteaded on adjoining acreage. They could escape the poverty awaiting a family of daughters and also gain the close companionship and support from each other that in Russia would have ceased upon the daughters' marriage: "It would have been virtually impossible for Christina and her daughters to have adjoining property in Russia unless the daughters married the owners next door. Thus it was that Christina happily approached old age in Dakota with her daughters and grandchildren nearby."[31]

The basic conservatism of the Germans from Russia revealed itself in matters of education as well as in questions of life-style and economics. In the Russian colonies, most children had gone to school during the five winter months from the ages of eight or nine until they were thirteen or fourteen, at which time they entered catechism school to prepare for confirmation.[32] In America, the immigrants often saw little reason why their children, whose labor they needed at home, should attend school any more than necessary to learn the rudiments of reading, writing, and reckoning and enough English to enable them to function adequately in the larger community. In the New World, too, children therefore often stopped attending school after their church confirmation.[33]

Many Germans from Russia also held the general opinion that an education beyond the most basic ability to learn the catechism and read the hymns was wasted on girls since they would marry and spend their lives at home. After all, it was frequently asked in the old country, "To whom are they going to write?"[34] American school attendance reflected the continuation of these attitudes. In contrast to other ethnic groups, fewer rural girls than boys among the Germans from Russia attended elementary and high school, even as late as the 1920s and 1930s.[35] In Ellis County, the priests opened an advanced course for boys, which eventually attracted enough students to become the Hays Catholic College. In general, however, the rural Germans from Russia did not value education until changing economic conditions made it difficult to give each son land. Advanced education for girls had been unknown in Russia and was uncommon in America, except among the more progressive of the Mennonites. Many Germans from Russia therefore looked askance at female schoolteachers and did not encourage their daughters to enter that profession.[36]

If women's subordinate position in certain areas did not change with immigration, we need not conclude that this was particularly stressful for them. Indeed, through immigration they might have gained some influence and authority because of their central position in the domestic sphere. Here their own instincts of conservation of the old ways could hold sway without excessive conflict with the outside world. Ample evidence exists that the women in this immigrant group were very successful in helping create a home environment that served as a haven in the New World. In their everyday activities of cooking and keeping house, women communicated to their families that they were members of a distinct ethnic group with an individual history. Eating such traditional German foods as sauerkraut and blood sausage and such adopted Russian dishes as borscht and *Bohne Beroggie* (bean-filled pastries) helped the immigrants feel at home in America and gave them a sense of continuity and communal identity. Serving kuchen and zwieback for *Faspa* (teatime lunch) when friends and relatives came visiting on Sunday was a tradition maintained long after the first generation of immigrant women passed on. Such food nourished group solidarity as well as the body, even if Anglo-Americans sometimes ridiculed it.[37]

Foodways are often closely associated with the celebration of holidays and other folk customs. Here, too, women helped solidify ethnic identity. They cooked the food for the holiday meals, and, along with their women neighbors and female relatives, they prepared refreshments for community weddings and funerals. They fashioned the traditional elaborate headpieces their daughters wore when they married or the Mennonite cap for the new bride. They supervised the coloring and hiding of Easter eggs. They helped their children learn Christmas verses and made or bought the gifts for their families. One of them portrayed the *Christkindchen* (Christ child) during the Christmas Eve visits that that figure and *Pelznickel* (a frighteningly shaggy version of St. Nicholas) made to children in Catholic and Lutheran communities. Certainly women's participation was crucial in perpetuating all the folk customs and celebrations that their descendants commemorate and carry on today.[38]

It is more difficult to document women's participation in church life among the Germans from Russia. The general position of women as "daughters of Eve" was symbolized spatially in all the Russian colonists' denominations by separating the sexes in church (a custom Lutherans from Germany had as well). Women sat on the left side of the church, "a spatial domain traditionally associated with evil and betrayal," as one anthropologist has put it.[39] Many immigrant churches in America continued this seating arrangement, as well as the separate entrances on the outside of the church that accompanied it.

Among the Volga German Catholics, women had few official roles (aside from joining a religious order) for a relatively long time because of the male-dominated hierarchy of that denomination. They were certainly pious, however, and must have supported the various church-related celebrations by supplying food and labor. The longevity of the tradition of parish processions on various church holidays in Ellis

County, Kansas, speaks to the force of family piety there. That "church-ing" women (i.e., blessing them in church after childbirth) was still a common practice in the 1940s may also be a sign of the strength of women's church life in that region.[40]

Even among the Mennonites, where women had at times played a significant role in church life, specific contributions to the continuation of those traditions in America are difficult to document. As mentioned earlier, Barbara Strohm Kraemer's home was used for church services, and later she and her husband donated land for a church and school. No doubt many women in this group gave that kind of support. Mennonite women were always important behind-the-scenes players in the life of their churches. They encouraged and inspired their husbands, brothers, and sons in the practice and propagation of their faith and endured the same tribulations their men did during times of persecution. They hosted and participated in prayer meetings and Bible study groups and doctrinal discussions at which church policy was formed or altered. Their personal, familial relationships were sometimes bonds that connected their spiritual community as well. Men's involvement in the public life of the church usually meant that women took up the slack at home. As indicated in the previous chapter, Christian Krehbiel's ability to give so much of his time and energy to Mennonite causes was due to the ability and willingness of his wife to take over his duties in the home and family.

The various Mennonite denominations had differing attitudes toward women's formal participation in church services and activities. Most did not allow women to take a public role in church services and congregational meetings. When the influence of American Protestantism led most Mennonite sects to introduce Sunday schools in the late nineteenth century, they soon called on women to teach classes for children and other women. Mennonite Brethren women were allowed to preach or teach classes with men in them only if they were missionaries abroad. Mennonite women began to found missionary societies and to hold prayer and Bible study meetings, perhaps again because of the example of American Protestant women. In America, these groups sometimes functioned as an auxiliary to the church and sometimes were almost parallel to the church, with a separate budget, program, membership list, and annual retreat. Women of all Mennonite denominations played a vital role in the disaster relief activities for which the churches are so well known. These developments indicate that the American environment allowed some Mennonite women opportunities for self-sufficiency in areas of spiritual activity and expression that had been closed to them before they immigrated.[41]

In Russia, the colonists had used German in the home and church as a barrier against the infiltration of Russian culture. It continued to have that function in America. Rural (and some urban) immigrant churches in the Midwest retained the use of German for services into the 1920s and 1930s, and a few even into the 1950s and 1960s.[42] Again, it is difficult to ascertain women's roles in the continued use of German in the church. As stated earlier, they generally had no direct voice in deciding such issues, but they would have had influence with the men in their families. We do know that immigrant women were generally slower than men to learn English, so many of them no doubt had a stake in retaining German-language church services.

It is also difficult to be sure how women helped perpetuate the use of German in the home. Women living in close communities of Germans from Russia did not learn much English and were therefore likely to maintain an environment in which their dialect was used for everyday communication. Some of the more progressive immigrants and those who lived in ethnically mixed communities, however, encouraged their children to become proficient in English, even if they did not do so themselves. Evaliz Meisner, for example, never learned English very well, yet she urged her husband to ask their rural Kansas school board to make a rule that the children speak only English at school because they were not learning it well enough. Later, she showed her pride in her husband's and children's growing Americanization by making a "show table" for her parlor, which had icons of the old and the new cultures. She covered the table with a snowy linen cloth brought from Russia and displayed the family Bible, a paper rose she had made, and a picture of George Washington that her husband had painted when he was preparing for citizenship. Americans, she believed, accepted her and her family better after viewing this visual representation of cultural accommodation and integration.[43]

In certain areas of female communal life, especially those having to do with key events in the female life cycle and folk healing, rural women among the Germans from Russia maintained a particularly closed culture. As in the Old World, marriages generally were arranged in the first years, often by *Fürsprecher* (go-betweens), and the mother of the girl played a significant role in the preliminary discussions. In some ethnic communities, she and the father then laid their hands in blessing on the young couple. Many of the customs surrounding the wedding celebration itself persisted long after the settlement period. They included rituals of invitation, *Polterabend* (shivaree) festivities on the evening before the wedding, traditions surrounding the order of the procession to and from the church, ceremonies recognizing the special status of cooks at the wedding feast, and the pinning of money, dry goods, and other gifts on the bride's dress at the wedding dance. Although many of these traditions involved the bridegroom and men in the community as much as they did the bride and women, it was women who made most of the arrangements for such events and who thus were probably most responsible for the maintenance of these traditions.[44]

More exclusively in the female domain was the care of women during and after childbirth. In rural areas, midwives from the immigrant community and female relatives and neighbors gave this care. Around Catherine, Kansas, it was the custom for nine neighbor women to cook for a family with a new baby, each for one day after the birth. Employing midwives is also evidence of the strength of the female community. Midwives were clearly preferred in most immigrant communities, even long after the early years of settlement. Some became famous, such as Sara Block Eitzen, who is said to have delivered more than eighteen hundred Mennonite babies after her arrival in Kansas in 1876. Although their low fees and the lack of doctors in general and of German-speaking doctors in particular during the early years of settlement no doubt contributed to the presence of midwives at births, these factors do not totally explain it. In Lincoln, Nebraska, where doctors were in plentiful supply, German women from Russia were still using midwives in the early part of the twentieth century. Even as late as 1970, at least one midwife was active in rural Ellis County, Kansas, and she was sometimes preferred over male doctors.[45]

Many of the Germans from Russia continued to practice folk medicine originating in medieval times. Women as well as men performed these acts of healing, called *Brauche*. The original traditions required that the various charms and remedies be passed on orally from a man to a woman and from that woman to another man. In more recent times, among the Volga Germans in America, in any case, folk healing, or *Brauchen*, was a family tradition, usually passed on from mother to daughter. Many of the female healers (*Braucher*) were also midwives who were respected, and sometimes feared, in their communities and who are still remembered in rural areas of the Great Plains.[46]

The clannish and conservative tendencies of the Germans from Russia affected their adaptation to America and influenced their economic success, for both good and bad. The closeness of communal life and the maintenance of religious and folk traditions also were a support to these groups. That they continued many of their ethnic-determined, characteristic behavior patterns after World War II suggests that women were active participants in the perpetuation of these patterns. There is strong evidence that rural women were indeed sheltered from the stress of acculturation by their residence in settlements of Germans from Russia, where they shared so many ties of family, faith, and culture.

* * *

In many ways, the outer contours and stresses of the lives of women among the Saxon Old Lutherans who came to found a colony in Missouri are parallel to those of other immigrant women. Most of the 612 colonists who survived the winter transatlantic voyage (one of their five ships went down in the crossing) went to their 4,400–acre tract of land in southeastern Perry County soon after their arrival in St. Louis in January and February of 1839. Of these, 274 (44.8 percent) were women, most of them part of family groups but also twenty-two maids, three midwives, and four seamstresses. The majority of the male heads of family were craftsmen (151) and farmers (34), but an educated core of clergymen (15), professionals and government employees (15), and merchants (8) had organized and supplied the main financing for the undertaking.[47]

The arrival of this contingent in St. Louis, soon followed by another 240 or so mostly poor colonists, caused an uproar in the St. Louis German community. The resident Germans believed the newcomers, with their shabby clothes and scanty resources, put all Germans in a bad light. Their alleged treatment of women also came in for criticism. In the 9 March 1839 edition of the *Anzeiger des Westens,* Heinrich Koch accused the Saxons of eating rotten meat, undercutting other German labor by working for twenty-five cents a day, and harnessing their women to carts. As a Dr. Gempp, a St. Louis physician attending some of the immigrants, wrote in the *Anzeiger des Westens* on 16 March 1839, it is likely the women simply pitched in to help move belongings from the riverfront to temporary residences as quickly and cheaply as possible. It is also certain, though, that women had to continue to do hard and often unwonted work in the group's efforts to become established in Missouri.

In Perry County, the colonists confronted terrible housing shortages, brutal weather, scanty supplies, and a lack of leadership and direction. Without the generosity, advice, and assistance of American neighbors, many would not have survived the first few months. To these problems was soon added the anguish of the exposure of their adulated leader, Martin Stephan, as a fornicator and mismanager of their pooled funds. The complete dissolution of the colony might well have followed from all of these negative experiences, but this did not happen. Although many of the Old Lutheran colonists went to St.

Louis to put their skills as craftspeople to better use, they continued their allegiance to the group and supported the colony's efforts with part of their wages. Only one of the leaders of the group eventually returned to Germany, and he did so largely at his wife's urging. Luise Marbach's husband, Franz, who was a lawyer, had been Stephan's right-hand man in making the plans and preparations for emigration. Luise had opposed the idea of emigration from the outset, to the extent that Stephan had had her confined to her cabin and separated from her husband on board ship because of her negative views and her influence on her husband. Family circumstances furnished her with additional ammunition: two of the Marbach children had died in Germany while their father was away making preparations for the trip, a toddler perished during the journey, and two of their remaining four children died in the Perry County colony.[48]

Families without the financial means and professional connections to return, of course, had no option except to remain and make the best of a difficult situation.[49] We have little direct testimony about how women and their families did this in concrete and in subjective terms, but we can surmise that these settlers, in whose lives religion played such a central role, were armed with weapons against despair and cultural alienation that other, "ordinary" immigrants did not always possess. The 1839 and 1840 letters from Perry County of Christiane Loeber, the unmarried sister of Pastor G. Heinrich Loeber, hint at this. Although she mentioned the miserable living conditions, the scarceness of food, and the illness and death in the colony, she also expressed her faith that God was overseeing the venture and had sent an abundant harvest in 1839 so that the Americans in the area could be especially generous to the colonists. She made her own contributions to the colony's efforts to establish itself by paying back the Americans with needlework, sharing her room and money with an impoverished widow with two children, and planning to earn her living by spinning and weaving cotton or making silk. The house Christiane Loeber built in the winter of 1839–40 became the first colony school building upon her death in April of 1840. A tone of cheerful confidence in God's grace and in the sustaining power of the Old Lutheran religious community speaks through her letters.[50]

Group solidarity was undoubtedly a support to the early Old Lutheran settlers. They aided each other materially and emotionally. Certain of their beliefs about family life and women's proper roles also helped them adjust successfully to their new environment while maintaining their religious and cultural identity. In 1872, Pastor Wilhelm Sihler spelled out the proper role for women and the threat to the

Missouri Synod home and faith posed by American attitudes about women. Women, Sihler said, should restrict their activities to the domestic sphere, maintaining silence in church and acting only in their Scripture-ordained capacities as subordinate helpmates to their husbands and as mothers to their children: "woman's destiny is fulfilled in the domestic and maternal callings, according to God's will and order." Sihler warned that the increasing number of unmarried Missouri Synod women pointed to the influence of American culture that suggested women should prepare themselves for professions other than that of wife and mother. This, Sihler claimed, was alienating serious young men, who were likely to turn into "gloomy, rancorous, misanthropic hermits" without female influence in their lives. Woman suffrage and women's entrance into higher education in preparation for inappropriate callings would result, he warned, in "a strange mixed breed of intellectual men-women and peace-amazons." Even deaconesses in their much-praised hospitals ran the risk of becoming too self-centered and losing sight of the proper motivations of Christian love and altruism for their work, said Sihler.[51]

Sihler's treatise makes clear the Old Lutherans' conservative view of proper female behavior. The dedication of women to home and family was not only part of their religious creed but also an important element in this immigrant group's adaptation to America. The immigrants could preserve many aspects of their way of life and tenants of their faith without the distraction of women's energies from these spheres and the disruptions that suffrage and changing gender roles were bringing to American society.[52]

The immigrant founders, male and female, of the Old Lutheran colony and of the Missouri Synod Lutheran church that developed out of it were in accord with the definition of the female role as Sihler's article outlined it. We know the most about the family and marital life of the early ministers in the colony and church. Their wives, who were to serve as role models to the congregations, found self-fulfillment in sacrificing their own needs to those of their husbands, families, and church. The death notice of Dorothea Benthien Craemer, for example, stated that she had been "known and honored throughout the bounds of Synodical Conference for her self-denial and motherly care" of her family of eight, as well as for her nursing work among Indian children and her (mostly unpaid) supervision of the kitchens at the Fort Wayne and St. Louis seminaries.[53]

Although Dorothea Craemer's supervisory work at the seminaries indicates that women did do work outside the home in the support of their church community, the Missouri Synod Lutheran church was quite slow to allow or encourage organized church work by women. Sewing clubs to aid indigent seminary students were organized in large cities even before the Civil War, but other church-sponsored outlets for women were not available until the formation of the Walther League in the 1890s. In 1919, the Missouri Synod finally witnessed its own deaconess movement, and in the 1920s Missouri Synod women began to organize a Lutheran women's national organization.[54]

Because of the church's teaching that it was improper for females to have preeminence over males, women were also not accepted as teachers in the early Missouri Synod Lutheran communities. The church did find, however, that the needs of the many German-language parochial schools it founded could not be met with male teachers alone, especially since the salaries many parishes could pay were so low. There is some indication that women teachers were present in small numbers before 1872. A discussion in 1873 about opening a seminary for women did not get very far, however. Official church policy on women parochial schoolteachers was not clarified for many decades. By the end of the nineteenth century, there was general agreement on the lack of conflict between the teaching profession and women's God-given gifts and duties. Yet no women were admitted for training in the Missouri Synod school system until 1919.[55]

If women could not serve their God directly through the church, they could do so through its ministers. As was true of other German-speaking Protestant ministers' wives, some women probably married pastors out of dedication to their faith rather than love for the man in question.[56] Frontier conditions often sorely tried their devotion, whether to husband or church. Lydia Buenger Lochner moved to a primitive, one-room log cabin at Pleasant Ridge, Missouri, after marrying an itinerate minister, J. F. K. Lochner. She wept upon seeing the cabin and had to get in bed under an umbrella to shelter herself from the snow drifting through the faulty roof. Nevertheless, we are told that she maintained her cheerfulness because of her love for her husband and her savior. Lydia Lochner, however, was not granted a long life to dedicate to her husband and church. A year and a half after coming to the Missouri backwoods and a month after giving birth for the first time, she died as a result of an illness contracted when spring rains flooded the Lochner cabin.[57]

Women married to ministers in rural areas had all of the difficult physical work of farm life and little or no assistance from their husbands, who often were gone much of the time, traveling long distances to several parishes. The pastors' poor salaries meant that their wives had no help in the garden and the house or with the cows and chickens, as one visitor to early Missouri Synod rural parishes noted. They therefore often had no choice except to "neglect" their children, who could seem, as the same visitor put it, "like little wild animals" (*wie kleine Wilde*).[58]

The support ministers' wives gave their husbands' efforts to establish the new church in America usually consisted of their being frugal, hardworking home managers, who took care of all family matters. This could result in domestic relations in which a woman deferred to her husband on many matters but also exercised a great deal of authority in household affairs. An example is Emilie Buenger Walther, the wife of C. F. W. Walther, the founder of the Missouri Synod church. Although of middle-class origins in Germany, she endured the same privations that others did in the Perry County colony and once confided that she never got past having to maintain a *Buschwirtschaft* (backwoods household). She is said to have idolized her husband, but she also was such a parsimonious housewife that in later years he sometimes smuggled in wood from the college to heat his home office because she thought he was too wasteful with fuel.[59]

Although she might have had no direct role in the development of the Missouri Synod church, Emilie Buenger Walther was certainly vitally interested in its teachings and practices. She might have been even more conservative than her husband. On one occasion, she told him that she found it inappropriate for seminary students to sing a rowdy song about sauerkraut since they were going to become pastors. He responded, "Yes, indeed, but not hypocrites." She also once expressed the belief that the Old Lutheran adherence to "plain simplicity, good morality, and . . . the beloved German language" had slipped after the Civil War.[60] In this conservatism and in her support for the teachings of the church for which she had left her homeland, she was no doubt like many other women of this group.

The link Emilie Walther saw between the cultivation of a simple German life-style and the moral standards of her church was one that the immigrant founders of the Missouri Synod Lutheran church came to view as fundamental. As Frederick Luebke put it, "German culture with all of its trappings was used to perpetuate the religious conservatism which had become their hallmark." Threatened by the religious diversity of American society, the church believed that only "through conservatism . . . could it preserve the religious identity of the group."[61] Women's acceptance of a Pauline subordination to their husbands and fathers and their strong support of the preservation of their German cultural identity thus had religious as well as ethnic implications. Their domestic duties included creating a home that would serve as a bulwark against the encroachment of American culture, thought to be synonymous with the loss of spiritual life. In this context, a mother's use of German in the home was not just an individual effort to maintain familiar family discourse but also a religious act.

* * *

Like the Saxon Old Lutheran colonists in Perry County, Missouri, the members of the Community of True Inspiration came to America to found a colony in which they could maintain their religious beliefs. The members of both groups used pooled resources to buy large tracts of land on which they established towns to accommodate the various elements of their populations. The basis for the distribution of the population and the naming of their towns indicate the differences between the two immigrant settlements, however. The residents of the Lutheran colony in Missouri grouped themselves according to the places from which their ministers originated, as the names of the towns they founded indicated: Altenburg, Frohna, Wittenberg, and Selitz.[62] The Inspirationists, who were even more diverse in their places of origin, had already had to rent several estates in Germany to minimize the vexations among people from various areas who spoke different German dialects. They established four villages in upper New York, where they first moved in 1843, and seven in Iowa after 1855. As a sign of the underlying unity of the Iowa colony, all of them (with the exception of the already existing village of Homestead) used the name Amana in combination with a designation of their locations in Amana Township. The Missouri Old Lutherans soon abandoned the goal of maintaining a self-contained religious colony and used their energies to develop into an expansionist American church centering on German ethnicity. This left the Perry County residents allied primarily with their local immigrant church, much as other German-speaking immigrants were elsewhere in the Midwest. The Inspirationists remained what they started out to be, at least until 1932: a largely self-contained, relatively static colony united by shared religious beliefs and a common life-style.[63]

The Inspirationists adopted a communal, agriculture-based life-style in America out of pragmatic economic considerations rather than a desire to imitate the lives of the early Christians. It seemed to them the most expedient way to attain and maintain their purpose for coming together. The first article of the constitution of the Amana Society, adopted in 1859, stated:

> The foundation of our civil organization is and shall remain forever God, the Lord, and the faith, which He worked in us according to His free grace and mercy. . . .

The purpose of our association as a religious Society is therefore no worldly or selfish one, but the purpose of the love of God in His vocation of grace received by us, to serve Him in the bond of union, inwardly and outwardly, according to His laws and His requirements in our own consciences, and thus to work out the salvation of our souls. . . .[64]

The policies of sharing property, guaranteeing support to all members of the Society, and engaging in agricultural and limited trades and manufacturing outlined elsewhere in the constitution were to be merely the framework enabling the attainment of this spiritual purpose.

Yet these conditions affected the lives of the colonists profoundly. They gave them the advantages of material security, shared work and wealth, and broad equality within the group. The guarantee of a subsistence living, with ample food and decent shelter, freed the immigrants from the stress of having to establish themselves independently in a strange land. Parents did not have to fear the economic consequences of the death of their spouse, and orphans were taken care of at community expense. The communal life-style had particular consequences for a woman. She was released from the economic near-necessity of marrying as well as from the difficulty of supporting her children in the event of her husband's death. The yearly maintenance allowance for each adult also gave women some discretionary funds for their personal use (within the narrow limits allowed by the Inspirationist emphasis on plain living).

The agricultural work of women and families was also different in Amana. Most of the work was done communally. Although girls and young women were called upon to help with field work during harvest times, particularly in the first decades after settlement, they did so in large crews. At the same time, other women took care of the food preparation and child care, which was a burden for women in independent nuclear families who did field work. An Amana woman with children under the age of two was exempt from the general village work, and she got her meals from the nearest kitchen-house. Until the early twentieth century, everyone ate in the community kitchens, where teams of women prepared five meals a day. Even this demanding work was easier than it might have been because the women worked in shifts (two weeks on duty and one week off), had a hired man for such heavy work as chopping wood and carrying water, and worked cooperatively.[65] The older women (again usually with help from a hired man and young girls and, during harvests, crews of women) did the less strenuous work involving poultry and the colony gardens. All of this communal labor was training in domestic skills for girls and young women. The team work also gave women opportunities to develop leadership and management skills, since each kitchen and garden had a female "boss," who was almost always a single woman or a mature woman with grown children, and an assistant boss.[66]

The inclusion of women in communal work affected other aspects of family life. Small children generally attended nurseries. School was held from seven in the morning until six in the evening, year-round. Men taught the morning session, the *Lehrschule* (teaching school). Then came a *Spielstunde* (recreational hour) and an afternoon *Arbeitsschule* (work school) for trades and crafts. Women taught some of the *Arbeitsschule* classes, which included needlework and gardening.[67] Although men, women, and children ate at separate tables and times in the communal kitchens during the day, families often took the evening meal from the kitchen and ate it in their own lodgings, especially in the last decades of the colony, when communal bonds were weakening. This practice reflects the Society's attempt to balance its emphasis on shared life and the anticommunal pull of the family.

The Community of True Inspiration recognized marriage as a necessary social institution, but it also considered celibacy the ideal state. Women could not marry until they had reached the age of twenty and men the age of twenty-four, and then only after a year-long engagement. Marriage and childbirth were viewed as falls from the state of grace. The Inspirationists signaled their disapproval of these events by "demoting" both marriage partners for a time in the seating hierarchy that indicated spiritual purity at the eleven weekly church meetings.

Inspirationist teachings treating husbands and wives as equally culpable in matters of marital sexuality mitigated against the Christian view of women as daughters of Eve and thus essentially sinful and seductive beings. The Inspirationist catechism followed Jacob Boehme's teaching of a double fall from grace. In this depiction of the origins of human sin, Adam was originally androgynous and could re-create himself magically. Satan then tempted Adam to desire earthly things, leading to a fall from grace and Adam's division into Adam and Eve, followed by the temptation of Eve. Childbirth and marriage were thus reminders of Adam's fall from his high estate in which he had possessed the powers of creation.[68]

The Community of True Inspiration was not, however, entirely free of teachings and practices that communicated women's inferior status and dangerous seductiveness. Number 13 of the "Twenty-Four Rules of True Godliness" holds, "The husband is the head of the household and should be a good spiritual example for his wife and children." Bertha Shambaugh noted "among the men an ample measure of the orthodox German sense of masculine superiority," although their desire to fulfill the precept to lead exemplary religious lives tempered this.[69] Number 18 of the "Twenty-One Rules for the Examination of Our Daily Lives" reveals a certain male-centeredness in Inspirationist teachings: "Fly from the society of womankind as much as possible, as a very highly dangerous magnet and magical fire." Although this rule reflects the traditional Christian origins of the group, the Community never applied it with any thoroughness. It probably was primarily part of the context of the two preceding rules that warn against meaningless conversation and activities.[70]

Certain Inspirationist church practices indicate a rough equality between the genders. Men still sit on one side of the church and women on the other, and when singing hymns, leaders from the two sides take turns in giving the beginning pitch.[71] The traditional church-going garb for Amana women communicates more than just a rejection of worldly fashion and vanity and an adherence to Old World dress, however. The somber colors, full skirts, small black caps, and long, concealing "shoulder-shawl" that hide from view "all lines of grace and beauty" minimize women's sensual appeal.[72]

We can view certain concrete aspects of life in old Amana as manifestations of the group's tendency to treat women and men as near-equals in spiritual matters. Families lived in houses that were almost identical to each other and that were meant to provide every adult family member her or his own room to facilitate spiritual self-examination. For nineteenth-century women, this was in itself a luxury. Most women in Amana married, but the high value the Inspirationists placed on the single state gave those who did not almost equal status with men in certain community matters. As stated in the constitutional bylaws, single women over the age of thirty and widows had the right to vote in the annual election of the Society's trustees. Since the trustees were elected from among the elders in each village, who were all men until very recently, women were effectively barred from attaining that position themselves, however.[73]

That a woman, Barbara Heinemann Landmann (1795–1883), was the last *Werkzeug* ("instrument") to speak God's inspired word to the Community indicates women could take on important roles in the spiritual life of the Inspirationists. She lived for sixteen years after the death of Christian Metz, the *Werkzeug* who had led the Inspirationists to America, but she never did have his status in the community. For example, the governing body of the colony, the Great Council of the Brethren, did not allow her to speak before them, as Metz had. That might have had as much to do with her lowly social origins and abrasive personality as with her gender, however. The Community's

acceptance of her as *Werkzeug* is proof of this sect's relative acceptance
of equality between the genders, at least in spiritual matters.[74]

The Amanists managed, by carefully admitting members and con-
trolling communal life, to maintain their communist life-style for three-
quarters of a century after coming to Iowa. They retained their identity as a unique group in American society even longer than that and
are capitalizing on it today.[75] Part of their success was because they
cultivated their ethnicity and re-created, in part, communal patterns
familiar to the immigrants from Europe. It could be argued that even
the insular quality of German village life was transplanted to Iowa, since
each village developed its own dialect differences and relatively little
social intercourse took place among the residents of the seven towns
before World War I.[76] Women's roles in the retention of certain ethnic qualities were substantial: using German in the home, preparing
German foodstuffs, and perpetuating holiday customs, for example.
Certain domestic, female-centered customs unique to the colony are
still in evidence: the preparation of certain traditional Christmas cook-
ies, the baking of a star-shaped marble cake for weddings, the bringing of other cakes to the wedding reception by the guests, and the
creation of a quilt in a typical Amana pattern for the bride.[77]

In the early 1980s, the Amana Heritage Society conducted an oral
history project. I have based much of my discussion of the implications of communal life for women on information contained in those
oral histories. Although many of the interviewees were just children
or teenagers when the communal economic structure was dissolved in
1932, their memories and their comments about their parents and
grandparents provide interesting insights into the advantages and disadvantages of communal life. They spoke positively of the financial
security of communal life, the support of others in accomplishing
domestic and group work, and the feeling of general equality among
the colony members. One Amana resident said that she preferred life
in Amana before 1932: "When you were done you were done. You
didn't have no worry; you didn't have to worry where the money came
from. . . ." But another said that her grandmother, an immigrant to
Amana from a well-off family in Germany, had found it hard to adjust
to the Amana way of sharing everything and having nothing of one's
own. She asserted that most people who left the community did so for
economic reasons.[78]

Work in the community kitchens meant that women were out of
their homes for lengthy periods every day. Some Amanists believed later
that it was better after 1932, when women could stay at home to take
care of their families. One informant had experienced vividly the neg-

ative repercussions for children whose mothers had to work. She had been badly scalded as a teenager soon after starting work in the community kitchen. Although she was in great pain and unable to walk for several weeks after the accident, she had had to take care of herself during the day while her mother was away.[79]

Other testimony indicates that the communistic basis of economic life was also the source of communal tensions and resentments when residents did not fully contribute to the group effort. One informant claimed that some men tried to avoid summer field work by doing unnecessary jobs in the furniture shop or elsewhere. Women with large families also sometimes came in for criticism. If they had one baby after another and thus did not have to work in the kitchens, some viewed them as shirkers. Such repeated "falls from grace" had social as well as spiritual implications. As one informant said resentfully, "They got their same allowance like from the store, could sit at home, walk around town with their kids, doing nothing and got just as much food and came with their baskets [to the community kitchens] and got their food."[80]

The community did provide a bulwark against the kind of catastrophes that could destroy or greatly burden family life. Upon the death of her mother, one fifteen-year-old had to take care of her father, grandmother, and two brothers. The elders assigned her a helper so she could continue to work in the community kitchen but also do her work at home. Others on her kitchen team pitched in to make her life a little easier. Because of her family situation, her husband moved to her village when they married, instead of her having to move to his, as was customary. It is perhaps not surprising that this woman believed that people cared more for each other and lived a closer life in old Amana.[81]

Most of the oral testimony concerning the community kitchens and women's communal work emphasizes the positive aspects. The kitchens were indeed centers of social life for female Amanists, and the decline in their use as eating places marked the decline in communal spirit. Each kitchen had its own ambience, according to the personalities of the boss and her helpers. Although one woman remembered the harsh strictness with which she was treated as a young girl learning the kitchen work, the majority of the women interviewed spoke more positively. One mentioned the fun she had had working in the kitchen, where "even" the older women "kidded around." Once a year, the workers in this kitchen went on a special picnic. The boss had to request a special allotment of sausage from the meat market and arrange for a horse and wagon to take them. Another woman believed that her time in the kitchens was important as well as enjoyable because she had acquired domestic skills and had learned discipline and respect for her elders. This woman also had fond memories of the traditional Easter egg hunts each kitchen organized for the families that ate there and for young relatives of the kitchen workers. Some women mentioned enjoying taking food out to the harvest workers and participating in large work crews, those that brought in, cleaned, and sorted the onion and potato harvests. The kitchens were a place for women to come together and share their joys and concerns as well as their labor. One young woman, for example, whose father was furious when she bobbed her hair in the early 1920s, followed the advice of her kitchen boss and had a braid made of the cut hair for her to wear until her wedding. The Amana oral interviews contain many indications that the female bonds and networks established in the kitchens played an important role in making communal and social life in the colony stronger and more pleasurable.[82]

Communal life at Amana also had its negative aspects for women, however. They might be moved temporarily to another village that needed female workers in a community kitchen. As communal ties weakened and contact with outsiders became more common, some female Amanists felt inferior to the visitors from "the world." One woman said, "They were dressed the way I would have liked to dress. They had all the things that I would have liked to have. They had the education that I would have wanted." Once in a great while, a young woman would have the courage to leave Amana to get some of the things the colony denied her. Speaking of one such rebel, a woman said, "She had the nerve to do it, where some of the others maybe wanted to, but didn't quite think they could handle it." A less drastic step was for women to take correspondence courses, which some of them did near the end of the communal period. After 1932, these women were likely to work outside the home. Although the interviewers asked many of the female informants if women felt discriminated against in old Amana, the answer was generally no. The comment of one is enlightening on that score. While acknowledging that women were generally in second place, she said, "We sort of were used to having that place in society that we had here. We didn't question it, let's put it that way."[83]

Certain Amana practices in the social sphere had negative repercussions for residents, especially, perhaps, in the last years of communal life. Women, like men, had to wait for the elders' permission to marry. The oral histories indicate that people sometimes felt irritated at having the wedding delayed by several weeks and at not being able to determine who would be guests at the ceremony. Some couples experienced the unhappiness of being separated to minimize the possibility of having sexual relations. In spite of such precautions, of course, premarital sex and out-of-wedlock births did take place. Although the young couple usually married eventually, they had to acknowledge their sin publicly. The consequences for the young woman could be quite unpleasant, as she was sometimes removed from her family and community and sent to a shack in the woods to await the birth. Perhaps as one might expect, however, the number of such negative reminiscences among the oral histories is relatively small.[84]

The longevity of Amana as a communistic society would indicate that its residents had the advantage of inner-group stability and cohesion to shield them from the changes brought about by contact with American society. Yet from the beginning, the demands of the American market economy influenced life at Amana. After the first years of settlement, the Amanists hired nonmembers (mostly of German origin) to do the heavy and dirty work. Outsiders were always present as workers in the colony's cloth and hotel enterprises, as customers in the Society's businesses, and, increasingly, as tourists.[85] The pressures to acculturate and the dangers of being seduced away from the community's beliefs and practices were also present. Many of those who "defected" did so because they did not feel the spiritual bonds of the community as strongly as they did the economic and personal lure of independence in the American society surrounding them. Such considerations motivated women as well as men. For example, Marie Burgy, born in Switzerland, had immigrated as a child with her family to the colony in Ebenezer, New York. After leaving school at the usual age of fourteen, she worked in an Amana community kitchen and at the age of twenty became its overseer, a job she continued for a time after marrying John Geiger. Eventually, however, the Geigers, "being of a more progressive nature," left Amana because they were not content with the "bare living" the colony offered them for their work. After years of hard work and "united effort," the Geigers bought their own 160 acres of prairie five miles south of South Amana.[86]

Charles Nordhoff, who visited Amana within a few decades of its settlement, believed that the advantages that the Inspirationists saw in their communal life-style—equality among members, security for their families, abundance of food, and independence from a master—were "dearer to the Germans than to almost any other nation." He went on to write:

hence they work more harmoniously in communistic experiments. I think I noticed at Amana, and elsewhere among the German communistic societies, a satisfaction in their lives, a pride in the equality which the communal system secures, and also in the conscious surrender of the individual will to the general good, which is not so clearly and satisfactorily felt among other nationalities. Moreover, the German peasant is fortunate in his tastes, which are frugal and well fitted for community living. He has not a great sense of or desire for beauty of surroundings; he likes substantial living, but cares nothing for elegance. His comforts are not, like the American's, of a costly kind.

I think, too, that his lower passions are more easily regulated or controlled, and certainly he is more easily contented to remain in one place.[87]

The example of the Amana defectors John and Marie Burgy Geiger suggests that the qualities that made German peasants relatively more successful in maintaining communistic communities were also those that led to success as individual family settlers. The choice of life-style for people like the Geigers depended on individual personalities and goals rather than on religious faith. The concrete difference was that the Geigers had to work a great deal harder than the Amanists to attain the "independence from a master" that the colonists found in communal life. Certainly Marie Burgy Geiger had a harder life as an isolated frontier wife than she would have had integrated into the Amana community.[88]

* * *

The nineteenth-century Midwest frontier could boast other utopian communities founded by German-speaking immigrants, although most of them were much shorter-lived and less successful than Amana. What settlements like Vandalia in Illinois or the Swedenborgian Colony in Benton County, Iowa, lacked was the unifying power of either an able and charismatic leader or an all-pervading philosophy or faith.[89] Amana had had both in Christian Metz and the Society of True Inspiration. Communism, however, was not the core of that central faith. It was incidental to the spiritual philosophy of Amana life, less a religious choice than one based on pragmatic economic considerations. For other utopian communities founded by German-speakers in the Midwest, communism was much more central to their philosophical reasons for coming together. Traditionally, communism has implied the equality of all members of society. To see if German-speakers established such truly egalitarian communist societies and how membership in them affected women and families, it is instructive to look at two such communities: Bethel in Missouri, with its Christian communism, and secular Communia in Iowa.

Bethel had both a charismatic leader and the unity of a common faith, which its residents sought to actualize through a form of Christian communism. Leadership and faith were centered in the person of "Dr." Wilhelm Keil, a breakaway Methodist minister who founded his own sect. From 1844 until Keil moved to Aurora, Oregon, in 1854 and subsequently drew away about 400 of the 650 persons gathered in Bethel, the colony enjoyed great prospects. Even after Keil's departure, Bethel continued to exist, albeit in a somewhat desultory fashion, a testimony to the power of Keil's leadership. It was not legally dissolved until 1881, three years after its founder's death.[90]

We know little about women's lives in Bethel. Written accounts say that Keil was such a powerful preacher that women would be carried away by his words and, "in a peculiar hypnotic state," would cry out, "Thou art Christ" (*Du bist Christus*).[91] At least one was so convinced of Keil's near-divinity (he was said to have supernatural powers) that she refused to marry John Roebling, the future builder of the Brooklyn Bridge, when he would not leave Pennsylvania to settle with her family in Bethel.[92] We do know that Keil extended his influence outside of the church and also exercised close control over his followers' daily lives. He discouraged contact with almost all printed material except the Bible and instituted the confession to him of intimate "sins," usually of a sexual nature. On at least one occasion, the perpetrators of such sins were forced to acknowledge their acts during a church service. Although this sort of control seems onerous to most modern American sensibilities, it might have given the colonists a sense of direction and clarity in moral issues. Unfortunately, we have no personal written testimony from women (or men) to document how they reacted to life under Keil's leadership.[93]

Most of the residents in Bethel were from German and Pennsylvania Dutch working and farming classes, although a few well-off families had contributed a good share of the original capital of $30,802.75 with which Keil and his followers bought about 4,000 acres in northeast Missouri. In some ways, Bethel operated in a truly communistic fashion. All property and monies were held in common, most field and factory work was done communally, and people received their clothing and some of their food staples from common stores. In other ways, however, particularly on the personal level, they lived rather conventional and individualistic lives. The domestic sphere was almost untouched by Bethel's version of communism. Women did not dress alike, as they did in Amana to demonstrate the equality of all (and to discourage vanity), but were free to choose the fabric and colors for their dresses and those of their family.[94] Everyone, with the exception of young single men, lived in individual family houses. The community gave each family enough cows for milk and butter and pigs for meat, and each had a garden plot to raise the other necessary foodstuffs. As was true in the outside world, processing dairy products and caring for small animals and the garden were part of women's work. It is interesting that the economic structure at Bethel recognized implicitly what was less commonly acknowledged in nineteenth-century society at large: the importance of women's labor in the home for family maintenance. Each family had to trade extra domestic products at the community store to obtain items they could not raise or produce themselves.[95]

In most ways, however, the economic structures at Bethel indicated that nineteenth-century women, even in a communistic society, had a subordinate position. Until women married and had children, they worked in community enterprises, for example, in the glove factory, and in other ways did their part. For their contributions to the common good, women members, like men, were entitled to support under the "Rules of the Christian Community," adopted in 1844 at Bethel. These rules, however, also established the lesser value attached to women's contributions. Number 4 dealt with the compensation due members who decided to leave the community. It granted single women eighteen years or older three-fifths ($12) of the amount of compensation for each year of service to the community given single men ($20).[96] When the community was dissolved, women received half of the compensation per year of service that men did ($3.88 versus $7.76) and half of the amount each man received from the sale of the church ($0.56 versus $1.12 per year of service).[97] Did they feel in any way that this inequity betrayed the principles of communal equality underlying their association? If so, no evidence exists to that effect. Probably they accepted this as the portion due them according to long-established patterns.

In addition to the unity that utopian societies gained through a charismatic leader or a common set of beliefs, a certain critical mass was probably also an important factor in determining whether they would survive. Like the German Swedenborgian Colony located north of Amana, Communia of Clayton County in northeast Iowa had only a shared philosophy and was quite small. Thirteen men signed the articles of association of "Community Colony, Clayton County" on 31 July 1850. Three years later, the constitution was filed, with the name of the association changed to "Communia Workingmen's League, Clayton County, Iowa." Within two years, the communal farming and associated industrial enterprises had failed, and the corporation was finally dissolved in 1864.[98]

Communia had its roots in the Fourierite movement of the early nineteenth century. Heinrich Koch, a Dreißiger and the publisher of the same anticleric newspaper in St. Louis that had criticized the newly arrived Saxon Old Lutherans, founded the original settlement in 1847. In 1846, Koch had mustered one of the first Missouri volunteer companies in the Mexican War from among St. Louis German immigrants. Several of the volunteers were former members of New Helvetia, a failed socialist utopian settlement of poor Swiss and German peasant and artisan immigrants near Westphalia in Osage County in central Missouri. Andreas Dietsch, an Alsacian, had led the New Helvetians to Westphalia, where they bought 363 acres of land from Jette Bruns's husband in September 1844, with the intention of establishing a self-sufficient agricultural society based on the Golden Rule. Dietsch's untimely death resulted in the group's dissolution within two years of its establishment. But the communist convictions of the core group of New Helvetians, along with Koch's influence and the incentive of land warrants for Mexican War veterans, led to the attempt to found another colony, this time in Iowa.[99]

Although Koch broke off his association with Communia in 1849, the colonists continued their efforts to achieve the agrarian utopia that Dietsch had envisioned. By 1850, after the signing of the articles of association, the colony owned more than a thousand acres of land and a sizable quantity of livestock and had built a large two-story frame house containing five apartments for families and a communal dining hall and kitchen. A year later, the value of the colony was reported at $6,500, with only $500 in outstanding debts.[100] The future of the colony seemed secure; however, Communia's course took a fateful turn in late 1850, when it came under the influence of the radical labor reformer Wilhelm Weitling, an old friend of Dietsch. Expelled from Switzerland, Weitling had founded the Workingmen's League (Arbeiterbund) in New York City, which in 1850 decided to foster colonies.[101] At first, it seemed that Communia might have found support from the outside world and the charismatic leader it needed. Weitling, however, proved to be dictatorial and mean-spirited in his methods and vacillating in his vision. He subverted the democratic processes of the colony, thus losing the trust of the members and contributing to its financial entanglements, and introduced capitalistic elements into Communia's economic structure. By 1855, dissension and financial pressures had split the colony into two camps, those wanting to continue the association and those who had come to believe this was no longer possible.

We learn something about what Communia's brief and turbulent history meant for the families involved in it through the Venus family. One of the leaders of the faction seeking the colony's final dissolution was Joseph Venus, who was also one of its founding members. A friend of Dietsch and seminarian-turned-blacksmith, Venus had been prominent in the early days of Communia, conveying about 840 acres to the Communia Colony in 1850 (part of this no doubt as an agent for other members) and acting as president of the colony during the time the articles of association were written. He continued his involvement in the colony, at first, it seems, supporting Weitling's efforts to integrate Communia into the Workingmen's League but in late 1854 acting as the colony administrator supporting dissolution.[102]

Correspondence received and sent by the Venus family between 1849 and 1874 is the only known personal documentation we have about Communia. With the exception of two letters sent by Joseph's wife, Christine ("Dina"), to her daughter Lina in 1872 and one Lina received from her sister Emma in 1874 after their mother's death, all of the letters were written by people outside of the immediate Venus family. Members of Dina Klein Venus's family wrote seventeen of the thirty-one extant letters. Her sister Katharine ("Käthchen") Klein Hamm from Ste. Genevieve, Missouri, sent thirteen of the seventeen.[103] The letters shed an indirect light on family life at Communia and give us certain insights into the impact of utopian ventures on families. Certainly Joseph Venus's steadfast support of Communia speaks for his socialist convictions. But what did his convictions mean for his wife and family? Did they share them? Or were they peripheral to life in the Venus family? Did Communia continue to exist in an informal, personal way for one of its member families even after it had formally been dissolved and the property divided? We have very little direct evidence with which to answer these questions, but the evidence we do have suggests an interesting contrast to what we know about the impact on women and families of life in longer-lasting utopian communities, such as Amana.

References in the letters to matters raised by Dina Venus tell us what was on her mind as she wrote from Communia. The only mention of the communistic society in the letters addressed to Dina is in a postscript to a letter from Käthchen dated 10 August (probably 1855, judging by the rest of the contents). Dina must have referred to her husband's activities as administrator seeking the colony's dissolution and probably also complained about Weitling's attempts to make good on League claims against its investments in Communia. Käthchen wrote, "We are sorry that you have so much trouble because of Weidling [*sic*], but I think it is better for your future, for none of this communist stuff lasts."

Beyond this, the letters sent to Dina Venus do not mention matters having to do with Communia Colony directly. From some of her family's letters and from one sent to Joseph Venus, however, we find collaboration that association with Communia did not ease the initial stress of immigration or ensure financial success. The earliest letter in the collection, from the New Helvetian Johan Bosshard, refers to difficulties he and Joseph Venus had incurred since emigrating: "It seems as if neither of us left Europe under a favorable star, for good fortune has not smiled warmly on either of us yet. Hard work and deprivations of all sorts have been our lot thus far" (30 August 1849). In time, and with the dissolution of the colony and the sale of its property to the members, things began to look up for the Venuses, at least in economic terms. The 1850 manuscript census of Volga Township in Clayton County lists Joseph Venus as heading a household of five men with real estate valued at $1,500.[104] Five years after the dissolution of the colony, the 1860 census lists the Joseph Venus household as consisting of his wife Dina, her daughter Marie (born in Germany in 1849), and six Venus children born in Iowa. The family valued their real estate at $1,200 and their personal property at $200. Among the German-born residents of Volga Township, the Venuses and the family of John Enderes, a former Communia member, were second in wealth only to that of another former colonist, Michael Baumann.[105]

The relative prosperity that the Venuses achieved in their first decade in Iowa was not, it seems, accompanied by complete contentment on Dina's part. We have no letters from the earliest period of the colony (1850–53), when communal life seems to have been strongest. According to Weitling's reports from this period, however, one of the main sources of strife among the colonists was the wives (seven of them in 1852), who then sowed dissent among their husbands.[106] Whether this was an accurate assessment on Weitling's part or whether he found the women's quarrels an easy target for blame is impossible to say. The friction among the women at least points to the difficulties that people living in communal dwelling situations can encounter. It may also point to a certain lack of communal goodwill and communist conviction on the part of the wives. The three wives of the founders Weitling mentioned were probably Dina Venus, Elsa Ponsar, and Barbara Enderes. All of them had infants or toddlers when they came to Communia or soon thereafter.[107] They were responsible for cooking, cleaning, washing, and gardening for the colony, which always included a large number of single men. It is no wonder they found few benefits in communal life and complained to their husbands. It may also be that the community house practice of sharing domestic property, including fine linens and silver, produced resentment and discord among the women. As Lina Venus Liers, born in 1854 in the community house, said many years later, women's dowries, as part of the family property, were also at risk in this venture.[108]

It is unlikely that Dina Venus was a committed communist. She probably did not even know Joseph Venus until shortly before they married. She seems to have immigrated to Missouri with her sister and brother-in-law and their two children sometime in 1849. The Hamms appear in the 1850 manuscript census for St. Louis. In the same census, a Christine Klein, twenty-eight years of age, from Darmstadt, Hesse, is listed as living in the household of the widower Oswald Benckendorf, evidently as housekeeper and nanny for his two young children. The year and place of birth are the same as Christine Klein Venus's. Her marriage to Venus must have occurred late in 1850 or early in 1851 (their oldest daughter Emma was born in 1851). Christine's daughter Marie, listed in the 1860 Clayton County, Iowa, manuscript census as born in Germany in 1849, does not appear in the 1850 Missouri manuscript census. Either the census taker missed Marie, or one of Marie's relatives brought her to America after Dina Venus's marriage. The fact that Marie was born several years after Joseph Venus immigrated to America speaks against her being Venus's child, as do various indications in Dina's correspondence that her family did not know her husband. For example, Käthchen Hamm uses the formal *Sie* form of address with Joseph Venus in a letter of 23 July 1862. Since she was Marie's godmother, she probably would have known Marie's father. It is tempting to speculate that the ex-seminarian and utopian activist Joseph Venus saw in marriage to Dina Klein a way to demonstrate his progressive thinking while gaining a wife to contribute women's labor to the new Communia settlement. For her part, Dina might have been willing to enter into this unusual venture to gain security for herself and legitimacy for her baby.[109]

During the early years at Communia, Dina Venus seems to have communicated to her sister how lonely she was for her parents and siblings and her feelings of being burdened by her work and her many children. In her responses, Käthchen Hamm lectured her on the need to have patience with her lot and to be grateful for the blessings and future assistance children brought. Käthchen wrote these sentiments after Communia's dissolution, just before and after thirty-seven-year-old Dina delivered her seventh child (letters of 21 December 1858 and 31 May 1859). Census records indicate that a few German-speaking women in the Venus neighborhood had domestic help during the 1860s and 1870s, but Dina does not seem to have been one of them. Käthchen wrote that, much as she would like to see Marie, the ten-year-old should stay at home and help her mother instead of taking a trip to Ste. Genevieve. Without the support of a communal division of women's labor or adult women relatives close at hand, Dina Venus had only her small female children to help her in what must have been at times overwhelming work. This hard labor, combined with frequent childbirth, probably contributed to her early death, at the age of fifty-two.

Although his wife did not have hired help, Joseph Venus seems to have had a hired man. Henry Pape, a wagon maker, was listed in the censuses of 1860 and 1870 as a resident in the Venus household. Pape was one of the four men who shared a house with Joseph Venus in 1850 and was also one of the signers of the 1850 and 1853 documents. He lived with the Venuses at least until 1870, when he was sixty-three years old.[110] By this time, the only surviving Venus son, Louis, was seventeen and probably able to take on a man's full share of work. We cannot know the type of relationship Pape had with the Venus family, but it was likely based on the brotherly ties formed during the two men's communal experiences.[111] Whether Dina Venus and her children had warm feelings for Pape is a question we cannot answer. His presence might have lessened the need for Dina to help her husband with field work, although we know that her daughters did do that kind of labor in later years (letter of 26 June 1872).

Besides Joseph Venus and Henry Pape, other members of the Communia Colony also remained in Volga Township. Like the Venuses, several bought communal land and buildings when the colony was dissolved. As far as we know, Dina Venus's letters to her relatives did not speak of these people, who must have figured large in her family's life. Instead, she used her letters to keep alive the ties to her parents and siblings. She wrote about her children and relatives and about her own and her sister's problems. She asked Käthchen for recipes and for a description of the death and funeral of Käthchen's infant daughter. It might have been because of insufficient schooling at Communia that Dina thought seriously about sending Marie to attend a school run by Catholic nuns in Ste. Genevieve (letters of 1 October 1854 and 10 August [1855]).[112] Or perhaps she felt it would be better for Marie to grow up with her godparents rather than in the home of her stepfather, in a neighborhood that knew of her illegitimacy. The letters Dina Venus received give us the impression that her emotional life remained strongly linked to her Old World family. Yet this indirect, one-sided evidence is only part of the story.

We have hints of the rest of Dina Venus's story in the only letters we have from her: two that she wrote in 1872 (15 May and 26 June) to her third daughter, Lina, who might have been the only Venus to make the trip to Ste. Genevieve. These indicate that Dina Venus came to feel at home in Clayton County, in spite of the hard life she had had when her children were small. In her letters, she expresses a lively interest in neighborhood and area events, speculating, for example, on why a young girl had run away from her place of employment and remarking on the large number of railroad workers in the little German settlement of St. Johann. Her letters also contain indications that some of the old colony connections endured as neighborly ties. Her children socialized with the children of at least two other Communia founding families, the Baumanns and the Kopps. The second generation thus inherited the old colony associations.

The Venus letters and the manuscript censuses indicate that Communia Colony became the core of a predominately German-speaking rural neighborhood. The letters Dina Venus wrote and three extant letters her daughter Lina (Caroline) received give the impression that all of their family associations were with German-speakers. Unlike the Hamms in Ste. Genevieve, who were speaking and reading almost exclusively in English just a few years after moving there (letter of 10 August [1855]), the Venuses retained the use of German as their primary language. The Venus children evidently spoke and wrote German in the family and in many of their other social contacts. On 26 June 1872, Dina reminded Lina to write the schoolteacher in English to thank him for the loan of a suitcase for her trip to Ste. Genevieve. A friend also wrote to Lina in German in 1872. Two years later, when Emma wrote to Lina from Clayton to ask her sister to send their mother's picture so copies could be painted from it, she wrote in German (19 November 1874).

Statistical evidence confirms the strength of the German-American community in Volga Township. In 1850, German-speaking immigrants headed only 4 (8.5 percent) of the 47 households in the township, while nonimmigrants headed 85.1 percent. Ten years later, the proportions had already changed dramatically. In 1860, German-speakers headed 50 (59.5 percent) of the 84 households, while only 11 American-born heads of households (13.1 percent) were listed. In 1880, the percentage of first- and second-generation farming households of German-speakers had increased to 72.5 percent (129 out of 178). The percentage of Anglo-American farm families had declined to only 6.7 percent (12 of 178).[113]

Although Communia did not succeed as the workers' cooperative Weitling and the Workingmen's League envisioned, it does seem to have maintained a kind of informal, shadow existence in the German-speaking neighborhood that developed around it. Some of the founding members became prosperous farmers in the community, who continued to associate with each other and transmitted certain aspects of their Germanic culture. A German-language church was not one of the central institutions of communal life here. An interview with Lina Venus Liers years later indicates the role women could play in the spiritual life of their families, even in secular Communia. She reported that the colony children were "taught the religious beliefs of their mothers" and that Catholics and Lutherans lived "in perfect harmony." Lina did not attend a church until she was thirteen, the age for confirmation in the German tradition.[114] The essentially secular nature of the colony might have been the basis for the *Turnverein* founded at Communia in 1883. Although small in terms of membership, this organization no doubt supported the members' Germanic identification into the twentieth century.[115]

From the evidence we have, it seems that the failed secular communist colony at Communia did not provide the women associated with it the benefits of cooperation in their domestic duties that women enjoyed in Amana. Women in Bethel also do not seem to have engaged in cooperative domestic labor as part of communal life there. Participation in the communist groups at Bethel and Communia had little effect on the outer contours of family life or on the domestic activities of women. By giving local residents a sense of separate identity and by drawing other German-speakers into their vicinity, however, Bethel and Communia probably contributed to the retention of cultural qualities and in that respect shielded the immigrants and their children from the immediate, stressful pressures from Anglo-American society.[116] This was especially true of rural Communia, because Bethel was integrated more closely into the dominant surrounding economic sphere early on.

The relative lack of success of both ventures in communistic living probably was not an important factor in the small impact they seem to have had on traditional nineteenth-century life for women and families. Neither community made or sought changes in gender relations or in the basic structure and dynamics of the family. Nor did their respective styles of communal life and the practices associated with them do much to make immigrant and frontier life easier for women. Certainly neither Bethel nor Communia established traditions granting or seeking greater social, economic, or political equality for women. In this respect, too, we may see essentially Germanic qualities of cultural conservatism in both communities.

*   *   *

Religious orders had traditionally offered women an alternative to marriage for leading meaningful lives and achieving self-fulfillment. They had also given women the opportunity to gain some independence from male hierarchical structures and to support each other in nondomestic areas of life. The American frontier was a natural place for religious congregations to continue these activities. It also offered the potential for an expansion of their activities and for greater individual and communal realization. The Midwest, with its large number of German-speaking immigrants, had obvious needs in education, health care, and spiritual life with which religious women could help. In the eyes of the American Catholic church, rural areas populated by Catholic immigrants were in particular danger of being lost to the many American Protestant sects, so the church called upon nuns to establish schools there. Life in America was quite different from that in Europe, though. Its stresses put into relief the strengths but also the cracks in the seams of communal religious life. The experiences of two groups of Catholic nuns in the rural Midwest, relatively well-documented in letters and chronicles, testify to the impact of immigration on their individual and communal lives and offer interesting contrasts to the experiences of women in families.[117]

The call for German-speaking religious women to meet the educational needs of immigrants on the rural Midwest frontier coincided with political pressures from the anti-Catholic *Kulturkampf* in Germany and Switzerland in the 1870s. In response, two groups of religious women established foundations in the midwestern states studied here: the Adorers of the Most Precious Blood from Gurtweil in Baden and the Benedictine Sisters of Perpetual Adoration from the Maria Rickenbach Convent in Switzerland. Both communities established themselves with small numbers at first: the Adorers with nine sisters at Belle Prairie in Hamilton County, Illinois, in 1870; the Benedictines with five at Maryville in Nodaway County, Missouri, in 1874. The early history of both foundations shows certain similarities in the privations and difficulties they faced.

The Adorers of the Most Precious Blood traveled the last fifty miles of their journey from Europe to Illinois in farm wagons provided by the Belle Prairie parishioners of the St. John Church. They had been relieved not to find blacks among the farmers who met their boat in Shawneeville, but they found little else to console them about the February landscape through which they were traveling:

The new world had not made a good impression on the sisters from the start in its wintry condition: it looked cold, dirty, bare. They also saw huts with holes instead of windows on this trip, where in general the first unpleasant impressions were awakened again and again, for they were going ever deeper into the bush and bare prairie. . . . At the time of their arrival, the surroundings looked bare and sterile; the forest, which could be seen a short distance away, lent the entirety an almost wild, primitive appearance.

. . . the first impressions are usually the most lasting, and the Fatherland left behind, compared to the uncultivated regions we passed through, seemed a blooming garden.[118]

Upon arriving in their rural parish, the sisters found a new two-story frame house awaiting them with five beds, a stove, and a table with two chairs. The parishioners, Badeners from the Pforzheim district, provided them with the necessities from their own scanty provisions, and the resident priest did what he could as well. They soon opened a school, took charge of the church sacristy and music, and set about settling into their new home.

One of the first adjustments the Adorers had to make was to get special permission from the bishop to teach boys, for that had been forbidden in their order in Germany. In this, as in so many other things, "America was different."[119] The bishop immediately pressured the teachers among them to learn English, so he could send some of them to other parishes to teach. The Adorers also suffered from a lack of spiritual sustenance. They saw four priests come and go in the first months of residence, and they sometimes had to go for weeks without the support of the sacraments.

Aside from the distress these changes caused in their spiritual life, most of the adjustments the German nuns faced in the first months were the same as those faced by other German-speaking immigrants in the rural Midwest. They suffered from the barrenness and poverty of their surroundings, the hard work of setting up a household and planting a garden, field work (cutting rye and plowing fields) in the Midwest summer heat and humidity, and malaria. It is no wonder that "many of the Sisters felt very discouraged and were sorry to have left their homeland."[120]

Some of the nuns repeated this early pioneer period only a few years later because of a split in the community. A year after the Adorers arrived in Illinois, they expanded their numbers with twelve more volunteers from the Gurtweil convent, including Mother Augusta Volk. This very capable leader objected to the restrictions the Illinois bish-

op put on the convent and began negotiations with Vicar General
Henry Muehlsiepen of St. Louis to establish a motherhouse in
O'Fallon, Missouri. When the German state dissolved the Gurtweil
convent and its missions two years later, in May 1873, Mother Augusta
Volk "decided to travel to Germany and encourage the sisters to come
to America, since she could guarantee them complete certainty of existence and a wide field of work."[121] Forty-eight of the Gurtweil sisters immigrated to Illinois in August of that year. By this time, the
Adorers had a sizable number of teaching assignments in German-
speaking and Anglo-American parishes in Illinois and Missouri. In July
of 1875, however, the group split in two over the consequences of the
establishment of the motherhouse in O'Fallon. Because of an early
agreement with the bishop in Alton, a move to the St. Louis diocese
would mean severing the community's ties with their order's headquar-
ters in Rome, which some of the nuns did not want. Most of the group
went on to found the order of the Sisters of the Adoration of the Most
Precious Blood in O'Fallon, Missouri, while eighteen sisters, novices,
and candidates stayed in Illinois with the Novitiate Mother Clementine Zerr. This small group endured the harshest conditions because
of its extreme poverty.

The Adorer convent archives in Illinois contain a lengthy description of the daily life of the sisters who remained at Belle Prairie and
who, a year later, moved to Ruma, Illinois, where the bishop had arranged their purchase of a former boys' college. The nuns' poverty was
so dire that in the winter of 1876–77 several priests in the neighborhood bet a keg of beer among themselves that the sisters would give
up and leave Ruma by the following March. The convent chronicle
states that this made the sisters even more determined to stick it out.
Their mutual support of each other and the structure and doctrine of
their communal life no doubt aided them in this. As the chronicle
emphasizes, their skimpy diet, makeshift shoes and clothing, and hard
labor were made bearable by their acceptance of it all as a sacrifice to
Christ and as a way of life in accord with their vows of poverty and
obedience. The narrative does not exclude testimony about how difficult this was, especially for the young immigrant novitiates, on whose
shoulders much of the hard physical labor fell.[122] Cheerful good humor also marks the text, however, as when the narrator relates the
difficulty the sisters had keeping their homemade corn-husk slippers
and wooden working clogs on their feet and how their skimpy skirts,
made from half of the normal amount of material, forced dainty, lady-
like steps upon them.[123]

One of the first immigrant sisters wrote the Ruma chronicle around

1912. By this time, the Adorers' foundation was flourishing, count-
ing 275 professed sisters and about 60 novices active in schools, hospitals, daughter convents, and missions in Illinois, Iowa, Missouri, and
Kansas.[124] From such a vantage point, the chronicler could view the
difficulties of the early days indulgently.

The immediate pain and stress the difficulties of frontier life caused
religious women are much more apparent in the extant letters written
by the Benedictine Sisters of Perpetual Adoration. The five Swiss sisters who arrived at Maryville in Nodaway County, Missouri, on 5 September 1874 came to help the missionary efforts of the Swiss Engelberg Benedictine Abbey, which had been instrumental in the founding
of their own home convent, the Maria Rickenbach Convent in Lucerne
Canton. We owe the completeness of the record of this immigrant
foundation to the reports the sisters and the mission priests wrote to
their superiors at Maria Rickenbach and Engelberg, who remained their
spiritual advisers and in charge of the missions for several years after
immigration.[125]

In Maryville, the sisters found themselves confronting a multitude
of new and difficult situations. Their lodgings consisted of two small
windowless rooms above a rickety rectory near the dilapidated church,
a half-mile out of town. Snow sifted through the roof and walls in that
first winter. On one occasion the following spring, the wind rocked
the rectory to such a degree that the women had to go to a neighbor's house for the night. They found the extremes of temperature in
the Great Plains autumn distressing and the landscape seemed barren,
especially compared with the mountains surrounding the Maria Rickenbach Convent.[126]

The unaccustomed hard work they had to do compounded the Swiss
sisters' homesickness. None of them was a trained cook, and some of
the first irritations and conflicts, which became increasingly frequent,
had to do with the allocation of these and other housekeeping duties
that took time away from their study of English and their teaching
preparations. The sisters also had not expected to have to assist the two
Benedictine priests as much as turned out to be the case. In addition
to teaching and taking care of their own household needs, they cooked,
cleaned, sewed, and washed for the priests, cleaned the church, provided the music and acted as acolytes at the services, and even took
care of the priests' horses. Mother Anselma Felber's first letter stated,
"They are here expecting more of us than I thought." A month later,
she wrote, "We have more work here than we can manage." At the
end of December, she described the work involved in preparing priz-
es for a fund-raising lottery for Father Adelhelm Obermatt's Maryville

church and concluded, "The Sisters don't get anything for it and we could use our time much better." A few weeks later she added a marginal note to the Maria Rickenbach mother superior: "We give to Father Adelhelm more work than the 60 Sisters in Maria Rickenbach to their confessor."[127]

This continuing and unaccustomed labor took its toll on the individual women. Sister Scholastica von Matt wrote a month after her arrival in Maryville, "I am so tired in the evening that I don't want to either stand or kneel to pray." Father Adelhelm reported that Sister Augustina Kuendig, a teacher with household duties in the rectory and also in charge of the church choir and the priests' two horses, was "severely tested—temptations to commit suicide, to run away, so that she can hardly stand it." Although the demands on their energies were somewhat different, the Benedictine nuns certainly experienced the physical stresses of frontier conditions that women in families often faced. The additional strain placed on these professional women by the men in their lives prompted a comment from Mother Anselma that also had its parallels in the gender relations in family life: "I often thought in Maria Rickenbach—and I am thinking it yet—the good Fathers have no idea how much work a household demands."[128]

Like the Adorers in Illinois, the founding Benedictine nuns felt the lack of the full spiritual life to which they were accustomed. The mission priests, who had to care for several parishes, gave them communion only three or four times a week, telling Mother Anselma, "It is not customary in this country to receive more often."[129] Mother Anselma's letters often bemoaned the impossibility of fulfilling the spiritual goal of the sisters' mission, the institution of the perpetual adoration of the Eucharist in America, because of their small numbers and the many demands on their time.

The needs of a frontier church and the lack of financial support in America forced such religious communities as the Benedictines, whose primary emphasis in Europe had been contemplative, to lead active and financially remunerative lives. Mother Anselma did what she could to maintain her order's spiritual life by resisting pressure from the local bishop and the missionary priests to take on more schools, something Father Frowin Conrad, the prior at the Conception Abbey and the sisters' spiritual and practical director in America, still complained about in 1879. She herself was deeply unhappy because she was unable to devote as much time to prayer and contemplation as she had in Switzerland. At one point, she feared Father Frowin would deprive the nuns of Holy Communion if he learned of strife between her and another sister: "and what can I do yet if this is taken away from me? Languish?

I am now already languishing under the pressure from within and from without." She was not like Mother Clementine of the Ruma Adorers, who accommodated her own attraction for the interior life by occupying herself with spinning whenever possible.[130]

The Benedictines' unceasing labor, along with their attempts to learn English and begin their teaching mission, no doubt exacerbated the personal tensions among the first five immigrant nuns. It is also possible that these five women were not particularly well-suited to their mission in America. Mother Anselma expressed her concern to Father Adelhelm that the sisters accompanying her had been selected not because they would be best able to carry out the mission but because they would be least missed at Maria Rickenbach. There are indications in the letters of this having been the case. Sister Beatrice Renggli was "sickly and weak" most of the time, "as at Maria Rickenbach," only there she had not had to teach every day. Mother Anselma herself had had a consumptive cough for ten years before emigrating, as well as other health problems, all of which persisted in America. According to Mother Anselma, Sister Agnes Dalie had been discontent at Maria Rickenbach and continued to be so in Missouri. Sister Adela Eugster had always had a tendency to oppose her superiors.[131]

Mother Anselma, an expert embroiderer and devoted to a life of prayer and introspection, found it difficult to assume the leadership role necessary for the establishment of the community. The other sisters challenged her authority, and this became even worse after the little community was split between the Maryville rectory and the rural parish at Conception, with its Benedictine monastery and the sisters' new convent. Matters did not improve when three more Maria Rickenbach sisters arrived in Missouri in June of 1876. One of these was Sister Bernardine Wächter, who had had emotional problems at Maria Rickenbach but was sent to be the superior at Maryville. She soon allied herself with the Maryville priest, Father Adelhelm, and wrote to Switzerland complaining about Mother Anselma's attempts to retain the higher authority of the foundation in Conception. For her part, Mother Anselma reported that the Maryville sisters engaged in conversations "for hours" with their confessor (Father Adelhelm) instead of pursuing their duties and taking their recreation quietly on their own. When she confronted Father Adelhelm and Sister Bernardine with her concerns about such behavior and what seemed to her the breakdown in convent discipline and order, they only gave her "good words but afterwards did the contrary."[132]

The intervention and manipulations of the Benedictine priests further complicated the relations between the two groups of nuns. Confusion about to whom the sisters owed their primary allegiance and competition between Father Adelhelm and Father Frowin for authority over the nuns, who represented an important missionary and economic resource, contributed to the growing rancor. In the summer of 1879, two of the Maryville sisters refused to come to Conception to renew their vows. Father Frowin blamed Father Adelhelm: "This schism is his worthless work." The Engelberg prior and Father Frowin forced a temporary patching-up of relations, moving the rebellious sisters, Adela and Bernardine, back to Conception, and Mother Anselma transferred the Maryville teaching sisters from Father Adelhelm's rectory and into a separate house. Eventually, however, they all were worn down by Sister Bernardine's insistence on feeling a divine call to work in Maryville and her continuing unhappiness and depression. Father Frowin anticipated a continuation of the troubles because of the unwillingness of Sister Bernardine and others to practice "humble obedience and quiet resignation." He wrote to Engelberg, "If a community is to prosper, all have to be one heart and soul with the leader. The smallest disharmony, if nourished, engenders factions which generally lead to the death of all spiritual life." His assessment was correct. Soon both Maryville and Conception had established a novitiate and were competing for the loyalties of the young German- and Irish-American women who joined their order.[133] A common purpose and faith, membership in a highly structured group, and the bonds of shared origin were not enough to hold this community together. The Benedictine letters offer valuable testimony to the conflict that religious communities could experience because of personality factors.[134]

In addition to the insights we gain about life in religious communities under the stressful conditions of the frontier and the establishment of new foundations, the Benedictine documents also inform us about the constructive possibilities available to immigrant religious women. On the frontier, personality could play a positive role in this. In 1880, Mother Gertrude Leupi, the founder of Maria Rickenbach, arrived in Missouri. This extraordinary woman brought seven nuns with her to America after being pressured to step down as the superior at the Swiss motherhouse. She set herself up as the superior in Maryville and rival to Mother Anselma at Conception, but in 1881 she made a mission at the Standing Rock Reservation in Dakota Territory. She then transferred the Maryville community to Mariazell at Vermillion in 1886 and finally to its new motherhouse in Yankton in 1887, where she officiated as superior until 1891. Upon her return to Switzerland, Mother Gertrude was inspired to purchase and restore her ancestral home at Wikon to found a school for girls, Marienburg, for the purpose of recruiting nuns for America.[135] Mother Gertrude's career in America illustrates the opportunities available to nineteenth-century religious women for personal and spiritual self-realization. They could capitalize on the needs of American society to expand their own fields of activity while advancing the cause of their community and their church.[136]

Members of religious communities were also individuals, as the Benedictine documents prove. As such, they were subject to the same pain of separation from family and homeland that secular immigrant women experienced. But having left the world behind, and with it their families, when they entered the convent, it was considered inappropriate or even sinful to allow family ties to interfere with what was considered primarily a spiritual decision to emigrate. There are, however, a few hints that such ties could play a role in emigration and adaptation to America. Adorer Sister Charlotte Zeller accompanied Mother Clementine on a recruiting trip in the spring of 1876 and then "was so ignoble as to remain in Germany, after Honorable Mother had granted her a longer stay there because of family matters." Several months after her immigration, Benedictine Sister Bernardine Wächter wrote that her mother was well again, having reconciled herself to her daughter's going to America.[137]

Family ties sometimes were maintained in America, although these could be the source of pain rather than support, just as in the world outside the convent walls. An example is the two sets of sisters separated by the split between O'Fallon and Ruma. The Ruma chronicle states that the older women, "sent by Sister Augusta . . . to bring back forcefully their blood sisters" to O'Fallon, "had to return home without accomplishing their mission in spite of their importunity which almost reached the point of violence."[138]

A happier example of family ties from the Ruma community is the Meier family. In 1877, Wilhelm Franz Meier, the brother of Sister Anna, came to work as a hired hand for the nuns. He worked free for the first two years and generally dedicated his life to assisting them. In 1891, he became the tenant of a farm they bought adjoining their convent. Five years before this, in 1886, his widowed mother, Mrs. Anton Meier, and his youngest sister, who subsequently joined the Adorers as Sister Frances, had joined Sister Anna and him in Illinois. Without charging anything, Mrs. Meier managed the house and farm that the congregation bought in the fall of 1886. The year before her mother and sister joined her in Illinois, Sister Anna Meier made a four-week trip to Germany, returning in November with two postulants and a younger brother, Otto, who celebrated his first mass in the convent chapel five years later.[139] The Meier family's experience might not have been common, but it does show that family ties could become intertwined with religious communal ties to strengthen the bonds of the group.

Besides serving as a link of shared experience, what role did ethnicity play in the lives of these German-speaking religious women? The structure and nature of their communities continued European traditions, traditions having sacred significance to these immigrants. The unwillingness of the Ruma Adorers to break with their general motherhouse in Rome and Mother Anselma's stubborn insistence on establishing a perpetual adoration of the Eucharist instead of dedicating more sisters to teaching are evidence of the strength of this self-identification. Although both foundations accepted English-speaking candidates from the beginning, many of their American-born candidates were the daughters of German-speaking immigrants. They also continued to use German in their communal lives well into the twentieth century, encouraging English-speakers who joined them to learn German.[140] Both orders also actively recruited new members in Europe. Mother Clementine Zerr and other Adorers traveled to Germany at least seven times between 1875 and 1910 to recruit postulants and solicit funds for the Ruma convent and its missionary work.[141] The "German connection" persisted strongly enough among the Benedictine sisters at Conception that in 1922 and 1923 Sister M. Bernard Willmann was successful in bringing back over forty candidates, most of whom professed vows with her order. Such activity is a variation of chain immigration. Like the secular communities discussed in this chapter, these family-like groups of women drew other members of their religious order to America after them or were successful in appealing to women with shared beliefs and purpose, as well as shared cultural heritage, to join them.

The retention of German as the community language must have been a comfort to those immigrant sisters who were forced to learn English quickly to establish schools for American Catholic children. In this respect, religious women immigrants certainly had things harder than most rural farm women, who often did not have to come into regular contact with English-speakers, much less function professionally in the foreign language. Mother Anselma Felber's letters offer poignant proof of the pain this necessity could cause. In her first letter from America, she wrote, "Please pray that God may loose my tongue and let me hear right." A month later she asked for prayers "that the Holy Ghost may come and teach us the English language." By the end of March of 1875, she concluded, "Without a miracle I shall never know English." She added that it was not so important for her, since she needed it only to instruct English-speaking novices. The next month, however, she reported that Father Adelhelm had insisted that she learn English and was working with her an hour a day to accomplish this. She must not have progressed very well with the language. In November of 1875, she wrote that the Americans thought she and Sister Agnes were not very bright because they still had not learned English. A year later, she said that she had been instructing five candidates in English ("which is very hard for me") and was still trying to learn the language. This was so onerous for her that she declared she would prefer only German-speaking novices, because having English-speakers was twice the work. Soon after this she sighed, "If there only would be an end to this—at least in heaven!"[142]

The sisters' work in American society meant that they could not isolate themselves within their community. I have already discussed the ways in which the demands of their mission contributed to inner-group conflict and the splitting of both the Adorer and Benedictine foundations into separate groups. At the same time, their ethnic identification could express itself as criticism of the dominant society around them. As immediate and personal expressions of opinion, the letters of the Benedictine sisters offer examples of this. Like many other German-speaking immigrants, Mother Anselma found American goods and housing far below German standards. "The stockings are poor; it seems they are made from cotton and paper," and in general, "America appears to be put together from tinsel." American values were materialistic and superficial, tied to transitory things: "So it is here usually: luxury in dresses and food, but the housing and furniture are poor. I think as to morality, this country must be like South America, a little better perhaps. The average American lives for one thing only: money is his god." Mother Anselma also expressed the belief that American girls probably could not stand a novitiate, for they only liked making visits and had "no mind for work." Later the same year she reiterated that opinion, citing the behavior of the Indiana Benedictine sister who was instructing them in English. Several years later, Mother Gertrude wrote much the same thing, saying that the young American women were mostly flighty in spirit and "therefore it is desirable to bring in genuine Swiss blood." A certain ethnic bias speaks in such statements. It is hard to know how much it might have affected communal life in German- or Swiss-founded communities. On the one hand, it might have served to strengthen communal bonds to some extent, at least among the German-speakers. On the other hand, to the extent that these sentiments might have been communicated to English-speaking members, they could have been a source of discord. No doubt prejudices against the American-born diminished as the immigrant sisters became more acculturated to America and as their communities became less heavily dominated by the foreign-born.[143]

These communities of nuns differed from the other special groups discussed in this chapter in one significant way: men were not integral members. What did this mean for their immigrant experiences? The absence of men, along with the sisters' lack of funds, meant the hard physical work associated with frontier conditions fell to them. The experiences of the Ruma Adorers illustrate this particularly well. In Conception, too, for example, Sister Agnes Dalie built the chicken coops for the new convent. The presence of priests as confessors did not necessarily lighten their labor and might even have added to it, as was the case with the Benedictine sisters in Maryville. The Ruma chronicle praises Father J. B. Neuhaus, parish priest and the convent confessor until his death in 1905, for his support of the fledgling community. Yet even he receives a bit of gentle criticism for supervising but not helping the sisters cut and gather wood in their first hard winters in Illinois.[144] Certainly, these religious women were not free of men's influence and domination. The American church hierarchy, as well as European ecclesiastical traditions, ensured that. The interaction of the Ruma Adorers and the Missouri Benedictines with bishops, monks, and priests shows that men continued to exert a good deal of control over nuns' lives and work. If anything, immigrant nuns might have lost some of their traditional power and independence when they left their European mother convents and exposed themselves to the demands and expectations of a church that had to function in an emphatically secular society.

The preceding discussion shows that the frontier experiences of immigrant religious women depended on their outer circumstances and individual differences, much as was the case with secular women. The leadership of the group, their own personalities, individual frictions and ambitions, the manipulations of tensions by outsiders, and stress because of the demands of the American church hierarchy affected the extent of the support they derived from communal life. Although the American religious hierarchy initially called them to establish schools and convents to serve rural German-dominated areas, it soon demanded that they also provide services to English-speakers and that they adapt their way of life to the needs and customs of the New World. Personal testimony and archival records of foundations of German-speaking nuns in Illinois and Missouri offer vivid proof of the pain and turmoil the forced acceleration of cultural adaptation caused both individuals and groups.

Roman Catholic immigrant nuns experienced certain advantages and disadvantages vis-à-vis other German-speaking women. They enjoyed a certain self-assurance about their identity as upholders of true religious practices. But, unlike the Old Saxon Lutheran women, for example, they could not connect this with their ethnic identity after their missionary foundations gained permanent status in the American church. Their professional life, while offering them opportunities to serve their faith and their own ambitions in a more direct fashion than was possible to many other women, also required them to adjust to American society much more quickly than other German-speaking women did. At the same time, however, they could shape their group life somewhat independently of the world around them and justify retaining some of its ethnic components because of the historical roots of their community.

* * *

Linguistic and cultural identity as German-speakers was an important part of the self-image of the groups discussed in this chapter. It formed the core of the spatial and cultural isolation of the Germans from Russia and found expression in the connection the Missouri Synod Lutherans made between their ethnicity and their religion. The Amana Inspirationists drew on their religious roots in German Pietism in shaping and governing their American colony, where they also continued certain aspects of a German village life-style. The German-speaking communities in Bethel and Communia grew out of communist utopian impulses with roots in Europe, but they persisted after the end of the utopian experiment because of their cultural and linguistic ties. Even the German-speaking religious women's foundations, forced though they were to confront the alien culture in their daily life and religious work, retained an awareness of their German or Swiss roots and maintained that identity in the relative isolation of their communal walls.

All of these groups resisted assimilation into American society because of common beliefs and life-styles that went beyond ethnic considerations. Sometimes, as was the case with some of the Germans from Russia and the Amanists, they even avoided contact with other German-speakers who did not share these. Such groups exhibited an especially strong retention of cultural differences and practices. In the secular groups, the preservation of traditional gender roles was part of this cultural retention. Teachings and practices within the Missouri Lutheran Synod professed this. It was also evident in the nonegalitarian communism of Bethel and Communia and in the lack of political or social advances for women in these communities. The positive side of this cultural conservatism in gender relations and family life was that it shielded women and the domestic sphere (or religious communal life of nuns) from many stresses and much pressure to change. The private sphere, over which women had dominion, became the core of self-identification for these groups, especially as time passed. Nuns perhaps had a more difficult time than secular women, but they still had the sanctuary of communal life, with its ethnic traditions and elements.

Several of the special groups discussed in this chapter sought support in the practice of organized communal life. This seemingly had real advantages for women only in Amana's sharing of the burdens of domestic life and in the communal sustenance religious women found in their convents. More typically, it made little difference in the day-to-day contours of women's lives, as at Bethel, or could bring disadvantages, as in the additional stress women at Communia experienced through being placed, perhaps unwillingly, in the position of having to share work and domestic resources.

The extent to which members of these groups clung to their ethnic, religious, or philosophical differences intensified their self-identification as strangers in a strange land. Such self-identification was a source of strength for most of them, but it could be a source of stress if, like the Catholic nuns, they could not avoid interacting with American society or if their isolationist impulses ended in a failure in communal life, as happened at Communia. Certainly, particular women in each of these groups had experiences that differed in varying degrees from the "norms" for each. In general, however, rural German-speaking women were likely to have been sheltered from cultural alienation by their membership in special groups. Such links were another network of support to them and their families that insulated them from the need to change their ideas and their way of life abruptly. Instead, they could draw on communal strategies for dealing with the inevitable pressures to conform to American expectations. Only members of religious orders, because of their professional activities, had to abandon or deemphasize their ethnic identity soon after arriving in America. Other women could consolidate their central importance to family, communal, and ethnic life within the safe confines of the home and a likeminded community. Their membership in these and similar immigrant subgroups made their experience as strangers in a strange land more bearable.

5

The Rural German-Speakers and Their Descendants: Reflections on Ethnicity in America

Ordinary lives are the true story of the West for men as well as for women.
—Susan Armitage, "Through Women's Eyes"

It is difficult to generalize about German-speaking women's experiences on the nineteenth-century Midwest frontier, as the preceding chapters have shown. Although we will never be able to reclaim fully the rich variety of these immigrants' lives, this study has given some indication of their diversity. In that diversity, rural German-speaking frontierswomen and their families were just like their neighbors of whatever ancestry. Yet some common patterns have also emerged, patterns that have helped me better understand relationships and conduct in my paternal family: their self-denying frugality, their reticence and aversion to emotional display, an Old World and rural-based separation of gender spheres, and the expression of inner and familial attachment through economic behavior, for example. I can now appreciate both my grandmother's uniqueness and the extent to which the expectations of the culture her parents transferred to America shaped her.

This study has other, less personal implications. By showing that it is inappropriate to approach rural German-speaking women as if they were all cut from the same pattern, I have extended to this group the warnings of some scholars of women's history against the stereotyping of (Anglo-American) western frontierswomen. Susan Armitage has noted the tendency to categorize women as belonging to one of three types: the refined lady ("who is too genteel for the rough and ready West"), the helpmate ("a workworn superwoman" who adapts to the West but loses "all her individuality"), and the fallen woman (who has "glamour and power" but suffers a bad end). The necessary antidote to such a distorted conceptualization of frontierswomen, asserts Armitage, is the examination of many "ordinary" women's experiences.[1] In the process of examining rural German-speaking immigrant women, I came to see clearly that other ethnically based oversimplifications and stereotypes are inadequate for the full understanding of "unremarkable" women. These stereotypes include the homesick frontier foreigner (who bears the extra burden of cultural alienation and linguistic isolation); the meek, self-effacing minister's or Latin farmer's wife (whose bourgeois conditioning and piety prevent her from voicing her unhappiness); the ignorant and browbeaten peasant woman (who serves her husband only as a fertile beast of burden); and the exemplary farmer's wife (who sacrifices all for her family but lacks the emotional warmth and courage to exercise any individuality or influence). Distant in the past though the ordinary lives examined here may be, they are distinct enough to prove that German-speaking women were much too complex to conform completely to any of these immigrant types.

Rejecting such stereotypes should not, however, prevent us from recognizing patterns of similarity in women's lives and experiences. All nineteenth-century women in the frontier Midwest lived in a man's world, but they also had had centuries of female modeling for how to do this as much as possible on their own terms. They not only acquiesced to their lot in life but also usually actively embraced it. To varying degrees, women in all circumstances and of all ancestries were able to exercise power over their own lives and within the dynamics of family and community life. Some final questions remain, however. Can we identify any differences between how rural German-speaking women and Anglo-American frontierswomen did this? If so, can we attribute any such differences to ethnicity? Finally, what influences on American life and culture can we trace to the immigrant women and their families studied here?

*   *   *

In chapters 2 and 3, we saw that after the first shock of a foreign environment, ethnicity proved to be a significant burden primarily to those families and individuals who lived isolated from other German-speakers and were in frequent, close contact with the dominant culture. Older women, women with small children, and women who lacked the support of female family members were especially susceptible to cultural alienation. In general, immigrants might have been at some disadvantage while they learned to deal with new situations on the American frontier, but this was minor and short-lived. Germans from Russia who came to the Great Plains armed with experience in living in a similarly difficult environment did not even have to adjust to the living and working conditions, geography, and weather of the Midwest frontier.[2]

Certain ethnic/cultural qualities common to most German-speakers were an advantage in rural frontier conditions. Woman's traditional subordination to family goals was an asset in a situation where her childbearing, domestic work, and self-sacrifice could help ensure a financially secure and improved future for herself and her children. The hard work in the house, garden, barnyard, and field that was expected of rural women helped families attain that goal and, given the possibility of family advancement, was not considered onerous. German-speaking women and their daughters were more fully engaged in all aspects of American farm labor than were most other women because of that European peasant tradition, and this was to the advantage of their families.

The family ethic of placing the economic good of all above individual profit stood rural German-speakers well on the Midwest frontier. They were more likely to pool their resources for the goal of increasing the family holdings than were Anglo-Americans. Children worked elsewhere and contributed their wages. The Old World strategy of passing land on to the next generation when the parents retired aided in this as well. Mothers and fathers trusted their children to care for them in their old age and did their best to guarantee their continued presence by helping set them up on neighboring farms, just as my own great-grandparents and grandparents attempted to do.[3]

Accumulating land for children contributed to the establishment of stable rural communities based on extensive family and immigrant networks. The immigrants' shared ethnic differences also might have made them more likely to cooperate with one another and more anxious than the Anglo-Americans to build rural communities, usually organized around immigrant churches and schools. Their basic conservatism and rejection of risk-taking for the sake of gain meant they were not as likely as their Yankee neighbors to "get ahead" quickly or to exhibit as high a degree of what the dominant culture viewed as progress in education and income. Their rejection of risk-taking in favor of stability and security for the family, however, enabled them to ride out hard times that broke other farming families around them. For many German-speakers in the Midwest, ethnic factors were a positive force for long-term, land-based economic success and rural family continuity.

Nineteenth-century rural life and culture were similar in many ways for all midwesterners. A certain degree of cautious conservatism typified most farmers, for such a philosophy was best suited to a livelihood that was hostage to the most unpredictable forces of nature and individual fate. Bad luck in the form of insect infestations, hail, flood, or drought could strike at any time, and the illness or death of a husband or wife could tip a precariously balanced household economy into ruin.

For all rural residents, the family was in practical as well as emotional terms "the quintessential principle of order" on the frontier.[4] Given the relatively weak reach of government on the nineteenth-century frontier, familial bonds and principles were crucial in influencing behavior and providing support in times of need. That some families disintegrated in the face of cruel blows of fate or simply from the stress of change should not surprise us. Unfortunately, we know as little about "failed" Anglo-American frontier families as we do about similar immigrant families.

Some scholars have identified more sinister economic reasons for the difficulties of frontier life. They have argued from a Marxist perspective that the West was developed not by individual men and women seeking land but by U.S. government land policy, which prohibited the development of large tracts of land except by private profit-making ventures and speculators at public expense. These scholars have asserted that this forced mode of individualistic and competitive capitalism, which institutionalized the nuclear family, private property, and dominate-subordinate relationships, found its human expression in the domestic exploitation of women and children within the patriarchal family.[5] One can debate to what degree the prominence of the nuclear, patriarchal family was due to capitalist market forces and policies. To the extent that this was the case, however, all rural families were more or less equally subject to those influences.

Interpersonal dynamics stemming from traditional rural family structure were also similar in most families. The father was generally the (nominal or actual) head of the family and was publicly empowered as such. The mother was under his dominion, although she was in control of domestic production. She was also usually perceived as the emotional heart of the family. Children were a source of labor as well as being objects of affection. They were expected to contribute to the family farming enterprise or to earn their own way as soon as the family economy could no longer accommodate them. Especially in the early years of settlement, farmers of all backgrounds were likely to keep their children out of school when they were needed at home and to deemphasize the importance of formal education. To be sure, we have seen that many variations on these patterns existed among individual German-speaking families, and it was not different for their neighbors.

Rural women lived generally similar lives. Their option in life was usually marriage to a farmer and childrearing or single lives dedicated to parents or siblings. Women of all ethnicities and ancestries performed the same house and yard tasks. Although many Anglo-American women did not work in the fields as their German-speaking sisters did, immigrant writers' criticism of them was ill-placed, as more reasonable observers noted.[6] All women worked hard and put their children to work as well. They were often confined to their farms while their husbands did the shopping in town, and they were unlikely to take a public role outside of their rural churches or, perhaps, in school-associated activities. Female relatives and neighbor women, usually of the same ancestry, formed their support network. Taken together, these female networks and the traditional culture of hearth and farmyard that they supported were important strengths in the lives of rural women, who otherwise were socially isolated and economically overlooked.[7]

Significant differences between rural German-speaking women and their nonimmigrant neighbors came about as a result of the Anglo-Americans' development of an entrepreneurial agricultural structure. German-speakers tended to retain a "yeoman" approach to farm management, in which diversification, labor intensiveness, risk absorption, heavy capital investment, and conservatism played important roles. The culture underlying this approach emphasized the innate value of an agrarian life, hard work, and the establishment of deep family and communal roots.[8] Many Yankee farmers, however, thought of farming as "a way to make a living, rather than a way of life."[9] They emphasized profits over landownership and were supportive of their children's entering occupations other than farming.

Women's roles developed differently under these two agricultural structures. Yeoman farming depends heavily on the contribution of women's (and children's) labor at crucial times and on income from their diversified enterprises on and off the farm to absorb risk. Although women and children were exploited by the patriarchal structure of yeoman agriculture, they were also attached to the ideology underpinning it. They might have had to work hard, but they did it for goals they understood and could see realized in their own lives and in the lives of those they loved.

Especially on the plains of the Midwest, entrepreneurial farmers engaged in monoculture agriculture in response to the opportunities of the capitalist economy. They consequently tended to participate in the industrialization of traditional areas of women's domestic production and to eliminate small-scale dairy and poultry production as "unprofitable." This left women less directly engaged in production and separated them from the goals of agricultural enterprise. The displacement of domestic production eventually turned the farm wife's primary role into that of consumer and creator of a home life similar to that of town dwellers, a life more in accord with the domestic ideology preached in publications centered in urban America.[10] Since this ideology kept women in the home and subordinate to men, it did not conflict with rural patriarchal family structures, until, of course, it promoted women's engagement in social action movements. While the wives of yeoman farmers generally embraced the goal of perpetuating rural family and community life, the wives of entrepreneurial farmers tended to encourage their children to pursue nonfarming careers and sometimes even pressured their husbands to move to town.

The differences in these ideologies no doubt contributed to a certain lack of understanding between women who adhered to each. The self-sufficiency of the yeoman farms, with their female networks of cooperation and mutual support, made it less important for immigrant women to learn English and accommodate themselves to the dominant culture. This might well have encouraged an Anglo-American woman to view her German-speaking neighbor as "some European peasant's wife, illiterate, impossibly shy, downtrodden," with whom she had little in common.[11] The native-born often viewed rural immigrants' efforts to establish ethnic communities, their support systems, and their desire to acquire more land for their children, all manifestations of the yeoman ideology, as "clannishness" or, more negatively, as a group conspiracy to squeeze "true" Americans out of an area.[12]

In actuality, of course, German-speaking immigrant farmers had no such nefarious plans. It was simply that the American agricultural environment was conducive to "the successful transplanting of the perennial bond between family, land, and community" that they valued above all else.[13] They did not have to change their values or their way of life to be successful in the terms that meant most to them. The freedom to shape immigrant communities, revolving around rural churches, was an important part of this. Rural churches in America provided many elements of the village life that German-speakers had enjoyed in the Old World, even enabling them to engage in the family Sunday *Gemütlichkeit* (relaxation and conviviality), complete with beer and wine, that was part of their social heritage.[14] As Walter Kamphoefner has shown, rural areas were more likely than urban neighborhoods to become ethnic "cocoons," providing immigrants with a relatively safe and stable environment in which to transplant Old World culture. Such neighborhoods were therefore quite different from the frontier "crucibles" Turner had postulated, which would force assimilation upon the immigrants. This was especially true of areas settled by chain migration and those that supported ethnic churches.[15]

Life in rural America also provided a safe environment in which all women could fulfill their traditional role as cultural "conservators and initiators."[16] Immigrant women probably often viewed this role as an especially important duty and service they could provide for families wrenched out of old surroundings and thrust into a new country. Writing of urban immigrants, Elizabeth Ewen has said that the female world in an immigrant community "created a web of personal, social, and familial relationships that mediated the world of culture left behind and the alien culture they had stepped into."[17] Reared to value domestic order and permanence, women naturally took on the task of retaining and adapting cultural practices in the home and ethnic community. The German-American press also recognized women's significance in this and urged them to preserve German traditions and family life by using German in the home, supporting immigrant churches, and maintaining connections to Old World customs and traditions.[18] These efforts proved to have particularly long-lasting results in rural immigrant communities, where high concentrations of German-Americans have endured.

In sheer numbers, the German-speaking immigrants of the last century left a strong mark on the rural Midwest. In 1980, 20,244,888 (41.13 percent) of the 49,224,146 persons in the United States who claimed German ancestry were located in the north-central region of the United States; 8,188,018 (40.4 percent) of these midwesterners claimed only German as their ancestry, while the others had a mixed ancestry that included German (see table 1).[19] The number and percentage of persons in our five-state area claiming a German-American heritage increased in the next census, perhaps partly because of the way questions about ancestry were asked and counted (compare tables 1 and 2). The summary of 1990 census information concerning ancestry in the United States as a whole and in the north-central region had not been released by the time I completed this study, but, judging by the pattern established in 1980, it is likely that the north-central region and these five states in it had a higher percentage of German-Americans than did the country as a whole. The percentage of single-ancestry German-Americans was probably also higher.

German-Americans have maintained a strong presence in rural areas. In 1980, 26.3 percent of the American population lived on farms or in communities under 2,500, and only 2.5 percent lived on farms; however, 30.4 percent of people categorized as German-Americans lived in rural areas, and 4.1 percent lived on farms. When one considers only single-ancestry German-Americans, the numbers are even more striking. Of these persons, 34.4 percent lived in rural areas, and 5.9 percent lived on farms. Among all farm residents in 1980, just under 36 percent were of sole or partial German ancestry. In that census year, German was second only to English as the strongest ancestry group reported by U.S. citizens, with 26.1 percent of the total population claiming German ancestry. This is certainly an impressive

Table 1. German-Americans in the United States, the North-Central Region, and the Midwest, 1980

Area or State	People with German Ancestry[a]		Single-Ancestry German-Americans	
	Number	Percentage	Number	Percentage
United States	49,224,146	26.1	17,966,813	36.5
North Central	20,244,888	34.4	8,188,018	40.4
Illinois	3,103,351	27.2	1,135,212	36.6
Iowa	1,331,624	45.7	599,421	45.0
Kansas	828,903	35.1	356,453	43.0
Missouri	1,575,432	32.0	633,291	40.0
Nebraska	724,165	46.1	352,873	48.7

Source: Derived from Bureau of the Census, *1980 Census of Population,* vol. 1, *Characteristics of the Population* (Washington, D.C.: GPO, 1983), parts 1, 15, 17, 18, 27, 29, table 60; Bureau of the Census, *Supplemental Report: Ancestry of the Population by State, 1980* (Washington, D.C.: GPO, 1983), tables 3 and 3a.
a. Single and multiple ancestries reported.

Table 2. German-Americans in the Midwest, 1990

State	People with German Ancestry[a]		Single-Ancestry German-Americans	
	Number	Percentage	Number	Percentage
Illinois	3,327,761	29.1	1,305,584	39.2
Iowa	1,394,939	50.3	680,105	48.8
Kansas	968,820	39.1	451,454	46.6
Missouri	1,844,192	36.0	821,492	44.5
Nebraska	795,177	50.4	395,301	49.7

Source: Derived from Bureau of the Census, *1990 Census of Population and Housing: Summary Tape File 3A* (Washington, D.C.: GPO, 1992).
a. Only single, first, and second ancestries reported.

figure, but it is markedly below that of farm residents claiming to have German ancestry.[20] Such numbers in themselves indicate a strong loyalty to the land among the descendants of the immigrants.

The number of German-Americans among persons engaged in farm-related occupations in the midwestern states studied here is also impressive. As table 3 shows, the percentage of persons of single or mixed German ancestry engaged in farm-related occupations was higher than the average for all employed persons in the United States and in each of the five states in 1980. Among all U.S. agricultural workers, German-Americans constituted 16.3 percent but had higher percentages in the five states studied here (41.5 percent to 45.8 percent). This is particularly striking because German-Americans were nationwide a strongly urban population. Although they made up 26.1 percent of the U.S. population, the proportion of them working in agriculture was almost 10 percent lower. The high number of them engaged in farm-related occupations (more than 4 in 10 workers in each of the five states studied) indicates the extent to which they have persisted in those occupations in this region during the past century and a half.

The proportion of women of German descent who were in farm-related occupations was also high in 1980, as table 4 shows. Even in Illinois and Missouri, with their large urban populations, the percentage of women of German ancestry engaged in farming was much higher than the national average. German-American women also made up

Table 3. Persons over Fifteen Employed in Farm-Related Occupations, 1980

Area or State	Percentage of Employed Persons in Farm-Related Occupations	Percentage of Employed German-Americans in Farm-Related Occupations	Percentage of German-Americans among Those in Farm-Related Occupations
United States	2.7	4.8	16.3
Illinois	2.1	3.3	45.8
Iowa	9.6	11.2	41.5
Kansas	6.2	7.8	41.7
Missouri	4.1	4.6	42.2
Nebraska	10.3	12.1	42.2

Source: Derived from Bureau of the Census, *1980 Census of Population,* vol. 1, chapter C, part 1, tables 104, 177, and 188, and parts 15, 17, 18, 27, and 29, tables 68 and 110.

Table 4. Women over Fifteen Employed in Farm-Related
Occupations, 1980

Area or State	Percentage of Employed Females in Farm-Related Occupations	Percentage of Employed German-American Females in Farm-Related Occupations	Percentage of German-American Females among Those Females in Farm-Related Occupations
United States	0.9	1.7	14.6
Illinois	0.6	0.9	43.3
Iowa	3.0	5.3	53.4
Kansas	1.5	4.3	43.6
Missouri	1.3	1.5	37.5
Nebraska	2.5	2.8	52.9

Source: Derived from Bureau of the Census, *1980 Census of Population,* vol. 1, chapter C, part 1, tables 104, 177, and 188, and parts 15, 17, 18, 27, and 29, tables 68 and 110.

very high percentages of all female agricultural workers, in Iowa and Nebraska more than half. These statistics indicate that among German-American women in the five-state midwestern region, the agricultural traditions of their female forebears were still strong in the latter half of this century.[21]

The relatively high percentage of German-Americans in the United States who claimed purely German ancestry in 1980 (36.5 percent) points to a persistent pattern of endogamy lasting well over a century after immigration. As we have seen, the percentage of single-ancestry German-Americans in the north-central region was even higher (40.4 percent). In the five midwestern states, the percentages of single-ancestry German-Americans ranged from 36.6 in Illinois to 48.7 in Nebraska (see table 1).[22] It seems that several generations after immigration, many German-Americans still preferred to marry within their ethnic group. In 1980, of the German-Americans claiming only German ancestry in the United States, 34.4 percent lived in rural areas and 65.6 percent in urban areas, whereas nationwide 30.4 percent of German-Americans lived in rural areas and 69.6 in urban areas.[23]

In predominantly rural counties with strong German-American populations, this preference for endogamy is particularly evident (see table 5). The number or percentage of German-Americans in all these counties except Ellis County in Kansas appears to have increased between 1980 and 1990 (see tables 5 and 6), although it is difficult to

Table 5. German-American Population in Selected Counties, 1980

County	Germans-Americans[a]		Single-Ancestry German-Americans	
	Number	Percentage	Number	Percentage
Effingham (Ill.)	17,846	57.7	11,830	66.3
Monroe (Ill.)	13,842	68.8	9,307	67.2
Randolph (Ill.)	16,833	47.2	9,875	58.7
Benton (Iowa)	12,960	54.8	6,990	53.9
Bremer (Iowa)	17,029	68.6	11,037	64.8
Clayton (Iowa)	14,155	67.1	8,689	61.4
Ellis (Kans.)	17,930	68.7	13,154	73.4
Finney (Kans.)	9,948	41.8	5,684	57.1
Marion (Kans.)	7,551	55.8	4,791	63.4
Cooper (Mo.)	7,069	48.3	4,127	58.4
Gasconade (Mo.)	8,392	63.7	5,599	66.7
Perry (Mo.)	10,692	63.7	7,257	67.9
Antelope (Nebr.)	4,651	53.6	2,657	57.1
Johnson (Nebr.)	3,431	64.9	2,181	63.6
Thayer (Nebr.)	5,287	69.7	3,842	72.7

Source: Derived from Bureau of the Census, *1980 Census of Population,* vol. 1, chapter C, parts 15, 17, 18, 27, and 29, table 60.

a. Single and multiple ancestries reported.

be sure since the questions concerning ancestry differed in the two censuses. In the 1990 questionnaire, respondents could indicate multiple ancestries, but only the first two listed were recorded. This may have simplified the responses and resulted in a slightly higher count for German-American ancestry. Nonetheless, the high value placed on land and the family-oriented, conservative values of the original German-speaking settlers still seem to be important factors influencing the marriage and career choices of contemporary residents in rural areas. These data also indicate that the concentration of German-Americans in the Midwest is due in no small measure to the large number of single- and multiple-ancestry German-Americans in rural areas like these.

Religious affiliation helps explain the high degree of endagomy in some of the counties in tables 5 and 6. For instance, the Catholic Germans from Russia in Ellis County, Kansas; the Mennonite Germans from Russia in Marion County, Kansas; and the Missouri Synod Lutheran Germans in Perry County, Missouri, would have had the extra incentive of shared religion to marry persons of German ancestry. Nevertheless, the percentages of single-ancestry German-Americans in counties settled by immigrants of mixed religious and geographic origins (Randolph County, Illinois; Benton County, Iowa; Finney County, Kansas; Cooper County, Missouri; and Antelope County, Nebraska, for example) are also much higher than the national average.[24]

This endogamy may be a sign of persistent ethnic identification, perhaps more surprising among German-Americans than in other immigrant groups because of what has appeared to many observers to be their seamless assimilation into American society.[25] In rural settings, to be sure, the choice of marriage partners was more limited than in cities. At the same time, however, persons of German ancestry in areas of strong immigrant settlement seem to have chosen wives and husbands from their own ethnic group more often than not and to have done so during more than a century of residence in those areas. The importance placed on keeping land within the family and community

Table 6. German-American Population in Selected Counties, 1990

County	Single-Ancestry Germans-Americans[a]		German-Americans	
	Number	Percentage	Number	Percentage
Effingham (Ill.)	20,754	65.5	14,225	68.5
Monroe (Ill.)	15,539	69.3	10,448	67.2
Randolph (Ill.)	18,832	54.5	11,464	60.9
Benton (Iowa)	13,677	60.9	7,437	54.4
Bremer (Iowa)	16,747	73.4	11,234	67.1
Clayton (Iowa)	14,042	73.7	8,874	63.2
Ellis (Kans.)	17,718	68.1	13,074	73.8
Finney (Kans.)	11,982	36.2	5,857	48.9
Marion (Kans.)	7,282	56.5	4,699	64.5
Cooper (Mo.)	8,537	57.5	4,851	56.8
Gasconade (Mo.)	9,448	67.5	6,456	68.3
Perry (Mo.)	11,261	67.6	8,096	71.9
Antelope (Nebr.)	5,176	65.0	3,693	71.3
Johnson (Nebr.)	3,247	69.5	2,203	67.8
Thayer (Nebr.)	4,807	72.4	3,482	72.4

Source: Derived from Bureau of the Census, *1990 Census of Population and Housing: Summary Tape File 3A.*

a. Single, first, and second ancestry reported.

and on maintaining ties within the ethnic and religious group no doubt played a role in these personal decisions.

Persons of English and Irish ancestry, who settled these rural counties at more or less the same time German-speakers did, have not practiced endogamy to the extent of the German-Americans (see table 7). This small sample indicates that English-Americans in certain areas of the Midwest, where German-Americans became dominant in the population, were better able to maintain a separate ethnic identity than the Irish-Americans. Neither group, however, matches the German-Americans in in-marriage patterns. This is no doubt in part a result of the ever-decreasing number of English- and Irish-Americans in these counties and the attractiveness and ease of intermarriage with native-born Anglo-Americans, who spoke their language. Perhaps partly because German-Americans were initially linguistically different, they

Table 7. English-American and Irish-American Populations in Selected Counties, 1980

| County | Percentage of English-Americans[a] | Percentage of Irish-Americans[a] | Percentage of Single-Ancestry Persons in Group | |
			English	Irish
Effingham (Ill.)	22.4	18.3	46.8	21.0
Monroe (Ill.)	15.2	28.3	29.2	10.1
Randolph (Ill.)	16.7	18.0	43.3	20.0
Benton (Iowa)	19.2	20.4	35.5	17.4
Bremer (Iowa)	16.1	14.9	29.6	14.5
Clayton (Iowa)	15.1	14.9	27.0	18.0
Ellis (Kans.)	13.8	12.5	41.8	21.9
Finney (Kans.)	20.8	16.9	47.0	26.2
Marion (Kans.)	19.9	12.3	39.2	16.2
Cooper (Mo.)	24.8	18.8	45.3	17.8
Gasconade (Mo.)	18.7	16.9	38.8	16.6
Perry (Mo.)	17.3	15.2	52.2	14.9
Antelope (Nebr.)	12.9	13.6	31.2	15.7
Johnson (Nebr.)	19.0	17.9	38.6	15.8
Thayer (Nebr.)	13.9	11.5	31.4	15.1

Source: Derived from Bureau of the Census, *1980 Census of Population,* vol. 1, chapter C, parts 15, 17, 18, 27, and 29, table 60.

a. Single and multiple ancestries reported.

seem to have maintained a stronger sense of ethnic identification than did the other large immigrant groups in their areas. Their "clannishness" had demographic results that are still evident.

The demographic information from the 1980 and 1990 censuses confirms once again that, to an extent that was disproportionate to their original numbers, German-speaking immigrants and their descendants stayed on the land they helped settle in the nineteenth century. The improvements they made there are still visible. They contributed to the introduction of crops and farming methods that made the midwestern states so important in the production of foodstuffs and livestock.[26] They left a distinctive mark on the landscape through the names and layout of the villages they founded, the architecture of the private and public buildings they constructed, and the characteristic neatness of their farmsteads.[27] Like other settlers, they planted trees, orchards, and windbreaks on the prairies, and everywhere they altered the landscape to suit agricultural purposes, forever changing the natural environment.[28]

Studies done in Illinois and Missouri indicate that German-American farmers are more likely to know about the history of their landholdings, to maintain and keep in use buildings built by the original settlers, to have more barns and outbuildings than their neighbors, to encourage their children to farm, and to be less likely than their "Yankee" neighbors to engage in trades other than farming or to participate in aid programs.[29] All of these qualities point to an Old World heritage: pride in the "home place" and in self-sufficiency, diversified farming that provides shelter for livestock, and a reluctance to break with the rural family traditions.

Other concrete evidence of German ethnicity is less visible. Contrary to Gert Goebel's confident assertion in 1877 that the German-American press would normalize dialect differences and even spread the use of German among English-speakers, language retention in the Midwest has decreased with each successive generation.[30] Only separatist communities, such as the Amish, Hutterites, and Old Order Mennonites, still use German in the home regularly. In Kansas, the Catholic communities and the Mennonite communities of Germans from Russia also show a relatively high degree of linguistic retention.[31] In Amana, adults in their thirties and forties speak German among themselves, but English is the community's first language. German is increasingly cultivated for nostalgic reasons as much as it is used as a matter of course.[32] A few persons in traditionally German rural areas and small towns still speak German in the home, but these are likely to be elderly people.[33] With the passing of this generation, most of the last vestiges of the language of the immigrants will have vanished from rural midwestern life.

Nevertheless, many rural communities have retained a sense of their German origins. In the last decades, the Midwest, like much of the rest of the United States, has witnessed a sentimental revival of interest in ethnicity. The proliferation of "German" festivals and pioneer days is proof of this. Some of these, like the annual month-long *Oktoberfest* and *Maifest* in Hermann, Missouri, promote ethnic retention primarily for commercial purposes. The Bavarian-style folk dancers and costumed inhabitants featured there bear little or no resemblance to the original immigrants. Other annual events, like the *Strassenfest* in St. Louis and the *Spassfest* in Germantown, Illinois, are forums for good times featuring beer and bratwurst. At most, they remind natives and visitors of the early immigrants' cultural practices, which were not originally as acceptable as they have become in our day.[34] The embracing of German-style *Gemütlichkeit,* the beer culture Americans associate with it, and the popularity of certain foodstuffs may be the most obvious areas in which the immigrants have left their mark on the Midwest and the United States.[35]

Some midwestern German-American communities have made a more serious effort to preserve and even revive ethnic culture. Deutschheim in Hermann, Missouri, is a state historic site commemorating German-American culture. Several structures and their gardens have been refurbished in a historically accurate manner. Recently, the Deutschheim Association of Hermann began publication of an informational newsletter. Bethel holds several yearly events at which scholars and local artisans demonstrate traditional colony and rural Missouri crafts. The commercial exploitation of Amana colony arts for the tourist trade takes on a positive aspect through the resulting revival in those arts. At a time when tinsmithing and basket-weaving were about to die out, young Amanists learned these crafts and others, such as woodworking, carpet making, and quilting. Young women were in the forefront of this movement, and they have entered crafts (willow basket construction, leather goods) that were earlier a male province. The new generation of Amanist handworkers has retained the patterns and styles traditional to the colonies. Their work also emphasizes the fine crafts skills that were part of the German heritage the colonists brought to America.[36]

In a much less self-conscious way, the perpetuation of local practices and celebrations stemming from the early years of settlement by German-speakers still characterizes rural life in many midwestern communities. As was true a century or more ago, family life and the (formerly ethnic) church are usually the foci of these activities. Many families still follow German traditions: celebrating St. Nicholas Day, not decorating (or perhaps not lighting) the Christmas tree until Christmas Eve, serving an afternoon coffee or snack, preparing holiday and traditional foods (*Fastnacht* donuts, homemade wurst, and white asparagus in southwestern Illinois, for example). Although not so common as they were twenty years ago, Saturday-night dances and potlucks for the whole family, held in a church basement or at a dance hall in a nearby town, still take place regularly in some rural communities. Bands with German names and instrumental configurations play polkas, waltzes, and the *Schottisch*.[37]

Rarer, but still persisting in a few rural areas, are publicly shared practices: "shooting in" the New Year, dancing traditional "mixers," hanging a dummy outside a saloon to mock the rejected boyfriends of a recently married woman, ringing the church bell to announce the death of a member of the parish (once for a child, twice for a woman, three times for a man), singing German hymns and folk songs on special occasions.[38] Much more common is the central importance the rural or small-town church, founded by immigrants, retains in community and family life. Compared with Anglo-American churches, fewer immigrant churches in the countryside have been abandoned. The well-kept condition of these churches, even if some are now used only for funerals, and the multiple purposes to which others are put testify to their importance in rural communities. They serve not only as social gathering places for the congregation but also as distribution centers for Meals on Wheels, polling places, and Red Cross blood donation centers. Church homecoming picnics in the summer, fall harvest festivals, and winter game dinners, often featuring such traditional foods as homemade sausage, German potato salad, and strudel, may serve as parish fund-raisers, but they also are events when families and neighbors gather, whether or not they belong to that particular parish. Even the city children and grandchildren come back for these occasions, when they are sure to see family and friends from their rural childhoods.[39]

In American public life, the influence of German-Americans is now less visible than it was a century ago. No longer do German immigrants form a political block to be reckoned with in politics. Their descendants' tenuous connection to modern Germany is a minor factor influencing American foreign policy. The retention of German as the language of instruction in schools is no longer a burning issue, and all German branches of the main American Christian church denominations have long since been absorbed. Even the Missouri Synod

Lutheran church has relinquished its insistence on the use of German as the language of worship and religious instruction.

Nevertheless, an awareness of a German-American identity persists in the Midwest. Residents of rural communities recognize certain qualities as characteristic of the "Germans" among them: conservatism, thrift, industriousness, cleanliness, self-reliance, and success and skill as farmers, homemakers, and craftspeople.[40] The German-Americans themselves often display a consciousness of and pride in their heritage that seem to go beyond a merely nostalgic cultural loyalty. Their deep-rooted, family-based stability on the land and in a locality is the core of their self-awareness.[41] They are one of the "success stories" of the rural Midwest. The extent to which their history of adaptation in American society can serve as a model for understanding or predicting a similar success for other, later immigrants is another question.

Let us return to Dietmar Kügler's assertions concerning the achievements and influence of the German immigrants in the Midwest that were discussed in the Introduction. Certainly, we can credit the German-speakers who came to the nineteenth-century rural frontier with accomplishing many things. They were indeed often extraordinary in the marginality of their initial farming enterprises and in their ability nevertheless to stick through difficult frontier times. They might have been more successful as Midwest farmers because of the extra measure of adventurousness typical of many immigrants and the narrowing of options that immigration entails. Probably their biggest asset in this frontier venture, however, was the concentration of family efforts on family progress. Like my great-grandparents, the Krauses and the Schelbitzkis, they could be "contented among strangers" because the attainment of those family goals was a realistic possibility. Women's dedication to family agrarian aims, rather than to bourgeois family or female ideals, was an important factor in the accomplishment of these goals.

Kügler's view of the German immigrants as "aggressive individualists" who trusted only themselves and "knew how to look after themselves" must be tempered by the strong evidence of family and community support systems in rural areas. Although the immigrants were perhaps more individualistic on the average than their compatriots who stayed in Europe, it is clear they also expended a great deal of effort in retaining family and community networks where they could and in fashioning new ones where they could not. They valued the freedom to do this that America gave them and that residence in rural America enabled in even greater measure. Their continued strong presence in rural midwestern areas is proof of an essentially conservative desire to build and preserve an ethnic group identity in the United States.

That American society allowed and even (if sometimes grudgingly) appreciated this rural immigrant presence indicates what I would like to call "cultural convergence," a concept related to what Kathleen Conzen has termed "parallel transformation."[42] The German-speaking immigrants exhibited values and behavior rural nineteenth-century Americans also found important: hard work, frugality, the centrality of family life, and an active church life. What are often viewed as "typical" midwestern values—an emphasis on family life and hard work, community stability, and conservatism—are convergent with those immigrant values. It would require a much more detailed study of many midwestern localities than is possible here to ascertain the degree to which the immigrant culture influenced the American and vice versa, particularly after the passing of the frontier era.[43] It seems likely, however, that the presence of numerous German-Americans in the central part of the nation was a factor that supported this development.

Because this midwestern value system is based in the home and the community, women were and are especially important in its support. The question then arises whether the strong tendency among immigrant German-speaking women to subordinate themselves to family has had an effect on gender relations throughout the Midwest. Certainly, such female behavior was very persistent in rural areas, where hardworking, self-sacrificing German-American farm women could still be found well past the middle of the twentieth century.[44] Patricia Lomire has suggested that the control of females in anti-assimilationist communities is a "means to limit integration of individual members of society."[45] Further demographic studies and oral interviews would be useful in exploring whether strongly German-American rural communities are still attempting to maintain a certain separateness from mainstream American society. If they are, the old gender dynamics of female subordination in rural German-speaking immigrant enclaves might still be at work and visible in fewer educational and career opportunities for women in those areas and in a generally lower-than-average participation by women in public life.[46] Whether such a pattern, if it exists, carries over in any perceptible fashion to other midwestern and rural women is yet another question.

The difficulty of answering these and related questions stems from the extent to which the vast majority of German-Americans have adapted and integrated themselves into American society and from the ways in which that society changed as a result. How this came about, in different ways at different times and in different localities, is a story that no single study can encompass, but it is a story that illustrates one of the great felicities of American history: the capacity for most foreign people to find a place in this relatively young nation without destruction or total loss of their own culture and identity. Frederick Jackson Turner conceived of a frontier crucible, which he thought forged a new composite American people. I would like to suggest another image, one in line with the female-centered interests of this study: a slow cooker, simmering various ingredients into a savory but somewhat lumpy stew, while allowing the flavor of the separate ingredients to be identified and appreciated.[47]

The new immigrants of the late twentieth century will probably have more difficulty than the German-speakers did in becoming part of that stew. Even more than the arrivals from south of the U.S. border, non-European, non-Christian peoples will find it hard to achieve a convergence with mainstream American life and culture, as has been true for the visibly "different" African Americans. Like the nineteenth- and early twentieth-century immigrants, the new immigrants are experiencing criticism and discrimination because of their high fertility, their attitudes toward women, their insistence on speaking their native tongues, and their attempts to build their own identity in U.S. society. In our modern cities, they will not be able to escape the most immediate pressures of direct confrontation with the dominant culture, and they do not generally have the option of escaping to rural enclaves, as many German-speakers did in the last century.

The new immigrants seem to be using the same strategies the earlier immigrants did, though: above all, a reliance on family and community life to sustain them during the transition. Studies that take into account women's roles in group adaptation would therefore offer particularly important insights into that process. Because of the interpersonal networks of support that are so central to women's lives in most cultures, many of the newest immigrants probably also feel content with their lot in this strange land, as did the German-speakers before them. With time, their descendants and the rest of American society may also reap the benefits of a convergence of the old culture with the new, as happened with the German-Americans.

Appendix A

Sources on German-Speaking Immigrant Women and Their Families

Since I could not interview the subjects of this study directly to learn about their frontier lives and the interplay between their European heritage and the American environment, I had to rely on a wide variety of resources, including the personal documents of such women. Directly and indirectly, my study also owes much to the work done by others.[1]

The most immediate information about people's lives and their concrete and subjective experiences is contained in their own words, but personal documents by nineteenth-century German-speakers are few and far between, considering the numbers who immigrated to America.[2] Even the sources we do have are far from being representative of the German-speaking immigrant. As is true of Anglo-Americans, more letters, diaries, and autobiographies by educated, urban, middle-class writers exist than by members of the more numerous urban and rural underclasses. Material written by women is even scarcer than that by men, although women never made up less than 40 percent of the German-speaking immigrant population. The reasons for these deficiencies in source material are obscure. Perhaps some members of the later generations did not keep German-language documents because they could not read the language or the old script. Perhaps relatives in Europe lost interest in old correspondence when the contact with the emigrants was weakened by time or broken by death. Perhaps the dominant American culture's ignorance of such material and general lack of interest in non-English documents were also factors.

There are probably other reasons for the small number of extant letters, diaries, and memoirs by rural German-speaking women. It is likely that a higher percentage of women immigrants than men were illiterate.[3] From what we know about the exploitation of female labor in Germanic culture, we can assume that most women had little leisure time and little reserve energy to devote to writing letters or diary entries on a regular basis. The dominant position of men in the family might have also been a factor. It was often the husband who wrote letters home, even to his wife's family. I cannot quantify this assertion, but it is a strong impression gained by reading many immigrant letters. As a concrete example, the two Neumeier sisters who wrote letters home from Iowa were married to men who could not write German well; one had come to America as a young boy, and the other had been born in America. The third sister, who had immigrated first with a husband from her home village, wrote almost no letters herself, whereas her husband wrote long letters at least annually to his wife's family.[4] Whatever the reasons, and in spite of the exploding interest in the personal documents of frontierswomen in the last decade, I have looked in vain for the letters, diaries, and memoirs of German-speaking women in collections of such writings.[5]

The known texts of this sort by women are variously accessible. Some have been published in German, either alone or in collections with other emigrant autobiographical texts. Of these, some appeared in nineteenth-century journals and newspapers that are often difficult to locate in this country. Local historical societies in German-speaking Europe are also publishing (or republishing) such texts, an interest spurred in part by the 1983 tricentennial of German settlement in America. A variety of archives throughout the United States and in a few locations in Europe contain other documents by women migrants, many of them unpublished. With a few notable exceptions, German-American women's personal writings have not been translated into English.

Other important sources of information about German-speaking women in rural nineteenth-century America include the personal writings of their male contemporaries and their descendants. These offer insights into women's roles in the family and immigrant community. Such sources, like those written by women, are also widely scattered, some translated and others not, some published and others not. The idiosyncratic and more intimate information contained in such personal documents can be supplemented by that found in public sources: census records, the dozens of German-language publications of nineteenth-century America, church records, probate court documents, and community history books.

These records of German-speaking women and their families have their strengths and limitations. Hard data, such as those contained in census records, are important in establishing the concrete reality of immigrants' lives. Where did they live? How many children did they have? How much property did they own? How long did they stay in an area? Church documents help clarify marriage patterns, women's contributions to building an ethnic community, and community dynamics in general. As I discovered in Cooper County, Missouri, wills may reflect the intersection of Old World and New World inheritance traditions. Court records, while often difficult to access, are treasure troves of knowledge about many facets of the immigrants' public and private lives. I came to regard German-language newspapers, at least in part, as prescriptive literature, for they communicated certain assumptions about proper female and male behavior, family life, and community dynamics.[6]

All of these sources are important in any attempt to understand nineteenth-century German-speaking immigrants, but they do not offer equally "hard" information. Church records are not comprehensive or totally objective records of an ethnic community's life. Newspaper articles, with their unspoken assumptions and regional and temporal biases, are far from being straightforward historical documents. The available personal writings pose other special problems. They are certainly valuable for the light they shed on the subjective dimensions of the immigrant experience and for their particularlistic, qualitative merits. But it was precisely their personal and subjective qualities that called for caution on my part. It is tempting, but wrong, to make sweeping generalizations about all immigrants on the basis of what *some* wrote in their letters, diaries, or memoirs.[7] It is more helpful to think of letters, diaries, and autobiographies and the knowledge they impart as historical *cases,* not historical *documents.* They gain value as cases when they can be placed, through census information, for example, in a socioeconomic context. They certainly are useful in an illustrative fashion and may take a central place in a study of attitudes, mentalities, or the everyday life of immigrants. They inform us about motivation, social and familial contacts and structures, self-confidence, barriers to and opportunities for adaptation, and the apperception of cultural difference on an individual level. They must, however, be approached with an awareness of their uniqueness, which makes them rich and rewarding sources but also difficult to evaluate properly.

The intended audience of the autobiographical text is always a complicating factor. In letters, it is the recipient(s). In diaries, it is the future (intended or accidental) reader or the future self whom the writer has in mind. Memoirs are directed at the descendants of the writer or at the broader society that shares the writer's past. Second-person memoirs, used extensively in my study, describe the experiences of others, inserting another layer of subjectivity and intentionality between the reader and the original persons, events, and circumstances. Oral histories are shared documents, in which the interviewer generates an account according to his or her view of what is relevant and the interviewee responds in greater or lesser degrees to that direction. Community history books, whether written by a single person or a committee, rely on the selective information that individuals and families submitted. In all cases, the writer shaped and censored the text with the intended audience in mind.

The autobiographical text is also shaped according to its perceived purpose. This is true of immigrant memoirs, whether they are first- or second-person testimonies. As family records, they may omit painful episodes and feelings that might diminish the sense of family accomplishment or that could cause discord. When they aim to be a "representative" example of a particular time, place, or group, they often show a restructuring of experience to reflect a generally valid or even mythic reality. Community history books clearly show this tendency. Immigrants wrote letters, too, not generally as records of all the details of daily life and emotion but to inform Old World friends and relatives of conditions in America, to ask for monetary help, or to maintain personal contact. Certain topics then were simply inappropriate for and even harmful to such purposes. A diary could contain the outpourings of the writer's soul, but among immigrants its purpose was likely to be more pragmatic: the recording of weather conditions and work accomplished or the documentation of a trip, intended to tell family members about the conditions encountered for their information or for purposes of future emigration.

A myriad of individual elements can play a role in all personal documents: for example, the variety of actual events recorded, the sex and age of the writer or speaker and his or her state of health and mind, the length of time between the described events and the narration, the positive or negative impact of the events and the concrete and emotional ability of the writer to deal with them, and the personal or public relationship between the individual and his or her audience. For all of these reasons, using such texts in writing history is challenging. In many respects, however, the possible pitfalls of dealing with personal texts are similar to those of writing history in general. This enterprise is essentially a reconstructive activity, in which the culture of the present reinterprets the culture of the past. Caution in using personal writings is necessary, but the insights gained are also important for a greater understanding of the past. The illustrative, particularistic richness of personal documents helps fill in the colors and the details of the broad picture that immigration and census records sketch.[8]

Before embarking on the research for this study more than a decade ago, I did not fully appreciate how difficult it would be to find primary sources by German-speaking women. Nor did I realize into what new areas of inquiry my search for information about them and their lives would lead me. Yet each of these areas, disparate though they may have seemed at first, has been important in filling in the crazy-quilt pattern of rural women's experiences.

German-Speakers as Immigrants and Midwest Residents: A Statistical Analysis

Statistical data of immigration, settlement patterns, intermarriage, childbirth, and employment contribute to a fuller understanding of German-speaking women and their families in the nineteenth-century Midwest. Such information can help us interpret and evaluate the influences they exercised and under which they lived. I begin an analysis of these kinds of data by looking at women as participants in the immigration. First, however, I must note several factors that inhibit the compilation of definitive data concerning emigration from German-speaking lands. European officials kept only spotty records during much of the nineteenth century, and the records they did keep were compromised by such factors as insufficient information about the emigrants and unsanctioned and unreported emigration. The lack of political centralization among German-speaking lands meant there was no consistent or universal emigration policy or record-keeping.

Other factors complicate the immigration information we have on the American side. It was not collected uniformly throughout the century. American immigration officials and census enumerators did not indicate the place of birth of immigrants reliably or consistently. The Bureau of Immigration began to classify the immigrants by "race or people" (roughly equivalent to language spoken) in 1899. Mother tongue was not noted in census enumerations until 1910. Before this, German-speakers from France (Alsace-Lorraine) or Denmark probably were counted among the French and Danish immigrants. The Germans from Russia were categorized as Russians rather than German-speakers. Italian-, French-, and German-speaking Swiss were lumped together. No one distinguished among the five language groups found in Belgium, Holland, and Luxembourg. The failure to distinguish among German-, Yiddish-, Polish-, and Hungarian-speaking citizens of Germany and Austria-Hungary is even more problematic because the numbers are larger, especially in the last two decades of the century. Wherever possible, I have used information that makes these distinctions. Nonetheless, the conclusions drawn from immigra-

tion and census data must be extrapolated from the incomplete information we have and therefore are less definitive than one might wish.[1]

The Numerical Strength of Women among the Immigrants

I begin by considering the number of German-speaking women in the
nineteenth-century migration to America. Women probably constituted
about 40 percent of the immigrants (see table B1). Similar statistics
have been compiled for Prussian emigrants between 1862 and 1871:
60 percent were males, and 40 percent were females.[2] The proportion
of males to females was less skewed in certain groups and in certain
periods. For example, between 1851 and 1857, 52.3 percent of the

Table B1. Male and Female Immigrants from German States,
1821–55 and 1871–1900

Years	Total	Number (%) of Males	Number (%) of Females
a. Immigrants from the German states, 1821–55			
1821–25	1,394	1,129 (81.0)	265 (19.0)
1826–30	5,367	3,462 (64.5)	1,905 (35.5)
1831–35	45,592	29,824 (65.4)	15,768 (34.6)
1836–40	106,862	67,923 (63.6)	38,939 (36.4)
1841–45	105,188	62,782 (59.7)	42,406 (40.3)
1846–50	329,152	203,694 (61.9)	125,458 (38.1)
1851–55	645,861	382,986 (59.3)	262,875 (40.7)
b. Immigrants from the German Empire, 1871–1900			
1871–75	508,394	294,734 (58.0)	213,660 (42.0)
1876–80	209,788	128,745 (61.4)	81,043 (38.6)
1881–85	814,753	462,876 (56.8)	351,877 (43.2)
1886–90	456,369	250,849 (55.0)	205,520 (45.0)
1891–95	387,349	214,054 (55.3)	173,295 (44.7)
1896–1900	119,597	66,195 (55.3)	53,402 (44.7)
Averages for 1821–55		65.1%	34.9%
Averages for 1871–1900		56.9%	43.1%
Overall		61.0%	39.0%

Sources: Part a was derived from Imre Ferenczi, *International Migrations,* vol. 1, *Statistics,*
ed. Walter F. Willcox (New York: National Bureau of Economic Research, 1929), table 9,
401–17; part b was derived from *Reports of the Immigration Commission,* vol. 3, *Statistical
Review of Immigration, 1820–1910* (Washington, D. C.: GPO, 1911), table 9, pt. 2: 30–
44.

emigrants from Bavaria were male, and 47.7 percent were female.[3] As table B1 indicates, the percentage of female immigrants increased as the century went on, when the peak periods of immigration occurred. The share of women in actual numbers in the century-long immigration was therefore probably somewhat higher than 40 percent.

Although men clearly outnumbered women, there is additional evidence that the male surplus of German-speakers was probably not as great as table B1 suggests. In emigrating *families,* females outnumbered males. Among Prussian emigrants between the years 1862 and 1871, 120,723 people traveled in families. Of these, 44 percent (53,162) were males and 56 percent (67,561) were females.[4] Similar percentages held true later in the century as well, as table B2 illustrates. As this table also indicates, the numbers of male and female family members were most nearly equal in the early 1880s, the years of the heaviest emigration. In 1881, the peak year of German emigration, an almost equal number of male and female family members emigrated (50.57 percent of the 135,077 people traveling in family units were female, and 49.43 percent were male).[5] One has the impression of near-panic gripping certain sectors of the German populace, as families left

Table B2. Male and Female Emigrants from Germany Traveling in Families and Alone, 1881–1900

Years	Emigrants in Family Units			Emigrants Traveling Alone		
	Total	Males	Females	Total	Males	Females
1881–85	497,720	237,792	259,928	318,833	225,104	93,729
		47.8%	52.2%		70.6%	29.4%
1886–90	236,611[a]	108,717	127,894	219,758	142,132	77,626
		45.9%	54.1%		64.5%	35.5%
1891–95	195,182	89,885	105,297	190,167	122,168	67,999
		46.1%	53.9%		64.2%	35.8%
1896–1900	45,422	19,798	25,624	74,175	46,367	27,808
		43.6%	56.4%		62.5%	37.5%

Source: Derived from Takenori Inoki, *Aspects of German Peasant Emigration to the United States, 1815–1914: A Reexamination of Some Behavioral Hypotheses in Migration Theory* (New York: Arno, 1981), table 13, 81–82.

a. A discrepancy exists in Inoki's listings of the numbers of emigrants traveling in families for the years 1886 and 1887. I have added Inoki's figures for men and women traveling in families during those years, resulting in new totals of 38,950 (1886) and 49,749 (1887).

in haste, without taking the time or using resources to send a (male) family member ahead to prepare the way.

Later in the century, the percentage of emigrants traveling in families diminished (see tables B2 and B3). This was a consequence of improving conditions in Germany, as the transition to industrialization became more complete and the economy there could absorb displaced workers from the agricultural sector. The more conservative elements of society—families, which had multiple obligations and responsibilities—became less willing to travel far away in the hope of material betterment when they could attain it in the closest large city.[6]

The high percentage of lone male emigrants, seen clearly in table B2, accounts for the overall surplus of males. Yet there is a discrepancy between the number of males documented in emigration data and the ratio of German-speaking male to female immigrants found in U.S. census data. In 1900, 46.3 percent of the German-born were female. Twenty years later, there were 110.4 German-speaking males for 100.0 German-speaking females in the age group of fifteen years and over. That is, 52.5 percent of the German-speaking foreign-born adults were males, and 47.5 percent were females.[7] Part of the reason for the greater numerical equality between the sexes than we might expect from nineteenth-century emigration data is that male migrants had greater mobility. Single men are almost always more numerous in international migrations than married men or women in general. They leave their homeland in greater numbers, but they also are more likely to return after temporary stays. Some single German-speaking men also returned to marry and then brought their brides back to America. Married men also often traveled to America ahead of their families to make preparations and sometimes then returned to accompany them. In such cases, they would have been counted twice as emigrants. Both single

Table B3. Emigrants from Germany Traveling in Families and Alone, 1881–1900

Years	Traveling in Families (%)	Traveling Alone (%)
1881–85	60.66	39.34
1886–90	51.82	48.18
1891–95	47.92	52.08
1896–1900	37.86	62.14

Source: Derived from Inoki, table 14, 83.

and married men also were more numerous among those returning to the Old World after they had accomplished their economic goals (or having failed to do so) or, in some cases, after the main reason for emigration no longer existed (e.g., military obligation). The larger proportion of men among German-speaking emigrants does not accurately reflect their presence in America.

In general, it was the young and able-bodied who emigrated. The age distribution of Bavarian emigrants between 1851 and 1857 shows that 88.9 percent were aged forty or under: 11.8 percent were under seven, 14.8 percent were between seven and sixteen years, and 62.3 percent were between sixteen and forty.[8] This age profile was also found on the American frontier in general. David J. Wishart's analysis of the 1860 census indicates that the "typical" frontier population had about two females for every male, with a disproportionately large number of young adults between twenty and thirty and children under ten years. The family unit of young adults with children dominated the initial phase of settlement. (More surprising is Wishart's finding that as the frontier "aged," the single male population increased.)[9] This contradicts widespread notions that women were a scarce commodity on the raw frontier and indicates that they played an important role in the earliest days of settlement. The overall population profile of first-generation German-speakers (and of most other immigrants) was at variance with this pattern, however, in regard to the proportion of women to men in frontier areas. Certainly single men were always more numerous among them. But in 1850 in St. Charles and Warren counties in Missouri, for example, the percentages of women (43 percent and 57 percent, respectively) among the German-born immigrants indicate a more nearly equal gender balance than in the population Wishart studied.[10]

Marriage Patterns

The imbalance between male and female German-speakers had an impact on marriage patterns in America. Germans were more likely to marry than most other European immigrants. In 1920, they ranked behind fourteen other ethnic groups in percentages of unmarried women (9.9 percent) and men (17.2 percent) fifteen years of age and over.[11] Although the number of single German-speaking women who came to the United States was relatively small, their proportion in the immigrant population, as in families, was greater than in the European populace.[12] The number of single women among German-speaking immigrants was, however, always less than that of single male immigrants, and their numbers in rural areas seem to have been even smaller. An analysis of census data showed that in 1920, 7.2 percent of German-speaking females in selected rural areas were single versus 10.8 percent in selected urban areas; 92.6 percent of all females living in rural areas were married, widowed, or divorced versus 89.1 percent in urban areas. In the same 1920 sample area, 15.7 percent of the rural and 17.7 percent of the urban German-speaking males were single; 83.8 percent of the males in rural areas were married, widowed, or divorced versus 81.9 percent in urban areas.[13] Some analysts have said that these statistics indicate that German-speaking men preferred not to marry at all rather than to marry a non-German-speaker, especially in rural areas. One could also argue, however, that given women's restricted opportunities for independence outside of marriage well into the twentieth century and German-speakers' traditional attitudes toward women's roles, women might have been more likely to marry than men were because women had fewer options to choose from, particularly in the rural areas. What is perhaps particularly surprising in these statistics is that there is not much difference between the percentages of rural and urban German-speaking males who married. Given the importance attached to female labor in rural areas, one might have expected a greater disparity. Some men evidently felt they could get along without a wife. What such data do not tell us, however, is the number of single men and women who lived with parents and siblings and thus were still part of families, although technically single. The minute analysis of enormous amounts of census data necessary for obtaining such information is impractical, if not impossible, at this time.

One consequence of males outnumbering females among the German-speaking foreign-born was a higher degree of endogamy among women, even into the twentieth century (see tables B4 and B5). In Missouri and Nebraska in 1880, many more German men than German women were married to Americans. Of the 39,180 children born in German-American unions in Missouri, 6,766 (17.3 percent) had a German mother and an American father. In Nebraska, 1,454 (22.2 percent) of the 6,550 children of mixed parentage had a German mother and an American father. Forty years later, the pattern, although weakened somewhat, still held throughout the United States. As indicated in table B5, immigrant women, still in the numerical minority, married their compatriots to a greater extent than did immigrant men. German-born women did so 1.43 times as often as German-born men. The difference was much smaller among Austrians, who were "newer" as an immigrant group than the Germans.

Tables B4 and B5 also indicate that both Austrian and German men were forced to marry outside of their national group to a much greater extent than native men were and that American women married

Table B4. Parentage of German-Americans in Missouri and
Nebraska, 1880

	Number of German-Americans	Number (%) with German-Born Parents	Number (%) with German-Born Mother, Native-Born Father	Number (%) with Native-Born Mother, German-Born Father
Born in United States, living in:				
Missouri	183,690	144,629 (78.8)	6,749 (3.6)	32,312 (17.6)
Nebraska	34,357	27,849 (81.0)	1,436 (4.2)	5,072 (14.8)
Born in foreign land, living in:				
Missouri	109,430	109,311 (99.89)	17 (0.01)	102 (0.10)
Nebraska	32,854	32,812 (99.87)	18 (0.06)	24 (0.07)

Source: Derived from U.S. Census Office, *U.S. Census Reports, Tenth Census, 1880* (Washington, D.C.: GPO, 1883), table 27, 680–92.

Table B5. Parentage as Indication of Intermarriage Patterns, 1920

Country of Birth of Mother	Country of Birth of Father		
	Austria[a]	Germany[b]	United States
Austria[a]	80.30	1.32	6.43
Germany[b]	3.03	42.16	43.13
United States	0.73	1.04	89.79

Country of Birth of Father	Country of Birth of Mother		
	Austria[a]	Germany[b]	United States
Austria[a]	77.25	0.81	15.76
Germany[b]	3.34	29.53	58.93
United States	0.30	0.56	95.07

Source: Derived from Niles Carpenter, *Immigrants and Their Children, 1920,* Census Monographs 7 (Washington, D.C.: GPO, 1927), tables 106–7, 234–35.

a. Includes Austrian Poland.
b. Includes German Poland.

Germans and Austrians twice as often as their male compatriots did. By 1920 the percentage of German-born women who had married native men was also high, in contrast to the data from 1880 in Missouri and Nebraska. We should keep in mind, however, that in 1920 a significant number of second-generation German and Austrian men, many of them German-speakers, were counted among the native-born Americans who married German-born women. The extent of the overlapping of Americans of native and of foreign parentage cannot be determined from the census compilation. Even taking this factor into consideration, we can attribute the high degree of intermarriage in 1920 to the century-long presence of the German-speakers in America, just as the fairly low rate of intermarriage between Austrian women and American men reflects the relative recentness of the main body of the Austrian immigration. Walter Kamphoefner's study of St. Charles and Warren counties in Missouri at midcentury supports the assumption that the longer an immigrant group resides in the United States, the higher the degree of intermarriage with the native-born. In 1850, in Kamphoefner's area of study, 87 percent of all the German women eighteen or older were married (or widowed), and 97 percent of these were married to German men. German men eighteen or older in these counties, who made up 57 percent of the German-born population, were also almost without exception married to German women (96 percent).[14]

German-Speakers in Rural Areas

Other important demographic information for this study is the relative strength of German-speakers in the nineteenth-century American rural population and women's numbers among agricultural workers. Scholars of German-American history disagree on the extent and significance of urbanization of the immigrants in the nineteenth century. Wolfgang Helbich and Ulrike Sommer point out that German-Americans in the 1870s were much less likely to have agricultural occupations than were either the Americans or the Germans in the Old World (see table B6). The high percentage of German-Americans in the trades probably included some farmers who gave their Old World profession to census enumerators or who were practicing their trade on the side to supplement income. Nevertheless, the disparity is striking. Part of the reason has to do with the economic pressures of immigration. Niles Carpenter has said that cities are "way stations for immigrants" and that therefore "immigrants have always been heavily represented in the cities." We know that many immigrants, whether

Table B6. Germans, Americans, and German-Americans by
Occupational Sectors, 1870s

	Agriculture (%)	Trades (%)	Commerce/Services (%)
Germans (1875)	49	30	21
Americans (1870)	47	22	31
German-Americans (1870)	27	37	36

Source: Wolfgang Helbich and Ulrike Sommer, *"Alle Menschen sind dort gleich . . .": Die Deutsche Amerika-Auswanderung im 19. und 20. Jahrhundert,* ed. Armin Reese and Uwe Uffelmann, Historisches Seminar, 10 (Düsseldorf: Schwann, 1988), 12.

traveling alone or in families, did not come directly to the rural frontier but stopped in cities for a time to earn money for land and equipment and to become acquainted with American ways. Kamphoefner points out that the urbanization index of German-Americans, based on their residence in the eight largest American cities, declined in each decade from 1850 to 1890. The same is true in the forty-four largest cities between 1870 and 1900, the period of increasing urbanization. While acknowledging the greater urbanization of the German-born, Kamphoefner sees this as a result of their tendency to settle first in cities before going on to farms. He points to shared places of origin of German-speaking immigrants who lived in cities and in the countryside surrounding those cities as proof that residence in a city was a mere prelude to residence on a farm. Similarly, Klaus J. Bade tries to explain why more than 51 percent of German-Americans lived in cities of over 25,000 in 1900, while 35 percent of citizens of the German Empire lived in cities of over 20,000 at that same time. He speculates this was because the impoverished families that made up the bulk of the immigration of the early 1880s went to cities to earn money to buy farms but then were unable to do so because of rising land prices and adverse economic conditions in the early 1890s.[15]

Some evidence from the early twentieth century suggests that urban areas continued to be way stations for immigrants and places for young rural people to earn money to help support their parents, siblings, and the family farm enterprise or to gain financial independence so they could undertake farming themselves. The urban population (incorporated areas of 2,500 and more) of both male and female German-speakers was markedly younger than the rural (see table B7). It is interesting that the percentages of the oldest group of rural and

Table B7. Populations by Age and Sex in Rural and
Urban Areas, 1920

Age	Rural			Urban		
	Both Sexes %	Females %	Males %	Both Sexes %	Females %	Males %
German-speakers						
Under 15	2.2	2.3	2.1	1.4	1.5	1.4
15 to 59	66.3	66.0	66.0	76.0	75.0	77.1
60 and over	31.4	31.6	31.2	22.4	21.5	23.4
Foreign-born whites						
Under 15	4.6	5.1	4.2	3.4	3.5	3.4
15 to 59	70.4	69.2	71.4	85.0	84.2	85.7
60 and over	24.8	25.6	24.2	11.4	12.2	10.8

Source: Derived from Carpenter, table 78, 172–73.

urban residents are higher for the German-speakers than for all other
white immigrants. On the one hand, this indicates the tendency for
the generation of those who settled in urban areas in the mid- and late
nineteenth century to move to rural areas in old age. On the other
hand, it also shows the high degree of urbanization among German-
speakers. The proportions of children in the German-speaking population are also interesting. The higher percentage of children in the
country than in the city, especially in view of the strength of the elderly rural population, indicates the persistence of fecundity patterns
among rural immigrants. Children were still an important source of
farm labor in 1920.[16]

German-Speakers and the Foreign-Born in Agricultural Occupations

Kathleen Conzen has calculated the number and percentage of German
immigrants engaged in agriculture for the years 1870 to 1900. Although
German-Americans were highly urbanized, they were also heavily represented among the foreign-born in the American agricultural sector (see
table B8). The percentage engaged in agriculture was higher for German immigrants than for foreign-born as a whole (the average percentage of all immigrant agricultural wage earners was 22.9 percent in 1870,
23.3 percent in 1880, 25.6 percent in 1890, and 13.1 percent in 1900).

Table B8. German Immigrants as Agricultural Wage Earners,
1870–1900

	1870	1880	1890	1900
Total number	244,531	293,722	389,993	363,004
As percentage of all U.S. agricultural wage earners	3.8	3.8	4.6	3.3
As percentage of all immigrant agricultural wage earners	36.3	36.1	35.8	33.7
As percentage of all German-born wage earners	26.8	28.4	26.0	25.2

Source: Derived from Kathleen Neils Conzen, "Deutsche Einwander im ländlichen Amerika: Problemfelder und Forschungsergebnisse," trans. Angela Adams and Klaus J. Bade, in *Auswanderer Wandererbeiter Gastarbeiter: Bevölkerung, Arbeitsmarkt und Wanderung in Deutschland seit der Mitte des 18. Jahrhunderts,* ed. Klaus J. Bade (Ostfildern: Scripta Mercaturae Berlag, 1984), table 1, 351.

Only the Scandinavians were more heavily engaged in agriculture than were the German-born.[17] In the midwestern states of the present study, the German-born made up a significant part of the agricultural sector by 1880 (see table B9). Chicago and St. Louis obviously drew German-born immigrants away from rural areas in Illinois and Missouri (see table B9). Nevertheless, the extent of agricultural occupation among the German-born even in these two states was above the 28.4 percent national average of German immigrants in U.S. agriculture in 1880 (see table B8). Certainly the agricultural sector was strong among German-born wage earners in these midwestern states, claiming the majority of wage earners in Iowa, Kansas, and Nebraska.[18]

Impressive though these statistics are, they pose certain problems for the purposes of this study. Census information about agricultural workers can give us only partial information about women in rural areas. Unless they were wage earners (sole owners of farms or paid farm laborers), they were not counted in the occupational statistics. Nonetheless, the census material from 1900 contains some useful information about the presence of foreign-born women among agricultural wage earners in general and in these midwestern states that can serve as an introduction to a more specific look at rural German-speaking women in this area. The limitations of each aspect of the analysis will be pointed out in the appropriate place, but a few words of general warning are also called for here. I have discussed the difficulties of clearly identifying German-speakers from immigration and census information. Other complications arise

Table B9. German-born in the Agricultural Sector in the Midwest, 1880

State	German-Born Agricultural Wage Earners	Percentage of German-Born among All Agricultural Wage Earners in the State	Percentage of Agricultural Wage Earners among German-Born Wage Earners	Percentage of Agricultural Wage Earners among All Wage Earners in the State
Illinois	42,356	9.7	34.3	43.6
Iowa	29,073	9.6	59.3	57.5
Kansas	10,380	5.0	65.4	63.9
Missouri	16,616	4.7	29.2	51.3
Nebraska	11,459	12.7	70.6	59.3

Source: Derived from U.S. Census Office, *U.S. Census Reports, Tenth Census, 1880,* table 34, 808–54.

from inconsistencies and inadequacies in the definitions and scope of census data. The terms *rural* and *urban,* which might have helped differentiate among population groups, were not used in early census enumerations, and later they meant different things at different times. Towns and cities of 4,000 population or more were set aside in the 1880 census. In 1920, "urban" was any incorporated place of 2,500 inhabitants or more, and "rural" was everything else. In 1900, the U.S. Census Bureau established a category of "semi-urban" for incorporated areas with populations of 1,000 to 4,000. In some of its tables, however, this census differentiates between cities having at least 50,000 inhabitants and all other areas ("smaller cities and country districts"). That 76.9 percent of the U.S. population residing in places smaller than 50,000 lived in communities of fewer than 2,500 in 1900 indicates the predominately rural nature of American society at the end of the century.[19] The term *rural* refers to communities under 2,500 in the following analysis of material drawn from the 1900 census.

The percentage of foreign-born women age sixteen or older who lived in smaller cities and country districts and were wage earners (all occupations) in 1900 was lower than the national average for all female wage earners (see table B10). White foreign-born females tended to be wage earners somewhat more often than white native-born women were but less often than women as a whole, which included

Table B10. Percentage of Female Wage Earners over
Fifteen, 1900

a. In cities under 50,000 population and country areas
   All females, continental United States   18
   Native white females, both parents native   13
   White foreign-born females   15

b. White female wage earners in the Midwest

	Native Parentage	Foreign-born
Illinois	12.6	11.5
Iowa	14.1	10.6
Missouri	9.5	9.5
Nebraska	13.1	9.5
Kansas	11.4	9.4

Source: Derived from *Statistics of Women at Work* (Washington, D.C.:
GPO, 1907), table 11, 152–53.

black women, half of whom were in the labor force in 1900. In four
of the five states I examined in my study, however, foreign-born females were less likely to be wage earners than were women of native
parentage. This may reflect more conservative attitudes toward wom-
en's roles outside the home among some immigrants in rural areas and
the strong integration of foreign-born women into family farming
enterprises, either as wives or daughters.

The age distribution among female foreign-born wage earners also
shows patterns that differ from those of the dominant culture (see table
B11). Foreign-born females were much more likely than white females
of native parentage to be wage earners between the ages of sixteen and
twenty-four and somewhat more likely to work for wages during the
peak childbearing years between twenty-five and thirty-four. They were
also somewhat less likely to work after the age of forty-five. The north-
central division and its two subdivisions, which encompass the Midwest, show the same pattern as that of the national population of foreign-born females, except that an even more conservative trend may
be discerned in the lower percentages of such women who worked for
wages between the ages of twenty-five and forty-four. I infer from these
data that young, probably unmarried immigrant women worked more
often outside the home in rural areas but somewhat less after marriage
than women of native parentage.

Table B11. Wage Earners in the Female Population in Small Cities and Country Districts, by Age and Nativity, 1900

White Female Population	Continental United States %	North-Central Division %	Eastern North-Central Division %	Western North-Central Division %
16 to 20 years of age				
Native parentage	18.0	18.4	19.9	16.2
Foreign-born	46.5	39.4	41.9	36.4
21 to 24 years of age				
Native parentage	18.7	20.4	20.8	19.8
Foreign-born	34.4	26.6	27.8	25.2
25 to 34 years of age				
Native parentage	11.9	11.7	12.1	11.1
Foreign-born	15.7	10.2	10.7	9.5
35 to 44 years of age				
Native parentage	10.2	8.8	9.2	8.1
Foreign-born	10.1	6.8	7.1	6.4
45 years of age and over				
Native parentage	10.2	8.4	8.5	8.2
Foreign-born	8.6	7.2	7.0	7.5

Source: Derived from *Statistics of Women at Work,* table 12, 154–57.

Note: The eastern north-central census division includes Ohio, Indiana, Illinois, Michigan, and Wisconsin; the western north-central division includes Minnesota, Iowa, Missouri, North Dakota, South Dakota, Nebraska, and Kansas.

Childbearing and Marital Status: Relation to Agricultural Occupations of Immigrant Women

One reason that mature immigrant women worked for wages less commonly than native-born American women did is that they had more children. In 1920, the national average for the number of children born to a white woman of native parentage was 3.0, with 2.9 children still living. Foreign-born white women had an average of 4.0 children, with 3.4 children surviving. For Austrian-born women, the numbers were 4.3 children born and 3.4 children still living, and for German-born women, 4.4 children born and 3.9 children living. The differences in child mortality are striking. In addition, other information indicates that a larger proportion of women of native parentage had families of one, two, or three children. In 1920, 689 children out of 1,000 born to women of native parentage were the first, second, or third child born in the family, compared with 454 children of Austrian-born mothers and 482 of German-born women.[20] German-speaking women were more likely to be pregnant or caring for young children for longer periods of their lives than were women of native parentage. Their children also had a greater chance of dying. Women in rural areas had more children than did those in urban areas, for children were a source of labor. One woman articulated the reasons for this. After eleven years on a Kansas farm, the Greving family opened a store in a small city in Idaho. Pauline Greving wrote that she would soon give birth to her sixth child and then "that is enough, for in the city there is not as much work for them as on a farm."[21]

As stated in chapter 1, illegitimacy had become increasingly common in some rural areas of northern and western Europe during the nineteenth century. This pattern was broken in America. Given economic opportunities, the lack of legal constraints, and changed social environments, most German-speakers married before having children. The close communal ties of the immigrant community might have also played a role in regulating sexuality. Whatever the reasons, the foreign-born generally had much lower illegitimacy rates than women of native parentage. In 1920, the national average of illegitimate births per 1,000 births among white women was 14.2. In the cities it was somewhat higher (15.9) and in rural areas lower (12.5). German- and Austrian-born women, however, gave birth out of wedlock on the average of 5.3 and 6.6 times in 1,000, respectively. In rural areas, the occurrences of illegitimacy were even less common: among women born in Germany as well as those born in Austria, 4.2 births in 1,000 were illegitimate.[22]

Statistics on female wage earners in the agricultural sector support the conclusion that marital status influenced the likelihood that a rural foreign-born woman would work outside the home. Of the 34,982 foreign-born women over fifteen years old who were listed as farmers, planters, and overseers in the agricultural sector in 1900, 56 percent were fifty-five years of age and over (see table B12). That is, they were most probably widows.[23] Several differences between women of foreign and native parentage are evident in table B12. The more equal distribution of foreign-born female agricultural laborers in all age groupings indicates a greater willingness on their part to do such labor throughout their lives. Table B12 also supports the assumption that foreign-born women of childbearing years were less likely to be agricultural wage earners. The relatively small percentage of those between the ages of sixteen and thirty-four who were engaged in all agricultural pursuits (5.45 percent versus 15.65 percent for women of native

Table B12. White Female Wage Earners in the Agricultural Sector, by Nativity and Age Groups, 1900

Occupation and Nativity	Number	Percentage by Age Groups				
		16–24	25–34	35–41	45–54	55+
All agricultural pursuits						
Native parentage	264,687	21.1	10.2	15.7	20.7	32.1
Foreign-born	40,926	5.6	5.3	12.7	25.4	50.9
Agricultural laborers						
Native parentage	82,584	62.0	16.8	10.0	6.7	4.3
Foreign-born	4,576	39.2	16.5	16.3	13.4	14.2
Farmers, planters, overseers						
Native parentage	179,475	2.3	7.1	18.3	27.2	44.9
Foreign-born	34,982	0.9	3.7	12.1	26.9	56.0
Other agricultural pursuits						
Native parentage	2,628	13.1	14.3	19.8	22.3	30.3
Foreign-born	1,368	11.3	7.0	15.8	24.4	41.2

Source: Derived from *Statistics of Women at Work*, table 17, 162–66.
Note: Percentages do not add up to 100 percent because the category "age unknown" has been omitted. There was an error in the original figure cited for foreign-born women engaged in all agricultural pursuits, which has been corrected.

parentage) implies this. The smaller percentages of foreign-born women under forty who were independent farmers also indicates that they were less likely to be independent agricultural wage earners when of childbearing age than were women of native parentage. That a consistently higher proportion of the foreign-born female wage earners belonged to the oldest age group in each of the agricultural occupations points to the more traditional work and role patterns for women among the foreign-born. Until her children were grown or her husband died, the married foreign-born woman was less likely than a woman of native parentage to be an agricultural wage earner.

Foreign-born women were, however, more likely to run farms themselves in the midwestern states of this study. In every state except Missouri, the percentage of female farmers among the foreign-born agricultural workers was markedly higher than among female workers of native parentage (see table B13). In four of the five states, the pro-

Table B13. White Female Farmers, Planters, and Overseers over Fifteen, by Nativity and Selected States, 1900

	Number	Percentage in U.S.	Percentage in State
Continental United States			
Native parentage	179,448	83.7	
Foreign-born	34,975	16.3	
Illinois			
Native parentage	6,269	3.5	72.4
Foreign-born	2,385	6.8	27.6
Iowa			
Native parentage	3,064	1.7	53.6
Foreign-born	2,653	7.6	46.4
Missouri			
Native parentage	10,993	6.1	88.6
Foreign-born	1,411	4.0	11.4
Nebraska			
Native parentage	1,322	0.7	48.0
Foreign-born	1,432	4.1	52.0
Kansas			
Native parentage	3,480	1.9	70.9
Foreign-born	1,427	4.1	29.1

Source: Derived from *Statistics of Women at Work*, Table 24, 180.

Note: The discrepancy between the numbers of white female farmers, planters, and overseers in the continental United States cited in this table and in table B12 is unaccounted for in *Statistics of Women at Work*, tables 17 and 14.

portion of foreign-born female farmers was well above the national average of 16.3 percent. Missouri, the exception to this pattern, had the smallest percentage of foreign-born female inhabitants in rural areas among the five states (see table B14). Why were foreign-born women more likely than women of native parentage to be independent farmers in 1900? A possible explanation for this may be that foreign-born women had shared more actively in farm work than women of native parentage and thus felt able to manage a farm if circumstances dictated. Another cultural factor was probably also at work here. As table B12 indicates, at least three-quarters of these independent farm women were forty-five years of age or older. The desire to preserve the farm as a family possession for the next generation would have strongly motivated many foreign-born widows to continue the family farming

Table B14. Foreign-born Females among Female
Population in Rural Areas of the United States
and the Midwest, 1900

	Number	Percentage
United States	2,308,288	13.1
Illinois	157,099	16.7
Iowa	126,201	19.3
Kansas	49,588	11.9
Missouri	31,466	4.8
Nebraska	63,493	23.9
Average of five-state area		15.3

Source: Derived from *Statistics of Women at Work,* table 11, 152–
53.

enterprise with the help of their children. Certainly women who had
emigrated from rural German-speaking Europe were likely to behave
according to this value system. Anglo-American women in similar circumstances were not under the same cultural influences.[24]

*German-Speakers and the Occupational Analysis of the 1900
Census*

This discussion of foreign-born women and their place in nineteenth-
century rural America can, of course, serve only as background material for this study. Until 1920, almost no detailed census compilation
or study separated German-speaking women from men in rural areas.
My demographic examination must therefore remain incomplete. Giv-
en the many similarities among immigrant women and the strong presence of rural German-speakers in the geographic area examined in this
book, however, the insights gained from data about the foreign-born
can be considered generally valid for that group as well.

One of the few areas offering detailed information separated by sex
about rural German-speakers is the occupational analysis of the 1900
census. This material, however, encompasses all persons "of foreign
parentage," that is, persons who had one or both parents born in a foreign land. The American-born children of immigrants are therefore included. Tables B15, B16, and B17 provide a broad overview of the
participation of first- and second-generation German-speakers in Midwest agriculture at the turn of the century. Since they no doubt include
non-German-speakers among the foreign stock (persons of the first and

Table B15. Males and Females over Nine in Agricultural Pursuits, by Region and Parentage, 1900

| | | | Place of Birth of Parent(s) | | | |
	Aggregate	Foreign Parentage	Austria	Germany	Russia	Switzer-land
a. Males						
Continental						
United States	9,404,429	2,124,108	16,104	775,254	23,761	37,442
Illinois	450,614	171,316	334	89,983	453	2,420
Iowa	363,472	183,992	612	79,009	91	2,739
Kansas	264,618	85,110	984	30,189	4,653	2,371
Missouri	447,315	74,346	448	45,767	65	2,530
Nebraska	182,338	99,832	1,451	42,551	1,732	1,452
b. Females						
Continental						
United States	977,446	71,565	993	26,823	909	1,124
Illinois	12,167	4,837	5	2,398	50	59
Iowa	8,132	4,490	17	1,807	—	44
Kansas	6,634	2,413	22	826	64	65
Missouri	15,978	2,978	24	1,781	1	78
Nebraska	4,249	2,533	35	902	62	41

Source: Derived from U.S. Census Bureau, *U.S. Census Reports: Occupations of the Twelfth Census, 1900* (Washington, D.C.: GPO, 1904), tables 38 and 39, 190–213.

Table B16. Males and Females over Nine in Agricultural Pursuits as a Percentage of All Occupations, by Region and Parentage, 1900

| | | | Place of Birth of Parent(s) | | | |
	Areawide Average	Foreign Parentage	Austria	Germany	Russia	Switzer-land
a. Males						
Continental						
United States	39.5	32.3	9.7	28.1	11.6	39.5
Illinois	29.6	20.1	3.0	27.8	3.0	32.4
Iowa	53.3	55.9	3.8	61.2	8.9	62.9
Kansas	58.5	61.4	46.1	65.0	80.0	74.9
Missouri	46.3	26.8	13.5	30.5	2.0	39.9
Nebraska	55.7	60.8	60.3	68.5	46.4	68.6

Table B16, continued

	Areawide Average	Foreign Parentage	Place of Birth of Parent(s)			
			Austria	Germany	Russia	Switzerland
b. Females						
Continental						
United States	18.4	3.5	3.9	4.8	2.2	7.4
Illinois	4.1	2.6	0.3	3.8	1.8	4.5
Iowa	7.6	8.5	8.1	9.6	—	8.6
Kansas	11.9	14.7	15.4	16.5	11.1	20.9
Missouri	10.3	5.5	5.3	6.4	—	8.2
Nebraska	9.1	10.9	10.3	12.3	13.0	19.6

Source: Derived from U.S. Census Bureau, *U.S. Census Reports: Occupations of the Twelfth Census, 1900,* tables 38 and 39, 190–213.

second generations), the information they contain is less precise than I would wish for the purposes of this study. For example, a sizable percentage of the descendants of those born in Austria residing in Nebraska would have been Czech-speakers, but the vast majority of the persons in tables B15, B16, and B17 would have had German-speaking parents. The relatively large number of immigrants born in Russia whose children were engaged in agriculture in Kansas and Nebraska, for example, were Germans from Russia. These tables establish for the second generation what has been noted earlier about the foreign-born: the strength of the German-born and their children among the agricultural foreign stock and their relatively strong overall engagement in agriculture in the five-state region of the Midwest. The rural clustering of immigrants from various regions is also evident in the relatively large percentage of the Austrian-born in Kansas and Nebraska, for example. The almost negligible number of Russian-born farm workers in Illinois and Missouri points to the inability of that group and other late nineteenth-century immigrants (including, to a somewhat lesser degree, the Austrians) to penetrate established agricultural areas. The foreign stock (except in Missouri) and the German-speaking stock made up higher percentages of the agricultural working population in each of the states in question than the respective national averages for the agricultural sector. The importance of both agriculture and the engagement of the foreign stock in each state is evident in these percentages.

Table B17. Persons over Nine in Agriculture, by Region,
Parentage, and Sex, 1900

		Agricultural Occupations			
				German-Speaking Parentage[a]	
	Aggregate, All Workers	Native Parentage %	Foreign Parentage %	Males %	Females %
Continental United States	29,073,233	37.7	7.6	2.67	0.09
Illinois	1,804,040	29.6	9.76	4.98	0.13
Iowa	789,395	53.3	23.88	10.01	0.23
Kansas	507,740	58.5	17.24	5.95	0.16
Missouri	1,121,392	46.3	6.9	4.08	0.16
Nebraska	373,970	55.7	27.37	11.38	0.24

Source: Derived from U.S. Census Bureau, *U.S. Census Reports: Occupations of the Twelfth Census, 1900,* tables 38 and 39, 190–213.
a. Excludes foreign stock of Austrian, Russian, and Swiss parentage.

The relatively small number of female agricultural wage earners from German-speaking stock and the fact that most farm women were not counted among them make it difficult to come to firm conclusions about women based on the statistics contained in tables B15, B16, and B17. Since women and girls of foreign parentage made up only 7.3 percent of all U.S. female agricultural workers in 1900, the even smaller number who were German-speakers seems insignificant. It is, however, still noteworthy that in 1900 persons of foreign parentage constituted 38.9 percent of all female wage earners in the United States.[25] Whereas women and girls of the foreign stock were working for wages in large numbers elsewhere in the economy, their numbers as farm laborers were far below what might have been expected from those statistics and from their numerical presence in rural society. This testifies to the unpaid nature of women's work in farm families, as well as to the failure of the agricultural community and census takers to acknowledge their labor. It also indicates the tendency for young, unmarried women to work in something other than the agricultural sector, if they worked outside the home. Indeed, about one-half of the German-born female work force in 1890 was in domestic service, although the proportion had diminished to about one-third by 1900.[26]

Bengt Ankarloo views the fact that young women did not find paid employment in the agricultural sector as one result of the movement to a capitalist, market economy and as proof that farm life did not and could not "better and more willingly keep and provide for all its members."[27] This judgment, however, may be too harsh. Without knowing how many of the women who worked outside of the agricultural sector returned to it upon marriage, we cannot be sure that their labor in towns and cities was truly divorced from farm and family life. It appears that the rural economies of Nebraska and Kansas were able to offer women and girls paid employment in 1900, perhaps because there were labor shortages in these relatively new areas and because other sectors of the economy were underdeveloped. It is likely in any case that many of the female foreign stock who were wage earners in rural areas gave part of their earnings to help support their families. In doing so, they would have been acting in accordance with Old World family economic structures and broadly accepted behavior in American society.[28]

Patterns of German-Speakers in Agriculture

The goal and economic rationale of the Germanic peasant family was the preservation and enlargement of the family holdings for future generations. The relative strength of the German-speaking stock in the midwestern states (see tables B15, B16, and B17) indicates that these immigrants and their children were attaining that goal in 1900. The success of German-speaking farm families in establishing long-term family holdings is seen more clearly in statistics from the mid-twentieth century. Their relative concentration among the foreign stock engaged as farmers and farm managers remained high (see table B18). Although by 1950 German-born males were less likely to be farmers than to be engaged in other occupations, the same was not true of the male descendants of earlier German immigrants. They, along with the Swiss male and female and the German female foreign stock, showed a remarkably strong propensity toward agricultural pursuits. The persistence of the descendants of German-speakers as farmers in America is evident here. These statistics also show the agricultural tradition to have been especially vigorous and long-lasting among women of German and Swiss heritage.[29]

Conclusions

Certain conclusions may be drawn from this statistical analysis. Among immigrant families, women were consistently in the numerical major-

Table B18. Concentration of German and Swiss Foreign Stock as Farmers and Farm Managers, 1950[a]

	Males	Females
German-Americans		
Foreign-born	80	188
Foreign or mixed parentage	150	195
Swiss-Americans		
Foreign-born	139	321
Foreign or mixed parentage	165	257

Source: E. P. Hutchinson, *Immigrants and Their Children, 1850–1950* (New York: Wiley, 1956), table 41, 224–39.

a. Base proportion = 100.

ity, although German-speaking males outnumbered them in the entire immigration (see tables B1 and B2). Demographic evidence in the rural Midwest reflects the transferal of Old World marriage and family patterns into their new lives. German-speaking women in rural areas in the early years of settlement were most likely to live in family units. When they married, and just about all of them did, they almost without exception married German-speaking men (see tables B4 and B5). Continuing to view children as sources of labor, they bore more children than Anglo-American women did. If young and single, they were wage earners in larger proportions than women of native parentage (see table B11). After marriage and during childbearing and child-rearing, they were less likely than Anglo-American women to work for wages (see tables B11 and B12). Yet they were proportionately much more numerous as independent farmers after the age of forty-five than women of native parentage (see table B13). Except for the numerical imbalance between the sexes, the demographic patterns of the rural German-speaking female population in the five-state area is what we might expect, given what we know about female and family life in Europe. That is, the demographics of the German-speaking female population of the five-state region reveal traits of cultural conservatism. Narrative and other evidence presented in this study generally confirms the traditional structure of women's and family life discernible in the statistical data.

The statistics confirm that Illinois, Missouri, Iowa, Kansas, and Nebraska constitute a rich area for the investigation of German-speaking rural immigrants. In all five states, the percentage of the German-born engaged in agriculture was higher than the national average (see table B9). Yet, between 1870 and 1900, the German-born only made up between 3.3 and 4.6 percent of all agricultural wage earners in the United States (see table B8). Thus, even if they were the second-most numerous group among immigrant agricultural workers, we cannot credit them with the primary settlement of the Midwest, as Dietmar Kügler did (see the Introduction). Nonetheless, their ability to outlast other groups, buy out their neighbors, and establish family holdings on the land surely identifies them as successful American farmers (see table B18, chapter 5, and tables 5–7 in chapter 5). Their conservatism, visible in their application of European patterns of rural family structures and values to the American situation, helped them in this (see chapter 1).

Notes

Abbreviations

AHSOHP   Amana Historical Society Oral History Project, Amana Heritage Society Library, Amana, Iowa

BABS   Bochumer Auswanderer-Briefsammlung (Bochum Emigrant Letter Collection), Ruhr University, Bochum, Germany

CCMPC   Cooper County, Missouri, Probate Court, Archives, Boonville, Missouri

CHI   Concordia Historical Institute, Clayton, Missouri

ISHD-HS   Iowa State Historical Department, Historical Society, Iowa City, Iowa

ISHD-MA   Iowa State Historical Department, Museum and Archives, Des Moines, Iowa

ISHL   Illinois State Historical Library, Springfield, Illinois

KSHS   Kansas State Historical Society, Topeka, Kansas

LDMC   Lilla Day Monroe Collection of Pioneer Stories, Kansas State Historical Society, Topeka, Kansas

NSHS   Nebraska State Historical Society, Lincoln, Nebraska

Tms   Typewritten copy of a handwritten document or oral interview

WHMC-C   Western Historical Manuscripts Collection, Columbia, Missouri

Introduction

1. Estelle Schelbitzki Freeman, letter of 1 August 1994, in my possession.

2. Lillian Schelbitzki Meistrell, letter of 14 July 1994, in my possession.

3. Dietmar Kügler, *Die Deutschen in Amerika: Die Geschichte der deutschen Auswanderung in die U.S.A. seit 1683* (Stuttgart: Pietsch, 1983), 182–83. Unless otherwise indicated, all translations from German to English are mine. I have normalized the spelling and punctuation of translations from personal writings when necessary to clarify meaning.

4. Frederick Jackson Turner, *The Significance of the Frontier in American History,* ed. Harold P. Simonson (New York: Ungar, 1963), 29, 57. Turner read this paper in 1893 before the American Historical Association.

5. The prominence of Germans in American agriculture is noted by Kathleen Neils Conzen, "Germans," in *Harvard Encyclopedia of American Ethnic Groups,* ed. Stephan Thernstrom (Cambridge, Mass.: Belknap Press of Harvard University Press, 1980): "Although Germans in 1870 were only 4 per-

232 Notes to Pages 5–6

cent of all American farm workers, slightly over a quarter of all employed
Germans were in agriculture, constituting over 33 percent of all foreign-born
farmers. By 1900 Germans owned nearly 11 percent of American farms and
accounted for almost 10 percent of the country's agricultural employment.
Fifty years later, the German-born and their children were still the single most
numerous immigrant group in agriculture" (415). Local concentrations of
farmers of German ancestry showed even more impressive growth. For example, Seddie Cogswell Jr.'s study of five counties in eastern Iowa showed
that in 1850, 23.1 percent of the population of this area was foreign-born but
that this had grown to 48.7 percent in 1880. Of the foreign-born in the six
Iowa counties, 62 percent were from the Continent in 1860, and by 1880,
63 percent were German-speakers (*Tenure, Nativity, and Age as Factors in
Iowa Agriculture, 1850–1880* [Ames: Iowa State University Press, 1975], 11).
The 1980 census indicates that 33 percent of the population of Indiana
claimed part German ancestry, as did 46 percent of the population of Iowa,
35 percent of the population of Kansas, 43 percent of the population of Minnesota, 32 percent of the population of Missouri, 46 percent of the population of Nebraska, 47 percent of the population of North Dakota, 33 percent
of the population of Ohio, 47 percent of the population of South Dakota,
and 52 percent of the population of Wisconsin.

6. Adolph Roenigk, *Pioneer History of Kansas* (privately published, 1933),
159–63.

7. Ibid., 159.

8. Few scholarly studies have focused on the immigrant woman in Amer-
ican history. Doris Weatherford's *Foreign and Female: Immigrant Women in
America, 1840–1930* (New York: Schocken, 1986) is one. Cecyle S. Neidle
surveys women of prominence in *America's Immigrant Women* (Boston:
Twayne, 1975). For a useful collection of related texts, see Maxine Schwartz
Seller, ed., *Immigrant Women* (Philadelphia: Temple University Press, 1981).
Other studies that examine the role of the family in the adaptation of ethnic
immigrants to America include Virginia Yans-McLaughlin, *Family and Com-
munity: Italian Immigrants in Buffalo, 1890–1930* (Ithaca, N.Y.: Cornell
University Press, 1977); Tamara Hareven, "The Laborers of Manchester, New
Hampshire, 1912–1922: The Role of Family and Ethnicity in Adjustment to
Industrial Life," *Labor History* 17 (Spring 1975): 249–65; Hasia R. Diner,
Erin's Daughters in America (Baltimore: Johns Hopkins University Press,
1983); and Stella DeRosa Trgoff, "Immigrant Women, the Family and Work:
1850–1950," *Trends in History* 2 (Summer 1982): 31–47. Trgoff's article is
a useful survey of studies that challenge the stereotype of immigrant women
as passive victims of their sex and ethnicity. Donna Gabaccia has challenged
scholars of history, the social sciences, and women's studies to investigate issues relating to immigrant women in a comparative, inclusive manner to bridge
the fragmented and isolated approach that has characterized many studies
("Immigrant Women: Nowhere at Home?" *Journal of American Ethnic History* 10 [Summer 1991]: 61–87).

9. Glenda Riley, *Frontierswomen: The Iowa Experience* (Ames: Iowa State

University Press, 1981), xv; Sandra Myres, *Westering Women and the Frontier Experience, 1800–1915* (Albuquerque: University of New Mexico Press, 1981), xvi. Other studies do not address the question of ethnicity at all. See, for example, Julie Roy Jeffrey, *Frontier Women: The Trans-Mississippi West, 1840–1880* (New York: Hill and Wang, 1979); John Mack Faragher, *Women and Men on the Overland Trail* (New Haven, Conn.: Yale University Press, 1979); and Joanna L. Stratton, *Pioneer Women: Voices from the Kansas Frontier* (New York: Simon and Schuster, 1981).

10. John Mack Faragher's *Sugar Creek: Life on the Illinois Prairie* (New Haven, Conn.: Yale University Press, 1986) is one of the few important historical studies to recognize and exploit this. The present study seeks to emulate the integrative nature of Faragher's work and to answer in a small way his call in "History from the Inside-Out: Writing the History of Women in Rural America," *American Quarterly* 33 (Winter 1981): 537–57. Nancy F. Cott and Elizabeth Pleck also pointed to the need for women's history studies that are comparative and cross-cultural (*A Heritage of Her Own: Toward a New Social History of American Women* [New York: Simon and Schuster, 1979], 21). Joan M. Jensen and Darlis A. Miller made the same point about the history of frontierswomen ("The Gentle Tamers Revisited: New Approaches to the History of Women in the American West," *Pacific Historical Review* 49 [May 1980]: 173–213). Paula Nelson's examination of western South Dakota is an excellent example of a study that takes women's and ethnic immigrants' contributions into account in the building of a frontier community (*After the West Was Won* [Iowa City: University of Iowa Press, 1986]). Diner concluded her examination of Irish immigrant women in the nineteenth century with a call for similar studies on other ethnic women (154).

11. Carol K. Coburn, "Ethnicity, Religion, and Gender: The Women of Block, Kansas, 1868–1940," *Great Plains Quarterly* 8 (Fall 1988): 222. Coburn's study of rural Block makes the same point (*Life at Four Corners: Religion, Gender, and Education in a German-Lutheran Community, 1868–1945* [Lawrence: University Press of Kansas, 1992], 4–5).

12. Kathleen Neils Conzen has done the most significant work on this topic. Her *Immigrant Milwaukee, 1836–1860: Accommodation and Community in a Frontier City* (Cambridge, Mass.: Harvard University Press, 1976) contains large segments on German immigrants. She first called for the need for rural studies in "Historical Approaches to the Study of Rural Ethnic Communities," in *Ethnicity on the Great Plains*, ed. Frederick C. Luebke (Lincoln: University of Nebraska Press, 1980), 1–18. She provides an overview of the particular problems and important questions associated with work on rural German-American history in "Deutsche Einwanderer im ländlichen Amerika: Problemfelder und Forschungsergebnisse," trans. Angela Adams and Klaus J. Bade, in *Auswanderer Wanderarbeiter Gastarbeiter: Bevölkerung, Arbeitsmarkt und Wanderung in Deutschland seit der Mitte des 18. Jahrhunderts*, ed. Klaus J. Bade (Ostfildern: Scripta Mercaturae Verlag, 1984), 350–77.

13. Mack Walker documents the background and nature of German regionalism and traditionalism in *German Home Towns, Communities, State and*

General Estate, 1648–1871 (Ithaca, N.Y.: Cornell University Press, 1971). Other studies examining the diversity of Germans in America are in Randall M. Miller, ed., *Germans in America: Retrospect and Prospect* (Philadelphia: German Society of Pennsylvania, 1984).

14. Georg Isernhagen, "The Story of My Life," in *Memoirs of Pioneers of Cheyenne County, Kansas: Ole Robert Cram, Georg Isernhagen, Nancy Moore Wieck,* ed. Lee F. Pendergrass (Hays, Kans.: Fort Hays Ethnic Studies Center, 1980), 71; Adolph Schock, *In Quest of Free Land* (San Jose, Calif.: San Jose State College, 1964), 151; Nicholas Gonner, *Die Luxemburger in der neuen Welt* (Dubuque, Iowa: Press of the "Luxemburger Gazette" for the author, 1889), 218. I did not discover the recent translated rendition of Gonner's book and newspaper articles until after this manuscript was completed, so all translations from *Die Luxemburger in der neuen Welt* are my own. The reader is referred to the two-volume edition by Jean Ensch, Jean-Claude Muller, and Robert Owen, *Luxembourgers in the New World* (Esch-sur Alzette, Luxembourg: Editions-Reliures Schortgen, 1987).

15. Psychological studies of present-day German emigrants show that personality and outer pressures can play a role in the decision to emigrate but most decisive are "relationships, whether these are fantasized or real, past or present, desired or rejected, too many or too few, conducive or inhibiting to emigration" (A. Cropley and Folkert Lüthke, "Endbericht: Zusammenfassung, Psychologie der Auswanderung," DFG-Projekt Cr71/2-1 [Hamburg: Psychologisches Institut II, University of Hamburg, 1988], 3).

16. Mack Walker's *Germany and the Emigration, 1816–1885* (Cambridge, Mass.: Harvard University Press, 1964) remains the classic work on the background of German emigration. Other relevant studies include Walter Kamphoefner, "At the Crossroads of Economic Development: Background Factors Affecting Emigration from Nineteenth-Century Germany," in *Migration across Time and Nations,* ed. Ira Glazier and Luigi De Rosa (New York: Holmes and Meier, 1986), 183–88; Leo Schelbert, "Emigration from Imperial Germany Overseas, 1870–1914," in *Imperial Germany,* ed. Volker Dürr, Kathy Harms, and Peter Hayes (Madison: University of Wisconsin Press, 1985), 112–33; Günther Moltmann, "The Pattern of German Emigration to the United States in the Nineteenth Century," in *America and the Germans: Assessment of a Three-Hundred-Year History,* vol. 1, ed. Frank Trommler and Joseph McVeigh (Philadelphia: University of Philadelphia Press, 1985), 14–24; Wolfgang von Hippel, *Auswanderung aus Südwestdeutschland: Studien zur württembergischen Auswanderung und Auswanderungspolitik im 18. und 19. Jahrhundert* (Stuttgart: Klett-Cotta, 1984); Klaus J. Bade, "Die deutsche überseeische Massenauswanderung im 19. und 20. Jahrhundert: Bestimmungsfaktoren und Entwicklungsbedingungen," in *Auswanderer Wanderarbeiter Gastarbeiter,* ed. Bade, 259–99; Klaus J. Bade, "German Emigration to the United States and Continental Immigration to Germany in the Late Nineteenth and Early Twentieth Centuries," *Central European History* 13 (December 1980): 348–77; Christine Hansen, "Die deutsche Auswanderung im 19. Jahrhundert—ein Mittel zur Lösung sozialer und sozialpolitscher Probleme?" in *Deutsche Ameri-*

kaauswanderung im 19. Jahrhundert, ed. Günther Moltmann (Stuttgart: Metzler, 1976); Rudolph Braun, "The Impact of Cottage Industry on an Agricultural Population," in *The Rise of Capitalism,* ed. David Landes (New York: Macmillan, 1966), 53–64; and Roger Daniels, *Coming to America: A History of Immigration and Ethnicity in American Life* (New York: Harper-Collins, 1990), 145–64. Reinhard R. Doerries provides a more general bibliographic resource in "German Emigration to the United States: A Review Essay on Recent West German Publications," *Journal of American Ethnic History* 6 (Fall 1986): 71–83. Guy Serge Metraux's "Social and Cultural Aspects of Swiss Immigration into the United States in the Nineteenth Century" (Ph.D. diss., Yale University, 1949) surveys French and German Swiss emigration. Gonner's survey of emigration from Luxembourg identifies similar patterns (95, 101–2, 126–28).

17. See Walter Kamphoefner's study of Tecklenburg, Oldenburg, and Hannoverian immigrants in these counties (*Westfalen in der neuen Welt: Eine Sozialgeschichte der Auswanderung im 19. Jahrhundert,* Beiträge zur Volkskultur in Nordwestdeutschland, Volkskundliche Kommission für Westfalen, 26 [Münster: Coppenrath, 1982]; also published in English as *The Westfalians: From Germany to Missouri* [Princeton, N.J.: Princeton University Press, 1987]).

18. Illinois became the twenty-first state in 1818, Missouri the twenty-fourth in 1821, Iowa the twenty-ninth in 1846, Kansas the thirty-fourth in 1861, and Nebraska the thirty-seventh in 1867.

19. Kamphoefner's studies of Westphalian immigrants in Missouri demonstrate this phenomenon clearly. Robert W. Frizzell traces a similar pattern in "Migration Chains to Illinois: The Evidence from German-American Church Records," *Journal of American Ethnic History* 7 (Fall 1987): 59–73. John C. Hudson found the same dynamics at work in the many ethnic groups that settled South Dakota in the late nineteenth and early twentieth centuries ("Migration to an American Frontier," *Annals of the Association of American Geographers* 66 [June 1976]: 242–65).

20. Michael P. Conzen analyzed settlement patterns for Germans and others in his *Frontier Farming in an Urban Shadow* (Madison: State Historical Society of Wisconsin, for the Department of History, University of Wisconsin, 1971). Kamphoefner examines the relationship between assimilation and chain migration ("'Entwurzelt' oder 'verpflanzt'? Zur Bedeutung der Kettenwanderung für die Einwandererakkulturation in Amerika," in *Auswanderer Wanderarbeiter Gastarbeiter,* ed. Bade, 321–49). K. Conzen assumes that the earliest chain migration settlements were probably more uniform in origin and in regional and ethnic identity than later ones, which were made by people who had often lived for some time in the United States or had even been born there ("Deutsche Einwanderer," 369). Gonner's comments on "first and second generation" Luxembourgian-American communities supports this (186–88).

21. Cited in Kathleen Neils Conzen, "Peasant Pioneers: Generational Succession among German Farmers in Frontier Minnesota," in *The Country-*

side in the Age of Capitalist Transformation: Essays in the Social History of Rural America, ed. Steven Hahn and Jonathan Prude (Chapel Hill: University of North Carolina Press, 1985), 265. The role U.S. agencies and institutions played in drawing Germans to the Midwest was also considerable, as Eleanor L. Turk shows in "Selling the Heartland: Agents, Agencies, Press and Policies Promoting German Emigration to Kansas in the Nineteenth Century," *Kansas History* 12 (Autumn 1989): 150–59.

22. Liz Schuster, "'Fleisch wird hier jeden Tag von der Früh bis des Abends gegessen,'" *Offenbach Post* 94 (23/24 April 1983): 23.

23. Gert Goebel, who emigrated as a boy with the Gießen Society, noted the long-term success of German-Americans in persisting on the farm, capitalizing on originally small and poor landholdings, and eventually buying out American neighbors (*Länger als ein Menschenleben in Missouri* [St. Louis: C. Witter, 1877], 23, 46–48). Gonner comments in a similar vein on Luxembourgian and German immigrants in general (147, 161). Kamphoefner noted the higher proportion of Germans who owned real estate in early Missouri, although their holdings were on the average half the size of the Americans' (*The Westfalians,* 124). K. Conzen refers to the most important literature on the topic of agricultural practices of German-speaking immigrants in "Peasant Pioneers" and discusses "the stereotype of the German-American farmer" in "Deutsche Einwanderer," 356–62. See also Alan E. Fusonie, "Our Rural German-American Heritage: A Selective List of Articles," *Journal of NAL Associates* 9 (1984): 37–40.

24. Kamphoefner discusses geographic persistence in his study of Warren and St. Charles counties, Missouri, and relates it to cultural persistence connected to attendance at parochial German-language schools and German-language churches (*The Westfalians,* 170–77). Studies of Scandinavian immigrant communities in the Upper Middle West draw the same conclusions. See Jon Gjerde, *From Peasants to Farmers* (Cambridge: Cambridge University Press, 1985), 114–15, 163–65 passim; and Robert C. Ostergren, *A Community Transplanted* (Madison: University of Wisconsin Press, 1988), 147, 184–85, 210–13 passim.

25. The most thorough study of this attempt is Terry Jordan, *German Seed in Texas Soil: Immigrant Farmers in Nineteenth-Century Texas* (Austin: University of Texas Press, 1966).

26. U.S. citizens now conceptualize this geographic area as the heart of the Midwest, if the cultural and cognitive maps that James R. Shortridge compiled are any indication (*The Middle West: Its Meaning and Culture* [Lawrence: University Press of Kansas, 1989], 84–95).

27. These five states, along with Indiana, Ohio, Wisconsin, Michigan, Minnesota, and the Dakotas, constituted the east and north-central divisions in Niles Carpenter's *Immigrants and Their Children, 1920,* Census Monographs 7 (Washington, D.C.: GPO, 1927). His analysis of census material from 1850 through 1920 shows that Germany was the most common country of birth of foreign-born white immigrants in those two divisions (table 162, 356).

28. Adolf Schroeder, *The Immigrant Experience: Oral History and Folk-*

lore among Missourians from German and German-speaking Groups, prepared by A. Schroeder (Columbia: Department of Germanic and Slavic Languages, University of Missouri–Columbia, 1976), 26; J. Neale Carman, *Foreign-Language Units of Kansas,* vol. 1, *Historical Atlas and Statistics* (Lawrence: University of Kansas Press, 1962), 9; Frederick C. Luebke, "Ethnic Group Settlement on the Great Plains," *Western Historical Quarterly* 8 (October 1977): 412.

29. The essays in James H. Madison, ed., *Heartland: Comparative Histories of the Midwestern States* (Bloomington: University of Indiana Press, 1988), make reference to the distinctive areas of German concentration and the importance of German-speakers' contributions in settling these states. See also Leopold Auburger, Heinz Kloss, and Heinz Rupp, eds., *Deutsch als Muttersprache in den Vereinigten-Staaten, Teil I: Der Mittelwesten,* Deutsche Sprache in Europa und übersee, 4 (Wiesbaden: Franz Steiner, 1979).

30. K. Conzen, "Deutsche Einwanderer," 366–69; Kamphoefner, *The Westfalians,* 86–122. Gonner's summary of Luxembourgian-American settlements in rural Jackson and Dubuque counties in Iowa also illustrates this pattern. Russel L. Gerlach identifies the area of dense German settlement in Missouri in his important study *Immigrants in the Ozarks: A Study in Ethnic Geography* (Columbia: University of Missouri Press, 1976), 35–39. Adolf E. Schroeder summarizes the pattern of German settlement in "The Survival of German Traditions in Missouri," in *The German Contribution to the Building of the Americas,* ed. G. K. Friesen (Hanover, N.H.: Clark University Press, 1977), 289–313. Robert Frizzell's map of Illinois counties, showing the number of German-born residents in 1870 and in 1890, illustrates the patchwork character of areas of rural German concentration ("Peopling the Prairie: Germans of Central Illinois" [Paper delivered at the Society for German-American Studies Thirteenth Annual Symposium, Chicago, April 1989], 21). The same is evident in James R. Dow's map of Iowa counties, showing the percentage of Germans among the foreign-born in that state in 1895 ("Deutsch als Muttersprache in Iowa," in *Deutsch als Muttersprache in den Vereinigten-Staaten,* ed. Auburger et al., 95). For Iowa, see also Robert E. Clark, "German Settlement in Iowa: Remnants on the Land," in *Culture and Civilization of the German-Speaking States,* Proceedings of the Tenth Annual Iowa Regional AATG, Workshop at the University of Northern Iowa, 1975 (Philadelphia: Iowa Chapter of AATG, 1976), 48. Carman's *Foreign-Language Units of Kansas,* one of the most thorough and important works of its kind, also reveals this pattern. Hildegard Bender Johnson's "The Location of German Immigrants in the Middle West," *Annals of the Association of American Geographers* 41 (March 1951): 1–41, includes a map of the distribution of the German-born population in 1900 that also illustrates this (7).

31. For studies of these groups, see Myrtle D. Fesler, *Pioneers of Western Kansas* (New York: Carlton Press, 1962); C. Henry Smith, *The Story of the Mennonites,* 4th ed. (Newton, Kans.: Faith and Life Press, 1957), 650–56; and Erich A. Albrecht, "Deutsche Sprache in Kansas," in *Deutsch als Muttersprache in den Vereinigten-Staaten,* ed. Auburger et al., 161–69.

32. Kamphoefner gives one of the more striking examples of this: the community of immigrants from Lippe-Detmold in Warren County, Missouri, who made up almost a fifth of the German-Americans in that county, although their small principality contributed less than one-third of 1 percent of the total population of the German lands ("'Entwurzelt' oder 'verpflanzt'?" 334).

33. Jay D. Eickemeyer, "Immanuel-God with Us: University of Iowa Student Paper, 1981," 7, Tms, Manuscript Collection, ISHD-HS.

34. Friedrich Julius Gustorf, *The Uncorrupted Heart* (Columbia: University of Missouri Press, 1969), 131.

35. Randy Brown, "From Germany to America: The Gabelmann Story" (15 December 1980), 12, Tms, Manuscript Collection, ISHD-HS.

36. Ostergren, *A Community Transplanted*, 224; Reinhard Doerries, "Church and Faith on the Great Plains Frontier: Acculturation Problems of German-Americans," *Amerikastudien/American Studies* 24, no. 2 (1979): 275–89. K. Conzen also notes the central importance of the immigrant church in building a cohesive and enduring ethnic community ("Deutsche Einwanderer," 368, 376).

37. Information derived from the family histories is contained in W. F. Johnson, *History of Cooper County, Missouri*, 2 vols. (Topeka and Cleveland: Historical Publishing, 1919; reprint, Fort Worth, Tex.: VKM Publishing, 1978). The King family from Holstein, prominant among the early immigrant settlers in the county, anglicized their name from Koenig (see will of John Adam King, 21 January 1890, folder 3126, CCMPC). The same was probably also true of "Squire" Nicolas Smith from Germany and the Fox family from Alsace (see W. F. Johnson, 1:448–49, 532–33, 578–82). The importance of the density of ethnic settlement has often been noted. See K. Conzen's studies (e.g., "Historical Approaches" and "Deutsche Einwanderer") for representative discussions. Kamphoefner notes the effect of wealth and social status on speed of assimilation as indicated by intermarriage with Americans ("'Entwurzelt' oder 'verpflanzt'?" 347). Doerries discusses the negative influence of competing religious affiliations on the development of ethnic community ("Church and Faith," 284–85).

38. Ihnke Kleihauer, letter of 5 May 1859, Tms, BABS.

39. Kamphoefner, *The Westfalians*, 66–67.

40. Friedrich Gillet Hillenkamp, letter of 4 May 1843, Tms, BABS. Gonner, in his contemporary analysis of Luxembourgian emigration, states that the main cause was "the constantly increasing impoverishment of the people, the disappearance of the middle class" (77).

41. Gottfried Duden, *Report on a Journey to the Western States of North America and a Stay of Several Years along the Missouri (during the Years 1824, '25, '26 and 1827): An English Translation*, trans. George H. Kellner, Adolf E. Schroeder, and W. M. Senner (Columbia: University of Missouri Press, 1980) (translation of *Bericht über eine Reise nach den westlichen Staaten Nord-Amerikas und einen mehrjährigen Aufenthalt am Missouri [in den Jahren 1824, 25, 26, und 1827], in Bezug auf Auswanderung und Überbevölkerung* [Elberfeld: Sam Lucas, 1829]).

42. Friedrich Muench, "Das Leben von Paul Follenius," *Gesammelte Schriften* (St. Louis: n.p., 1902), and "The Duden Settlement in Missouri," *Der deutsche Pionier* 2 (September and October 1870): 197–98. See also Kamphoefner, *The Westfalians,* 95.

43. Carl E. Schneider summarizes the history of the Dreißiger contributions to German immigration history in Missouri and Illinois in *The German Church on the American Frontier: A Study of the Rise of Religion among the Germans of the West, Based on the History of the "Evangelischer Kirchenverein des Westens"* (St. Louis: Eden Publishing House, 1939), 19–24. William G. Bek translated the Steines letters and other documents of Dreißiger in Missouri under the title "The Followers of Duden" in the *Missouri Historical Review* 14–19 (1919–25).

Chapter 1: *"The Best Household Utensil"*

1. Karl Friedrich Wander, *Deutsches Sprichwörter-Lexikon,* 5 vols. (Leipzig: Brockhaus, 1867–80), 3:419. Further citations from this standard reference source are in the main body of the text. Many legal practices of earlier days were similarly formulated in folk sayings. See, for example, J. H. Hillebrand, *Deutsche Rechtsprichwörter* (Zurich: Meyer and Zeller, 1858); and Eduard Graf and Mathias Dietherr, *Deutsche Rechtsprichwörter,* 2d ed. (Nördlingen: C. H. Beck, 1869).

2. Horst Beyer and Anneliese Beyer, *Sprichwörterlexikon* (Munich: Beck, 1985), 382. Further references to this collection (based heavily on Wander) are cited in the main body of the text.

3. Eda Sagarra summarizes most of the classical literature on this topic in her chapter "The Other Half: Women in German Society," in *A Social History of Germany, 1648–1914* (New York: Holmes and Meier, 1977), 403–23. Dirk Blasius makes clear the connection between legal authority, social structures, and female subordination ("Scheidung und Scheidungsrecht im 19. Jahrhundert: Zur Sozialgeschichte der Familie," *Historische Zeitschrift* 241 [October 1985]: 329–60). Elizabeth H. Pleck cites studies that document the disproportionately high number of German and other European immigrants arrested for wife-beating in certain American cities in the nineteenth and early twentieth centuries ("Challenges to Traditional Authority," in *The American Family in Social-Historical Perspective,* 3d ed., ed. Michael Gordon [New York: St. Martin's Press, 1983], 504).

4. Silvia Bovenschen's study of middle- and upper-class German women's social status and history in the eighteenth century and early nineteenth makes reference to the most important literature on this topic (*Die imaginierte Weiblichkeit* [Frankfurt: Suhrkamp, 1979]). A thorough summary of the origins and development of the nineteenth-century women's movement is contained in Margrit Twellmann's *Die deutsche Frauenbewegung: Ihre Anfänge und erste Entwicklung, 1843–1889,* 2 vols., Marburger Abhandlungen zur Politischen Wissenschaft, 17/1 (Maisenheim am Glan: A. Hain, 1972; abridged ed., Königstein: Athenäum, 1976). See also Werner Thönnessen, *The Emancipation of*

Women: The Rise and Decline of the Women's Movement in German Social Democracy, 1863–1933, trans. Joris de Bres (London: Pluto, 1973).

5. Louise A. Tilly and Joan W. Scott's *Women, Work and Family* (New York: Holt, 1978) is the classic analysis of the impact of industrialization on women and family life in the modern (post–seventeenth century) period. The reader is referred to their sections on women in preindustrial France and England (44–55). Robert Lee's study of the nineteenth-century peasant family in Bavaria also provides an excellent overview of the subject and pertinent German sources ("Family and 'Modernization': The Peasant Family and Social Change in Nineteenth-Century Bavaria," in *The German Family*, ed. Richard J. Evans and W. R. Lee [London: Croom Helm, 1981; Totowa, N.J.: Barnes, 1981], 84–119). Lee states, "Despite the increased discussion of female emancipation in the eighteenth century within enlightened circles, the position of women in rural society remained subject to the mode of production of material life" (95).

6. Sagarra, 410–11. Joan W. Scott points out the political implications of gender roles and relationships as a way of signifying relationships of power in her important article "Gender: A Useful Category of Historical Analysis," *American Historical Review* 91 (December 1986): 1053–75.

7. David Warren Sabean, *Property, Production, and Family in Neckarhausen, 1700–1870*, Cambridge Studies in Social and Cultural Anthropology, 73 (Cambridge: Cambridge University Press, 1990). Particularly enlightening are Sabean's third and fourth chapters, "The Ideology of the House" and "Patterns of Marital Conflict" (88–146). His study, based largely on court documents, shows that while officials emphasized hierarchy and vertical relationships in the family, "from the beginning, women, as they appeared in court protocols, challenged official discourse by inserting words of horizontal relationships, exchange, and reciprocity into the argument" (114).

8. Hainer Plaul estimated that the proportion of annual income spent on food by the average lower-class, working family in protoindustrial Germany was 60 percent ("The Rural Proletariat: The Everyday Life of Rural Labourers in the Magdeburg Region, 1830–80," trans. Cathleen S. Catt, Richard J. Evans, and W. R. Lee, in *The German Peasantry*, ed. Richard J. Evans and W. R. Lee [New York: St. Martin's Press, 1986], 119).

9. For the effect of industrialization on German women and on family life and structures, see Ingeborg Weber-Kellermann, *Die deutsche Familie: Versuch einer Sozialgeschichte* (Frankfurt: Suhrkamp, 1974); Ute Gerhard, *Verhältnisse und Verhinderungen: Frauenarbeit, Familie und Rechte der Frauen im 19. Jahrhundert*, 2d ed. (Frankfurt: Suhrkamp, 1981); Heidi Rosenbaum, *Formen der Familie: Untersuchungen zum Zusammenhang von Familienverhältnissen, Sozialstruktur und sozialem Wandel in der deutschen Gesellschaft des 19. Jahrhunderts* (Frankfurt: Suhrkamp, 1982); Ingeborg Weber-Keller, *Frauenleben im 19. Jahrhundert* (Munich: Beck, 1983); Ursula Frevert, *Frauen-Geschichte zwischen bürgerlicher Verbesserung und neuer Weiblichkeit* (Frankfurt: Suhrkamp, 1986); and Reinhard Sieder, *Sozialgeschichte der Familie* (Frankfurt: Suhrkamp, 1987).

10. Rosenbaum, 340–43; Gerhard, 63; Hayke Lanwert, "Deutsche Emigrantinnen in den USA: Arbeit und soziale Lage im Spiegel ihrer Briefe, 1850–1900" (M.A. thesis, Ruhr University, Bochum, 1988), 20. Dorothee Wierling writes of the burgeoning number of housemaids as a sign of the growing gap between the classes, a symbol of the rejection of manual labor by the "new" middle class (*Mädchen für alles* [Berlin: Dietz, 1987], 14).

11. John Demos, *Past, Present, and Personal: The Family and the Life Course in American History* (Oxford: Oxford University Press, 1986), 12. Similar conclusions are drawn by Rosenbaum, 294; Weber-Kellermann, *Die deutsche Familie*, 124; and Karin Hausen, "Family and Role-Division: The Polarisation of Sexual Stereotypes in the Nineteenth Century—An Aspect of the Dissociation of Work and Family Life," in *The German Family*, ed. Evans and Lee, 51–83. Reinhard Sieder and Michael Mitterauer assert that "the development of the ideology of the character of the sexes around 1800 may have been an important means" of perpetuating "the traditional dominance of the husband in the now 'private' family" (*The European Family: Patriarchy to Partnership from the Middle Ages to the Present*, trans. Karla Oosterveen and Manfred Horzinger [Oxford: Blackwell, 1982], 131). They also describe the rapid spread of this ideology among the lower middle class and even the industrial proletariate.

12. Karin Walser, *Dienstmädchen: Frauenarbeit und Weiblichkeitsvorstellungen um 1900* (Frankfurt: extrabuch, 1985), 23–24. See also Sieder, 109–10.

13. Louise A. Tilly, Joan W. Scott, and Miriam Cohen, "Women's Work and European Fertility Patterns," *Journal of Interdisciplinary History* 6 (Winter 1976): 470. John Knodel and Mary Jo Maynes concluded that in the late nineteenth century, after industrialization was well established in Germany, men and women in cities tended to marry later or not at all. They explained this by the difficulty of becoming financially established in the city and the large number of extra women who had come to urban areas as housemaids ("Urban and Rural Marriage Patterns in Imperial Germany," *Journal of Family History* 11 [Winter 1976]: 129–68).

14. Hans Medick's discussion of "das ganze Haus" (the whole house) is particularly important here ("The Proto-industrial Family Economy," in Peter Kriedte, Hans Medick, Jürgen Schlumbohn, *Industrialization before Industrialization*, trans. Beate Schempp [New York: Cambridge University Press, 1981], 38–73).

15. Braun examines how protocapitalist ventures ("the putting-out system") altered inheritance and marriage patterns and family structures in the Swiss Highland by increasing family wealth and security. See Walker's analysis of the influence of industrialization on the lower echelons of society (*Germany and the Emigration, 42–69*) and that of John H. Clapham (*The Economic Development of France and Germany, 1815–1914,* 4th ed. [Cambridge: Cambridge University Press, 1966], 29–52, 195–231). More recent studies detailing the regional complexities of this subject include Wolfgang Mager's "Haushalt und Familie in protoindustrieller Gesellschaft: Spenge (Ravensberg) während der ersten Hälfte des 19. Jahrhunderts—Eine Fallstudie," in *Fam-*

ilie zwischen Tradition und Moderne, ed. Neithard Bulst, Joseph Goy, and Jochen Hoock, Kritische Studien zur Geschichtswissenschaft, 48 (Göttingen: Vandenhoeck, 1981), 141–81; and Plaul's.

16. Rosenbaum, 48; Frevert, 26–27. R. Lee shows the extent to which peasant life in Bavaria remained largely untouched by what on the surface seemed to be important changes in economic structures and political life.

17. Joan W. Scott and Louise A. Tilly's study of nineteenth-century working- and peasant-class women (primarily in England, France, and Italy) offers a model for German-speaking women of the same backgrounds ("Women's Work and the Family in Nineteenth Century Europe," *Comparative Studies in Society and History* 17 [January 1975]: 36–64).

18. Sagarra, 350.

19. Takenori Inoki, *Aspects of German Peasant Emigration to the United States, 1815–1914: A Reexamination of Some Behavioral Hypotheses in Migration Theory* (New York: Arno, 1981), 86, 93–96. See the complete analysis of the occupations of emigrants from the German lands contained in his chapter 3 (86–100).

20. See Klaus Tenfelde's study of Prussian agricultural workers and the laws to which they were subject ("Ländliches Gesinde in Preußen: Gesinderecht und Gesindestatistik 1810 bis 1860," *Archiv für Sozialgeschichte,* vol. 19, ed. Friedrich-Ebert Stiftung [Braunschweig-Bonn: Neue Gesellschaft, 1979], 189–229). Dietmar Sauermann's outline of the development of a two-class rural society during the nineteenth century, in the introduction to the collection of testimonials about the lives of rural hired help which he edited, is particularly helpful (*Knechte und Mägde in Westfalen,* 2d ed. [Munster: Coppenrath, 1979], 10–20). For other examinations of these changes, see Plaul; Mager; R. Lee; and Rosenbaum, 102–4.

21. Rosenbaum, 80–81. See also Plaul, 113, 125; and R. Lee, 95, note 63. Ingeborg Weber-Kellermann's *Landleben im 19. Jahrhundert* (Munich: Beck, 1987) contains detailed information on certain areas of women's work, for example, dairy production (146–50) and flax (186–88).

22. Regina Schulte's study was particularly helpful in this summary ("Peasants and Farmers' Maids: Female Farm Servants in Bavaria at the End of the Nineteenth Century," trans. Cathleen S. Catt, in *The German Peasantry,* ed. Evans and Lee, 158–73; also published in German as "Bauernmägde in Bayern am Ende des 19. Jahrhunderts," in *Frauen suchen ihre Geschichte,* ed. Karin Hausen [Munich: Beck, 1983], 110–27). For comparative purposes here and in general, see also Pamela Horn's *Victorian Countrywomen* (London: Blackwell, 1991), 103–63 passim.

23. M. Bidlingmaier, "Die Bäuerin in zwei Gemeinden Württembergs" (Ph.D. diss., Tübingen University, 1918), 157, cited in Rosenbaum, 147.

24. For a discussion of how public roles and rural economics determined the power relationships between the sexes, see Rosenbaum, 79–86; and Sieder, 32–38. Again, Sabean's *Property, Production, and Family* is enlightening on women's resistence to male control of them and their property and earnings. His study shows that women were sometimes able to wrest concessions from

their husbands and the authorities in these areas. Gerhard Wilke's analysis of the power structures of village life during and after the Weimar Republic shows that women continue to play a subordinate role in rural German communities ("The Sins of the Fathers: Village Society and Social Control in the Weimar Republic," in *The German Peasantry*, ed. Evans and Lee, 193). The contemporary attitudes toward rural women that Wilke notes are typical of the patriarchal society Sabean's study documents in the eighteenth and nineteenth centuries.

25. Albert Ilien and Utz Jeggle, *Leben auf dem Dorfe* (Wiesbaden: Opladen, 1978), 76, quoted in Rosenbaum, 98; Sieder, 45. R. Lee cites some of the relevant sources on women's inferior status in rural society (95–96).

26. Sieder and Mitterauer, 7–10; R. Lee, 92, 99; Mager, 146.

27. R. Lee, 91, 96–98; Rosenbaum, 91–92.

28. One study asserts that female farm servants were paid one-half to two-thirds the wages of male farm workers (Ruth Roebke, "Informationen für Frauen und das Frauenbild in den Auswanderungsratgebern aus dem 19. Jahrhundert" [M.A. thesis, Philipps-Universität, Marburg, 1986], 20). Sauermann also concludes that women were paid less than men (15).

29. The soaring rates of illegitimacy in nineteenth-century Europe were also seen in German-speaking lands. For various interpretations of the reasons for this phenomenon, see Sieder and Mitterauer, 124–26; Edward Shorter, "Illegitimacy, Sexual Revolution, and Social Change in Modern Europe," in *The Family in History*, ed. Theodore K. Rabb and Robert I. Rotberg (New York: Harper, 1973), 48–84; and Tilly, Scott, and Cohen. Peter Laslett discusses the complexity of the influences on illegitimacy rates and their regional and temporal variations throughout Europe ("Introduction: Comparing Illegitimacy over Time and between Cultures," in *Bastardy and Its Comparative History*, ed. Peter Laslett, Karla Oosterveen, and Richard M. Smith [Cambridge, Mass.: Harvard University Press, 1980], 1–65). John Knodel and Steven Hochstadt document the same complexity ("Urban and Rural Illegitimacy in Imperial German," in *Bastardy and Its Comparative History*, ed. Laslett et al., 284–312). In some rural areas, where bastardy accounted for a high percentage of the births (50–60 percent in parts of Styria, Austria, in the 1830s to 1870s, for example), such offspring and their mothers could be fully integrated into family and farm life. See the important study by Michael Mitterauer, "Familienformen und Illegitimität in ländlichen Gebieten Österreichs," in *Archiv für Sozialgeschichte*, ed. Stiftung, 123–88. For comparisons with areas of high illegitimacy in nineteenth-century Sweden, see Ostergren, *A Community Transplanted*, 64–65.

30. Essential literature on legal impediments to marriage includes the study by Klaus-Jürgen Matz, *Pauperismus und Bevölkerung: Die gesetzliche Ehebeschränkung* (Stuttgart: Klett, 1980), 29–32 passim. See also Walker, *Germany and the Emigration*, 54.

31. Rosenbaum, 88; Sieder and Mitterauer, 7–10. This is still true in many areas of German lands, including parts of northwest Germany, where a man marrying into a farm takes his wife's name, as well as that of the farm. (I appreciate Walter Kamphoefner's drawing my attention to this.)

32. See Lutz K. Berkner, "The Stem Family and the Developmental Cycle of the Peasant Household: An Eighteenth-Century Austrian Example," in *The American Family in Social-Historical Perspective,* ed. Michael Gordon (New York: St. Martin's Press, 1973), 34–58. Mager also discusses this in relation to Westphalia (144). A somewhat later study by Berkner of late seventeenth-century tax records from the Göttingen area (where largely partible inheritence patterns prevailed) and Calenburg (largely impartible) concludes that stem family households were more common in areas of impartible inheritance and nuclear family households in areas of partible inheritance ("Inheritance, Land Tenure and Peasant Family Structure: A German Regional Comparison," in *Family and Inheritance: Rural Society in Western Europe, 1200–1800,* ed. Jack Goody [Cambridge, Mass.: Cambridge University Press, 1976], 71–95). Michel Verdon argues, however, that the stem family was always a minority type, even in areas of impartible inheritance ("The Stem Family: Toward a General Theory," in *The American Family in Social-Historical Perspective,* 3d ed., ed. Michael Gordon, [New York: St. Martin's Press, 1983], 24–37). On the role of long-lasting family holdings in building rural community, see Rosenbaum, 75, 112; and K. Conzen, "Peasant Pioneers," 264–65.

33. Louis Osterholt, letter of 16 February 1884, BABS.

34. R. Lee discusses intergenerational conflict and sibling rivalry (94), as does Josef Mooser ("Soziale Mobilität und familiale Plazierung bei Bauern und Unterschichten: Aspekte der Sozialstruktur der ländlichen Gesellschaft im 19. Jahrhundert am Beispiel des Kirchspiels Quernheim im östlichen Westfalen," in *Familie zwischen Tradition und Moderne,* ed. Bulst et al., 193–95). Rosenbaum cites studies that put the average age of marriage in areas of impartible inheritance at twenty-nine to thirty for men and twenty-five to twenty-eight for women (70–71). Similar statistics were obtained for Sweden and Norway during this period (Ostergren, *A Community Transplanted,* 65–68; Gjerde, *From Peasants to Farmers,* 99). Mooser discusses in detail the difficulties rural women had in marrying on their social level, and R. Lee's table showing the social origin of marriage partners in several Upper Bavarian villages reveals the same pattern (100). R. Lee also comments on the traditional marriage patterns in rural Bavaria and the concomitant closeness of communal ties (101–7). Mooser suggests that the marriage between those of different levels of rural society, brought about largely by women's disadvantaged position, may also explain the lack of significant social conflict in rural areas, even as economic disparity between groups increased in the nineteenth century (188).

35. Berkner, "The Stem Family," 53; Mooser, 193; Rosenbaum, 86–89, 103–4.

36. Rosenbaum concludes that children generally agreed with the marriage choices their parents made for them (75).

37. Ilien and Jeggle, 79, cited in Rosenbaum, 73.

38. See Braun, 57–59; Tilly and Scott, *Women, Work and Family,* 93, 116; and Sieder, 82–90.

39. Cited in Rosenbaum, 88. Much the same saying survived in America in Pennsylvania Dutch, according to Martha K. Wallach ("German Immigrant Women," *Journal of German-American Studies,* 13 [Winter 1978]: 101). It was also common among the Germans who settled along the Volga, according to Fred C. Koch (*The Volga Germans in Russia and the Americas, from 1763 to the Present* [University Park: Pennsylvania State University Press, 1977], 173).

40. For relevant sources, see R. Lee, 96–97; Mooser, 193–94; and Sieder and Mitterauer, 127.

41. Rosenbaum, 251–309. Peter N. and Carol Z. Stearns have pointed out the complicated and delicate problem the historian faces in attempting to assess emotional life in past times ("Emotionology: Clarifying the History of Emotions and Emotional Standards," *American Historical Review* 90 [October 1985]: 813–36).

42. Tilly and Scott, *Women, Work and Family,* 58; R. Lee, 97–98; Rosenbaum, 90.

43. Writing of eastern Prussia in the early nineteenth century, W. R. Lee states that "peasant families . . . may well have had to rely on a greater reserve of emotional capital to cope with the frequent casualties in wasted infant and child lives that occurred with such increasing regularity" ("The Impact of Agrarian Change on Women's Work and Child Care in Early Nineteenth-Century Prussia," in *German Women in the Nineteenth Century,* ed. John C. Fout [New York: Holmes and Meier, 1984], 248). In his discussion of the relationship between rural adults and their children, Sieder warns against the danger of assuming there are eternal norms by which we can evaluate the emotional life of earlier times (39–43).

44. Wilhelm Niggemeier, letter of 20 July 1848, BABS; Amalia Rückels, letter of 4 February 1861, Rückels-Kessel Letters, 1859–92, BABS; Gottfried Rückels, letters of 7 March 1875 and 9 March 1877, BABS.

45. Johannes Gillhoff, ed. and comp., *Jürnjakob Swehn der Amerikafahrer* (Berlin: Steinigerverlag, 1939), 162–63, 166–67, 296. See also Joachim Reppmann's comments in the *Society for German-American Studies Newsletter* 14 (December 1993): 29.

46. Inoki summarizes the history of land tenancy in German lands and the major nineteenth-century legislation and its consequences in Prussia in his fourth chapter (101–50). For Luxembourg, see also Gonner, 78–80. Sieder's overview of the many economically based layers of rural society at this period is also helpful (14–17).

47. W. R. Lee, "The Impact of Agrarian Change," 234–55. Plaul's study of one Prussian area illustrates the deleterious effect the early and strong development of a one-crop economy (sugar beets) had on its landless residents, particularly women (113, 125).

48. E. Sax, *Die Hausindustrie in Thüringen,* 3 vols., 2d ed. (Jena: Fischer, 1884–88), 49, quoted by Rosenbaum, 204.

49. See Gonner's comments on the diet of the Luxembourgian poor as early as 1852 (77).

50. Rosenbaum, 56–57, 206.
51. Walker, *Germany and the Emigration,* 69.

Chapter 2: Arriving, Settling In, and Surviving

1. Not one of the forty-seven letter writers in Lanwert's study states the reasons for immigrating to America (16). Agnes Bretting concludes, on the evidence of women's personal writings, that women's motives for emigration were probably usually a mixture of the personal and the economic ("Deutsche Einwandererfrauen im 'Land der unbegrenzten Möglichkeiten'—Wunsch und Wirklichkeit: Autobiographische Quellen in der Frauenforschung," in *Frauen wandern aus: Deutsche Migrantinnen im 19. und 20. Jahrhundert,* ed. Monika Blaschke and Christiana Harzig [Bremen: Labor Migration Project, University of Bremen, 1990], 14).

2. Elsie B. Hass Stickney, "Hass-Stickney Family History" (1962), folder 2, box 5, Donald F. Danker Personal Papers, NSHS; Ludwig Kurz, *Wege des Schicksals* (Erbach im Odenwald: August Franz, 1926), 4–12; Mathias Blommer, letter of 2 May 1873, BABS.

3. Mark Wyman views this as one of the important reasons for the flood of German emigration after 1830 (*Immigrants in the Valley* [Chicago: Nelson-Hall, 1984], 50).

4. Sonya Pohlman, "John H. Pohlman, Nebraska Pioneer" (1962), folder 6, box 5, Danker Personal Papers; Joseph Suppiger, Salomon Koepfli, and Kaspor Koepfli, *Journey to New Switzerland,* ed. John C. Abbott, trans. Raymond J. Spahn (Carbondale: Southern Illinois University Press, 1987), xxvii; Hermann Steines, letter of 8 November 1833, in William G. Bek, trans. and comp., "The Followers of Duden," *Missouri Historical Review* 14 (October 1919): 70; Louise Sophia Gellhorn Boylan, "My Life Story" [ca. 1942], Manuscript Collection, ISHD-HS.

5. Cited in Lutz Röhrich, "German Emigrant Songs," in *Eagle in the New World,* ed. Theodore Gish and Richard Spuler (College Station: Texas A & M University Press, 1986), 63–64.

6. Prominent examples in Missouri of women who convinced their husbands to leave America are Luise Marbach of the Stephanite group of Saxon immigrants and Mrs. Nicolas Hesse of Westphalia. For a related discussion, see Linda S. Pickle, "Stereotypes and Reality: Nineteenth-Century German Women in Missouri," *Missouri Historical Review* 79 (April 1985): 302–5.

7. Helene Friesen Eitzen, "Erinnerungen aus meinem Leben" (4 April 1919), 16, 17, duplicate copy, Inman, Kans. I am grateful to Duane Kroeker of Columbia, Missouri, for permission to quote from his grandmother's autobiography. An English translation, "A Remembrance of My Life" (Tms, n.d.), also in Mr. Kroeker's possession, contains a few omissions and inaccuracies; therefore, the translations are my own.

8. Ibid., 17–19.
9. Ibid., 19, 20.
10. Sophie Luise Duensing Weitbrecht, "Neun schwere Aufbaujahre in

deutschen Gemeinden der Vereinigten Staaten von Nordamerika (1848–1857)," comp. Hans-Thorald Michaelis, *Genealogie* 2 (1980): 52–63. Mary Cresence Berhalter Maichel, an orphan trained in nursing, also came to America to escape an unwanted marriage (microfilm roll 5, LDNC). More independent than Sophie Weitbrecht, probably because she had supported herself for a time, she paid her own fare, traveled with a friend, and after four years married a New York grocer. They later moved to Kansas for her husband's health.

11. "Da würdet Ihr Euch wundern. . . ," *Die Zeit*, 21 May 1976.

12. J. Sanford Rikoon, "The Reusser House: A Log Structure in Iowa's 'Little Switzerland,'" *Annals of Iowa* 45 (Summer 1979): 6.

13. John Michael Kunz, an impoverished nobleman, married Christina Winegar and brought her to Illinois and then Nebraska (Mary Miller, "Cass County Settlers Who Were Ancestors of Marvin, Carol Ann, and Debra Kay Miller" [1962], Tms, folder 8, box 5, Danker Personal Papers). Regina Rückels Kessel and her brothers sold the family holdings and became prosperous farmers in Illinois (Rückels-Kessel Family Letters, 1859–92, BABS). In Kansas, an eighteen-year-old wrote her brother about working off her passage as a kitchen maid (Pauline Kull Fischer, letter of 23 April 1882, BABS). The eighteen-year-old Magdalena Schnack Fahrenbrink came to America with the family of a neighbor and worked one year to pay her transportation costs of sixty-six dollars (W. F. Johnson, 2:703).

14. Kamphoefner, *The Westfalians*, 43, 49.

15. "Was erwartet die auswandernde Frau," 4 970, D-Archiv, Institut für Auslandsbeziehungen, Stuttgart, Germany. Roebke's thesis discusses the most important material printed to advise nineteenth-century emigrants.

16. Britta Fees's recent study on prostitution in San Francisco makes no mention of German-speakers among the prostitutes and in general adds nothing to earlier studies of the subject ("Einwanderinnen als Prostituierte in San Francisco, 1848–1870," in *Frauen wandern aus*, ed. Blaschke and Harzig, 65–81). Jacqueline Baker Barnhardt states that "the most likely victims [of white slave operations] were unattached young immigrant women, whose disappearance would raise no outcry from their families . . ." (*The Fair but Frail: Prostitution in San Francisco, 1849–1900* [Reno: University of Nevada Press, 1986], 71). Barnhardt adds that it is likely the large body of late nineteenth-century literature on white slavery overemphasized this phenomenon and that most women probably went into prostitution because of the lure of "easy" money, the life-style, and pleasure. Anne Firor Scott has found evidence of attempts by native-born women's associations to keep or save young immigrant women from a life of sin (*Natural Allies: Women's Associations in American History* [Urbana: University of Illinois Press, 1991], 38–43, 104).

17. Hannah Aschman Harms remembered her mother's chest of linen (microfilm roll 3, LDMC), and Barbara Graw Wahl recalled saving the family featherbeds (microfilm roll 9, LDMC). Frederick Steines wrote that his newly arrived mother missed her furniture (letter of 15 September 1834, in William G. Bek, trans. and comp., "The Followers of Duden," *Missouri Histori-*

cal Review 15 [April 1920]: 538). Matthew Hermann's bride, Mary Krausz, had brought her bedroom furniture with her (letter of October 1871, in Walter W. Hermann, "Germany to USA: Migration of the Matthew Hermann Family" [n.d.], 22, Tms, Nebraska United Methodist History Center, Lincoln). On 27 August 1869 Henry Ruegg went to St. Louis from his Highland, Illinois, farm to sell "two silver cups and the Bernese clock" (Diaries and Papers, 1848–1877, trans. Othmar Stutz, Tms, KSHS). Elizabeth Bigler's silver and copper-bottomed pots went down in a shipwreck on the transatlantic voyage, a loss she mourned "for all her days" (Ruth Harbecke Jewett, "The Story of Emilie Joss-Bigler," *Swiss American Historical Society Newsletter* 21 [November 1985]: 3, 13).

18. Auswanderung Deutschland-USA, Ratschläge zur Auswanderung, 4 971, D-Archiv, Institut für Auslandsbeziehungen, Stuttgart, Germany.

19. Faragher, "History from the Inside-Out," 550–51. Other scholars of ethnic groups in the United States also defined the basic patriarchal structure of the ethnic family in similar ways. See, for example, William L. Warner and Leo Srole, *The Social Systems of American Ethnic Groups,* Yankee City Series, 3 (New Haven, Conn.: Yale University Press, 1960), 103–4.

20. Glenda Riley, *The Female Frontier: A Comparative View of Women on the Prairie and the Plains* (Lawrence: University Press of Kansas, 1988), 2.

21. Among the studies of women's work on the agricultural frontier and in agriculture in general, the following are particularly worthy of note: Mary Meek Atkeson, "Women in Farm Life and Rural Economy," *Annals of the American Academy of Political and Social Sciences* 143 (May 1929): 188–94; Dorothy Schwieder, "Labor and Economic Roles of Iowa Farm Wives, 1840–80," in *Farmers, Bureaucrats and Middlemen,* ed. Trudy Huskamp Peterson (Washington, D.C.: Howard University Press, 1980), 152–68; Joan M. Jensen, *With These Hands: Women Working on the Land* (Old Westbury, N.Y.: Feminist Press, 1981); Corlann G. Bush, "The Barn Is His, the House Is Mine," in *Energy and Transport,* vol. 52, ed. George H. Daniels and Mark H. Rose (Beverly Hills, Calif.: Sage Focus Education, 1982), 235–59; Carol Fairbanks and Sara Brooks Sundberg, *Farm Women on the Prairie Frontier: A Sourcebook for Canada and the United States* (Metuchen, N.J.: Scarecrow, 1983); Scott G. McNall and Sally Allen McNall, *Plains Families: Exploring Sociology through Social History* (New York: St. Martin's Press, 1983); Riley, *The Female Frontier* and *Frontierswomen;* Deborah Fink, *Open Country, Iowa: Rural Women, Tradition and Change* (Albany: State University of New York Press, 1986); and Seena B. Kohl, "Image and Behavior: Women's Participation in North American Family Agricultural Enterprises," in *Women and Farming: Changing Roles, Changing Structures,* ed. Wava G. Haney and Jane B. Knowles (Boulder, Colo.: Westview, 1988). A useful bibliography for the more recent period is Colette Moser and Deborah Johnson, *Rural Women Workers in the Twentieth Century,* Central Rural Manpower and Public Affairs, Special Paper, no. 15 (East Lansing: Michigan State University Press, 1973). The best general study of women's work in the home is Susan Strasser, *Never Done: A History of American Housework* (New York: Pantheon, 1982).

22. Cornelia B. Flora and Jan L. Flora, "The Structure of Agriculture and Women's Culture in the Great Plains," *Great Plains Quarterly* 8 (Fall 1988): 197. Almost everyone who has written about the work of women and children on the agricultural frontier has acknowledged their central role. A skeptical view of the governmental policies that supported patriarchal family structures, thereby encouraging families to place themselves in stressful frontier situations, is offered by Rosalinda Mendez Gonzales, "Commentary," in *Western Women: Their Land, Their Lives,* ed. Lillian Schlissel, Vicky Ruiz, and Janice Monk (Albuquerque: University of New Mexico Press, 1988), 102–4. Related works include John Stitz, "A Study of Family Farm Culture in Ellis County, Kansas, and the Relationship of That Culture to Trends in Farming" (Ph.D diss., University of Kansas, Lawrence, 1983); Susan A. Mann and James M. Dickinson, "Obstacles to the Development of Capitalist Agriculture," *Journal of Peasant Studies* 5 (July 1978): 466–81; Glenda Riley, "Farm Women's Roles in the Agricultural Development of South Dakota," *South Dakota History* 13 (Spring/Summer 1982): 83–121; Max J. Pfeffer, "Social Origins of Three Systems of Farm Production in the United States," *Rural Sociology* 48 (Winter 1983): 540–62; and Jan L. Flora and John Stitz, "Ethnicity, Persistence, and Capitalism of Agriculture in the Great Plains during the Settlement Period: Wheat Production and Risk Avoidance," *Rural Sociology* 50 (Fall 1985): 341–60. Rachel Ann Rosenfeld has shown that the work of contemporary farm women is as varied, important, and unrenumerated as it was a century ago (*Farm Women: Work, Farm and Family in the United States* [Chapel Hill: University of North Carolina Press, 1986], 5–11).

23. Goebel noted this in his memoir of his life in early Missouri (45–48). See also R. Lee, 95; and K. Conzen, "Deutsche Einwanderer," 373.

24. This according to the leaflets "Was erwartet die auswandernde Frau" and "Gegenstände, welche die auswandernde Frau notwendigerweise mitbringen muß," Auswanderung nach USA, Liste für die Auswanderung, Institut für Auslandsbeziehungen, Stuttgart.

25. Hillenkamp, letter of 4 May 1843, Tms, BABS; Clara M. Shields, "The Lyon Creek Settlement," *Kansas Historical Collections* 14 (1915–18): 163. Women whose husbands were incapable of hard labor sometimes took over that role. Frederick W. Pehle's mother split rails for fences (Kamphoefner, *The Westfalians,* 161), and Karolina Miller Krause worked as a hired hand (Estelle Schelbitzki Freeman, "Anton and Karolina Krause" [1986], Tms, in author's possession).

26. Roebke, 89. See J. M. Jensen's discussion of the changes in agricultural economy and production that lay behind the eighteenth- and early nineteenth-century decrease in American women's participation in field work (*With These Hands,* 36–37, 46–48, 81–85). Lanwert also discusses these developments (56–59). Allan G. Bogue surmises that immigrant (German and Scandinavian) women and children in nineteenth-century Iowa took a greater part in field work than Americans did, in spite of the negative pressure of the dominant society (*From Prairie to Cornbelt* [Chicago: University of Chicago Press, 1963], 238). In confirmation of Bogue's assertion, the letters of Amalia Rück-

els, Regina Kessel, Wilhelmine Neumeier-Herbold, Christine Neumeier-Rock, and Friederike Neumeier-Hinkhaus (all in BABS) and the diary of Henry Ruegg (KSHS) all contain many references to such work of women and children. See also Louis H. Siekmann, "The German Element and Its Part in the Early Development of Otoe County, Nebraska" (M.A. thesis, University of Nebraska, 1930), 21.

27. Katharina Tiek, letter of 21 February 1869, Tms, BABS.

28. 1870 U.S. Manuscript Census, Madison County, Illinois, 305A, lines 8–13.

29. Tiek, letter of 18 March (1880?).

30. The children of many immigrants blamed hard work and the strain of numerous births for their mothers' poor health and early deaths. See, for an example, J. C. Ruppenthal, "Anna Barbara Immendorf, a Pioneer of Lincoln and Russell Counties, Kansas" (1925), Tms, microfilm 7, LDMC.

31. The reminiscences of Friederika Oesterreich Staatz are included in Shields, 148–50. Pearl Donnelly also wrote of Mrs. Staatz in "Pioneer Women of the Lyon Creek Settlement, Dickinson County" (n.d.), microfilm 2, LDMC.

32. Ruppenthal reported that his thirteen-year-old brother helped his mother deliver her seventh child because her husband and other children were on their second farm, eight miles away (8).

33. Hermann, 20; Tildy Kiest Heitman told this of her mother, Caroline Fette Kiest ("Notebooks," 8, ISHL).

34. Lucy Steinhaus, *I Remember When* (Sacrament: J. Rad, 1980), 74. Among the many documents that mention children's contributions to the family income are Emil Pieschl, "My Memoirs, 1882–1976," 36–37, Tms, Manuscript Collection, ISHD-HS; Irene DeBettignies, "An Old Settler's Story" (n.d.), box I, Manuscript Collection, ISHD-HS; and Albert Parks Butts, "A Calhoune County Pioneer: Sabine Kropf" (1973), Tms, Manuscript Collection, ISHD-HS. Mari Sandoz documented best the pain of growing up in an unhappy family, beset by economic problems (*Old Jules* [Lincoln: University of Nebraska Press, 1962]). In contrast, John Ise remembered the warmth and sharing among the children in his large family (*Sod and Stubble* [Lincoln: University of Nebraska Press, 1936]). Interestingly, Ise recorded experiences from his mother's impoverished childhood in America much less positively ("Mother's Recollections of Her Early Life" [n.d.], Tms, Kansas Collection, University of Kansas, Lawrence).

35. On the treatment of children in rural Europe, see Braun, 62; R. Lee, 96–99; Sieder, 43–45; Rosenbaum, 93–95; W. R. Lee, "The Impact of Agrarian Change," 338–40; Weber-Kellermann, *Landleben*, 243–63; and Frevert, 27–28. To illustrate the low status of even the wives of relatively well-off peasants, Weber-Kellermann cites the 1857 instance of a peasant woman left to give birth alone while her husband and servants attended All Saints' services (*Landleben*, 145).

36. Carl Köhler, "Eight Weeks on a St. Clair County Farm in 1851: Letters by a Young German," ed. and trans. Frederic Trautman, *Journal of the Illinois State Historical Society* 75 (Autumn 1982): 178; Hillenkamp, letter of

8 January 1846, Tms, BABS; J. D. Wilkins, letter of 19 January 1886, Kleihauer Family Letters, BABS. The system Köhler and Hillenkamp describe was still working in the early twentieth century, as Nancy Wieck's memoir about her family's efforts to save money and accumulate land proves ("The Life of a Pioneer Girl," in *Memoirs of Pioneers of Cheyenne County, Kansas,* ed. Pendergrass, 123, 126, passim).

37. Albine Schelbitzki, untitled ms. (ca. 1967), Tms, in my possession.

38. Gillhoff, 46; Maichel, microfilm 5; Mariam S. Wiederstein, *The Pioneer Obstetrician: A Country Midwife,* ed. James Klassen (Newton, Kans.: United, 1972); Coburn, *Life at Four Corners,* 92–93; Charlotte Borst, "Wisconsin Midwives as Working Women: Immigrant Midwives and the Limits of a Traditional Occupation, 1870–1920," *Journal of American Ethnic History* 8 (Spring 1989): 24–59.

39. Ada Oliva, "The Story of My Grandmother" (n.d.), box 15, Manuscript Collection, ISHD-HS; *Marion County Anzeiger,* Hillsboro, Kansas, 21 September 1888. German immigrants in Plank Township, Keokuk County, Iowa, made baskets for extra income (Sophia Stanfield, "History of Plank Township" [1927], 40, Tms, Manuscript Collection, ISHD-HS).

40. On this, see Riley, *The Female Frontier,* 102–3, 121, passim. For the domestic production of nineteenth-century women in the eastern United States, see Joan M. Jensen, "Cloth, Butter, and Boarders: Women's Household Production for the Market," in her *Promise to the Land: Essays on Rural Women* (Albuquerque: University of New Mexico Press, 1991), 186–205.

41. Maria Wolf Förschler to Mina Wolf, n.d., Tms (1868–1908), Langendorf-Tiek/Foerschler/Freitag/Faust Letters, BABS.

42. Goebel wrote of the female and child labor in the families of poor rural immigrants that led to eventual financial security and said that the girls in such families benefited by their exposure to better housekeeping methods when they worked out (47–49). The most important study of domestics in America is David Katzmann, *Seven Days a Week* (New York: Oxford University Press, 1978). Two fine studies of domestic service have recently appeared in Germany: Karin Walser, *Dienstmädchen. Frauenarbeit und Weiblichkeitsbilder um 1900* (Frankfurt: extrabuch, 1985); and Dorothee Wierling, *Mädchen für alles* (Berlin: Dietz, 1987). See also Silke Wehner, "Auswanderung deutscher Dienstmädchen in die USA, 1870–1920," in *Frauen wandern aus,* ed. Blaschke and Harzig, 29–50; and Silke Wehner, "Auswanderung deutscher Dienstmädchen in die Vereinigten Staaten, 1850–1914" (Ph.D. diss., University of Münster, 1992). One North Dakota woman's memoir documents her premarital work for wages. After emigrating from Bessarabia with her sister's family, Mary Gellner worked as a dishwasher, harvest hand, and domestic before marriage (Mary Gellner Weisz, "Cloudy Skies: Gellner Family Saga," *Heritage Review* 18 [November 1988]: 3–13). On the quite different purposes and consequences domestic work had for third-generation German-American women, see Coburn, *Life at Four Corners,* 121–26.

43. Edith Connelley Ross, "The Bloody Benders," *Kansas Historical Collections* 17 (1926–28): 464–79.

44. Strasser gives a price of $30 (171). See chapter 3 herein for evidence of higher prices paid by farm women in the 1870s. At the 1880 estate sale of Emma Blank in Cooper County, Missouri, her sewing machine sold for $25, while her four cows brought between $14 and $18 each (folder 2090, CC-MPC).

45. Boylan, 2. See also Ise, *Sod and Stubble,* 81–82.

46. Mrs. Wayne Shaneyfelt, "Mrs. Rebecca Stege Beins," in *Sod House Memories,* ed. Frances J. Alberts (Hastings, Nebr.: Sod House Society, 1972), 205; Isernhagen, 74.

47. Pauline Greving, letter of 30 December 1888, Pauline and Henry Greving Letters, 1884–1923, Tms, BABS: "This year the harvest was quite good, but the prices are too low, except eggs and chickens now cost 2–3 dollars the dozen 20 cents. Last fall I sold 12 dozen chickens and now every week I sell eggs for $2.50."

48. Gilbert Fite points out the importance of butter as a cash crop in lean years (*The Farmers' Frontier, 1865–1900* [New York: Holt, 1966], 47). Joan M. Jensen has shown the significance of women's butter income for the family economy, especially when farm income was low ("Butter Making and Economic Development in Mid-Atlantic America, 1750–1850," in *Promise to the Land,* 170–185; "Cloth, Butter, and Boarders"). Jensen has also investigated the autonomy women gained through their role in butter making in the Brandywine valley (*Loosening the Bonds: Mid-Atlantic Farm Women* [New Haven: Yale University Press, 1986], 79–113). Fink found that women's income and domestic productivity were what supported many Iowa families during the Great Depression (57–71). In 1935, the egg and poultry sales on one Michigan farm nearly equaled that from the dairy herd (John L. Shover, *First Majority—Last Minority* [DeKalb: Northern Illinois University Press, 1976], 120).

49. U.S. Census Office, *Tenth Census, 1880: Productions of Agriculture* (Washington, D.C.: GPO, 1883), tables 9 and 14.

50. This was said of Rosa Felt and the fifty pounds of butter she made every week (Lorna Reichenberg, "History of My Ancestors" [1962], 4, folder 3, box 3, Danker Personal Papers). Bernie Zerfass, a second-generation Bukovinia German in Kansas, acknowledged, "We would have starved to death if we wouldn't have had cows to milk and chickens. You'd take a can of cream and some eggs to town, and that's what you bought your groceries with" (Irmgard Hein Ellingson, *The Bukovina Germans in Kansas: A 200 Year History,* Ethnic Heritage Studies, 6 [Fort Hays, Kans.: Fort Hays State University, 1987], 36). Elise Isely remembered that her dairy and egg income "was the main reliance for household expenses" (Bliss Isely, *Sunbonnet Days by Elise Dubach Isely* [Caldwell, Idaho: Caxton, 1935], 171). Caroline Fette Kiest also paid for the family groceries with her butter and eggs (Heitman, 8). In contrast, and perhaps reflecting a male viewpoint, Gonner wrote that Luxembourgian-American women's poultry and dairy earnings contributed "to the support of minor needs of the household" (157).

51. Hillenkamp, letter of 4 May 1843.

52. J. M. Jensen has documented the power dynamics underlying such behavior (*Promise to the Land,* 181–83, 196). For a discussion of women's wage earning, see Kohl, "Image and Behavior," 94. Kohl has also analyzed the power base farm women gain through their contributions to family farm enterprise ("Working Together: Husbands and Wives in the Small-Scale Family Agricultural Enterprise," in *The Canadian Family,* ed. K. Ishwaran [n.p.: Gage, 1983], 234–43). Flora and Flora wrote of women among the Germans from Russia in Kansas having to resist their husbands' efforts to discourage their poultry and butter production (13). In Germany, also, some nineteenth-century analysts of agricultural economy found women's participation in the weekly markets unprofitable and detrimental to their proper work at home (Johann Gottfried Kinkel, "Die Heimatlosen," in *Dorfgeschichten aus dem Vormärz,* vol. 2, ed. Hartmut Kircher [Cologne: Informationspress, C. W. Leske, 1981], 275). Fink's chapter on egg production makes clear men's disdain for poultry until, during World War II, egg production became a viable market industry (135–59).

53. General descriptions of women's household production may be found in many sources. See, for example, Everett Dick, *The Sod-House Frontier* (Lincoln, Nebr.: Johnsen, 1954), 238–39; Riley, *Frontierswomen,* 64–67; Riley, *The Female Frontier,* 118–19; and Fairbanks and Sundberg, 52–55.

54. Shaneyfelt, 205; Isely, 166; *Hillsboro Post,* 25 March 1898. Roenigk wrote that in the first years of settlement, no one, including the merchants, had any money, so trade in goods was the usual form of commerce (312–13).

55. The same thing was true for Anglo-American rural women. Susan Armitage's interviews with twenty women who lived on the Colorado frontier showed that all were poor but that none went out to work for wages. Instead, they "engaged in home food production as a direct contribution to the uncertain farm economy" ("Housework and Childrearing on the Frontier: The Oral History Record," *Sociology and Social Research* 63 [April 1979]: 468). The patterns of these women's lives were similar to those already noted for German-speaking women. Barter for needed goods was common. They also made clothes for the family. They integrated child care into work, having the children help them and then leaving them on their own when the work was done.

56. Dorothee Schneider, "'For Whom Are All the Good Things in Life?' German-American Housewives Discuss Their Budgets," in *German Workers in Industrial Chicago: A Comparative Perspective,* ed. Hartmut Keil and John B. Jentz (DeKalb: Northern Illinois University Press, 1983), 145–60.

57. Francis Dischner, *The Franciscans in Nebraska* (Humphrey and Norfolk, Nebr.: Humphrey Democrat, Norfolk News, 1931), 54.

58. J. Neale Carman, "Foreigners of 1857–1865 at Schippel's Ferry, Saline County," *Kansas Historical Quarterly* 24 (Autumn 1958): 307, 310; Elvira Getzmeier, "The Story of My Grandmother" (n.d.), box 14, Manuscript Collection, ISHD-HS. Widowed Pauline Roedel Bremmer Downs's brother-in-law helped her and her two toddlers complete the five-year residency requirement under the Homestead Act and lay claim to the land she

and her husband had settled on (Lester Harsch, *Grandfather Stories* [n.p, n.d.], 23–24).

59. H. Elaine Lindgren, "Ethnic Women Homesteading on the Plains of North Dakota," *Great Plains Quarterly* 9 (Summer 1989): 157–73. A German-born woman who gained land in Kansas under the Homestead Act was Nancy Moore Wieck's mother-in-law, but she probably would not have done so if she had not been left a widow. Mother Wieck used the $1,300 she received when she sold the homestead to pay for her keep with her son and daughter-in-law (Wieck, 113). Jules Sandoz's mother-in-law also invested in a homestead relinquishment, at Jules's urgings (Sandoz, 218). One German widow from Russia immigrated to Nebraska with her children, where they worked in the sugar beet fields until she could successfully homestead with them in Wyoming in 1912 (Harold D. Kauffman, "A Mother's Quest for a Better Life," *Journal of the American Historical Society of Germans from Russia* 9 [Spring 1986]: 33–38). Katherine Harris has asserted that women gained status and opportunities for self-realization through this experience, whether they participated in it as a partner in a family venture or as an independent settler ("Homesteading in Northeastern Colorado, 1873–1920," in *The Women's West*, ed. Susan Armitage and Elizabeth Jameson [Norman: University of Oklahoma Press, 1987], 165–78). She does not refer to foreign-born women among those she studied, however, and her positive evaluation of women as homesteaders is contradicted by negative information elsewhere.

60. Ise, "Mother's Recollections," 5.

61. Jacob Sieck, "Die Amerikafahrer," *Jahrbuch für die Schleswigsche Geest*, vol. 15 (Schleswig: Heimatverein Schlewegsche Gust, 1967), 144. Mark Friedberger has pointed out that monetary shares for daughters probably were inequitable, since the land was devalued when sold or given to sons ("The Family Farm and the Inheritance Process: Evidence from the Corn Belt, 1870–1950," *Agricultural History* 57 [January 1983]: 12). A variation on this pattern is recorded in Iowa. One family of nine accumulated enough land for each of the three sons to inherit 160 acres, while the six daughters got an education (three became teachers) and some cash, "so they pretty much came out the same" in the view of their descendant (Myrne Detloff Bogh, "Oral Interview," 11 July 1978, Remsen, Iowa, with Rebecca Conard and Mary Jo Wallace, Oral History Project, Earthwatch, #23, tape 1, Manuscript Collection, ISHD-HS). Given the relatively low level of education needed to become a teacher in the nineteenth century and the short time most women remained in the profession, however, we might ask how equal this inheritance was.

62. Sonya Salamon has contributed several especially pertinent studies of farming practices and inheritance traditions in communities of various ethnic heritages in central and southern Illinois ("Ethnic Differences in Farm Family Land Transfers," *Rural Sociology* 45 [Summer 1980]: 290–308; "Sibling Solidarity as an Operating Strategy in Illinois Agriculture," *Rural Sociology* 47 [Summer 1982]: 349–68; "Ethnic Communities and the Structure of Agriculture," *Rural Sociology* 50 [Fall 1985]: 323–40).

63. Kamphoefner, *The Westfalians,* 124. See also W. R. Lee, *Population Growth: Economic Development and Social Change in Bavaria, 1750–1850* (New York: Arno, 1977), 276.

64. Lindgren (173, note 22) cites the Russian-language source A. A. Klaus, "Obshchina-sobstvennik i eia iuridicheskaia organizatsiia," *Vestnik Evropy,* no. 3 (March 1870): 82, 103, trans. Liya Vinograd. Other sources indicate that in the Volga colonies, the Russian "mir" system prevailed, whereby land was apportioned according to the number of adult males in the household. In the Black Sea and Caucasus areas, ultimogeniture was the case. See Theodore Hummel, *100 Jahre Erbhofrecht der deutschen Kolonisten in Russland* (Berlin: n.p., 1936), 41–42, 64, 129; and Adam Giesinger, *From Catherine to Khrushchev: The Story of Russia's Germans* (Battleford, Saskatchewan: Marian Press, 1974), 69.

65. A. G. Roeber has examined the inheritance customs among Germans in eighteenth-century colonial America ("The Origins and Transfer of German-American Concepts of Property and Inheritance," in *Perspectives in American History,* n.s., vol. 3, ed. Bernard Bailyn, Donald Fleming, and Stephan Thernstrom [Cambridge, Mass.: Cambridge University Press, 1986]: 115–71). His study shows a great deal of variation stemming from local and regional differences, with further layers of complexity due to the several legal systems that had influenced these customs. The picture in German lands became increasingly complex in the nineteenth century, especially in areas of partible inheritance, as Sabean's study in Württemberg indicates (201–7). An example of the clear transferal of inheritance customs within a homogenous immigrant community, in this case Swedish-American, can be found in Robert C. Ostergren, "Land and Family in Rural Immigrant Communities," *Annals of the Association of American Geographers* 71 (September 1981): 400–411.

66. K. Conzen discusses the relationship between American inheritance patterns and the family economic strategies of German settlers and their descendants in Minnesota ("Peasant Pioneers," 266, 280–81).

67. W. F. Johnson, vols. 1 and 2. I am grateful to Westminster College for support in the form of a summer study grant to conduct this research in 1989 and to Kenton G. Askren, the Cooper County associate circuit judge, and Jammey Brandes and Terry Wolfe, probate clerks, for their assistance in gathering the pertinent material.

68. Georg Neff, will dated 5 August 1854, folder 690, CCMPC. Friedberger noted similar documents among the wills of second-generation Germans in Illinois (8–9).

69. Theresa Schmidt, will dated 20 August 1902, folder 3737, CCMPC. See also Neff will; and Jacob Schilb, will dated 18 December 1855, folder 785, CCMP. John Hoerl deeded his oldest son only personal property, but he had earlier sold him the home place and resided there with him (will dated 6 October 1928, folder 5573, CCMPC; W. F. Johnson, 2:674). In another case, John King gave his only son the opportunity to buy an additional eighty acres of family land (will dated 3 April 1914, folder 4394, CCMPC).

70. Wilhelm Kahle, will dated 16 October 1916, folder 4654; Ernst Wallje, will dated 6 March 1905, folder 4395, both in CCMPC.

71. Theobald Theiss, will (n.d.), folder 3798; Henry A. Renkin, will dated August 1925, folder 5221; Johann Jacob Blank, will dated 25 April 1888, folder 2741; Albert Muntzel, will dated 5 March 1902, folder 3674, all in CCMPC.

72. W. F. Johnson, "August Stegner," 1:566–67; August Stegner, will dated 17 April 1914, folder 5343, CCMPC.

73. Margaretha Brueckner, will dated 24 August 1910, folder 4392; Ida Joeger, will dated 10 February 1932, folder 6718, both in CCMPC.

74. Blasius Efinger, will dated 30 July 1897, folder 3476, CCMPC; W. F. Johnson, 2:648–49.

75. Theodore Brandes, will dated 25 May 1925, folder 5143, CCMPC; the wills that seek to protect the daughter's legacy from her husband are those of Johann Peter Huth, will dated 17 August 1892, folder 2950; John Langlotz, will dated 28 June 1909, folder 3829; and King will, all in CCMPC. Sonya Salamon and Anna Mackey Keim examined the relationship between landownership and women's power in a contemporary Illinois German-American community and concluded that "women appear to make a trade-off of lower status and less power for male management of the family enterprise which assures them a financially secure widowhood" ("Land Ownership and Women's Power in a Midwestern Farming Community," *Journal of Marriage and the Family* 41 [January 1979]: 109).

76. Andrew Steigleder, will dated 13 April 1907, folder 3854, CCMPC. Other testaments in which daughters seem to be rewarded for the care of parents are those of John Henry Quint, will (n.d.), folder 2241; Theiss will; Elizabeth Mittelbach, will dated 25 April 1907, folder 3937; Ferdinand Ohlendorf, will dated 28 April 1904, folder 3989; Elizabeth Spieler, will dated 28 May 1925, folder 5168; John J. Walther, will dated 8 February 1937, folder 6823, all in CCMPC. Anna Katharine Felton designated $400 for masses for herself, her husband, and her deceased son and daughter and $300 to "the child who shall care for and provide for me in my old age and in my last sickness and shall furnish me with such things that are necessary for my comfort" (will dated 6 August 1898, folder 3451, CCMPC).

77. Hoerl will.

78. Maria Bechtold, will dated 30 April 1938, folder 6368, CCMPC.

79. King will.

80. Sophia King, will dated 27 March 1918, folder 5001, CCMPC. Sophia King disposed of the remainder of her personal property (including money, clothes, household furnishings, an incubator, and two buggies and harnesses) equally among her children and granddaughter. Each received $1,464.94 in the final settlement.

81. Another interesting document is the handwritten will of Fannie Eppstein, who split up her jewelry, clothing, household goods, and family pictures among her daughters and granddaughters (her two sons, she said, had got-

ten their father's watch and sword, after all) (will dated 8 November 1903, folder 3751, CCMPC).

82. John Schnuck, will dated 1 August 1880, folder 2111; Katharine Schnuck, will dated 5 September 1911, folder 5119; Cooper County probate court record of jury trial, 24 May 1927, folder 5119, all in CCMPC.

83. Louis Roth, will dated 1 September 1899, folder 3175, CCMPC. A similar case is that of Christian Kosted, whose two farms were deeded to a son and a daughter, with the proviso that the daughter would pay her two sisters $500 each and that the son would pay off $3,100 in debt and $500 to each of his two brothers (will dated 10 September 1884, folder 2342, CCMPC).

84. Ostergren saw both influences at work in his study of seven Swedish-American communities in Minnesota ("Land and Family").

85. The estates involved are Henry Fricke, folder 848; and Henry Robien, folders 1606 and 1993, both in CCMPC.

86. In addition to Gerlach's *Immigrants in the Ozarks* and Jordan's *German Seed in Texas Soil,* the following studies are particularly relevant: Joseph Schafer, "The Yankee and the Teuton in Wisconsin," *Wisconsin Magazine of History* 6 (1922–23): 125–45, 261–79, 386–402; James C. Malin, "The Turnover of Farm Population in Kansas," *Kansas Historical Quarterly* 4 (November 1935): 339–72; Robert G. Wingate, "Settlement Patterns of La Crosse County, Wisconsin, 1850–1875" (Ph.D. diss., University of Minnesota, 1975); Douglas E. Bowers, "American Agriculture: The Contributions of German-Americans," *Journal of NAL Associates* 9, no. 1–4 (1984): 1–12; Donald L. Winters, *Farmers without Farms: Agricultural Tenancy in Nineteenth-Century Iowa,* Contributions in American History, 79 (Westport, Conn.: Greenwood, 1978); Robert C. Ostergren, "European Settlement and Ethnicity Patterns on the Agricultural Frontiers of South Dakota," *South Dakota History* 13 (Spring 1983): 49–82; and Bogue. Gonner (162–63) asserted that Luxembourgian-Americans had chosen wooded land rather than prairie in Iowa because in the old country, a piece of forest meant the difference between a *Schibebauer* (a poor peasant in a traditional work shirt) and a *Herrebauer* (a wealthy peasant).

87. Lanwert cites a letter from a woman in Michigan, whose family had moved to a larger farm three and a half miles from their first. The woman lamented the distance from the "good neighbor ladies" in the old neighborhood and the lack of anyone but bachelors close by, saying that she had never missed her family in Germany as much as she did now. She consoled herself with the fact that they had twice as much land and a much better farm now, with "nothing lacking in the household" (128).

88. Gerlach noted typically "German" village construction in the Ozarks (*Immigrants in the Ozarks,* 83–85). The Amana and Bethel colonists had some success in re-creating rural villages in America, but in Kansas the Germans from Russia for the most part did not (see chapter 3 herein).

89. Anna Kroos, undated letter from near Lincoln, Nebraska, in "*So be-*

sint euch doch nicht lange und kommt herrüber . . ." Briefe von Amerikaauswanderern aus dem Kreis Lübbecke aus zwei Jahrhunderten, ed. Heinz-Ulrich Kammeier (Lübbecke: n.p., 1985), 80.

90. Darlene M. Ritter, *The Letters of Louise Ritter from 1893–1925: A Swiss-German Immigrant Woman to Antelope County, Nebraska* (Fremont, Nebr.: Siegenthaler-Ritter, 1980), 25; "Letters to Landshut Ursuline Convent," German Tms, folder 2, box II H, Kirkwood, Ursuline Archives, Central Province, Crystal City, Mo.

91. Letter of 12 July 1876, in *Letters from Mother M. Anselma Felber, OSB, and Others,* trans. M. Dominica Bonnenberg (St. Louis: Benedictine Sisters of Perpetual Adoration, 1977); M. Beatrice Renggli, "From Rickenbach to Maryville: An Account of the Journey," *American Benedictine Review* 27 (Fall 1976): 266. See my comments on similar reactions of Swiss and German nuns to climatic and geographic changes in "German and Swiss Nuns in Nineteenth-Century Missouri and Southern Illinois: Some Comparisons with Secular Women," *Yearbook of German-American Studies,* vol. 20 (Lawrence, Kans.: Society for German-American Studies, 1985), 74–76.

92. Ellingson, 21, 23.

93. E. P. Hutchinson, *Immigrants and Their Children, 1850–1950* (New York: Wiley, 1956), table 14, 34–37.

94. For example, frontier ministers' wives were generally unprepared by their upbringing for such primitive living. See the experiences of Sophie Luise Weitbrecht (52–55); Adelheid von Borries-Garlich (Henry Bode, *Builders of Our Foundations* [Webster Groves, Mo.: privately pubished, 1940], 49–50); and Albertina and Gottlieb Eisen ("Personal Biographies, Plus Letters," comp. David Schoen, Tms, #11–1/Eis 8, Eden Theological Seminary, St. Louis). Other women responded with disbelief or tears when first seeing their future home, as did Frederica Hecker Fischer and Hannah Aschman Harms's mother (microfilm 3, LDMC).

95. See Gustorf, 131.

96. Ise, *Sod and Stubble,* 23.

97. Edward E. Hirschler, "The Story of a Pioneer Family" (M.A. thesis, Fort Hays Kansas State College, 1937), 27.

98. Ise, *Sod and Stubble,* 17–18; Wieck, 115.

99. Rose Marie Eidam, "History of Maternal Ancestors of Rose Marie Eidam" (1961), Tms, folder 20, box 1, Danker Personal Papers. Even in a sod house, the cold could be life-threatening, as Rebecca Beins discovered during the Nebraska blizzard of 12 January 1888 (*Sod House Memories,* ed. Alberts, 205).

100. Strasser, 58.

101. Jewett, 18. Emilie did not record if Elizabeth Bigler's prayers were answered that summer. Rosie Ise's might have been when her husband agreed to borrow money to buy a windmill, to save her from drawing water by hand for their cattle in the hot Kansas summers (Ise, *Sod and Stubble,* 195–97).

102. Duden, 72.

103. C. C. Regier, "Childhood Reminiscences of a Russian Mennonite Immigrant Mother 1859–1880," *Mennonite Quarterly Review* 15 (January

1941): 93. A letter written by a Kansas Mennonite woman from Russia described the devastation settlers experienced during the 1874 grasshopper plague, when a woman could not even keep her houseplants safe from the insects (*Mennonitische Blätter,* Danzig, Germany [March 1875], cited by Melvin Gingerich, "The Reactions of the Russian Mennonite Immigrants of the 1870s to the American Frontier," *Mennonite Quarterly Review* 34 [January 1960]: 144). Gingerich's article lists a number of adjustments and difficulties the Mennonite Germans from Russia faced on the Great Plains, including prairie fires, recalcitrant oxen, and dust storms.

104. Howard Raid, "Migrations from Germany to Iowa by Mennonite Settlers, Excerpt Taken from the 'Tagebuch' Written by the Reverend David Ruth and Katherine Strohm" (1855), Tms, Manuscript Collection, ISHD-HS.

105. Ruppenthal, 10; Susanna Amalia Ruth Krehbiel, "Autobiography" (1979), 24, Tms, Mennonite Historical Library, Bethel College, North Newton, Kansas (original manuscript begun 9 January 1911 in Geary, Oklahoma); Gillhoff, 104. Nancy Wieck's humor and optimism are strong elements in her memoir, qualities she seems to have shared with her German mother-in-law (115, 125).

106. Related scholarly commentaries include McNall and McNall, 85; and Nelson, 170–71, 175, 177.

107. Bradley H. Baltensperger, "Agricultural Change among Nebraska Immigrants, 1880–1900," in *Ethnicity on the Great Plains,* ed. Luebke, 173–82. Kamphoefner notes that almost no Americans grew barley or buckwheat in 1850 in the area of his study in Missouri, but some Germans did (*The Westfalians,* 129). John C. Weaver shows the connection between the tendency of German-born farmers in southwest Illinois to grow more wheat than Anglo-Americans did and their origins in wheat-growing parts of Germany ("Changing Patterns of Cropland Use in the Middle West," *Economic Geography* 30 [January 1954]: 9). Gonner noted that the Luxembourg immigrants raised a great deal of wheat but were switching to corn and pig feeding in Iowa because it was proving more profitable (150, 156). Ostergren speculates that the greater amounts of wheat planted by Swedes and Germans than by Anglo-Americans in Isanti County, Minnesota, during the settlement period (1860–80) could be attributed to the early successes they had had with that crop (*A Community Transplanted,* 197–98). As K. Conzen has asserted, however, immigrants adopted American farming methods and crops quickly as a means to achieving their ultimate goals and saw no inherent value in their native practices ("Deutsche Einwanderer," 366).

108. Bogue's study of two Iowa counties in 1880 shows that immigrants lagged behind the native-born in animal husbandry as it grew in response to specialized market demands (211).

109. Among the many German-speaking immigrants who spun and knit their own wool were Minnie Sanders Volker in Kansas (Mrs. Henry Volker Jr., "Minnie Sanders Volker" [n.d.], Tms, microfilm 9, LDMC), and Mathilda Bortz's and Ella Hein Sillars's grandmothers in Iowa (Mathilda Bortz, "The Story of My Grandmother" [n.d.], box 13, Manuscript Collection, ISHD-HS; Ella Sillars, Oral History Interview [28–30 July, 4 August 1976], tape 5,

Manuscript Collection, ISHD-HS). For further comment on this, see Boylan, 5, 12; and Stanfield, 35, 38. On flax and rye production as examples of "cultural rebound" among Germans from Russia in Nebraska, see Baltensperger, 177. Ostergren noted that immigrants in South Dakota also returned to familiar European crops after some years in America ("European Settlement and Ethnicity Patterns," 80). Brown called the wine distilled in Iowa basements "a part of the daily meal" (17). Gonner wrote about growing flax in western Iowa and sheep being kept for family use, even though they were not profitable (153, 156).

110. Kamphoefner found that 95 percent of the German-born in Warren and St. Charles counties, Missouri, listed potatoes among the crops they had planted in 1850, but only 5 percent had grown sweet potatos (*The Westfalians,* 129). Louis Geiger, writing of rural Cooper County, Missouri, said that the German-speaking immigrants there and their children never developed a taste for roast raccoon or oppossum ("At Century's Turn, 1880–1930: Billingsville" [May 1991], 15, Tms, Collection 5051, WHMC-C).

111. Roebke, 108. See her listing of emigrant guidebooks (231–38). Among the more significant, in addition to that by Duden already cited, are Friedrich Vulpius, *Amerikanische Erfahrungen* (Frankfurt am Main and St. Goar: Verlagsbuchhandlung zu Belle-Vue, 1847); Ottomar von Behr, *Guter Rath für Auswanderer nach den Vereinigten Staaten von Nordamerika* (Leipzig: R. Friese, 1847); Ludwig von Baumbach, *Briefe aus den Vereinigten Staaten von Nordamerika in die Heimath mit besonderer Rücksicht auf deutsche Auswanderer* (Cassel: Theodor Fischer, 1851); Gustav Struve, *Wegweiser für Auswanderer* (Bamberg: Buchner, 1866); and Gustav Struve, *Kurzgefaßter Wegweiser für Auswanderer...* (Bamberg: Buchner, 1867).

112. Goebel said that the wives of the Missouri Dreißiger learned handy cooking techniques from backwoods American women (68). Anna Kroos, working as a maid on a farm outside of Lincoln, Nebraska, wrote that she had had to learn to cook, bake and sew, "for here everyone does everything herself" (letter, undated, in Heinz-Ulrich Kammeier, *"Ich muß mir ärgern, das ich nicht ehr übern Großen Ozean gegangen bin": Auswanderer aus dem Kreis Lübbecke und Umgebung berichten aus Amerika* [n.p.: Mittwalddruck Espelkamp, 1988], 78). Elise Isely, whose mother died soon after the family arrived in Missouri, learned all of her frontier housekeeping skills from American neighbors (75–79). Louise Gellhorn Boylan remembered the picniclike atmosphere of molasses-making, a skill her northeast German family no doubt learned from their American neighbors (5).

113. August Rauschenbusch warned women that they would have to bake their own bread in the American backwoods (*Einige Ausweisungen für Auswanderer nach den westlichen Staaten von Nordamerika und Reisebilder,* 3d ed. [Eberfeld und Iserlohn: Bädeker, 1848], 61). Gustorf, after meeting the daughters of a German immigrant trial lawyer in Missouri, found it incredible "that women of such culture have come here to milk cows" (137). Goebel described how discouraged his mother became when her rice pudding, a special treat for which she had saved milk, spilled into the flames of the open

hearth (48–49). The German-born Adorers of the Most Precious Blood in Ruma, Illinois, spoiled new foodstuffs because they did not know how to handle them properly. These nuns also disliked the morning snack of parched corn available to them and their pupils. For a further discussion of similar problems, see Pickle, "Stereotypes and Reality," 296; and Pickle, "German and Swiss Nuns," 75–76.

114. Dick describes the procedure for making soap out of lard (238–39). Women in German-American farm families in Nebraska were still making their own soap well after World War II, as I and no doubt many others can attest.

115. Roenigk, 113, 238–39, 277. The descendants of German-speaking women on the Nebraska frontier recorded different reactions to Indians on the part of their ancestors (see, for example, Catherine Ballow March, "A Story of the Ballow Family and the Heldt Family in Saunders County, Nebraska" [1962], folder 15, box 4, Danker Personal Papers; and Judy Blecher, "My Ancestors" [1961], folder 16, box 1, Danker Personal Papers). Immigrant children could find Indians attractive (Jewett, 15). Even when the frontier era was past, however, a newly arrived immigrant might still be frightened by a small group of Indians in wagons who stayed overnight on her farm (Ritter, 25).

116. In Kamphoefner's study of German immigrants in Warren and St. Charles counties in 1850, he found that 28 out of 1,000 households owned slaves, and half of these had only one slave. Many of those Germans who owned slaves were married to Americans (*The Westfalians,* 115–17).

117. Isely, 78; William Arndt, "Several Episodes from the Life of the Sainted Pastor F. J. Biltz," *Concordia Historical Institute Quarterly* 6 (July 1933): 41–50. One of the episodes in the Arndt article figures prominently in Robert Frizzell's "'Killed by Rebels': A Civil War Massacre and Its Aftermath," *Missouri Historical Review* 71 (July 1977): 369–95. German-speakers formed several home guard units in Missouri. For activities and casualties of the German-dominated Boonville home guard, see W. F. Johnson, 1:190–202. On the stance of German-speakers before and during the Civil War, see James A. Bergquist's "People and Politics in Transition: The Illinois Germans, 1850–60," Jay Monaghan's "Did Abraham Lincoln Receive the Illinois German Votes?" and Frederick C. Luebke's Introduction, all in *Ethnic Voters and the Election of Lincoln,* ed. Frederick C. Luebke (Lincoln: University of Nebraska Press, 1971). See also Steven Rowan and James Primm, *Germans for a Free Missouri* (Columbia: University of Missouri Press, 1983); and Richard J. Jensen, *The Winning of the Midwest: Social and Political Conflict, 1888–1896* (Chicago: University of Chicago Press, 1971), 96, 142–43, 294–95, passim.

118. Thomas C. Coulter, "A History of Woman Suffrage in Nebraska, 1856–1920" (Ph.D. diss., Ohio State University, 1967), 50. Frederick Luebke discusses Nebraska Germans' views on suffrage as well (*Immigrants and Politics* [Lincoln: University of Nebraska Press, 1969], 127–30). See also the exchange between the German-born pioneer Fred Hedde and the suffragist Harriet Brooks in the Grand Island, Nebraska, *Times,* May–September 1881.

119. Friedrich Muench, a prominent Dreißiger in Missouri, wrote that

woman's "greatest perfections can only be manifested in Domestic Life" and that her nature is "love, innocence, tact, fineness, delicacy, in short, amiability" (*Spirit of the Age* 1 [3 November 1849]: 12). Wilhelm Sihler sets forth the prevailing attitude in the Missouri Synod in the late nineteenth century ("Über den Beruf des Weibes und seine Entartung," *Der Lutheraner* 28 [1 February 1872]: 65–67).

120. Margretta Stewart Dietrich, *Nebraska Recollections* (Santa Fe: Dietrich, 1957), 9.

121. I checked listings of woman's rights organizations at the Kansas State Historical Society and the Nebraska State Historical Society. Irene Häderle, however, found reference to the founding of a *Frauen-Stimmrechtsverein* (women's franchise club) in St. Louis County in June 1871 ("Deutsche Frauenvereine in den USA, 1840–1930: Ein Zwischenbericht," in *Frauen wandern aus*, ed. Blaschke and Harzig, 88). On the German-American women's press, see Monika Blaschke, "Die deutschamerikanische Presse für Frauen: Bestand, Prognosen und Probleme," in *Frauen wandern aus*, ed. Blaschke and Harzig, 98, 101–2, 107; and Christiane Harzig, "Elemente einer deutschamerikanischen Frauenkultur: Deutschamerikanerinnen in Chicago vor der Jahrhundertwende," in *Frauen wandern aus*, ed. Blaschke and Haezig, 116, 118. June O. Underwood notes only that immigrant women were the objects of philanthropic efforts by some Anglo-American women's groups ("Civilizing Kansas: Women's Organizations, 1880–1920," *Kansas History* 7 [Winter 1984–85]: 291–306). See also Luebke, *Immigrants and Politics*, 129–31, 138–41. For a related discussion of the connection between views of women's nature and attitudes toward suffrage among German-American socialists, see Ruth Seifert, "The Portrayal of Women in the German-American Labor Movement," in *German Workers' Culture in the United States, 1850 to 1920*, ed. Hartmut Keil (Washington, D.C.: Smithsonian Institute Press, 1988), 109–36. On the antiforeigner sentiments among suffragists, see Barbara Berg, *The Remembered Gate: Origins of American Feminism* (New York: Oxford University Press, 1978), 269.

122. An interesting history of one such family recreation spot is Robert Perry's *Schimmer's Sand Krog: Resort on the Platte* (Grand Island, Nebr.: Prairie Pioneer Press, 1984). See also Percy G. Ebbutt, *Emigrant Life in Kansas* (London: Swan Sonnenschein, 1886), 204. Paul Kleppner discusses various stances toward temperance (mostly oppositional) taken by German-American voters during the period of his study (*Cross of Culture: A Social Analysis of Midwestern Politics, 1850–1900* [New York: Free Press, 1970]). Luebke notes that the only German-Americans who supported temperance were those who joined American Protestant churches (Baptist, Methodist, Congregationalist, and Evangelical) and some Mennonites (*Immigrants and Politics*, 66).

123. C. Carnahan Goetsch, "The Immigrant and America: Assimilation of a German Family," *Annals of Iowa* 42 (Summer and Fall 1973): 17–27, 114–25. For a "strong-minded lady" in Plank Township, Iowa, who found and took away the jug her menfolk had taken care to hide from her, see Stanfield, 47.

124. Wiemar Stommel, letter of 24 June 1850, BABS.

125. See, for example, August P. Richter, *Geschichte der Stadt Davenport und des County Scott,* 2 vols. (Davenport, Iowa: privately printed, 1917), 1:453. Roebke noted the same disapproval in the emigrant advisers (181). A subtle warning to women is contained in an *Abendschule* piece on the Amazons (6 October 1881), who awaken admiration for their courage and bravery but at the same time give "the impression of the unnatural and the immoral."

126. Blommer, letter of 25 February 1874, BABS.

127. Frederick Steines, letter of 24 April 1835, in William G. Bek, trans. and comp., "The Followers of Duden," *Missouri Historical Review* 15 (July 1921): 677. Rural Anglo-American women also "did not mount much sustained criticism, nor much evident resistance to male rule" (Faragher, "History from the Inside-Out," 551).

128. Steinhaus, 74; Goetsch, 23.

129. J. R. Buchanan reported the incident of the recalcitrant wife in "The Great Railroad Migration into Northern Nebraska," *Proceedings and Collections of the NSHS,* 2d ser., 10 (1907): 28–29. Pleck's "Challenges to Traditional Authority" shows that in urban areas German immigrants were the worst offenders for wife beating and child abuse. See also Seller, 65. For particularly disturbing evidence of wife and child abuse among poor immigrants from Russia, see Pauline Neher Diede, *Homesteading on the Knife River Prairies,* ed. Elizabeth Hampsten (Bismarck, N.D.: Germans from Russia Heritage Society, 1983). On this score, see also Sandoz, *Old Jules,* 215–16, 230–31, 279.

130. Timothy J. Kloberdanz has said that the one place where men, women, and children were equal was in the field ("Volksdeutsche, the Eastern European Germans: Hungry for Land, Hungry for a Home; North Dakota's 'Other Germans,'" in *Plains Folk: North Dakota's Ethnic History,* ed. William C. Sherman and Playford V. Thorson [Fargo: North Dakota Institute for Regional Studies, 1988], 150).

131. See, for example, Pieschl, 35; and Ritter, 71. Rosenfeld writes that such reciprocity is still very rare on American farms today (10–11). In her study of Block, Kansas, Coburn found that the kind of work necessary at any time was more important than gender in determining what a child did in the family. She also concluded that first- and second-generation German-American men rarely helped their wives with household work (*Life at Four Corners,* 86–90, 97).

132. See the 10 June 1837 letter to the editor on this subject in the St. Louis *Anzeiger des Westens.* Similarly, the Evangelical minister Johann Gottfried Buettner was scandalized by the unkept, blunt-speaking, bareback-riding German midwife he met in the Missouri backwoods while going to baptize the child she had helped deliver. According to Buettner, Americans held all German women in low esteem because of women like her and were prone to say, "The dutchwomen are worse than the squas." Buettner also reported having heard that the German women around Belleville, Illinois, rode to town bareback on market days. His conclusion: "It is a true disgrace!" (*Die Vereinigten Staaten von Nord-Amerika* [Hamburg: M. Geber, 1844], 1:199).

133. Stanfield, 48–49. It would be interesting to know if immigrant women in rural areas, removed from the pressure to conform to American women's fashions, retained the midcalf skirts from their homelands for field and yard work.

134. Nancy Wieck's engaging memoir contains several instances of her going against her mother-in-law's advice by making decisions and taking actions in her husband's absence that he had expressly forbidden (114–15, 121–22). Nancy, unlike her mother-in-law, was not German-born, which may partly explain her open independence and the older woman's inclination to go along with her son's wishes. Nonetheless, Nancy's German husband seems to have accepted this in her, telling her, "You say and I'll do" (118).

135. Autograph book epigram, written around 1890 by Pauline Lehner Hoffmann (born in 1855 in Ohio) in Battle Creek, Nebraska, in autograph book of her daughter Clara Hoffmann (later, Uhlmann, born in 1876), in the possession of Rachel Uhlmann Ehrman of South Amana, Iowa.

136. Isernhagen, 77–78; Kloberdanz, "Volksdeutsche," 150; Coburn, *Life at Four Corners,* 155.

137. Lauren Ann Kattner, "Growing Up Female in New Braunfels: Social and Cultural Adaptations in a German-Texas Town," *Journal of American Ethnic History* 9 (Spring 1990): 49–72; Ellingson, 27; Coburn, *Life at Four Corners,* 76.

138. "Jürnjakob Swehn" and his wife seem to have chosen each other without direct intervention from others and agreed to marry when they had $550 saved between them (Gillhoff, 46). August Raasch reported laconically in his diary of the steps taken between his father and the father of his future wife over the period of a week before he got the news that he "could have Marie, also that it was her will and that she had nothing against the whole matter" (Personal Diary, 19 November 1871, NSHS).

139. Schock, *In Quest of Free Land,* 55.

140. See Salamon, "Ethnic Differences," "Sibling Solidarity," and "Ethnic Communities."

141. Bretting rejects Seller's contention that women came to America to emancipate themselves: "Not an attempt to break away, but a wish for continuity was at the basis of their decision to emigrate" (28). The vast majority of "ordinary" immigrants did not redefine their role in family or society because of the new activities they had to assume.

142. *Central Missourier,* 24 December 1874.

143. Gillhoff, 206–7.

144. Pieschl, 36–37; Blommer, letter of 20 July 1871, BABS. Kamphoefner notes that in 1850 a higher proportion of the German immigrants in Warren and St. Charles counties owned property than did any other ethnic group, although the value of that property was less than half that owned by Anglo-Americans (*The Westfalians,* 142). See also K. Conzen, "Peasant Pioneers," 282.

145. Bogue concluded this on the basis of his study of Wapello County and Warren Township in Bremer County, Iowa (25–27). Coburn's study of

the Block community in Miami County, Kansas, confirms this as well (*Life at Four Corners*, 16–23).

146. Studies that examine the significance of the rural immigrant church include August Hollingshead, "The Life Cycle of Nebraska Rural Churches," *Rural Sociology* 2 (June 1937): 180–91; Frederick Luebke, "German Immigrants and Churches in Nebraska, 1889–1915," *Mid-America* 50 (April 1968): 116–30; Doerries, "Church and Faith"; Robert C. Ostergren, "The Immigrant Church as a Symbol of Community and Place in the Upper Midwest," *Great Plains Quarterly* 1 (Fall 1981): 224–38; and Jon Gjerde, "Conflict and Community: A Case Study of the Immigrant Church in the United States," *Journal of Social History* 19 (Summer 1986): 681–970. Doerries points to the dual role the church played in providing cultural continuity and stability while also serving as a vehicle for accommodation to the immigrants' new world ("Church and Faith," 286–87), a point K. Conzen has also made (*Immigrant Milwaukee*, 155; "Deutsche Einwanderer," 369, 374). Studies noting the connection between the existence of immigrant churches and the persistence of ethnic communities include H. B. Johnson, 40; Gerlach, *Immigrants in the Ozarks*, 118; Peter A. Speek, *A Stake in the Land* (New York: Harper, 1921); Gjerde, *From Peasants to Farmers*, 163–65, 227–31; and Ostergren, *A Community Transplanted*, 210–11.

147. "Diary of Julie Wall, née Turnau, 1842" (n.d.), trans. Armin Saeger, 25, #12–1/WA 11, Eden Theological Seminary Archives, St. Louis.

148. Historical studies of German immigrant churches in the five-state region include Otto E. Kriege, Gustav Becker, Matthäus Hermann, and C. L. Korner, eds., *Souvenir der West Deutschen Konferenz der Bischöflichen Methodistenkirche* (Cincinnati: Jennings and Graham, 1906); George Eisenach, *A History of the German Congregational Churches in the United States* (Yankton, S.D.: Pioneer Press, 1938); C. E. Schneider; and Bode. Although Coburn's study of Block, Kansas, takes gender roles in rural immigrant communities into account, she, too, acknowledges the difficulty of ascertaining women's roles and contributions to immigrant church life because they were so much a part of the fabric of assumptions about women and their work (*Life at Four Corners*, 48–49). The archives of foundations of German-speaking Catholic nuns, however, contain many valuable sources on women's contributions to religious life (see chapter 4 herein).

149. Howard Ruede's letters contain many references to such frontier gatherings, without more than the following oblique acknowledgement of women's contributions: "It seems to be thought no imposition for fifty or more to take dinner at a place" after such a meeting (*Sod-House Days: Letters from a Kansas Homesteader, 1877–78*, ed. John Ise [New York: Columbia University Press, 1937], 32). The letters of Christian Helmreich, pastor for a time to a colony of East Frisians near Lodgepole, Nebraska, attest to the long struggle small ethnic communities faced in founding their own congregations ("Letters of Christian Helmreich [1866–1945]," ed. and trans. Ernst C. Helmreich, *Nebraska History* 58 [Summer 1977]: 175–92).

150. The records of the Smithton Methodist Church, Smithton, Missou-

ri, recording the building of a new church in 1897, are an example of this (Smithton Methodist Church, Records, 1867–1951, 2:83–87, #C3704, WHMC-C). The 1871 articles of incorporation of the Brunswick, Missouri, "Deutsche protestantische evangelisch-lutherische Johannes Gemeinde" list only men as signatories (German Lutheran Church, Record Book, 1869–1888, #C3825, folder 542, Benecke Family Papers, WHMC-C).

151. Raid, 3, 4; Stickney, 22. Fink stated of the mixed-ethnic area she studied in Iowa, "The church replicated the social organization of the family and, in turn, served as a model for its dual organization. Women, responsible for social reproduction, were the backbone of the church membership, and their dedication to church life kept it a vital part of the community. Although men had less overall involvement in religious life than women did, men were the public face of the church, its formal leaders" (41). Häderle also notes the behind-the-scenes importance of women in the functioning of immigrant churches (87). Arthur J. Vidich and Joseph Bensman's study of a twentieth-century rural community also shows that Anglo-American women played a vital but hidden role in church life (*Small Town in Mass Society* [Princeton, N.J.: Princeton University Press, 1968], 232–33).

152. Gillhoff, 191. Similarly, Gonner noted the intensification of church life among Luxembourgian immigrants in America (166–71).

153. Siekmann, 55; Henry W. Casper, *History of the Catholic Church in Nebraska*, 3 vols. (Milwaukee: Bruce, 1960–66), 1:136.

154. Concrete evidence of the contributions of immigrant church women's groups in the Midwest include the minutes of the Ladies Aid Society (1922–24) of the Smithton, Missouri, Methodist Church, vols. 6 and 7, WHMC-C. Louis Geiger's 1991 history of the St. Johannes Deutsche Evangelische Kirche (St. John German Evangelical Church) at Oak Grove–Billingsville in rural Cooper County, Missouri, contains much information about women's activities in this small country church ("St. Johannes Deutsche Evangelische Kirche" (10 May 1991), Tms, folder 1, Collection 5051, WHMC-C). Coburn's study of the rural Missouri Synod Lutheran community and church of Block, Kansas, also attests to the many unsung and unrecorded contributions women made to the maintenance of ethnic community through their church-related activities (*Life at Four Corners*, 49–55). Gjerde offers evidence of parallel activities by Norwegian women in the upper Midwest (*From Peasants to Farmers*, 230). Similarly, a Ladies Aid Society was the founding core of the rural Norwegian First Lutheran Church of Bruce, South Dakota (Elizabeth Hampsten, "Sterling Township Women Built a Church," comp. Janet Hovey Johnson, *Plainswoman* 8 [September 1984]: 6–7, 15).

155. This was true for a long time. The art historian Charles Van Ravenswaay, who grew up in Cooper County, Missouri, remembered the German-American farm women in the 1920s, whose isolation was broken almost solely by church attendance and family and neighborhood visits on Sunday (*The Arts and Architecture of German Settlements in Missouri* [Columbia: University of Missouri Press, 1977], vii–viii).

156. For example, the Evangelical Church Board of Missions refused to

authorize the formation of a woman's missionary society until 1880 (Kriege et al., 47). In Block, Kansas, the Trinity Lutheran Ladies Aid was not formed until 1912 (Coburn, *Life at Four Corners,* 49).

157. Brown, 13.

158. Geiger, "St. Johannes Deutsche Evangelische Kirche," 13–14.

159. *Kansas Staats-Anzeiger* (Atchison), 14 July 1881.

160. Goetsch, 24–25; Gottfried Walz, letter of 12 February 1897, BABS. See also Speek, 65–66, 156–57, 203–18, passim.

161. Hutchinson, table 35b, 182–85. Speek noted that immigrants did not take seriously the typically young, single female American teachers in rural, one-room public schools (207).

162. An example was Trinity Lutheran School at Block, Kansas, which hired its first such female teaching assistant in 1906. The fact that she was the unmarried daughter of the pastor made the school board feel it was not as bad as it might have been (Coburn, *Life at Four Corners,* 73–74). One of the most important studies of the Missouri Synod school system is August C. Stellhorn, *Schools of the Lutheran Church-Missouri Synod* (St. Louis: Concordia Publishing House, 1963).

163. Boylan, 8, passim.

164. Sillars, tape 3.

165. See Speek, 156–65; and Coburn, *Life at Four Corners,* 226. Some school districts in Kansas and Nebraska were allowed to teach in German as well as English (A. F. Buechler, R. J. Barr, and Dale P. Stough, *History of Hall County, Nebraska* [Lincoln, Nebr.: Western Publishing, 1920], 350–51). This led to complaints from state education officials about the diversion of public funds to non-English-language schools (Heinz Kloss, "German-American Language Maintenance Efforts," in *Language Loyalty in the United States,* ed. Joshua A. Fishbein and Mary E. Warschauer [The Hague: Mouton, 1966], 234–35). Luebke discusses German immigrants' opposition to compulsory school laws in Nebraska in the 1890s (*Immigrants and Politics,* 143–50). In contrast, J. Olson Anders suggests that in other regions, immigrants were eager to cooperate with public school policy so their children could become integrated into American society ("Educational Beginnings in a Typical Prairie County," *Rural Sociology* 7 [December 1942]: 423–31). On teacher training for these schools, see LaVern J. Rippley, "The German-American Normal Schools," in *Germanica-Americana, 1976: Symposium on German-American Literature and Culture,* ed. Erich A. Albrecht and J. Anthony Burzle (Lawrence, Kans.: Max Kade Document and Research Center, 1977), 63–71.

166. Gillhoff, 300. See also Dorothy Weyer Creigh's comments in *Nebraska: A Bicentennial History* (New York: Norton, 1977), 153.

167. Harley Ransom, comp., *Pioneer Recollections* (Cedar Rapids, Iowa: Historical Publishing, 1941), 262. This society, located in a small community a few miles north of the Amana colonies, endured well past World War II (Ransom, 263–65). See also Reinhard Doerries, *Iren und Deutsche in der neuen Welt: Akkulturationsprozesse in der amerikanischen Gesellschaft im späten 19. Jahrhundert,* Beiheft 76, Vierteljahrschrift für Sozial-und Wirtschaftsge-

schichte (Stuttgart: Steiner, 1986), 90–91); and Wolfgang Helbich and Ulrike Sommer, *"Alle Menschen sind dort gleich . . .": Die deutsche Amerika-
Auswanderung im 19. und 20. Jahrhundert,* ed. Armin Reese and Uwe Uffelmann, Historisches Seminar, 10 (Düsseldorf: Schwan, 1988), 46, 52–53.

168. According to an 1847 letter quoted by Schuster (23). For the location of secular German-American clubs, see Heinz Kloss, *Atlas of Nineteenth
and Early Twentieth Century German-American Settlements* (Marburg: Elwert,
1974), map series F.

169. Brunswick Turn-Verein, 1866–69, #C3825, folder 574–82, Benecke
Family Papers, WHMC-C. The Boonville, Missouri, *Central Missourier* listed three women among the nine actors performing "Ein toller Tag" on 28
January 1875 during a "Turn- und Gesang-Verein" benefit. Häderle gives a
general overview of the formation of nineteenth-century German-American
women's clubs (89–91). For an introduction to the history of the *Turner*
movement in Germany and the United States, see Henry Metzner, *A Brief
History of the North American Gymnastic Union,* trans. Theodore Stempfel
Jr. (Indianapolis: National Executive Committee of the North American Gymnastic Union, 1911). Ralf Wagner discusses the increasing diversity among
German-American *Turner* societies ("Turner Societies and the Socialist Tradition," in *German Workers' Culture,* ed. Keil, 221–40).

170. Ralph Gregory, *The German-Americans in the Washington, Missouri, Area* (Washington, Mo.: Missourian Publishing, 1981), 54–57, 66–74. For
a study of Washington, Augusta, and Hermann, Missouri, see Karen Jean
DeBres, "From Germans to Americans: The Creation and Destruction of
Three Ethnic Communities" (Ph.D. diss., Columbia University, 1986). Related sources and studies of German-American secular clubs include Carl
Wencker, "History of the 'Augusta Harmonie Verein'" (February 2, 1906),
as told to Reinhard A. Hoffmann, Missouri History Manuscript Collection,
Missouri Historical Society, St. Louis; Paul Adams, "The Topeka Turn Verein," *Bulletin of the Shawnee County Historical Society* 58 (November 1981):
87–98; Daniel Padberg, "German Ethnic Theatre in Missouri: Cultural Assimilation" (Ph.D. diss., Southern Illinois University at Carbondale, 1980);
Roland Binz, "German Gymnastic Societies in St. Louis, 1850–1913: Emer-
gent Socio-Cultural Institutions" (Master's thesis, Washington University,
1983); William Roba, *The River and the Prairie: A History of the Quad-Cit-
ies* (Davenport, Iowa: Hesperion, 1986), 78–79, 101; Siekmann, 64; and
Creigh, *Nebraska,* 154. The influence of the *Turnverein* in German-American life continued among the children of immigrants (see, for example, Roba,
101; and Goetsch, 26, 118–19).

171. On the club-sponsored refuges for country women and their children,
see Scott, *Natural Allies,* 145–46.

172. Kloss discusses the main factors contributing to language maintenance
in the United States, most of which were more common in rural areas ("German-American Language Maintenance Efforts," 206–52). Useful discussions
of women's and rural immigrants' adaptation to American culture include Alan
Bayer, *The Assimilation of American Family Patterns by European Immigrants*

and Their Children (New York: Arno, 1980), 135–36; and Richard Kolm, *The Change of Cultural Identity: An Analysis of Factors Conditioning the Cultural Integration of Immigrants* (New York: Arno, 1980). For related comments, see Coburn, *Life at Four Corners,* 6–7; Bogue, 278; and Grace DeSantis and Richard Benkin, "Ethnicity without Community," *Ethnicity* 7 (April 1980): 137–43.

173. See Dorothy W. Creigh, *Adams County: A Story of the Great Plains* (Hastings, Nebr.: Adams County–Hastings Centennial Commission, 1972), 333. Carman noted that "the Germans very frequently emigrated as families, a conservative linguistic trait," and linked the large number of women in German families to this conservatism (*Foreign Language Units,* 93). Dow observed as late as the 1970s that older female residents of Amana used German exclusively when among themselves, whereas elderly men used English, although the men also spoke German fluently (112). Häderle stated that the women's branch of the short-lived Deutschamerikanischer Nationalbund (founded in 1904 and dissolved in 1918) believed women to be "predestined" through their maternal role to preserve German language and culture (91). Gonner claimed that the dialect preference of the wife determined language usage in the homes of Luxembourgian-Americans (186). An unusual example of the linguistic conservativism of a male immigrant is Francis Arnold Hoffmann, who even persuaded his Anglo-American wife to learn German. The family spoke German exclusively from the time they married in 1844 until he died in 1903 (Minna Hoffman Nehrling, "Papapa" [n.d.], folder 4, Francis A. Hoffmann Papers, ISHL). Much more recently, Kurt Rain noted the conservative aspect of Hutterite women's language usage, in that they speak primarily the basic dialect of the home, not the standardized or "elevated" dialects reserved for business and church usage ("German Dialects in Anabaptist Colonies on the Great Plains," trans. Paul Schach, in *Languages in Conflict,* ed. Paul Schach [Lincoln: University of Nebraska Press, 1980], 108).

174. See, for example, Freeman, "Anton and Karolina Krause"; James A. Schelbitzki, interview with Linda S. Pickle, Columbia, Missouri, 30 December 1986; Elise Boyd, Oral History Interview, April 5, 1977, Clinton, Iowa, with Jay Naftager, tape 79, Manuscript Collection, ISHD-HS. The 1900 census for Benton Precinct, in Nemaha County, Nebraska, shows that Meta Mannott, Ihnke Kleihauer's sister, did not speak English after having lived thirty-two years in America.

175. Pauline Gauß Wendt, letter of 9 February 1897, Gauß-Rogosch Letters, 1865–1903, BABS; Ritter, 149, 37, 151, 163. Even under the most favorable conditions, language retention was difficult and often stunted. For a discussion of the factors favoring language maintenance, see Kloss, "German-American Language Maintenance Efforts," 206. Jürgen Eichhoff has noted the tendency for dialect usage to ossify upon transplantation to American rural areas ("The German Language in America," in *America and the Germans,* 2 vols., ed. Frank Trommler and Joseph McVeigh [Philadelphia: University of Pennsylvania Press, 1985], 1:234.

176. Jewett, 18.

177. On featherbeds and goose down, see Stanfield, 35, 43. Siekmann writes of the Old World brick ovens (22), as does Allie Wallace, *Frontier Life in Oklahoma* (Washington, D.C.: Public Affairs Press, 1964), 22. On retention of Old World foods, see Gonner, 156; and Goetsch, 116.

178. Speek, 51; Mela Meisner Lindsay, *Shukar Balan: The White Lamb* (Lincoln, Nebr.: American Historical Society of Germans from Russia, 1976), 180; Isely, 72.

179. According to Albine Krause Schelbitzki, her parents and their children had eaten in this communal fashion while still in Austria. Blommer also pointed out that families who had eaten with wooden spoons from a common bowl in Germany used porcelain and silverware daily in America (letter of 13 September 1874, BABS). Gonner noted the other changes in Luxembourgian peasant customs (148–49). J. J. Teten, however, reported a kind of community bread-breaking, which seems to have commemorated the end of the old life and the beginning of the new. When Teten's family arrived at his uncle's farm near Nebraska City in 1867, the entire neighborhood of German immigrants was invited to share in the loaves of rye bread his mother had brought along, "because it symbolized old friendships" (Siekmann, 81).

180. "Diary of Julie Wall," 23; Lindsay, 138–40; Wallace, 22; Jewett, 10, 18.

181. See Plaul's comments on European preemigration dress (120–21). Roebke found that the immigrant advisers were aware of the relative equality in dress among American women and often disapproved when young German-American women, especially of the lower classes, assumed it (106, 181). For examples of German-American views of servant girls' inappropriately independent behavior in America, see Lanwert, 99–101. Elizabeth Ewen's study of Italian and Jewish women on the Lower East Side of New York offers interesting parallels in this regard (*Immigrant Women in the Land of Dollars* [New York: New Feminist Library, 1985], 67–71, 197). Rural women would not, however, have experienced the constant pressure to conform that the women in Ewen's study did.

182. Jewett, 20–21.

183. Steve Parsons, "A German-Style Ozarks Christmas: Before Santa There Was Scary Old Belsnickels," *Ozarks Mountaineer* 40 (November/December 1992): 32–35; Gonner, 149–50, 166–68, 216–17; Schuster, 23; Geiger, "At Century's Turn," 10–11. Ellingson mentions the traditional visits of *Pelzenickel* among the Kansas Bukovinia Germans and the retention of many other domestic and folkway customs. Mary Alicia Owen suggested that the Germans brought the Christmas tree to Missouri, where it was adopted by Anglo-Americans ("Social Customs and Usages in Missouri during the Last Century," *Missouri Historical Review* 15 [October 1920]: 181).

184. Jewett, 27–28.

185. On *Brautbitter* and shivarees, see Stickney, 10–12; Geiger, "At Century's Turn," 8; William G. Bek, "Survivals of Old Marriage Customs among the Low Germans of Western Missouri," *Journal of American Folk-lore* 21 (January–March 1908): 60–67; Coburn, *Life at Four Corners,* 106–7; and

Adolf E. Schroeder, "The Persistence of Ethnic Identity in Missouri German Communities," in *Germanica Americana, 1976,* ed. Albrecht and Burzle, 38. Schroeder reports a variety of other holiday and folk customs that German-American communities in Missouri retained, in some cases until the 1970s (36–38). See also his "Deutsche Sprache in Missouri," in *Deutsch als Muttersprache in den Vereinigten-Staaten,* ed. Auburger at al., 125–59). A good general source on German and German-American folklore and traditions is LaVern Rippley, *Of German Ways* (Minneapolis: Dillon, 1970). See also John F. Streng, "Remainders of Superstitions among German-Americans in Nebraska" (M.A. thesis, University of Nebraska, 1929).

Chapter 3: Adventure, Alienation, and Adaptation

1. Ellen Kiechel Partsch, *Howard County, the First One Hundred Years* (n.p.: n.d.), 25–26.

2. Friedrich Muench, *Der Staat Missouri, geschildert mit besonderer Rücksicht auf teutsche Einwanderung* (New York and St. Louis: Press of the Farmers' and Vinegrowers' Society, 1859), 99–100.

3. Adelheid von Borries-Garlich and Hermann Garlich, Tagebuch 1835–1839, Femme Osage, Amerika, in private possession of Reyner von Borries; Weitbrecht, 52–63.

4. Demos, 16–17.

5. Röhrich, 73.

6. Boylan, 1–12.

7. Isely, 60. Elise Isely's son Bliss said that he wrote "this narrative largely in Mother's own words," after rearranging the sequence of her narration and verifying dates and matters of records "by reference to personal letters, diaries, and documents in her possession" (7–8).

8. Ibid., 98. At that time, St. Joseph had a population of less than 9,000.

9. Ibid., 109.

10. Ibid., 72, 171–72, 214.

11. Ibid., 181–83, 205–9, 213–14.

12. Barbara Rueß, letters of 21 June and August [?] 1868, May and 20 September 1869, and 27 February 1871, Letters of Barbara Rueß and Others, 1868–71, BABS.

13. Ibid., letter of 16 March 1869.

14. Ibid., letter of 20 September 1869. Barbara Rueß seems to consider the term *Weib* a negative designation for a lower-class woman, perhaps parallel to *wench.*

15. Karl Zeller, letter of [April] 1869; J. G. Zeller, letter of 21 May 1869.

16. Rueß, letter of 11 September 1870.

17. Maude Griffis, "Mrs. John Krebs: The Flower Woman of Haiwatha" (1927), microfilm 4, LDMC. The 1880 census lists the Krebs family as living in Hiawatha with their four children. John was employed as a stone mason (1880 U.S. Manuscript Census, Brown County, Kansas, 429, lines 17–22).

18. Pauline Greving, letter of 14 September 1884, Pauline and Henry Greving Letters, 1884–1923, Tms, BABS.

19. Ibid., letter of 30 December 1888.

20. Ibid., autobiographical letter to "All meine lieben Verwandten" (n.d. [after 1920]).

21. Gillhoff, 158.

22. Wendt, letters of 1 October 1891, 7 March 1899, 13 March 1903, and 9 February 1897.

23. Käthe Gauß Baumann, letter of 29 January 1897, Gauß-Rogosch Letters, 1865–1903, BABS.

24. Wendt, letters of 7 March 1899 and 9 February 1897.

25. Baumann, letter of 11 December 1900.

26. Wendt, letter of 20 September 1889.

27. Ibid., letter of 9 February 1897.

28. Ibid., letter of 7 March 1899.

29. Ruppenthal, 4–5.

30. Ibid., 8–10.

31. Ritter, 92, 46, 64, 125.

32. Ibid., 24–25 (first and second quotes), 30, 32 (third, fourth, and fifth quotes), 26, 29, 53, 61, 103, 140 (sixth quote), 39 (seventh quote), 64 (eighth quote), 66 (ninth quote), 82 (tenth quote).

33. Ibid., 50, 54, 71 (first quote), 73 (second quote).

34. Ibid., 37 (quote), 123, 121.

35. Ibid., 149 (quotes), 151, 163.

36. Gillhoff, 96, 102; Mrs. Frank (Nettie) Schroeder, notation about her mother, Christina Barbara Brei Wiegert, on a picture in Frederich L. Wiegert folder, Nebraska United Methodist Historical Center, Lincoln, Nebraska; Frederic Trautmann, "Missouri through a German's Eyes: Franz von Löher on St. Louis and Hermann," *Missouri Historical Review* 77 (July 1983): 388.

37. Nannie L. Gander, "Frederica Hecker Fischer" (n.d.), Tms, microfilm 3, LDMC.

38. Frederica Fischer probably found it somewhat easier to adjust to life in Kansas than she might have otherwise because her husband was relatively well-off. He is listed in the 1870 census as owning real estate valued at $4,700 and personal property at $1,000 (1870 U.S. Manuscript Census, Jefferson County, Kansas, 413, line 29). In 1900, after Ludwig had died, Frederica was still living on the farm in Kentucky Township with a married daughter and her husband and her two youngest children, while renting out part of the land to another son and his wife. Few foreign-born lived in Kentucky Township; a sign of the Fischers' integration into the dominant culture is that both second-generation marriages recorded in this census were to Anglo-Americans.

39. Raid, 5.

40. See the evidence of such female networks in ethnic families and neighborhoods that Coburn found in Block, Kansas (*Life at Four Corners*, 94–95). The letters of the three Neumeier sisters, Wilhelmine Herbold, Christine Rock, and Friederike Hinkhaus, also attest to the assistance and support a close fe-

male family network gave immigrant women (BABS). In the northwest Iowa area to which they immigrated, two of the sisters married sons of families that had emigrated from their home village as much as forty years earlier, a rather remarkable instance of the persistence of patterns of chain immigration.

41. Gottfried Rückels, letter of 7 March 1875, Rückels-Kessel Letters, 1859–92, BABS.

42. In the 1860 census, both families were listed as owning $500 worth of real estate and $450 (Rückels) and $600 (Kessel) of personal property (1860 U.S. Manuscript Census, Jones Creek Township, Randolph County, Illinois, 407–8). Ten years later, the value of their personal property had increased to $1,000, and the Rückelses owned real estate worth $5,000, while the Kessels' was worth $4,000 (1870 U.S. Manuscript Census, Randolph County, Illinois, 66, and Jackson County, Illinois, 149, respectively).

43. Gottfried Rückels, letter of 7 March 1875.

44. Regina Kessel, letter of 2 October 1859, Rückels-Kessel Letters, 1859–92; Amalia Rückels, letters of 4 February 1861 and 27 January 1862.

45. Regina Kessel, letters of 2 October 1859 and 3 February 1861.

46. Ibid., letter of 1 January 1875.

47. Hirschler, 26.

48. Ibid., 27.

49. Ise, *Sod and Stubble*, 12.

50. Ibid., 91, 20, 167, 298.

51. Ibid., 82.

52. Ibid., 178, 269–70.

53. Ibid., 122.

54. Ibid., 313.

55. In 1910, Tilden, Nebraska, where the Ritters shopped and eventually retired, had a German men's lodge, and 20.4 percent of the residents of Madison County were German-born. Brown County, where Elise Isely lived, had a German-born population of 5.3 percent in 1910, and Osborne County, where Rosie Ise settled, had 6.0 percent in the same year (Kloss, *Atlas of Nineteenth and Early Twentieth Century German-American Settlements,* Series B [Foreign White Stock from Germany in Farming Communities and Small Towns] and F [Secular German Clubs]).

56. In 1910, Hodgeman County had 7.8 percent German stock among its residents (Ibid., Series B).

57. The figure for Randolph County is derived from *U.S. Census Reports, Ninth Census, 1870,* vol. 1, *Population* (Washington, D.C.: GPO, 1872), table 7, Selected Nativities by Counties, 352; for Calhoun County, from Kloss, *Atlas of Nineteenth and Early Twentieth Century German-American Settlements,* Series B.

58. Henrietta Geisberg Bruns, *Hold Dear, As Always: Jette, a German Immigrant Life in Letters,* ed. Adolf E. Schroeder and Carla Schulz-Geisberg (Columbia: University of Missouri Press, 1988), 123.

59. Ibid., 40–43.

60. Ibid., 88.

61. Ibid., 77.
62. Ibid., 223, note 7.
63. Ibid., 92, note 35; 80; 103–4; 125; 136–37.
64. Ibid., 105.
65. Ibid., 75 (first quote), 100, 131 (second quote).
66. Ibid., 197–98.
67. Ibid., 107.
68. Ibid., 255 (first quote), 144 (second quote), 222 (third quote).
69. S. Krehbiel, "Autobiography."
70. Ibid., 19, 14 (first quote), 20 (second quote).
71. Ibid., 19.
72. Ibid., 12, 24 (first quote), 11–12 (second quote).
73. Ibid., 25 (first quote), 12 (second quote)
74. Ibid., 12; Christian Krehbiel, *Prairie Pioneer* (Newton, Kans.: Faith and Life Press, 1961).
75. S. Krehbiel, 38 (first quote), 47 (second quote).
76. Bruns, 142.
77. S. Krehbiel, 17, 12.
78. Muench, *Der Staat Missouri,* 100.
79. Baumann, letters of 29 January 1897 and 11 December 1900.
80. Trienke Rahmann, letters of 5 April 1855, 20 January 1856, and undated [probably 1858], Kleihauer Family Letters, 1855–1895, BABS. In the 1860 census, Henry and Margaret "Raymond" (ages sixty-four and forty-four, respectively) are listed as living in Menard County, Illinois, with their sons James (eighteen) and George (eight) and a (foster?) child, Ann Folschers (two). No value of personal property or real estate was listed, perhaps indicating that they were still renting land (1860 U.S. Manuscript Census, Township 17, Range 8, Menard County, Illinois, 41, lines 25–29).
81. (Karl) Adolf Frick Letters, 1856–1868, BABS. The Fricks and their first daughter appear in the 1860 census for Boeuf Township (1860 U.S. Manuscript Census, Franklin County, Missouri, 9, line 7). Their real estate was valued at $1,200 and their personal property at $3,600. John E. Vitt, Alwina's father, claimed real estate in Boeuf Township valued at $3,200 and personal property worth $7,000 (Ibid., 8, line 29). Twenty years later the Fricks had given up their store and were living on a farm in Franklin County with their eight children and three hired men (1880 U.S. Manuscript Census, Franklin County, Missouri, 144B).
82. Lee F. Pendergrass, preface, *Memoirs of Pioneers of Cheyenne County,* ed. Pendergrass, iv–x.
83. Gillhoff, 207. See also ibid., 231, 314.
84. S. Krehbiel, 33; Isely, 217–18 (quotes).
85. Emma Wyneken, "Memoirs of the Wyneken Household," ed. Julia Ronecker, *Concordia Historical Institute Quarterly* 14 (January 1942): 100.
86. Hermann, 29.
87. H. Boeckers, Letters, 29 December 1859–22 December 1861, Tms, BABS.

88. Frick, letter of 9 December 1865; 1850 U.S. Manuscript Census, St. Louis, Missouri, 202b, lines 12–15; Käthchen Hamm, letter of 2 October 1853, "4 Letters, 1853–1866"; letter of 27 May 1856, "Ten Letters, 1856–1874"; undated letter (probably fall 1860), "Corresp[ondence] received 1849–70?" Josef Venus Manuscript Collection, ISHD-HS.

89. Ritter, 101–2.

90. Amy Bilsland, "Oral Interview, 31 July 1978, Archer, Iowa, with Michael Mendelson and Elizabeth Ongley," Oral History Project, Earthwatch, Manuscript Collection, ISHD-HS.

91. Herman Quandt and Emma (Quandt) Schneider, "Oral Interview, 16 August 1976, Denison, Iowa, with Rebecca Conard," Manuscript Collection, ISHD-HS.

92. Roenigk, 116.

93. Sandoz, 216.

94. Ruegg, diary entries of 3 and 6 October 1867. Maria Metzger is listed in the 1870 census as residing in Riley County, Kansas, with her husband and two small children (U.S. 1870 Manuscript Census, Jackson Township, Riley County, Kansas, 502, lines 1–4).

95. Jessie Benton Frémont, *The Story of the Guard: A Chronicle of the War* (Boston: Ticknor and Fields, 1863), 58–59 (first quote), 55 (second quote). Ralph Gregory, a journalist and local historian, believes that the unnamed woman was the wife of the early settler Bernhard Fricke, who ran a smithy and a hotel in the town (*Washington Missourian,* 2 May 1968).

96. Gillhoff, 292–93.

97. Ibid., 316–17 (first quote), 332 (second quote).

Chapter 4: Strangers in a Strange Land

1. Norman E. Saul, "The Migration of the Russian-Germans to Kansas," *Kansas Historical Quarterly* 42 (Spring 1976): 39–41. Many professional and amateur historians have studied the Germans from Russia. The first chapter of Schock's *In Quest of Free Land* gives a good overview of the immigration to Russia in the eighteenth century and then examines the colonists' life along the Black Sea and in the Dakotas. The historian Karl Stumpp wrote the basic source on the Volga Germans *(The German-Russians: Two Centuries of Pioneering,* trans. Joseph Height [Bonn: Atlantic-Forum, 1967]). Two other extensive studies are Giesinger; and Koch. A briefer summary is found in Timothy Kloberdanz, "Plainsmen of Three Continents: Volga German Adaptation to Steppe, Prairie, and Pampa," in *Ethnicity on the Great Plains,* ed. Luebke, 54–72. Valuable works on the Mennonite colonists and settlers include C. Henry Smith, *The Coming of the Russian Mennonites: An Episode in the Settling of the Last Frontier, 1874–1884* (Berne, Ind.: Mennonite Book Concern, 1927); Karl Stumpp, *Die deutschen Kolonien im Schwarzmeergebiet dem früheren Neu-(Süd)-Russland* (Stuttgart: Ausland und Heimat Verlag, 1922); and Cornelius Krahn, ed., *From the Steppes to the Prairies (1874–1919)* (Newton, Kans.: Mennonite Publication Office, 1949). American journals

devoted to the history and folkways of these immigrants include the *Journal of the American Historical Society of Germans from Russia, Mennonite Life,* and *Heritage Review.* In this study, I employ the term *Germans from Russia* (rather than *German-Russians* or *Russian-Germans*), in accordance with the usage of the American Historical Society of Germans from Russia.

2. Saul, 41–45; Krahn, 3–4.

3. Saul, 46–47. The Mennonite group led by Cornelius Jansen chose to settle in south-central Nebraska because "it more nearly resembled South Russia in the open character of its land, than any other place they had visited" (cited in Hattie Plum Williams, *The Czar's Germans* [Lincoln, Nebr.: American Historical Society of Germans from Russia, 1975], 191).

4. Saul, 43–44; Alberta Pantle, "Settlement of the Krimmer Mennonite Brethren at Gnadenau, Marion County," *Kansas Historical Quarterly* 13 (February 1945): 262.

5. Pantle quotes at length from stories written in the *Marion County Record* (16 January 1875; 11 August 1876), the Topeka *Commonwealth* (20 August and 19 December 1875), and the Atchison *Daily Champion* (4 May 1882) recounting visits to Gnadenau ("Settlement of the Krimmer Mennonite Brethren," 267–72). See also Alberta Pantle, "A Mennonite Village in Kansas," *Mennonite Life* 2 (October 1947): 20–22; and Kendall Bailes, "The Mennonites Come to Kansas," *American Heritage* 10 (August 1959): 103.

6. Pantle states, "Factors contributing to the breakdown of the village system included: absence of the necessity for banding together for safety as they had been forced to do along the Turkish border in South Russia; improved agricultural machinery which made 'strip' farming impracticable; the spirit of the American frontier which tolerated no barriers; close contact with non-Mennonite neighbors; confusion which arose over the allocation of taxes" ("Settlement of the Krimmer Mennonite Brethren," 267, note 31). On group clustering among the Mennonite settlers, see Dennis D. Engbrecht, *The Americanization of a Rural Immigrant Church: The General Conference Mennonites in Central Kansas, 1874–1939* (New York: Garland, 1990), 59–60.

7. Mary Eloise Johannes, *A Study of the Russian-German Settlements in Ellis County, Kansas,* Catholic University of America Studies in Sociology, 14 (Washington, D.C.: Catholic University Press, 1946), 34–35; Saul, 57; Francis S. Laing, "German-Russian Settlements in Ellis County, Kansas," *Kansas State Historical Society Collections,* vol. 11 (Topeka: State Printing Office, 1909–10), 489–528.

8. Eduard Seib, in his extensive study of German colonists in Russia, emphasized the importance of the church in their lives ("Der Wolgadeutsche im Spiegel seines Brauchtums," *Heimatbuch der Deutschen aus Rußland* [Stuttgart: Landsmannschaft de Deutschen aus Russland, 1967–68], 198). Engbrecht's listing of the origins of the thirty-four Mennonite churches belonging to the Central Kansas General Conference reveals the homogeneity of the congregations (51).

9. Ellingson, 30, 50.

10. John B. Terbovich, "Religious Folklore among the German-Russians

in Ellis County, Kansas," *Western Folklore* 22 (April 1963): 82. Johannes also noted the endogamy in the Volga German settlements in Ellis County (74–75). Amy B. Toepfer and Agnes C. Dreiling wrote about the exclusivity of the Volga Germans in the Ellis area (Victor C. Leiker, ed., *Conquering the Wind* [Garwood, N.Y.: Victor C. Leiker, 1966], 130).

11. Laing recorded the "rivalry" among the immigrants in various Kansas settlements modeled after those they had left in Russia (516). Leiker noted the "jealousy among individuals and families as well as between the various settlements" in the first decades of settlement (vii). Timothy J. Kloberdanz has examined the persistent sense of exclusivity among the Volga Germans of the Great Plains a century after the immigration ("'Unsre un' die Andre': Ingroup Affiliation among the Volga Germans of Russia and the Great Plains," *Plains Anthropologist* 31 [June 1986]: 281–93). One wonders if the animosities between the Oberdorf and Unterdorf sections of the Russian colonies carried over to the rural villages in Kansas and Nebraska. See Koch, 175; and Seib, 157.

12. Toepfer and Dreiling, viii; Barbara Handy-Marchello, "Assimilation of German-Russian and Norwegian Immigrants," *Heritage Review* 17 (May 1987): 30–31; Pantle, "Settlement of the Krimmer Mennonite Brethren," 276. As Pantle and others note, the Mennonites were opposed by doctrine to political activity.

13. Schock, *In Quest of the Land,* 135; Lindsay, 138–43. This was not the case in the Hastings, Nebraska, Volga German community, however (George G. Bruntz, *Children of the Volga* [Ardmore, Penn.: Dorrance, 1981], 70).

14. Johannes interpreted this latter behavior as a sign of cultural adaptation (42). For collaborative evidence of female conservatism in matters of clothing, see Handy-Marchello, 32.

15. For a study of such structures still extant in the northern Great Plains, see Michael Koop and Stephen Ludwig, *German-Russian Folk Architecture in Southeastern South Dakota* (Vermillion, S.D.: State Historical Preservation Center, 1984). Various accounts indicate that immigrants in both Kansas and Nebraska first constructed housebarns and used sunbaked brick such as they had known in Russia. See Creigh, 154; Saul, 56; Stanley E. Voth, *Henderson Mennonites: From Holland to Henderson,* 2d ed. (Henderson, Nebr.: Service Press, 1981), 62; and Regier, 92–93. Summer kitchens might have been used for a longer period after immigration (Koch, 79).

16. Johannes, 32.

17. Voth, 48; Smith, *The Story of the Mennonites,* 655; Lawrence Weigel, *From the Rhine to the Volga to Kansas, 1763–1984: The Story of My Volga German Ancestors and Their Descendants* (n.p., 1984), 5. Laing reported in 1909, however, that small amounts of tobacco were still being harvested, mainly near Herzog (523).

18. Johannes, 38. See also a larger-scale statistical study of fertility among Germans from Russia living in Lincoln, Nebraska, in Hattie Plum Williams, "A Social Study of the Russian Germans," *University Studies of the University of Nebraska* 16 (July 1916): 164–76. Although Plum's study examined ur-

ban immigrants, the high rates of fertility she documented, for a group that would likely have fewer children than would rural families, support the general impressions about family size among Germans from Russia.

19. Schock, *In Quest of the Land,* 144; H. P. Williams, "A Social Study," 195.

20. The farm duties women carried out in Russia (Seib, 185–87) continued to be in their purview in America (Voth, 54–57; Koch, 179–82; Johannes, 44, 51; Weigel, *From the Rhine to the Volga to Kansas,* 5). Lindgren speculates that German women from Russia who took out a homestead were more likely interested in increasing family holdings than in setting up an independent household (168–69).

21. Flora and Flora, 197, 199, 202.

22. C. Henry Smith wrote a moving memorial to his mother in *Mennonite Country Boy* (Newton, Kans.: Faith and Life Press, 1962), saying her death at the age of fifty-four was "a sacrifice to her family and to the traditions of her people" (175). Pauline Neher Diede's chronicle *Homesteading on the Knife River Prairies* contains, in its depiction of her family's difficulties, a (perhaps unconsciously) negative view of gender relations and the traditional female role among impoverished Germans from Russia. See Elizabeth Hampsten's discussion of Diede's work ("The Nehers and the Martins in North Dakota, 1909–1911," in *Far from Home,* ed. Lillian Schlissel, Elizabeth Hampsten, and Byrd Gibbens [New York: Schocken, 1989], 175–229).

23. Seib, 175.

24. Johannes, 51, 74, 118.

25. Laing, 519; H. P. Williams, "A Social Study," 213, 217; Lawrence A. Weigel, "Childhood Folklore from Ellis County, Kansas," *Journal of the American Historical Society of Germans from Russia* 1 (Spring 1978): 38. Toepfer and Dreiling wrote that the Capuchins instituted a "virtual medieval Catholicity" among the isolated Volga Germans in Kansas" (133). On the comment by the Mennonite elder, see Carolyn L. Zeisset, *A Mennonite Heritage* (Lincoln, Nebr.: Carolyn L. Zeisset, 1975), 98.

26. Hummel's study of inheritance customs among the Germans in Russia is the standard work on the subject. As Sonya Salamon and Karen Davis-Brown have shown in their study of contemporary Illinois farmers of German heritage, long-held yeoman values favoring farm continuity and the desire among (Mennonite) farmers to give all their children equal inheritances have either social or economic costs to women family members ("Farm Continuity and Female Land Inheritance: A Family Dilemma," in *Women and Farming,* ed. Haney and Knowles, 195–210).

27. Toepfer and Dreiling, 63.

28. Seib discusses this aspect of Volga German family life (180–82). See also Koch, 191; and Irene Rader, "The Folklore of German-Russian Women," *Journal of the American Historical Society of Germans from Russia* 7 (Summer 1984): 32. Johannes assumed on the basis of oral informants that generational quarreling had led to the breakdown of the old patrilocal system (40).

29. Weigel, "Childhood Folklore," 38.

30. Bruntz, 13, 35, 62–63. Aganetha Wiens Suderman, a Kansas Mennonite immigrant, also had conflicts with her son and his wife after going to live with them as a widow in 1907, for she "was used to being the boss" (Zeisset, 36).
31. Carol Halverson Just, "The Inheritance: A Salute to My Foremothers in Honor of Mothers Day 1988," *Heritage Review* 18 (May 1988): 7.
32. Seib, 152.
33. Ellingson, 27. This was true for other rural immigrants, for example, the Lutherans around Block, Kansas (Coburn, *Life at Four Corners,* 76).
34. Koch, 143; Toepfer and Dreiling, 82. Marie Suderman Unruh, a Mennonite immigrant in Kansas, "could read printed German, but not the written script; nor could she write" (Zeisset, 75).
35. See Johannes, 87–95; Rader, 33–34; and Solomon L. Loewen, "History of the Ebenfeld Public School in Marion County, Kansas," *Journal of the American Historical Society of Germans from Russia* 10 (Winter 1987): 31.
36. Laing, 512; Adolph Schock, "In Quest of Free Land," *Rural Sociology* 7 (December 1942): 441. Engbrecht states that many Mennonite communities did not accept women as teachers until the 1890s (167).
37. Zeisser, 120; Toepfer and Dreiling, 202; Lindsay, 180–81; Voth, 48–49, 60–62; Milton W. Goering, "Ein Volk unterwegs: Swiss-Germans in Kansas," in *Germanica-Americana, 1976,* ed. Albrecht and Burzle, 103. See the collection of recipes in Leiker, 200–206. Timothy J. Kloberdanz says that along with the *Dakota Freie Presse* and Lawrence Welk, the *Fleischkiechla* (meat pies) served in the homes of the immigrants' descendants symbolized cultural continuity for Germans from Russian in the Dakotas during the twentieth century ("Symbols of German-Russian Ethnic Identity on the Northern Plains," *Great Plains Quarterly* 8 [Winter 1988]: 3–15).
38. Koch, 189–90, 192–94; Rader, 34, 36; Voth, 60–62, 85; Ellingson, 28; Laing, 518–21; Johannes, 110–11; Toepfer and Dreiling, 135–39; Terbovich, 81–83; Timothy J. Kloberdanz, "Cross Makers: German-Russian Folk Specialists of the Great Plains" (Ph.D. diss., Indiana University, 1986), 299–302. On marriage customs among Volga Germans from Russia, see especially Phyllis A. Dinkel, "Old Marriage Customs in Herzog (Victoria) Kansas," *Western Folklore* 19 (April 1960): 99–105. Seib's testimony shows that many of these customs were carried over into the New World (160–78).
39. Kloberdanz, "Cross Makers," 177.
40. Laing, 508–10; Johannes, 70, 77–78.
41. Much of this is drawn from Katie Funk Wiebe, "Mennonite Brethren Women: Images and Realities of the Early Years," *Mennonite Life* 36 (September 1981): 22–28. The Ruth family of immigrants (which included Susanna Ruth Krehbiel) illustrates the importance of female family members in establishing and maintaining links in the religious community. Many of the eighteen men who signed the 1860 Document of Secession of the Mennonite Brethren Church in Russia were related through their wives, for example. See Alan Peters, "Brotherhood and Family: Implications of Kinship in Mennonite Brethren History," in *P. M. Friesen and His History,* ed. Abraham

Friesen (Fresno, Calif.: Center for Mennonite Brethren Studies, 1979), cited in Wiebe, "Mennonite Brethren Women," 24. On the rise of Sunday schools, see Engbrecht, 89–90; and Zeisset, 97.

42. Daniel J. Classen, "Meade—A Changed Community," *Mennonite Life* 4 (July 1951): 14; Johannes, 70, 101; Engbrecht, 77; Zeisset, 119; William G. Chrystal, "German Congregationalism," *Journal of the American Historical Society of Germans from Russia* 6 (Summer 1983): 35; LaVern J. Rippley, "Zur sprachlichen Situation der Russlanddeutschen in den USA," in *Deutsch als Muttersprache in den Vereinigten-Staaten,* ed. Auburger, 216, 218.

43. Lindsay, 152, 188, 198–201. On the use of German in Kansas Volga German communities, see Laing, 522; Johannes, 70, 96, 101; and Rippley, "Zur sprachlichen Situation," 215.

44. For Old World marriage and wedding customs among the Volga Germans, see Seib, 160–78; Koch, 189–90; and Alfred Thilemann, "Looking for a Wife (*Brautschau*)," trans. Thomas A. Welk, *Heritage Review* 13 (September 1983): 45. On related customs in America, see Rader, 36; Voth, 60–62; and Johannes, 108–11.

45. Johannes, 48–49, 118; Esther Loewen Vogt, "Horse and Buggy Midwife: Sara Block Eitzen (1840–1917)," in *Women among the Brethren,* ed. Katie Funk Wiebe (Hillsboro, Kans.: General Conference of Mennonite Brethren Churches, 1979), 75; H. P. Williams, "A Social Study," 190–91; Weigel, "Childhood Folklore," 38–39.

46. For a discussion of *Brauchen* as it was practiced in the Russian colonies, see Seib, 203–7; and Koch, 163–67. See also Gerda Stumpp, "Volksmedizin und Volksglaube bei den Schwarzmeerdeutschen," in *Heimatbuch der Deutschen aus Rußland* (Stuggart: Landsmannschaft der Deutschen aus Russland, 1956), 119–22. Many chronicles of the Germans from Russia in America mention folk remedies, *Brauchen,* and *Braucher,* including Weigel, "Childhood Folklore," 38; Rader, 34; Johannes, 48–50; and Mrs. Fred Lock, "They Came to Kansas as Farmers . . . and Then," in *Germanica-Americana, 1976,* ed. Albrecht and Burzle, 119). Kloberdanz's "Cross Makers" is the basic scholarly study of *Brauchen.*

47. Walter O. Forster, *Zion on the Mississippi: The Settlement of the Saxon Lutherans in Missouri, 1839–1841* (St. Louis: Concordia Publishing House, 1953), 540–63. Forster's is the most thorough and dispassionate study of the Old Lutheran immigration. See also Gotthold Guenther, *Die Schicksale und Abenteuer der aus Sachsen nach Amerika ausgewanderten Stephanianer* (Dresden: Heinrich, 1839); Carl Eduard Vehse, *Die Stephan'sche Auswanderung nach Amerika* (Dresden: Teubner, 1840); G. A. Schieferdecker, *Geschichte der ersten deutschen lutherischen Ansiedlung in Altenburg, Perry County, Missouri* (Clayton County, Iowa: Wartburg Seminary Press, 1865); J. F. Köstering, *Auswanderung der sächsischen Lutheraner im Jahre 1838,* 2d ed. (St. Louis: Wiebusch and Son, 1867); P. E. Kretzmann, "The Saxon Immigration to Missouri, 1838–1839," *Missouri Historical Review* 33 (January 1939), 157–70; and William A. Kramer, "The Saxons in Missouri," *Concordia Historical Institute Quarterly* 60 (Spring 1987): 2–18.

48. Forster, 175, 284, 529–30.

49. The St. Louis congregation did, on rare occasions, organize aid for poor people who wanted to return but did not have the funds to do so. One example is Johanna Christiana Nagel, who had left her husband and other children to accompany a twenty-two-year-old son on the emigration ("Bittschrift" [12 March 1842], folder 16, Saxon Immigration Documents, Manuscript Collection, CHI). Perhaps the congregation gave her petition a positive hearing because it had had a role in splitting the family.

50. Christiane Loeber, undated letter of fall 1839 and letter of 4 December 1839, in *Von Altenburg (Sachsen-Altenburg) nach Altenburg in Nordamerika (Missouri) Ein Briefwechsel aus den Jahren 1838–1844*, ed. Heinrich Loeber-Eichenberg (Kahla: J. Beck, 1912), 28–32, 38–43; Stella Wuerffel, "Women in the Saxon Immigration," *Concordia Historical Institute Quarterly* 35 (Fall 1962): 88–92.

51. Wilhelm Sihler, "Über den Beruf des Weibes und seine Entartung," *Der Lutheraner* 28 (1 February 1872): 65–67.

52. The tenacity with which the American church founded by the Old Lutheran Germans has clung to these traditional attitudes about women's role is seen in the relatively recent decision, at the 1969 Lutheran Church–Missouri Synod conference, to allow women a vote and a voice in church matters (Resolution 3–09). The Fellowship of Lutheran Congregations' break with the Lutheran Church–Missouri Synod that followed this change and others related to it shows that it is still a controversial issue. See R. J. Lietz, *What Does the Bible Teach about Woman Suffrage in the Christian Congregation?* (Oak Park, Ill.: FLC Tract Center, 1992). I am grateful to Lietz for bringing this text to my attention.

53. *Lutheran Witness* 3 (7 December 1884): 109.

54. See Ruth Brauer, "Tracing Women's Services in the Missouri Synod," *Concordia Historical Institute Quarterly* 36 (Spring 1963): 5–13; and Ruth Fritz Meyer, *Women on a Mission* (St. Louis: Lutheran Women's Missionary League, 1967).

55. George J. Gude Jr., "Women Teachers in the Missouri Synod," *Concordia Historical Institute Quarterly* 44 (Winter 1971): 163–70. For further information, see Stellhorn, especially 210, 424–26.

56. For an example of such a marriage, the reader is referred to that between Wilhelm Sihler and Susanna Kern (Linda S. Pickle, "Women of the Saxon Immigration and Their Church," *Concordia Historical Institute Quarterly* 57 [Winter 1984]: 152–54).

57. Unidentified clipping, *Aus dem Pionierleben eines amerikanischen Landpastors*, included in *Materialien zur Fortführung der Lochner'schen Familienchronik*, folder 10, box 2, CHI.

58. Margarethe Lenk, *Fünfzehn Jahre in Amerika* (Zwickau: Johannes Hermann, 1911), 68.

59. Ibid., 39, 43.

60. Ibid., 48, 34.

61. Frederick C. Luebke, "The Immigrant Condition as a Factor Contrib-

uting to the Conservatism of the Lutheran Church," *Concordia Historical Institute Quarterly* 38 (Spring 1965): 22, 27.

62. Letter of Christiane Loeber, undated, in *Von Altenburg,* ed. Loeber-Eichenberg, 30–31.

63. Important sources on Amana include the *Jahrbücher der wahren Inspirations-Gemeinden* (Amana, Iowa: Community of True Inspiration, 1842–present); Gottlieb Scheuner, *Inspirations-Historie,* 3 vols. (Amana, Iowa: Community of True Inspiration, 1884–1900); William R. Perkins and Barthinius L. Wick, *History of the Amana Society or Community of True Inspiration* (Iowa City: State University of Iowa, 1891; reprint, Westport, Conn.: Hyperion Press, 1976); Bertha M. H. Shambaugh, *Amana: The Community of True Inspiration* (Iowa City: State Historical Society of Iowa, 1908); Bertha M. H. Shambaugh, *Amana That Was and Amana That Is* (Iowa City: State Historical Society of Iowa, 1932; reprint, New York: B. Blom, 1971); Albert Shaw, "Life in the Amana Colony," ed. William Peterson, *Palimpsest* 52 (April 1971): 161–224; Jonathon Andelson, "Communalism and Change in the Amana Society, 1855–1932" (Ph.D. diss., University of Michigan, 1974); Robert Clark, "A Cultural and Historical Geography of the Amana Colony, Iowa" (Ph.D. diss., University of Nebraska–Lincoln, 1974); B. Richling, "The Amana Society: A History of Change," *Palimpsest* 58 (March/April 1977): 34–47; Diane Barthel, *Amana: From Pietist Sect to American Community* (Lincoln: University of Nebraska Press, 1984); and Frank M. Moore, "The Amana Society, 1867–1932: Accommodation of Old World Beliefs in a New World Frontier Setting" (Ph.D. diss., Vanderbilt University, 1988). Dolores Hayden's chapter on Amana offers interesting insights into the way the colony's architecture and design reflected its religious philosophy and communal life (*Seven American Utopias: The Architecture of Communitarian Socialism, 1790–1975* [Cambridge, Mass.: Massachusetts Institute of Technology Press, 1976]).

64. Shambaugh, *Amana: The Community of True Inspiration,* 380.

65. Shambaugh asserts that women's work was lightened by the use of some up-to-date conveniences in the kitchens (Ibid., 152–53, 156), but Hayden holds that "Inspirationists do not seem to have taken advantage of mechanization or economies of scale to free women's time" (242).

66. *How It Was in the Community Kitchen* (Fairfax, Iowa: R. Trumpold, n.d.), 5.

67. Because Amana encompassed an entire township, the schools were German-language. This was also true in Homestead, which was outside Amana Township.

68. Moore, 66–67.

69. Shambaugh, *Amana: The Community of True Inspiration,* 161.

70. Moore, 95–96; Barthel, 7.

71. For this and other information on contemporary Amana customs and usages, I am indebted to Barbara Hoehnle of the Amana Historical Library.

72. Shambaugh, *Amana: The Community of True Inspiration,* 159–60. Amana women still wear the black cap and shawl to church.

73. In November of 1987, Kristie Berger was elected the first female elder (Moore, 262). She has since married, left Amana, and resigned her position for family reasons.

74. Barbara Heinemann narrated her life story to Gottlieb Scheuner (*Barbara Heinemann Landmann Biography*, trans. Janet W. Zuber [Lake Mills, Iowa: Graphic Publishing, 1981]). See also Perkins and Wick, 34–38; Shambaugh, *Amana: The Community of True Inspiration*, 39–43; Cecyle S. Neidel, *America's Immigrant Women* (Boston: Twayne, 1975), 64–66; and entries in *Liberty's Women*, ed. Robert McHenry (Springfield, Mass.: Merriam, 1980), and in *Notable American Women, 1607–1950: A Bibliographic Dictionary*, ed. Edward T. James, Janet W. James, and Paul S. Boyer, 3 vols. (Cambridge, Mass.: Belknap Press, 1971), 2:175–77. Jonathan Andelson has analyzed Metz's and Heinemann's differing personalities and status in Amana ("Routinization of Behavior in a Charismatic Leader," *American Ethnologist* 7 [November 1980]: 716–33).

75. Clark ("A Cultural and Historical Geography") and Barthel discuss the importance of tourism in Amana history. Steven Ohrn has asserted that the community's recent revitalization of traditional crafts is less an economic response to opportunities tourism offers than a desire to renew and preserve Amana culture ("Conserving Amana's Folk Arts: A Community Remaining Faithful," *Palimpsest* 69 [Spring 1988]: 16–33.

76. Shambaugh, *The Community of True Inspiration*, 356, note 142.

77. See the collection of brief memories by Marie Stuck Selzer, *Hobelspaen* (Amana, Iowa: Hobelspaen Publications, 1985) for examples of the perpetuation of German customs and cooking long into the twentieth century. Many of the Amana oral histories collected in the early 1980s also make reference to such traditions (see, for example, MS #OH-30, OH-33, OH-34, OH-84, AHSOHP). Indications that women in Amana retained the use of German for interpersonal communication longer than did men hints at women's relative isolation from outside contacts and their greater adherence to cultural traditions (see Dow, 109–10; and Barbara J. Selzer, "A Description of the Amana Dialect of Homestead, Iowa" [M.A. thesis, University of Illinois, 1941]). Selzer, a Homestead native, said that older people rarely spoke English and that old women had never really learned it and would run into their homes to avoid embarrassing themselves by having to speak it. Clark's study shows that during the first two decades in Iowa, the Amanists raised crops, livestock, and foodstuffs that reflected Germanic domestic consumption and agricultural practices ("A Cultural and Historical Geography," 128–32). At the present time, Amanists celebrate one German and one English church service every Sunday, a "Sängerbund" (choral club) is active, and at least one family plays the zither.

78. MS #OH-34, OH-29, AHSOHP.

79. MS #OH-55, OH-34, AHSOHP.

80. MS #OH-34, OH-29, OH-30, AHSOHP.

81. MS #OH-7, AHSOHP.

82. MS #OH-29, OH-55, OH-91, OH-30, OH-33, AHSOHP.

83. MS #OH-91, OH-29, OH-7, AHSOHP.

84. MS #OH-34, OH-71, AHSOHP.

85. As early as the 1880s, English words had infiltrated Amana German. By the 1920s, intercolony communication was largely in English (Clark, "A Cultural and Historical Geography," 263).

86. Lydia Gunzelhauser, "The Story of My Grandmother" (n.d.), 3–5, Tms, SHD-MA.

87. Charles Nordhoff, *The Communistic Societies of the United States* (New York, 1875; reprint, New York: Schocken, 1965), 41.

88. Both Nordhoff (40) and Shambaugh (*Amana: The Community of True Inspiration*, 173, 187) asserted that the Amanists did not work hard. They cited abuses of communal trust when workers begged off strenuous work details and the long-standing tradition of hiring outsiders for especially demanding and dirty work. The tendency to pay others rather than force some group members to work harder than others and to slack off from the commitments to the community was an important factor in the eventual need to revise Amana's economic basis (Moore, 219–21). Gunzelhauser relates some of the hardships in her grandmother's life in her narrative (5–6).

89. The Vandalia colony (1820–22) had a strong leader in Ferdinand Ernst, but the colony was tied only by temporary financial obligations to him (Paul E. Stroble Jr., "Ferdinand Ernst and the German Colony at Vandalia," *Illinois Historical Journal* 80 [Summer 1987]: 101–10). The eighteen Swedenborgian families in Benton County, Iowa, could maintain their community only from 1851 until 1853, although they founded a church and a school in that period (Ransom, 251).

90. Bethel has been the subject of two lengthy studies: William G. Bek, "A German Communistic Society in Missouri," *Missouri Historical Review* 3 (October 1908): 52–74, (January 1909): 99–125 (also published as "The Community at Bethel, Missouri, and Its Offspring at Aurora, Oregon," *German American Annals* 7 [September and October, November and December 1909]: 257–76; 8 [January and February, March and April 1910]: 15–44, 76–81); and Robert J. Hendricks, *Bethel and Aurora: An Experiment in Communism as Practical Christianity* (New York: Press of the Pioneers, 1933; reprint, New York: AMS Press, 1971). Nordhoff also visited Bethel and Aurora (326–30). The utopian activist Wilhelm Weitling spent a few days in the Missouri colony in 1852 and wrote a (largely uncomplimentary) report to J. A. Macdonald (H. Roger Grant, "The Society of Bethel: A Visitor's Account," *Missouri Historical Review* 68 [January 1974]: 223–31). H. Roger Grant included Bethel in "Missouri's Utopian Communities," *Missouri Historical Review* 66 (November 1971): 21–48. Milton D. Rafferty's *Historical Atlas of Missouri* (Norman: University of Oklahoma Press, 1982) contains a map locating Missouri's utopian communities.

91. Bek, "A German Communistic Society," 59.

92. Hendricks, 9–11.

93. A Bethel resident reported the public confession of "illicit carnal intercourse" to Bek ("A German Communistic Society," 70). Nordhoff believed

that the "monotonous and dreary impression" Aurora's residents made on him and the general atmosphere of "carelessness and decay" in the community were due in part to "the stern repression of the whole intellectual side of life by their leader" (322).

94. Lisa Whittle Horn, "Textile Production in the Communalistic Colony at Bethel" (M.A. thesis, University of Missouri–Columbia, 1988), 68, 110–11.

95. Nordhoff, 322. During his 1876 visit to Bethel, W. A. Hinds noted the mixture of individualism and communism that existed in the colony (*American Communities* [Oneida, N.Y.: Office of the American Socialists, 1878; reprint, Glouchester, Mass.: Peter Smith, 1971], 40–41).

96. The rules are cited in Hendricks, 16–17.

97. Bek, "A German Communistic Society," 123–24.

98. Clayton County Deed Records, vol. F, 137–39 (July 31, 1850); vol. I, 39ff. (July 23, 1853). The Joseph Venus file entitled "Memory Books, ca. 1836–1845," ISHD-HS, includes a typed summary of the incorporation of the colony and the county records of land transfers. For the most comprehensive study of Communia, see George Schulz-Behrend, "Communia, Iowa, a Nineteenth-Century German-American Utopia," *Iowa Journal of History* 48 (January 1950): 27–54. See also the *History of Clayton County, Together with Sketches of Its Cities, Villages and Townships* (Chicago: Inter-State Publishing, 1882), 1116–18; and Joseph Eiboeck, *Die Deutschen von Iowa und deren Errungenschaften* (Des Moines: Verlag des Iowa Staats-Anzeiger, 1900), 96–101. Ruth S. Beitz's brief piece on Communia adds nothing new ("Communia," *The Iowan* 15 [October 1966]: 40–42).

99. On New Helvetia and Dietsch, see George Schulz-Behrend, "Andreas Dietsch and New Helvetia, Missouri," *Swiss Record* 2 (March 1950): 5–31. Howard B. Furer seems to be in error when he says Koch's establishment of a colony in Clayton County, Iowa, occurred in 1832 (*The Germans in America, 1607–1970*, Ethnic Chronology Series, 8 [Dobbs Ferry, N.Y.: Oceana, 1973], 24).

100. Reported by Wilhelm Weitling in the *Arbeiterbund* publication *Die Republik der Arbeiter* (18 October 1851), cited in Schulz-Behrend, "Communia," 33.

101. The best sources on Weitling are Carl Wittke's biography, *The Utopian Communist* (Baton Rouge: Louisiana State University Press, 1950); and Hans-Arthur Marsiske's more recent study *"Eine Republik der Arbeiter ist möglich": Der Beitrag Wilhelm Weitlings zur Arbeiterbewegung in den Vereinigten Staaten von Amerika* (Hamburg: Hamburger Institut für Sozialforschung, 1990).

102. Clayton County Deed Records (Elkader, Iowa), vol. F, 171–74 (15 August 1850) and 489 (16 November 1850), cited in Schulz-Behrend, "Communia," 29–30 (see also 35 and 51). Venus was also involved in a public altercation between old and new colonists in the spring of 1855, after which he filed suit against another man (Clayton County Court Records, Vertical File, 1855, cited in Gary Armstrong, "Utopians in Clayton County, Iowa," *Annals of Iowa*, 3d ser., 41 [Spring 1972]: 936).

103. Located in the ISHD-HS, the Joseph Venus correspondence fills three folders of material entitled "Corresp. received 1849–70?" "Four Letters, 1853–1866," and "Ten Letters, 1856–1874." In the following discussion, I indicate letters by their date only.

104. 1850 U.S. Manuscript Census, Clayton County, Iowa, 148.

105. 1860 U.S. Manuscript Census, Clayton County, Iowa, 585. In the 1870 census, the Venus real estate is valued at the same amount as the Baumanns' ($6,000), while the Endereses' is $3,000 (1870 U.S. Manuscript Census, Clayton County, Iowa, 472).

106. *Die Republik der Arbeiter,* 21 August 1852, cited in Schulz-Behrend, "Communia," 35. Armstrong also says that "the women continually grumbled over having to do work for people outside their family" (930). His source seems to be Weitling's reports, however.

107. 1850 U.S. Manuscript Census, Clayton County, Iowa, 148; 1860 U.S. Manuscript Census, Clayton County, Iowa, 585–86.

108. "Village of Communia in Clayton County Founded as Socialist Colony in 1845" (interview of Caroline Venus Liers by Kathleen M. Hempel), *Cedar Rapids Gazette,* 23 November 1930, found in Clippings File (Cities and Towns), ISHD-HS.

109. 1850 U.S. Manuscript Census, St. Louis, Missouri, 179, 202; 1860 U.S. Manuscript Census, Clayton County, Iowa, 585.

110. 1850 U.S. Manuscript Census, Clayton County, Iowa, 148; 1860 U.S. Manuscript Census, Clayton County, Iowa, 585; 1870 U.S. Manuscript Census, Clayton County, Iowa, 472. Dina Venus does not mention Pape when she writes to her daughter about the field work in the summer of 1872 (letter of 26 June).

111. In his letter of 30 August 1849, Johan Bosshard addresses Joseph Venus as "Dear Brother" and concludes with the salutation "Greetings and a handshake from your brother."

112. Weitling's 1853 New Year's address to the colony in *Die Republik der Arbeiter* mentioned that the children would soon get a male teacher, indicating that they had probably been taught until then by a woman—perhaps another task the colony wives had to perform (cited in Schulz-Behrend, "Communia," 37).

113. A sizable number of Irish immigrant farmers resided in Volga Township in these years. In 1850, 3 of 47, or 6.4 percent; in 1860, 22 of 84, or 26.2 percent; in 1880, 34 (including 4 second-generation Irish farmers) of 178, or 19.1 percent. One Norwegian-born farmer resided in Volga Township in 1860, and in 1880, one Scottish and two English immigrant farmers were recorded. The 1880 data exclude the villages of Elkhart and East Elkhart and the Gifford addition to Littleport. In my survey of the 1880 census, I counted only single households with the given profession of farmer for the head of household and therefore counted some two-generation households, in which the inheriting son and his family resided with his parents, as one family. I included retired farmers as heads of households, although there were very few. In 1880, 4 of the 129 German-speaking farmers were second gen-

eration (1850, 1860, and 1880 U.S. Manuscript Censuses). The 1990 census reveals the continuing strong German heritage of this locality. Single- and multiple-ancestry German-Americans numbered 569 of the 669 residents of Volga Township (85.1 percent). Of these 569, 402 (70.7 percent) declared themselves to be of solely German ancestry. Fifteen persons above the age of five (2.24 percent) spoke German in the home (Bureau of the Census, *1990 Census of the Population and Housing: Summary Tape File 3A* [Washington, D.C., GPO, 1992]).

114. "Village of Communia."

115. In his 1900 statistical report on the Upper Mississippi Turner Region, Eiboeck reported that the Communia *Turnverein* had twenty-five members, ten of whom were active, and a net worth of $1,800. There is conflicting evidence concerning the club's meeting place. Eiboeck's report states that the club did not own its own hall, but Grant's article reproduces a picture said to have been taken outside the Communia *Turnverein* around 1890 (15). Armstrong also includes a picture of the building, taken in the early 1970s, shortly before it was torn down. This building had the date 1883 painted on the central structure, which looks as if it had been a small church converted to secular usage with the addition of a kitchen and meeting room. This was probably the "public hall" said to be still in use at Communia in the 1920s, but what entity owned it is not clear (David C. Mott, "Abandoned Towns, Villages, and Post Offices of Iowa," *Annals of Iowa*, ser. 3, 17 [October 1930]: 461).

116. In her study of Bethel textiles, Horn points out that the retention of German weaving patterns and techniques in coverlets produced at Bethel, as well as the safe-guarding of these as treasured articles as late as a century and a half after they were made, points to the perpetuation of a German cultural heritage by the colonists and their descendants (106–8).

117. See Pickle, "German and Swiss Nuns," 61–82. Barry J. Coleman's *The Catholic Church and German Americans* (Milwaukee: Bruce, 1953) is the basic work on the topic. Richard M. Lenkh includes sections on German-Americans in *American Catholicism and European Immigrants (1900–1924)* (New York: Center for Migration Studies, 1975). The third chapter of Emmet H. Rothan's *The German Catholic Immigrant in the United States (1830–1860)* (Washington, D.C.: Catholic University of America Press, 1946) deals with the Midwest. Parts of the third volume of Casper's *History of the Catholic Church in Nebraska* survey late nineteenth-century German Catholic immigration. A valuable general source on the history of Catholic women in America is Mary Ewens, "The Role of the Nun in Nineteenth-Century America: Variations on the International Theme" (Ph.D. diss., University of Minnesota, 1971).

118. "Chronicles, O'Fallon, Missouri, 1870–1881," 7, 10, folder 9, Collection I, D, Transition to America, Archives of the Sisters of the Adoration of the Most Precious Blood, O'Fallon, Missouri; "Entstehung und Entwicklung der Kong[regation] der Schw[estern] vom K[östlichsten] Blut," trans. M. Albert Kaufmann, 13, Archives of the Adorers of the Most Precious Blood, Ruma, Illinois.

119. "Chronicles, O'Fallon," 5. This translation does not correspond precisely to the German original: "wie jedoch dies für Amerika unerläßlich ist" (original German manuscript in same folder, 12).

120. Ibid., 6.

121. Ibid., 17.

122. This tradition of hard physical labor continued into the 1880s, when the novices spent weeks breaking up several wagon loads of stones for the new convent wing ("Entstehung," 38).

123. Ibid., 18–31.

124. Ibid., 22.

125. Several histories and accounts of the early history of the Maryville and Conception missions exist, including Edward E. Malone, *The History of Conception Colony, Abbey and Schools*, Benedictine Series (Omaha: Interstate Publishing, 1971); M. Pascaline Coff, M. Carmelita Quinn, M. DeSales Markert, Mary Jane Romero, and M. Valeria Scott, *100 Years for You: The Story of the Benedictine Sisters of Perpetual Adoration* (St. Louis: Congregation of the Benedictine Sisters of Perpetual Adoration, 1974); Renggli, 247–69; and Dolores Dowling, *In Your Midst* ([St. Louis]: Congregation of Benedictine Sisters of Perpetual Adoration, 1988). The most informative sources are the letters sent to Switzerland and the daybooks kept by the heads of the new American foundations. These have been compiled and translated in several publications: *Letters from Mother M. Anselma Felber, OSB, and Others*, trans. Dominica Bonnenberg (St. Louis: Benedictine Sisters of Perpetual Adoration, 1977); *Early Chronicled History of the Benedictine Sisters of Perpetual Adoration: Relationship between Maryville and Conception (Clyde), 1874–1893*, ed. Kathleen M. Gorman, trans. Dominica Bonnenberg (St. Louis: Benedictine Sisters of Perpetual Adoration, 1982); and *Early Chronicled History of the Benedictine Sisters of Perpetual Adoration: Biographical Notes*, ed. Kathleen M. Gorman, trans. Dominica Bonnenberg (St. Louis: Benedictine Sisters of Perpetual Adoration, 1984). I did not have access to all of the German originals of the Benedictines' letters and daybooks.

126. Coff, 11; Renggli, 266; *Letters from Mother M. Anselma*, 29 May 1875, 15 February 1875, and 12 September 1874: "Would do us good to be every night for a little while on the dear mountains!" Unless otherwise noted, the citations from the Benedictine letters are located in this collection.

127. Benedictine letters of 12 September, 12 October, 29 December 1874; 17 January 1875.

128. Ibid., 17 July 1876, 5 March 1877, 19 July 1876.

129. Ibid., 12 October 1874.

130. Ibid., May 1877, 3 May 1879, 10 August 1876; "Entstehung," 29 (quote).

131. Benedictine letters of 10 August 1875, 21 February 1876.

132. Ibid., 21 February 1876, 26 July 1877, end of August 1877 (quote).

133. Ibid., 11 August 1879, 9 June 1880.

134. The chronicles of the Ruma and O'Fallon communities also hint at such conflicts, but they receive very little attention, probably out of the de-

sire to remember the most positive qualities of the community history and to grant all participants in it the Christian benefit of the doubt (see Pickle, "German and Swiss Nuns," 69).

135. For a biography of this strong-willed, enterprising woman mystic and founder, see Moritz Jäger, *Schwester Gertrud Leupi (1825–1904)* (Freiburg, Switzerland: Kanislus, 1974).

136. Sister Bernardine Wächter and Father Adelhelm Obermatt also went on to make new foundations in the West: Queen of the Holy Angels Convent in 1881 and Mount Angel Abbey in Oregon in 1882.

137. "Entstehung," 17 (quote); Benedictine letter of 31 December 1876.

138. "Entstehung," 16–17.

139. Ibid., 32–33, 36.

140. Mother Anselma mentioned to Abbot Anselm in Switzerland that the English-speaking novices had to learn German (Benedictine letter of February 1877). This practice continued in the Benedictine community until after World War I (personal communication to the author by Sister M. Domitilla Dirig, Benedictine Sisters of Perpetual Adoration, St. Louis, March 1984). In their language loyalty, the Adorers and the Benedictines were in the conservative camp of German-American Catholics, who held that too rapid assimilation and language loss would endanger the faith. See Lenkh's discussion of the strife between the German-speaking elements of the American Catholic church and its Irish-dominated hierarchy, which sought an "Americanization" of the church (4–14).

141. "Entstehung," 33–50.

142. Benedictine letters of 12 September 1874 (first quote); 12 October 1874 (second quote); March 1875 (third quote); 30 April 1875; November 1875; 10 September 1876 (fourth quote); 5 January 1877; *Early Chronicled History . . . Biographical Notes*, ca. February 1877 (fifth quote).

143. Ibid., 12 October 1874 (first quote); 17 January 1875 (second quote); 30 May 1875 (third quote); 24 January 1881 (fourth quote).

144. "Entstehung," 25.

Chapter 5: The Rural German-Speakers and Their Descendants

1. Susan Armitage, "Through Women's Eyes: A New View of the West," in *The Women's West*, ed. Armitage and Jameson, 12. For one of the better discussions of the diversity of farm women and their frontier lives, see also Fairbanks and Sundberg, 37–70.

2. For a discussion of the labor common to frontierswomen of all European ancestries, see Riley, *The Female Frontier*, 114–47. Ethnic and religious factors might have encouraged or inhibited women's participation in homesteading in some immigrant groups (Lindgren, 163–66, 171–72). Carl Degler has asserted that any differences between nineteenth-century Anglo-American families and immigrant families were due primarily to ethnicity rather than to class and that even these differences were relatively minor (*At Odds: Women and Family in America from the Revolution to the Present* [New York: Oxford University Press, 1980], 134–43).

3. Anton Totemeier, who had come to the United States in 1853 and had managed to give each of the twelve children from his first marriage eighty acres or more of Iowa farmland, was continuing to accumulate land for the children from his second marriage, even though he was in his seventies at the time (Letters, 1882–1908, BABS). Friedrich Muench noted the success of such a family strategy in "What Influence upon the Moral and Social Life of Our German Population Has Its Transfer from the Old to the New World Shown to Date?" *Der deutsche Pionier* 3 (January 1872): 338ff., cited in William G. Bek, "The Followers of Duden," *Missouri Historical Review* 19 (January 1925): 345. K. Conzen examined the cultural roots of generational succession among German-speaking farmers in frontier Minnesota in "Peasant Pioneers."

4. The term is Lillian Schlissel's ("Family on the Western Frontier," in *Western Women*, ed. Schlissel et al. 88). Her argument that the fate of the "disfunctional" Westering family she chronicles in this article was due to isolation and therefore vulnerability to the lawlessness of the frontier, however, downplays the negative effects that bad luck and individual personalities seem to have also had. Fink, among others, has also recognized the centrality of the family as "the most salient organizing unit" of the frontier, a centrality that was reinforced in the home and the church and by government policies (41).

5. Rosalinda Mendez González has articulated this viewpoint most convincingly ("Distinctions in Western Women's Experience: Ethnicity, Class, and Social Change," in *The Women's West*, ed. Armitage and Jameson, 237–51; "Commentary" [on the previously cited article by Lillian Schlissel], in *Western Women*, ed. Schlissel et al., 99–105).

6. For negative comments about Anglo-American women, see Wilhelm Fischer's 1851 letter from the prairie outside Davenport, Iowa, cited in Richter, 1:453. Nicolas Hesse, however, praised the cleanliness and "unostentatious" domestic work of Anglo-American women in Missouri in *Das westliche Nord-Amerika* (Paderborn, 1838; excerpts translated in William G. Bek, "Nicolas Hesse, German Visitor to Missouri, 1835–1837," *Missouri Historical Review* 41 [April 1946–47]: 291). Roebke provides an excellent overview of the opinions Germans expressed about American women (82–95).

7. The limited political activity allowed women before passage of the Nineteenth Amendment was generally available only to women in towns and cities (e.g., the female municipal suffrage law passed in Kansas in the late 1880s). See Rosalind Urbach Moss, "The 'Girls' from Syracuse: Sex Role Negotiations of Kansas Women in Politics, 1887–1890," in *The Women's West*, ed. Armitage and Jameson, 253–64. On the importance of rural women's networks and traditional culture, see Faragher, "History from the Inside-Out," 552–55.

8. For good discussions of the differences between yeoman and entrepreneurial agriculture and how the differences relate to German-American agricultural history, see Flora and Flora; and Salamon, "Ethnic Communities." For a related discussion of German-American farming traditions, see Douglas E. Bowers, "American Agriculture: The Contributions of German-Americans,"

Journal of NAL Associates 9, no. 1–4 (1984): 1–12. Fink also analyzes the prevalent model of the yeoman-style "family-based household production unit" that settled the West (24–37).

9. Flora and Flora, 24.

10. For discussion of the effects of the capitalist cash economy on farmers and their wives, see McNall and McNall, 23–27; and Carolyn Sachs, *The Invisible Farmers: Women in Agricultural Production* (Totowa, N.J.: Rowman and Allanheld, 1983), 49–53. Norton Juster attributes what he sees as "the disproportionate statistics of insanity and mental aberration among rural women" in the late nineteenth century to the propagation of the domestic ideology of the home as a safe haven, while a rural woman "was denied, in her narrowly circumscribed life, the essential ingredients necessary to create a logical rationale for that life—beyond embracing those sentimental, exploitative myths that kept her in her place" (*So Sweet to Labor: Rural Women in America, 1865–1895* [New York: Viking, 1979], 6, 5). Robert L. Griswold offers a more balanced view of the power the domestic ideology had in women's lives ("Anglo Women and Domestic Ideology in the American West in the Nineteenth and Early Twentieth Centuries," in *Western Women*, ed. Schlissel et al., 15–33; see also Richard Griswold del Castillo's commentary on this article, in ibid., 43–46). Faragher's discussion of conflict between rural women's traditional culture and the new "scientific" methods of farming and of the disparity between the stereotypes of antebellum farm women as either victims or advocates of "true womanhood" and the reality of their lives is also instructive ("History from the Inside-Out," 554–55, 538–43).

11. Speek, 227. Speek's study on acculturation stressed the importance of reaching immigrant women in any effort to bring immigrants into mainstream American culture, for "they live in the Old World" (227). An Anglo-American frontierswoman in the Dakotas remembered how alienated she was at first when she saw immigrant women working in the fields, something she had not seen at home in Michigan. "I rather resented it as an insult to my sex, but later years I became accustomed to it and even came to realize that the girls and women enjoyed the freedom of outdoor life. Many girls preferred working outside" (Nina Farley Wishek, *Along the Trails of Yesterday* [Ashley, N.D.: Ashley Tribune, 1941], 235, cited by Lindgren, 170–71).

12. Ruegg reported evidence of interethnic conflict even in the earliest days of settlement in the Fancy Creek area near Manhattan, Kansas. He wrote that two American families had taken land in the largely German and Swiss area, and the immigrants would have liked to see them leave. The feeling was evidently mutual: "These Americans do not like it near the Germans and their wives like it still less" (diary entry of 4 October 1867). August de B. Hollingshead noted the persistence of prejudice and dislike between the descendants of Yankee and immigrant settlers in Nebraska, which he attributed to the practices associated with differing agricultural ideologies ("Changes in Land Ownership as an Index of Succession in Rural Communities," *American Journal of Sociology* 43 [March 1938]: 776).

13. Conzen, "Peasant Pioneers," 285.

14. See Karl Theodor Griesinger's comments on the "Sacred Concerts" (named thus to get around nineteenth-century Sunday drinking laws) held in New York City's German beer gardens on Sundays (Furer, 129).

15. Walter Kamphoefner, "The German Agricultural Frontier: Crucible or Cocoon," *Ethnic Forum* 4 (Spring 1984): 21–35. In this study, Kamphoefner successfully challenges Oscar Handlin's pessimistic view that immigrants' cultural alienation was inescapable on farms (O. Handlin, *The Uprooted* [Boston: Little, Brown, 1951]).

16. On women in general, see Riley, *The Female Frontier,* 72–73, 98. Speaking of the descendants of German colonists in the Soviet Union, whose language and culture came under attack during Stalin's regime, Schock has written, "The mother of a family was the only carrier of German culture after the destruction of the German schools, so that the young still could learn something about German religion and morals" (*In Quest of Free Land,* 53). Similarly, Kolm has asserted that the immigrant woman "becomes usually the main bearer of the ethnic culture" (127–28).

17. Ewen, 37. John E. Bodnar's discussion of the development of a "culture of everyday life" among immigrants as a means of adaptation is also helpful (*The Transplanted* [Bloomington: University of Indiana Press, 1985]).

18. See, for example, Blaschke's discussion of the women's pages (entitled *"Hausfrau"*) of the *Acker- und Gartenbauzeitung* (106–7). Brent O. Peterson's study of *Die Abendschule,* the long-lived weekly centered in the Midwest, is also informative on this score (*Popular Narratives and Ethnic Identity* [Ithaca, N.Y.: Cornell University Press, 1991]). See also K. Conzen's important study "German-Americans and the Invention of Ethnicity," in *America and the Germans,* ed. Trommler and McVeigh, 131–47.

19. Bureau of the Census, *Supplemental Report: Ancestry of the Population by State, 1980* (Washington, D. C.: GPO, 1983), tables B and 3.

20. Bureau of the Census, *1980 Census of Population,* vol. 1, *Characteristics of the Population* (Washington, D.C.: GPO, 1983), chapter C, part 1, table 76; *Supplemental Report: Ancestry of the Population by State, 1980,* table 2.

21. See table B18 in appendix B for comparative data from 1950. If we compare the percentages of all employed German-American females in farm-related occupations in 1980 in table 4, we see that German-American women were 5.89 times as likely to be engaged in farm-related occupations as were all women nationwide. In Kansas, they were 4.78 times, in Nebraska 3.11 times, and in Missouri 1.64 times more likely than the national average to be farm workers.

22. Derived from *Supplemental Report: Ancestry of the Population by State, 1980,* tables 2, 3, and 3a. By way of contrast, the percentages of single-ancestry Austrian- and Swiss-Americans in the United States were, respectively, 35.8 percent and 24 percent and in the north-central region 31.3 percent and 22.3 percent. The percentages of single-ancestry persons in these groups were also lower than the national average in each of the five states studied here. Using marriage license information of the early part of this century from Nebraska, Wisconsin, and New York, Edmund de S. Brunner established a

clear preference (+ 50 percent) for in-group marriage through the second generation of residence in the United States. His study also showed that the tendency to marry outside the group increased with the length of residence (*Immigrant Farmers and Their Children* [Garden City, N.Y.: Doubleday, Doran, 1929], 54–91). At least for strongly German-American rural areas in the Midwest, however, the trend toward intermarriage might never have been so marked and certainly seems to have leveled off in the late twentieth century. As Kamphoefner has shown, rural immigrant districts formed by chain migration initially were especially immune to marriage outside the group ("'Entwurzelt' oder 'verpflanzt'?" 345–47). These early marriage patterns probably depressed the number of subsequent out-group marriages for a long time.

23. Bureau of the Census, *1980 Census of Population,* vol. 1, chapter C, table 76.

24. See Russel Gerlach's study of population origins in Missouri, based on the 1980 census (*Settlement Patterns in Missouri: A Study of Population Origins with a Wall Map* [Columbia: University of Missouri Press, 1986], 47–77). Richard M. Bernard's study of intermarriage in early twentieth-century Wisconsin is also generally informative on this topic (*The Melting Pot and the Altar* [Madison: University of Wisconsin Press, 1980]).

25. As one study has put it, "If ever an American ethnic group vanished, it is the Germans" (Andrew M. Greeley and William C. McCready, *Ethnicity in the United States* [New York: Wiley, 1974], 112).

26. In addition to the hard winter wheat that the Germans from Russia are said to have introduced to the Great Plains, amateur German-speaking horticulturists, such as Jules Sandoz, took part in the adaptation of European plant life to the midwestern environment. Swiss immigrants contributed to the development of the cheese industry in southern Wisconsin and northwest Illinois in the 1840s and 1850s, and Wendelin Grimm brought alfalfa seed from Baden and acclimatized it to grow through Minnesota's severe winters (Theodore Saloutos, "The Immigrant Contribution to American Agriculture," *Agricultural History* 510 [January 1976]: 52, 55, 66).

27. Studies dedicated to tracing German influence in midwestern architecture include Van Ravenswaay; Philippe Oszuscik, "Germanic Influence upon the Vernacular Architecture of Davenport, Iowa," *Pioneer America Society Transactions,* vol. 10 (Akron, Ohio: Pioneer America Society, 1987): 17–27; and Howard W. Marshall, "The Pelster Housebarn: Endurance of Germanic Architecture on the Midwestern Frontier," *Material Culture* 18 (Summer 1986): 65–104. An entire issue of the magazine *OzarksWatch* (3 [Summer 1989]) was dedicated to the German heritage of the "north Ozarks border" (i.e., south-central Missouri), with references to architecture. Studies include James M. Denny, "Persistence in the Built Environment," 4–7; Gary Kremer, "Persistence and Change in the German Ozarks," 8–10; Mimi Stiritz, "Preservation Corner River Town," 11–13; Russel Gerlach, "The German Presence in the Ozarks," 14–17; Claire F. Blackwell, "The Pelster House Barn," 18–21; and Bill Nunn, "A Song from the Third Floor," 22–24. Pa-

tricia Rice's "The Missouri Rhineland: Church and Community," *St. Louis Post-Dispatch Magazine,* 18 July 1993, previews a photography exhibit and book on the German-American churches of central and eastern Missouri being prepared by John Wickersham of Maryville University. K. Conzen ("Germans," 424) also comments on qualities of German-American rural architecture, as do Gerlach (*Immigrants in the Ozarks,* 67–69, 82, 95, 117), Clark ("German Settlement in Iowa"), and Rikoon ("The Reusser House").

28. Butts's narrative about Sabine Drushel Kropf contains several good examples of the changes this immigrant and her family made in the northwest Iowa territory they came to in the early 1880s and how this effected the fish in the streams and the wild birds, including whooping cranes, in the sloughs.

29. Gerlach, *Immigrants in the Ozarks,* 82–83, 87–88, 95–96; Gary Foster, Richard Hummer, and Robert Whittenbarger, "Ethnic Echoes through 100 Years of Midwestern Agriculture," *Rural Sociology* 52 (Fall 1987): 365–78); Salamon, "Sibling Solidarity," 357, 366.

30. Goebel, 170.

31. In Ellis County, 2,319 persons age five and older of a total population of 26,004 (8.9 percent) used German at home in 1990, and in Marion County, 713 of 12,888 (5.5 percent) (Bureau of the Census, *1990 Census of Population and Housing: Summary Tape File 3A*). Albrecht cites the Mennonite hymnal *Gesangbuch der Mennoniten,* published in 1965, as proof this group retained its language (164).

32. In 1990, 764 persons (5.2 percent) above the age of five spoke German at home in Iowa County, Iowa, where the Amana colonies are located. In Lenox Township, the heart of the Amana colonies, 348 (24.1 percent) of the 1,442 people age five or older spoke German at home (Bureau of the Census, *1990 Census of Population and Housing: Summary Tape File 3A*).

33. Albert Heinrich refers to such older people ("Bevölkerung deutscher Herkunft in Südwest-Illinois," in *Deutsch als Muttersprache in den Vereinigten Staaten,* ed. Anburger et al., 1, 26). According to the 1990 census, the following numbers of persons age five and above used German at home in the midwestern counties listed below (the percentages of German-speakers among the total county populations are given in parentheses):

Illinois: Effingham County, 318 (1.0 percent); Monroe County, 693 (3.1 percent)

Iowa: Benton County, 142 (0.6 percent); Clayton County, 237 (1.2 percent)

Kansas: Finney County, 300 (0.9 percent); Trego County, 217 (5.9 percent)

Missouri: Gasconade County, 373 (2.7 percent); Osage County, 375 (3.1 percent)

Nebraska: Cedar County, 96 (0.9 percent); Thayer County, 181 (2.7 percent).

(Bureau of the Census, *1990 Census of Population and Housing: Summary Tape File 3A*).

34. As John M. Coggeshall has put it, the superficial trappings of German culture at such "ethnic" festivals "add authenticity but not validity as ethnic markers" ("'One of Those Intangibles': The Manifestation of Ethnic Identity in Southwestern Illinois," *Journal of American Folklore* 99 [April–June 1986]: 185). DeBres expressed a more negative view of similar phenomena when she wrote that the ethnic heritage on view at Hermann is "the kind of past Americans want to have today": sanitized, selective, and essentially nonexistent, reflecting how we want to view the past, not how it actually was (41).

35. See Helbich and Sommer's comments on the German influence of "a Sunday dedicated to pleasure and relaxation and a taboo-free, relaxed attitude toward alcohol" (*Alle Menschen sind dort gleich*, 47).

36. See Jonathan G. Andelson's discussion of the connection between ethnicity and handicrafts in Amana ("Tradition, Innovation, and Assimilation in Iowa's Amana Colonies," *Palimpsest* 69 [Spring 1988]: 2–15); and Ohrn.

37. Coggeshall, "'One of Those Intangibles,'" 192–95; Fink, 91. Lock noted that the seven-member "Dutchmasters" band was invited to play at the 1976 Oktoberfest in Munich and that two plane-loads of German-Americans from the Russell, Kansas, area accompanied them there (118).

38. Coggeshall, "'One of Those Intangibles,'" 195, 200–201, 204; Rice, 9. A century ago, "Jürnjakob Swehn" wrote that because their children mostly spoke English, he and his wife tried to keep them German "in their hearts" by singing folk songs and hymns with them (Gillhoff, 299–300).

39. Hollingshead, "The Life Cycle of Nebraska Rural Churches," 188–90; Lenore Salvaneschi, "Mission Festival," *Palimpsest* 64 (May-June 1983): 103–8; Rice, 8, 10; Gerlach, *Immigrants in the Ozarks*, 113–18; Salamon, "Ethnic Differences," 295; Geiger, "St. Johannes Deutsche Evangelische Kirche," 26. The attachment some German-Americans feel for their rural churches is illustrated by the efforts made to keep the West Boonville Evangelical Church in Cooper County, Missouri, functioning, even if on a half-time basis (Sara Ervanian, "A Century of Worship," *Columbia Daily Tribune*, 14 June 1993).

40. A. Schroeder, "Deutsche Sprache in Missouri," 157; Bowers, 3. John M. Coggeshall examined the dynamics of German-American ethnic identification within and between interacting groups ("Ethnic Persistence with Modification: The German-Americans of Southwest Illinois" [Ph.D. diss., Southern Illinois University, 1984]).

41. John M. Faragher has written that if one studies the early settlers who did not persist on the land, one finds "the geographic mobility and loss of community that have become the hallmarks of modern America" ("Open Country Community: Sugar Creek, Illinois, 1820–1850," in *The Countryside in the Age of Capitalist Transformation*, ed. Hahn and Prude, 252).

42. See Kathleen Neils Conzen, *Making Their Own America: Assimilation Theory and the German Peasant Pioneer*, German Historical Institute Annual Lecture Series, 3 (New York: Berg, 1990), 33; and Jörg Nagler's comments on this term ("Ethnic Persistence and Transformation: A Response to Kathleen N. Conzen," in *Making Their Own America*, 41).

43. K. Conzen's comments relating to the German Catholic settlement in

Stearns County, Wisconsin, are instructive (*Making Their Own America,* 32–33). Frederick C. Luebke has questioned the extent to which the Midwest today may "still reflect a residue of German immigrant values," especially the emphasis on "family values, self-help, and work for its own sake" (*Germans in the New World* [Urbana: University of Illinois Press, 1990], 176). Gregory has asserted that the German heritage in Washington, Missouri, made this small town "a more industrious, more socially diverse, happy, progressive and tolerant community than is generally found in Missouri" (*The German-Americans,* 92).

44. See Fink, 63–65; and Oscar F. Hoffman, "Cultural Change in a Rural Wisconsin Ethnic Island," *Rural Sociology* 14 (March 1949): 39–50.

45. Patricia Wasely Lomire, "An American Gender Dilemma: A Weberian Approach to the Politics of Ethnic and Gender Status" (Ph.D. diss., Notre Dame University, 1986), 264.

46. The family-centered orientation of German-American women, noted by some social scientists, is indicated by their slightly greater tendency to marry and be members of male-headed households. See K. Conzen, "Germans," 406; and Hinda Winawer-Steiner and Norbert A. Wetzel, "German Families," in *Ethnicity and Family Therapy,* ed. Monica McGoldrick, John Pearce, and Joseph Giordno (New York: Guilford Press, 1982), 258–62.

47. Don H. Tolzmann has noted that "recently the melting-pot concept has been replaced by the more realistic idea of cultural pluralism as the key to understanding American history" ("Frederick Jackson Turner's Frontier Thesis and the German-Americans," *Heritage Review* 10 [August 1980]: 21). Loretta K. Matulich has written, "Perhaps the greatest contribution of the immigrants to American society . . . was their very presence and identity. They were a challenge to America to enlarge her thinking and activity . . . , to grow and adapt their government and culture according to the needs of the time" (*A Cross-Disciplinary Study of the European Immigrants of 1870 to 1925* [New York: Arno, 1980], 236).

Appendix A: Sources on German-Speaking Immigrant Women and Their Families

1. Such debts are acknowledged throughout this study. Among the most important general works on German-speakers in the Midwest and elsewhere are Gustav Körner, *Das deutsche Element in den Vereinigten Staaten von Nordamerika, 1818–1848* (Cincinnati: Wilde, 1880); A. B. Faust, *The German Element in the United States* (New York: Houghton Mifflin, 1909); Frederick F. Schrader, *The Germans in the Making of America* (Boston: Stratford, 1924); John A. Hawgood, *The Tragedy of German-America* (New York: Putnam, 1940); Carl F. Wittke, *We Who Built America* (New York: Prentice, 1940); Richard O'Connor, *The German-Americans: An Informal History* (Boston: Little, Brown, 1968); and LaVern J. Rippley, *The German-Americans* (Boston: Twayne, 1976). Frederick C. Luebke's studies of German-American political structures deserve special mention (*Bonds of Loyalty: German-*

Americans and World War I, Minorities in American History [DeKalb: Northern Illinois University Press, 1974]; *Immigrants and Politics*). Bibliographies of sources on German-Americana include Don Heinrich Tolzmann, *German-Americana: A Bibliography* (Metuchen, N.J.: Scarecrow Press, 1975); Henry A. Pochmann and Arthur R. Schultz, eds., *Bibliography of German Culture in America to 1940,* rev. ed. (Millwood, N.Y.: Kraus International Publications, 1982); and Arthur A. Schultz, ed., *German-American Relations and German Culture in America: A Subject Bibliography of German-American Sources, 1941–1980* (Millwood, N.Y.: Kraus International Publications, 1984).

2. Wolfgang Helbich has estimated 100 million private letters were written from the United States to Germany in the nineteenth century ("The Letters They Sent Home: The Subjective Perspective of German Immigrants in the Nineteenth Century," *Yearbook of German-American Studies,* vol. 22 [Lawrence, Kans.: Society for German-American Studies, 1987]: 11). Yet the archive of emigrant letters Helbich established at the University of Bochum contains only about 6,000 letters ("Bochumer Auswandererbrief-Sammlung," herein referred to as BABS).

3. Rosenbaum's comments about the casual and often dismissive attitudes toward education and the practice of formal education in rural areas are instructive (91–97, 243–45). General illiteracy rates in Bavaria were 40–50 percent in the 1840s, despite education reforms (W. R. Lee, *Population Growth,* 344–46). By 1871 illiteracy in the new German nation was probably around 5 percent, at least among men (Wolfgang Helbich, Walter D. Kamphoefner, and Ulrike Sommer, eds., *Briefe aus Amerika: Deutsche Auswanderer schreiben aus der Neuen Welt, 1830–1930* [Munich: Beck, 1988], 36). Concrete evidence of higher illiteracy among German-speaking women is found among the documents associated with the case study of wills of German-speaking immigrants in Cooper County, Missouri. Only one man was unable to sign his own name, whereas seven women could not. What J. M. Jensen has said of the writings of nineteenth-century Anglo-American women applies to German-speaking rural women as well: "These factors then,—illiteracy, long and exhausting work hours, scarcity of uninterrupted leisure, and the absence of a practical need for written communication—all affected the amount of written material that has come down to us" (*With These Hands,* xviii).

4. Neumeier Family Letters, 1892–1915, BABS.

5. See, for example, the following collections and studies: Sandra L. Myres, ed., *Ho for California! Women's Overland Diaries from the Huntington Library* (Malibu, Calif.: Museum Reproductions, 1980); Lillian Schlissel, ed., *Women's Diaries of the Westward Journey* (New York: Schocken, 1982); Elizabeth Hampsten, ed., *Read This Only to Yourself: The Private Writings of Midwestern Women, 1880–1910* (Bloomington: Indiana University Press, 1982); Kenneth L. Holms, ed., *Covered Wagon Women: Diaries and Letters from the Western Trails,* vol. 1, *1840–1849* (Glendale, Calif.: Clark, 1983); and Ruth B. Moynihan, Susan Armitage, and Christiane Fischer Dichamp, eds., *So Much*

to Be Done: Women Settlers on the Mining and Ranching Frontier (Lincoln: University of Nebraska Press, 1990). Only three German women's diaries are listed in Joyce D. Goodfriend's annotated bibliography *The Published Diaries and Letters of American Women* (Boston: Hall, 1987), and all of these are by middle-class women. A better source (although not for rural German-speaking women) is Donna Gabaccia's bibliographical compilation *Immigrant Women in the United States* (Westport, Conn.: Greenwood, 1989).

6. Roebke's thesis is a good example of the insights that can be gained from such public material. Carol Smith-Rosenberg called for combining the imagery underlying prescriptive literature and the testimony of personal writings to arrive at the whole reality of women's history ("The New Woman and the New History," *Feminist Studies* 3 [Spring 1975]: 193). Kathleen N. Conzen discusses the many difficulties associated with locating and preserving the documentation of German-American and other immigrant experiences in this country ("Hunting the Snark; or, the Historian's Quest for Immigrant Documentation," in *Documenting Diversity: A Report on the Conference on Documenting the Immigrant Experience in the United States of America*, ed. Rudolph Vecoli [St. Paul, Minn.: Immigrant History Research Center, 1991], 77–89).

7. The generalizations with which Kammeier concludes his collection of emigrant letters serve as negative examples (*"So besint euch"*).

8. A large body of literature on the interpretation of personal documents exists. The most relevant works for the topic of this study include Charlotte Erickson, *Invisible Immigrants: The Adaptation of English and Scottish Immigrants in Nineteenth Century-America* (Coral Gables: University of Florida Press, 1972); Wolfgang Helbich and Ulrike Sommer, "Immigrant Letters as Sources," in *The Press of Labor Migrants in Europe and North America, 1880–1930*, ed. Christiane Harzig and Dirk Hoerder (Bremen: University of Bremen, 1985), 39–58; W. Helbich, ed., *"Amerika ist ein freies Land . . ."* *Auswanderer schreiben nach Deutschland* (Darmstadt: Luchterhand, 1985); Thomas Finkemeier, "Assimilation im Spiegel deutsch-amerikanischer Auswander-Autobiographien im 19. Jahrhundert" (M.A. thesis, Ruhr University, Bochum, 1986); Bretting, 9–28; Personal Narratives Group, ed., *Interpreting Women's Lives* (Bloomington: Indiana University Press, 1989); Katherine Jensen, "Oral Histories of Rural Western American Women: Can They Contribute to Quantitative Studies?" *International Journal of Oral History* 5 (November 1984): 159–67; Nancy Thym-Hochrein, "'Peter Left Home Because . . .': A Comparative Study of Oral Family Histories," *Arv* 37 (1981): 61–68; James C. Holte, "The Representative Voice: Autobiography and the Ethnic Experience," *Melus* 9 (Summer 1982): 25–46; and William Boelhower, "The Brave New World of Immigrant Autobiography," *Melus* 9 (Summer 1982): 5–23. See also Lanwert, 6–13. Seena B. Kohl has been particularly interested in the subjective, autobiographical nature of community history books and has dealt with this topic in several studies ("Image and Behavior"; "Memories of Homesteading and the Process of Retrospection," *Oral History Review* 17 [Fall 1989]: 25–45; "Writing Popular History: Contrasting

Approaches from Rural Mississippi and Rural Canada," in *Cultural Heritage Conservation in the American South,* ed. Benita J. Howell [Athens: University of Georgia Press, 1990], 42–53). Her long-term study with John W. Bennett also uses these documents as sources (*Settling the Canadian American West, 1890–1950: Pioneer Adaptation and Community Building* [Lincoln: University of Nebraska Press, 1995]).

Appendix B: Demographic Aspects of the Female Component of German-Speaking Settlement in the Midwest

1. Günther Moltmann has calculated the percentage of "remigrants" (persons who had intended to settle permanently in the United States but then returned to Europe) as approximately 4 to 5 percent of the emigration rate for any given year ("American-German Return Migration in the Nineteenth and Early Twentieth Centuries," *Central European History* 13 [December 1980]: 378–92). This rate of return is not calculated into any of the figures cited here.

2. Inoki, table 11, 76.

3. Ibid., table 8, 73, derived from *Jahrbuch für Volkswirtschaft und Statistik,* vol. 7, ed. Otto Hübner (Leipzig: n.p., 1861), 148. These figures include 5,530 Bavarians (out of the total of 91,663 emigrants) who migrated to other German states between 1851 and 1857.

4. Ibid., table 11, 76.

5. Ibid., 81.

6. Bade asserts that the economic boom in Germany during the 1890s was much more important in keeping Germans in Europe than was the end of American frontier ("German Emigration," 365). The impact of industrialization and the development of an agricultural market economy came later in Austria. Increasing numbers of German-speaking Austrians therefore made up for some of the diminishing German emigration between 1880 and 1920, as Carpenter's table 150 shows (324–25).

7. Joan Y. Dickinson, *The Role of the Immigrant Women in the United States Labor Force, 1890–1910* (New York: Arno, 1980), 61; Carpenter, table 101, 218.

8. Inoki, table 9, 74.

9. David J. Wishart, "Age and Sex Composition of the Population on the American Frontier, 1860–1880," *Nebraska History* 54 (Spring 1973): 109–11.

10. Kamphoefner, *The Westfalians,* 108.

11. Carpenter, table 101, 218.

12. This was particularly true of those who emigrated from the poorer groups of agricultural workers. Kamphoefner found this population profile among the Missouri Osnabrück immigrants he studied (*The Westfalians,* 25, 43).

13. Carpenter, table 180, 424–27.

14. Kamphoefner, *The Westfalians,* 106–34. Bernard found similar patterns in his study of intermarriage in early twentieth-century Wisconsin (44–68).

15. Carpenter, 147; Kamphoefner, "'Entwurzelt' oder 'verpflanzt'?" table 2, 330, 332; Bade, "The German Emigration to the United States," 365.

16. The seemingly low proportion of children among German-speakers in relation to the average of all immigrant groups is due to the high proportion of children among Mexican immigrants in the sample area Carpenter considered, which skewed the figures for the average.

17. See K. Conzen, "Deutsche Einwanderer," table 3, 353.

18. The same is shown by Max Hannemann, *Das Deutschtum in den Vereinigten Staaten: Seine Verbreitung und Entwicklung seit der Mitte des 19. Jahrhunderts,* Petermanns Mitteilungen 1936, Ergänzungsheft Nr. 224 (Gotha: J. Perthes, 1936), table 13.

19. *Statistics of Women at Work* (Washington, D.C.: GPO, 1907), 17. In another way of figuring the rural population at the turn of the century, the Census Bureau calculated that 51.9 percent of the population lived in unincorporated areas with fewer than 4,000 inhabitants (*U.S. Census Reports, Twelfth Census, 1900,* vol. 1, *Population* [Washington, D.C.: GPO, 1901], part 1, lxxxix).

20. Carpenter, tables 82 and 83, 183–84. The Austrian and German women include those born in areas that had been Poland. A study of Saginaw County, Michigan, between 1850 and 1880 reveals that German-born women continued to have large numbers of children throughout this period, at the same time that the fertility of native-born women and women of other nativity declined markedly (G. Alexander Ross, "Delaying the Fertility Decline: German Women in Saginaw County, Michigan, 1850–1880," *Journal of Family History* 14 [April 1989]: 157–70). Although lumber rather than farming was the primary industry in Saginaw County at this time, the cultural and social backgrounds of the German women there were generally representative of most immigrants in the Midwest.

21. Pauline Greving, letter of 25 June 1895, Pauline and Henry Greving Letters, 1884–1923, Tms, BABS. Second-generation women broke the pattern of high fertility rates established by their mothers, as an analysis of a large sampling of women from the 1900 census shows (Miriam King and Steven Ruggles, "American Immigration, Fertility, and Race Suicide at the Turn of the Century," *Journal of Interdisciplinary History* 20 [Winter 1990]: 347–69).

22. Carpenter, table 113, 245. Other patterns of Old World rural reproductive life might have been perpetuated in the New World. J. M. Jensen, for example, tells that her immigrant grandmother followed an "old German custom" and was pregnant on both of her wedding days (*Promise to the Land,* 40, 73).

23. Dickinson notes that in 1890 almost one of three widows who were native-born but of foreign parentage worked, and she explains this high work rate by the fact that they were largely in the agricultural sector and probably had become farm proprietors as widows (49).

24. That is not to say that families headed by widows with children were unknown in other groups and other frontier areas. A study of a six-county Texas frontier region showed that in 1850 the majority of widows who had

land and an average of 3.5 children did not remarry (Blaine T. Williams, "The Frontier Family: Demographic Fact and Historical Myth," in *Essays on the American West*, ed. Harold M. Hollingsworth and Sandra L. Myres [Austin: University of Texas Press, 1969], 50–60).

25. Census Bureau, *U.S. Census Reports: Occupations of the Twelfth Census, 1900* (Washington, D.C.: GPO, 1904), table 73, cxcii-cxciv.

26. Dickinson, 89.

27. Bengt Ankarloo, "Agriculture and Women's Work: Directions of Change in the West, 1700–1900," *Journal of Family History* 4 (Summer 1979): 120.

28. For a discussion of the continuance of such patterns in the Great Plains, see Flora and Flora. Elizabeth Pleck has shown that for all women in America, the worlds of work and home coexisted well past World War I, with unmarried women generally expected to give their wage earnings to parents ("Two Worlds in One," *Journal of Social History* 10 [Winter 1976]: 178–95).

29. See chapter 5 for a discussion of such persistence in the decades since 1950.

Index

abolition: German-American opposition to, 72

acculturation: role of ethnic clubs in, 83–84, 85; women's role in, 85. *See also* adaptation to America, factors affecting; assimilation

adaptation to America, factors affecting: age, 93–104; clannishness, 132, 144; communal life, 150–80 passim; contact with Americans, 94–95, 113, 115, 169, 172, 176–77, 178; domestic conditions, 129–30; family and female networks, 99–100, 104–11, 113, 116, 117, 164–65; finances, 112, 115, 170, 171; health, 98, 99–100, 103, 105, 112, 125, 126, 127; husband, 122–25, 128; misfortune, 125, 126, 127; recurring cultural alienation, 128–30; social institutions, 83–84, 85, 186. *See also* acculturation; assimilation

Adorers of the Most Precious Blood, 168–71, 261n113. *See also* nuns

agrarian ideology: in America in general, 48–49; among foreign-born (1900), 223–24; in 1950, 228–29; nineteenth-century German peasant, 14, 31, 33, 40; women's subordination, 48–49; yeoman agricultural practices, 185

agricultural practices: yeoman vs. entrepreneurial, 185–86

Amana, Iowa: child care, 152; clothing, 153; communistic economy, 151, 155; community kitchens, 154–56; equality of sexes, 152, 153; ethnic heritage, 195; ethnic retention and group identity, 154; ethnic retention and women, 154; family life, 152, 153; language retention in twentieth century, 294n32; marriage, 152, 156–57; religious teachings about women, 152–53; schools, 152; wedding customs, 154; women and communal life, 156; women's communal work, 151–52; women's subordination, 156; mentioned, 20, 66, 132

Amish, 15, 194

Antelope County, Nebr., 191, 192, 193

assimilation: rapidity of, among German-Americans, 131–32; role of parochial schools, 83; separatist immigrant groups, 179. *See also* acculturation; adaptation to America

autobiographical texts. *See* personal writings

Bartsch, Louisa, 67, 108

Baumann, Käthe Gauß, 99–100, 122

Baumann, Michael, 163

beer, 73–74, 195. *See also* diet

Bender, Kate, 54

Benedictine Sisters of Perpetual Adoration: alienation from environment, 66, 171; constraints on spiritual life, 172; living conditions, 171; strife within community, 173–74; work, 171–72. *See also* nuns

Benton, Thomas Hart, 114, 128

Benton County, Iowa, 191, 192, 193, 294n33

Berlin Society, 20

Bethel, Mo.,: domestic production, 160; family and domestic life, 159; public confessions of sin, 159; residents shielded from cultural alienation, 167; subordination of women, 160; women as wage earners, 160; mentioned, 20, 66, 132, 158, 159, 195

Beulke, Augusta (Holtz), 42

Beulke, Ferdinand, 42
Biehler-Meyer, Elisabeth Beckbird, 49
Bigler, Elizabeth, 68, 88, 248*n17*
Bigler, Emilie, 86
Bilsland, Amy Holmes, 126
Block, Gesche Mahnken, 53
Block, Kans.: female networks, 272*n40;*
  female teacher, 267*n162;* rejection of
  public displays of emotion, 76; wom-
  en's church activities, 265*n148,*
  266*n154,* 267*n156;* mentioned, 76,
  77, 265*n145*
Blommer, Mathias, 42, 74, 78, 270*n179*
Bock, Wilhelm von, 20
Boeckers, Clara, 125
Boeckers, Heinrich, 125
Borries-Garlich, Adelheid von, 92–93
Bossard, Johan, 163, 286*n111*
Brauchen, 144
Brautbitter, 88
Bremer County, Iowa, 191, 192, 193,
  264*n145*
Brown County, Kans., 273*n55*
Bruns, Bernhard, 112–15 passim, 120
Bruns, Henriette ("Jette") Geisberg:
  cultural alienation 113, 115, 116;
  homesickness, 116, 128; lack of fe-
  male network, 113–14, 115; person-
  ality, 121–22; physical work done,
  114, 118; relationship with husband,
  120; subjective experience, 116, 120–
  21; mentioned, 125, 161
Brunswick, Mo., 84, 266*n150*
Bruntz family (Hastings, Nebr.), 139
Buchow, Mr. (Archer[?], Iowa), 126
Buchow, Mrs. (Archer[?], Iowa), 126
Buettner, Johann Gottfried, 263*n132*
Bukovina Germans, 77, 136, 270*n183*
Butler County, Iowa, 17
butter, 55–56

Calhoun County, Iowa, 99, 111
Catherine, Kans., 144
Cedar County, Nebr., 294*n33*
census information: limitations of, 214,
  218, 224, 226
chain migration, 12, 131, 176, 186,
  235*nn19–20,* 273*n40*
Charter Oak, Iowa, 126
cheese, 55–56

childbearing: among German-Americans
  (1920), 216; comparisons between
  native- and foreign-born, 220–21; effect on women's wage earning, 221–
  22
childbirth: customs accompanying, 142,
  144; hazard on frontier, 50
children: care of, on frontier, 50–51;
  mortality, 36–37, 39, 50–51, 220;
  objects of affection, 36–38; source of
  labor, 31, 50–51, 56, 140, 184–85,
  216, 221
churches: community institutions, 17,
  78–81; role in ethnic retention, 196;
  sources of conflict, 16–17, 109–10;
  women's contributions to, 79–81,
  141–42, 147–48, 168
cities: as way stations for rural immigrants, 214–16
Clarinda, Iowa, 16, 17
Clayton County, Iowa, 191, 192, 193,
  285*n102,* 294*n33*
Clinton County, Iowa, 56
clothing: adapted to American expectations, 87; in Amana, 153
clubs, ethnic, 78, 83–85. *See also Turnverein*
communal life: benefits for women,
  151–52, 155–56; conservative, in
  matters of gender, 179–80; control in
  personal sphere, 159; disadvantages
  for women, 156, 163–64; effect on
  domestic sphere, 167; support for
  ethnic retention, 167, 179, 180
Communia, Iowa: core of ethnic community, 165, 166; economic failure,
  163; friction among wives, 163–64;
  influence of mother on church affiliation, 167; residents shielded from
  cultural alienation, 167; *Turnverein,*
  167; wives taught school, 286*n112;*
  mentioned, 132, 158
communistic colonies. *See* Amana, Iowa;
  Bethel, Mo.; Communia, Iowa; New
  Helvetia, Mo.
communistic societies: congenial to Germans, 157–58; cultural conservatism of,
  167; minor effect on domestic life, 167
Community of True Inspiration. *See*
  Amana, Iowa

Cooper County, Mo.: diversity of German-American residents, 17–18; ethnic population (1980 and 1990), 191, 192, 193; St. John's German Evangelical Church, 81; study of wills of German-speaking immigrants, 60–65; mentioned, 203, 266*n155*, 295*n93*

Craemer, Dorothea Benthien, 147

cultural conservatism: congenial setting in rural Midwest, 197; visible in demographics, 229–30

cultural convergence, 198–99

cultural retention, 21, 70, 128, 179–80, 236*n24*

Darmstadt, Ill., 12, 16, 88

Deutschheim Association (Hermann, Mo.), 195

diaries. *See* personal writings

diet: beer and wine, 73–74; change and continuity of, in America, 70–74 passim, 195, 196; meat, 40, 50; in rural nineteenth-century Europe, 39–40

Dietsch, Andreas, 161, 162

Dietzenbach, Ill., 84

diversity: in immigrant communities, 17–18, 109–10

domestic servants, 26, 28, 29, 96, 227, 241*n10*, 251*n42*

Down, Pauline Roedel Bremmer, 253–54*n58*

dowry: at risk in communistic colonies, 164; importance of, for marriage, 46; linens as part of, 47; as recompense to husband's siblings, 33; mentioned, 138

Dreißiger: as political emigrants, 14; in Missouri, 12–20; mentioned, 15, 17, 19, 20, 43, 114, 121, 161, 261*n119*

Duden, Gottfried, 19, 68, 112

dugouts, 3, 67–68

education: in Amana, 152; attitudes toward, 101, 115, 140; attitudes toward, for women, 23–24, 81

education, American: German-Americans' opinions of, 103

Effingham County, Ill., 191, 192, 193, 294*n33*

Efinger, Blasius, 62–63

eggs, 55–56

Eitzen, Helena Friesen: homesickness, 105; personality, 122; role in decision to emigrate, 44–45

Eitzen, Sarah Block, 144

Ellis County, Kans.: ethnic population (1980 and 1990), 191, 192, 193; language retention (1990), 294*n31*; persistence of church-related customs, 141–42; mentioned, 135

Emanuel, Caroline, 68

emigration: advantages for women, 96–97; advice to women, 46–48, 49; complexity due to regionalism, 8; as conservative act, 40; economic motivations for, 9, 12–13, 14–15, 18–19, 134; as family venture, 5–6; political motivations for, 14, 134; problems of enumeration, 207; religious reasons for, 15, 145, 150–51, 168; utopian motivations for, 20, 159–61; women's monetary contributions to, 46; women's role in decision to emigrate, 41–46

emotional life: influence of bourgeois domestic ideology, 27; rejection of public displays of emotion, 2–3, 36, 38, 76

Enderes, Barbara, 163

Enderes, John, 163

endogamy: among German-speaking immigrants (1880 and 1920), 212–14; among rural German-Americans (1980 and 1990), 190–93; among rural Irish- and English-Americans (1980), 193–94

Eppstein, Fannie, 256–57*n81*

Erhardt, Ferdinand, 127

ethnic conflict: with Anglo-Americans, 94, 109, 177–78, 185–86

ethnicity: in frontier life, 182–83; impact on American society and culture, 21–22, 192, 194–99 passim; role in frontier success, 89–90, 193; twentieth-century revivals of, 195; in twentieth-century rural Midwest, 194–96, 197

ethnic retention: supporting group identity, 140–41, 154; women's roles in, 89–90

Ewy, Mary, 108, 111

Books in the Statue of Liberty–Ellis Island Centennial Series